D1560562

Guide to Elliptic Curve Cryptography

H. D'Souza

Darrel Hankerson
Alfred Menezes
Scott Vanstone

Guide to Elliptic
Curve Cryptography

With 38 Illustrations

 Springer

QA
76.9
.A25
H37
2004

Darrel Hankerson
Department of Mathematics
Auburn University
Auburn, AL 36849-5107, USA
hankedr@auburn.edu

Alfred Menezes
Department of Combinatorics and
  Optimization
University of Waterloo
Waterloo, Ontario, N2L 3G1 Canada
ajmeneze@uwaterloo.ca

Scott Vanstone
Department of Combinatorics and
  Optimization
University of Waterloo
Waterloo, Ontario, N2L 3G1 Canada
savansto@uwaterloo.ca

IPFW

WITHDRAWN
AUG 2009

HELMKE LIBRARY

Library of Congress Cataloging-in-Publication Data
Hankerson, Darrel R.
    Guide to elliptic curve cryptography / Darrel Hankerson, Alfred J. Menezes, Scott Vanstone.
      p. cm.
    Includes bibliographical references and index.
    ISBN 0-387-95273-X (alk. paper)
      1. Computer security.   2. Public key cryptography.   I. Vanstone, Scott A.
  II. Menezes, A. J. (Alfred J.), 1965–   III. Title.
  QA76.9.A25H37 2003
  005.8′2–dc22
                                                    2003059137

ISBN 0-387-95273-X   Printed on acid-free paper.

© 2004 Springer-Verlag New York, Inc.
All rights reserved. This work may not be translated or copied in whole or in part without the written permission of the publisher (Springer-Verlag New York, Inc., 175 Fifth Avenue, New York, NY 10010, USA), except for brief excerpts in connection with reviews or scholarly analysis. Use in connection with any form of information storage and retrieval, electronic adaptation, computer software, or by similar or dissimilar methodology now known or hereafter developed is forbidden.
The use in this publication of trade names, trademarks, service marks, and similar terms, even if they are not identified as such, is not to be taken as an expression of opinion as to whether or not they are subject to proprietary rights.

Printed in the United States of America.   (HAM)

9 8 7 6 5 4 3 2

Springer-Verlag is a part of *Springer Science+Business Media*

springeronline.com

Contents

List of Algorithms

List of Tables

List of Figures

Acronyms

AES	Advanced Encryption Standard
AIA	Almost Inverse Algorithm
ANSI	American National Standards Institute
ASIC	Application-Specific Integrated Circuit
BEA	Binary Extended Algorithm
DES	Data Encryption Standard
DH	Diffie-Hellman
DHP	Diffie-Hellman Problem
DL	Discrete Logarithm
DLP	Discrete Logarithm Problem
DPA	Differential Power Analysis
DSA	Digital Signature Algorithm
DSS	Digital Signature Standard
ECC	Elliptic Curve Cryptography
ECDDHP	Elliptic Curve Decision Diffie-Hellman Problem
ECDH	Elliptic Curve Diffie-Hellman
ECDHP	Elliptic Curve Diffie-Hellman Problem
ECDLP	Elliptic Curve Discrete Logarithm Problem
ECDSA	Elliptic Curve Digital Signature Algorithm
ECIES	Elliptic Curve Integrated Encryption Scheme
EC-KCDSA	Elliptic Curve Korean Certificate-based Digital Signature Algorithm
ECMQV	Elliptic Curve Menezes-Qu-Vanstone
EEA	Extended Euclidean Algorithm
FIPS	Federal Information Processing Standards
FPGA	Field-Programmable Gate Array
gcd	Greatest Common Divisor
GHS	Gaudry-Hess-Smart
GMR	Goldwasser-Micali-Rivest
HCDLP	Hyperelliptic Curve Discrete Logarithm Problem

HMAC	Hash-based Message Authentication Code
IEC	International Electrotechnical Commission
IEEE	Institute of Electrical and Electronics Engineers
IFP	Integer Factorization Problem
ISO	International Organization for Standardization
JSF	Joint Sparse Form
KDF	Key Derivation Function
KEM	Key Encapsulation Mechanism
LD	López-Dahab
MAC	Message Authentication Code
NAF	Non-Adjacent Form
NESSIE	New European Schemes for Signatures, Integrity and Encryption
NFS	Number Field Sieve
NIST	National Institute of Standards and Technology
OEF	Optimal Extension Field
PKI	Public-Key Infrastructure
PSEC	Provably Secure Elliptic Curve encryption
RSA	Rivest-Shamir-Adleman
SEC	Standards for Efficient Cryptography
SECG	Standards for Efficient Cryptography Group
SHA-1	Secure Hash Algorithm (revised)
SIMD	Single-Instruction Multiple-Data
SPA	Simple Power Analysis
SSL	Secure Sockets Layer
STS	Station-To-Station
TLS	Transport Layer Security
TNAF	τ-adic NAF
VLSI	Very Large Scale Integration

Preface

The study of elliptic curves by algebraists, algebraic geometers and number theorists dates back to the middle of the nineteenth century. There now exists an extensive literature that describes the beautiful and elegant properties of these marvelous objects. In 1984, Hendrik Lenstra described an ingenious algorithm for factoring integers that relies on properties of elliptic curves. This discovery prompted researchers to investigate other applications of elliptic curves in cryptography and computational number theory.

Public-key cryptography was conceived in 1976 by Whitfield Diffie and Martin Hellman. The first practical realization followed in 1977 when Ron Rivest, Adi Shamir and Len Adleman proposed their now well-known RSA cryptosystem, in which security is based on the intractability of the integer factorization problem. Elliptic curve cryptography (ECC) was discovered in 1985 by Neal Koblitz and Victor Miller. Elliptic curve cryptographic schemes are public-key mechanisms that provide the same functionality as RSA schemes. However, their security is based on the hardness of a different problem, namely the elliptic curve discrete logarithm problem (ECDLP). Currently the best algorithms known to solve the ECDLP have fully exponential running time, in contrast to the subexponential-time algorithms known for the integer factorization problem. This means that a desired security level can be attained with significantly smaller keys in elliptic curve systems than is possible with their RSA counterparts. For example, it is generally accepted that a 160-bit elliptic curve key provides the same level of security as a 1024-bit RSA key. The advantages that can be gained from smaller key sizes include speed and efficient use of power, bandwidth, and storage.

Audience This book is intended as a guide for security professionals, developers, and those interested in learning how elliptic curve cryptography can be deployed to secure applications. The presentation is targeted to a diverse audience, and generally assumes no more than an undergraduate degree in computer science, engineering, or mathematics. The book was not written for theoreticians as is evident from the lack of proofs for mathematical statements. However, the breadth of coverage and the extensive surveys of the literature at the end of each chapter should make it a useful resource for the researcher.

Overview The book has a strong focus on efficient methods for finite field arithmetic (Chapter 2) and elliptic curve arithmetic (Chapter 3). Next, Chapter 4 surveys the known attacks on the ECDLP, and describes the generation and validation of domain parameters and key pairs, and selected elliptic curve protocols for digital signature, public-key encryption and key establishment. We chose not to include the mathematical details of the attacks on the ECDLP, or descriptions of algorithms for counting the points on an elliptic curve, because the relevant mathematics is quite sophisticated. (Presenting these topics in a readable and concise form is a formidable challenge postponed for another day.) The choice of material in Chapters 2, 3 and 4 was heavily influenced by the contents of ECC standards that have been developed by accredited standards bodies, in particular the FIPS 186-2 standard for the Elliptic Curve Digital Signature Algorithm (ECDSA) developed by the U.S. government's National Institute for Standards and Technology (NIST). Chapter 5 details selected aspects of efficient implementations in software and hardware, and also gives an introduction to side-channel attacks and their countermeasures. Although the coverage in Chapter 5 is admittedly narrow, we hope that the treatment provides a glimpse of engineering considerations faced by software developers and hardware designers.

Acknowledgements We gratefully acknowledge the following people who provided valuable comments and advice: Mike Brown, Eric Fung, John Goyo, Rick Hite, Rob Lambert, Laurie Law, James Muir, Arash Reyhani-Masoleh, Paul Schellenberg, Adrian Tang, Edlyn Teske, and Christof Zalka. A special thanks goes to Helen D'Souza, whose artwork graces several pages of this book. Thanks also to Cindy Hankerson and Sherry Shannon-Vanstone for suggestions on the general theme of "curves in nature" represented in the illustrations. Finally, we would like to thank our editors at Springer, Wayne Wheeler and Wayne Yuhasz, for their continued encouragement and support.

Updates, errata, and our contact information are available at our web site: http://www.cacr.math.uwaterloo.ca/ecc/. We would greatly appreciate that readers inform us of the inevitable errors and omissions they may find.

Darrel R. Hankerson, Alfred J. Menezes, Scott A. Vanstone
Auburn & Waterloo
July 2003

CHAPTER 1

Introduction and Overview

Elliptic curves have a rich and beautiful history, having been studied by mathematicians for over a hundred years. They have been used to solve a diverse range of problems. One example is the congruent number problem that asks for a classification of the positive integers occurring as the area of some right-angled triangle, the lengths of whose sides are rational numbers. Another example is proving Fermat's Last Theorem which states that the equation $x^n + y^n = z^n$ has no nonzero integer solutions for x, y and z when the integer n is greater than 2.

In 1985, Neal Koblitz and Victor Miller independently proposed using elliptic curves to design public-key cryptographic systems. Since then an abundance of research has been published on the security and efficient implementation of elliptic curve cryptography. In the late 1990's, elliptic curve systems started receiving commercial acceptance when accredited standards organizations specified elliptic curve protocols, and private companies included these protocols in their security products.

The purpose of this chapter is to explain the advantages of public-key cryptography over traditional symmetric-key cryptography, and, in particular, to expound the virtues of elliptic curve cryptography. The exposition is at an introductory level. We provide more detailed treatments of the security and efficient implementation of elliptic curve systems in subsequent chapters.

We begin in §1.1 with a statement of the fundamental goals of cryptography and a description of the essential differences between symmetric-key cryptography and public-key cryptography. In §1.2, we review the RSA, discrete logarithm, and elliptic curve families of public-key systems. These systems are compared in §1.3 in which we explain the potential benefits offered by elliptic curve cryptography. A roadmap for the remainder of this book is provided in §1.4. Finally, §1.5 contains references to the cryptographic literature.

1.1 Cryptography basics

Cryptography is about the design and analysis of mathematical techniques that enable secure communications in the presence of malicious adversaries.

Basic communications model

In Figure 1.1, entities A (Alice) and B (Bob) are communicating over an unsecured channel. We assume that all communications take place in the presence of an adversary E (Eve) whose objective is to defeat any security services being provided to A and B.

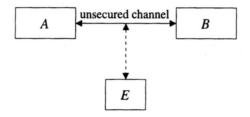

Figure 1.1. Basic communications model.

For example, A and B could be two people communicating over a cellular telephone network, and E is attempting to eavesdrop on their conversation. Or, A could be the web browser of an individual $\tilde{A}$ who is in the process of purchasing a product from an online store $\tilde{B}$ represented by its web site B. In this scenario, the communications channel is the Internet. An adversary E could attempt to read the traffic from A to B thus learning $\tilde{A}$'s credit card information, or could attempt to impersonate either $\tilde{A}$ or $\tilde{B}$ in the transaction. As a third example, consider the situation where A is sending an email message to B over the Internet. An adversary E could attempt to read the message, modify selected portions, or impersonate A by sending her own messages to B. Finally, consider the scenario where A is a smart card that is in the process of authenticating its holder $\tilde{A}$ to the mainframe computer B at the headquarters of a bank. Here, E could attempt to monitor the communications in order to obtain $\tilde{A}$'s account information, or could try to impersonate $\tilde{A}$ in order to withdraw funds from $\tilde{A}$'s account. It should be evident from these examples that a communicating entity is not necessarily a human, but could be a computer, smart card, or software module acting on behalf of an individual or an organization such as a store or a bank.

Security goals

Careful examination of the scenarios outlined above reveals the following fundamental objectives of secure communications:

1. *Confidentiality*: keeping data secret from all but those authorized to see it—messages sent by A to B should not be readable by E.

2. *Data integrity*: ensuring that data has not been altered by unauthorized means—
   B should be able to detect when data sent by A has been modified by E.

3. *Data origin authentication*: corroborating the source of data—B should be able
   to verify that data purportedly sent by A indeed originated with A.

4. *Entity authentication*: corroborating the identity of an entity—B should be
   convinced of the identity of the other communicating entity.

5. *Non-repudiation*: preventing an entity from denying previous commitments or
   actions—when B receives a message purportedly from A, not only is B convinced that the message originated with A, but B can convince a neutral third
   party of this; thus A cannot deny having sent the message to B.

Some applications may have other security objectives such as *anonymity* of the
communicating entities or *access control* (the restriction of access to resources).

Adversarial model

In order to model realistic threats faced by A and B, we generally assume that the
adversary E has considerable capabilities. In addition to being able to read all data
transmitted over the channel, E can modify transmitted data and inject her own data.
Moreover, E has significant computational resources at her disposal. Finally, complete descriptions of the communications protocols and any cryptographic mechanisms
deployed (except for secret keying information) are known to E. The challenge to cryptographers is to design mechanisms to secure the communications in the face of such
powerful adversaries.

Symmetric-key cryptography

Cryptographic systems can be broadly divided into two kinds. In *symmetric-key
schemes*, depicted in Figure 1.2(a), the communicating entities first agree upon keying
material that is both secret and authentic. Subsequently, they may use a symmetric-key
encryption scheme such as the Data Encryption Standard (DES), RC4, or the Advanced
Encryption Standard (AES) to achieve confidentiality. They may also use a message authentication code (MAC) algorithm such as HMAC to achieve data integrity and data
origin authentication.

   For example, if confidentiality were desired and the secret key shared by A and B
were k, then A would encrypt a plaintext message m using an encryption function ENC
and the key k and transmit the resulting ciphertext $c = \text{ENC}_k(m)$ to B. On receiving c,
B would use the decryption function DEC and the same key k to recover $m = \text{DEC}_k(c)$.
If data integrity and data origin authentication were desired, then A and B would first
agree upon a secret key k, after which A would compute the authentication tag $t = \text{MAC}_k(m)$ of a plaintext message m using a MAC algorithm and the key k. A would
then send m and t to B. On receiving m and t, B would use the MAC algorithm and
the same key k to recompute the tag $t' = \text{MAC}_k(m)$ of m and accept the message as
having originated from A if $t = t'$.

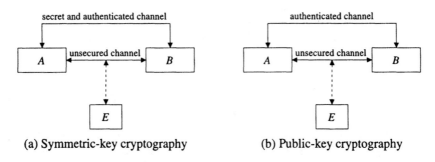

(a) Symmetric-key cryptography   (b) Public-key cryptography

Figure 1.2. Symmetric-key versus public-key cryptography.

Key distribution and management   The major advantage of symmetric-key cryptography is high efficiency; however, there are significant drawbacks to these systems. One primary drawback is the so-called *key distribution problem*—the requirement for a channel that is both secret and authenticated for the distribution of keying material. In some applications, this distribution may be conveniently done by using a physically secure channel such as a trusted courier. Another way is to use the services of an on-line trusted third-party who initially establishes secret keys with all the entities in a network and subsequently uses these keys to securely distribute keying material to communicating entities when required.[1] Solutions such as these may be well-suited to environments where there is an accepted and trusted central authority, but are clearly impractical in applications such as email over the Internet.

A second drawback is the *key management problem*—in a network of N entities, each entity may have to maintain different keying material with each of the other $N-1$ entities. This problem can be alleviated by using the services of an on-line trusted third-party that distributes keying material as required, thereby reducing the need for entities to securely store multiple keys. Again, however, such solutions are not practical in some scenarios. Finally, since keying material is shared between two (or more) entities, symmetric-key techniques cannot be used to devise elegant *digital signature schemes* that provide non-repudiation services. This is because it is impossible to distinguish between the actions taken by the different holders of a secret key.[2]

Public-key cryptography

The notion of public-key cryptography, depicted in Figure 1.2(b), was introduced in 1975 by Diffie, Hellman and Merkle to address the aforementioned shortcomings

---

[1]This approach of using a centralized third-party to distribute keys for symmetric-key algorithms to parties as they are needed is used by the Kerberos network authentication protocol for client/server applications.

[2]Digital signatures schemes can be designed using symmetric-key techniques; however, these schemes are generally impractical as they require the use of an on-line trusted third party or new keying material for each signature.

of symmetric-key cryptography. In contrast to symmetric-key schemes, *public-key schemes* require only that the communicating entities exchange keying material that is authentic (but not secret). Each entity selects a single key pair (e, d) consisting of a *public key e*, and a related *private key d* (that the entity keeps secret). The keys have the property that it is computationally infeasible to determine the private key solely from knowledge of the public key.

Confidentiality If entity A wishes to send entity B a confidential message m, she obtains an authentic copy of B's public key e_B, and uses the encryption function ENC of a public-key encryption scheme to compute the ciphertext $c = \text{ENC}_{e_B}(m)$. A then transmits c to B, who uses the decryption function DEC and his private key d_B to recover the plaintext: $m = \text{DEC}_{d_B}(c)$. The presumption is that an adversary with knowledge only of e_B (but not of d_B) cannot decrypt c. Observe that there are no secrecy requirements on e_B. It is essential only that A obtain an authentic copy of e_B—otherwise A would encrypt m using the public key e_E of some entity E purporting to be B, and m would be recoverable by E.

Non-repudiation Digital signature schemes can be devised for data origin authentication and data integrity, and to facilitate the provision of non-repudiation services. An entity A would use the signature generation algorithm SIGN of a digital signature scheme and her private key d_A to compute the signature of a message: $s = \text{SIGN}_{d_A}(m)$. Upon receiving m and s, an entity B who has an authentic copy of A's public key e_A uses a signature verification algorithm to confirm that s was indeed generated from m and d_A. Since d_A is presumably known only by A, B is assured that the message did indeed originate from A. Moreover, since verification requires only the non-secret quantities m and e_A, the signature s for m can also be verified by a third party who could settle disputes if A denies having signed message m. Unlike handwritten signatures, A's signature s depends on the message m being signed, preventing a forger from simply appending s to a different message m' and claiming that A signed m'. Even though there are no secrecy requirements on the public key e_A, it is essential that verifiers should use an authentic copy of e_A when verifying signatures purportedly generated by A.

In this way, public-key cryptography provides elegant solutions to the three problems with symmetric-key cryptography, namely key distribution, key management, and the provision of non-repudiation. It must be pointed out that, although the requirement for a secret channel for distributing keying material has been eliminated, implementing a *public-key infrastructure* (PKI) for distributing and managing public keys can be a formidable challenge in practice. Also, public-key operations are usually significantly slower than their symmetric-key counterparts. Hence, hybrid systems that benefit from the efficiency of symmetric-key algorithms and the functionality of public-key algorithms are often used.

The next section introduces three families of public-key cryptographic systems.

1.2   Public-key cryptography

In a public-key cryptographic scheme, a key pair is selected so that the problem of deriving the private key from the corresponding public key is equivalent to solving a computational problem that is believed to be intractable. Number-theoretic problems whose intractability form the basis for the security of commonly used public-key schemes are:

1. The integer factorization problem, whose hardness is essential for the security of RSA public-key encryption and signature schemes.

2. The discrete logarithm problem, whose hardness is essential for the security of the ElGamal public-key encryption and signature schemes and their variants such as the Digital Signature Algorithm (DSA).

3. The elliptic curve discrete logarithm problem, whose hardness is essential for the security of all elliptic curve cryptographic schemes.

In this section, we review the basic RSA, ElGamal, and elliptic curve public-key encryption and signature schemes. We emphasize that the schemes presented in this section are the basic "textbook" versions, and enhancements to the schemes are required (such as padding plaintext messages with random strings prior to encryption) before they can be considered to offer adequate protection against real attacks. Nevertheless, the basic schemes illustrate the main ideas behind the RSA, discrete logarithm, and elliptic curve families of public-key algorithms. Enhanced versions of the basic elliptic curve schemes are presented in Chapter 4.

1.2.1   RSA systems

RSA, named after its inventors Rivest, Shamir and Adleman, was proposed in 1977 shortly after the discovery of public-key cryptography.

RSA key generation

An RSA key pair can be generated using Algorithm 1.1. The public key consists of a pair of integers (n, e) where the *RSA modulus n* is a product of two randomly generated (and secret) primes p and q of the same bitlength. The *encryption exponent e* is an integer satisfying $1 < e < \phi$ and $\gcd(e, \phi) = 1$ where $\phi = (p-1)(q-1)$. The private key d, also called the *decryption exponent*, is the integer satisfying $1 < d < \phi$ and $ed \equiv 1 \pmod{\phi}$. It has been proven that the problem of determining the private key d from the public key (n, e) is computationally equivalent to the problem of determining the factors p and q of n; the latter is the *integer factorization problem* (IFP).

Algorithm 1.1 RSA key pair generation

INPUT: Security parameter l.

OUTPUT: RSA public key (n, e) and private key d.

1. Randomly select two primes p and q of the same bitlength $l/2$.
2. Compute $n = pq$ and $\phi = (p-1)(q-1)$.
3. Select an arbitrary integer e with $1 < e < \phi$ and $\gcd(e, \phi) = 1$.
4. Compute the integer d satisfying $1 < d < \phi$ and $ed \equiv 1 \pmod{\phi}$.
5. Return(n, e, d).

RSA encryption scheme

RSA encryption and signature schemes use the fact that

$$m^{ed} \equiv m \pmod{n} \tag{1.1}$$

for all integers m. The encryption and decryption procedures for the (basic) RSA public-key encryption scheme are presented as Algorithms 1.2 and 1.3. Decryption works because $c^d \equiv (m^e)^d \equiv m \pmod{n}$, as derived from expression (1.1). The security relies on the difficulty of computing the plaintext m from the ciphertext $c = m^e \bmod n$ and the public parameters n and e. This is the problem of finding eth roots modulo n and is assumed (but has not been proven) to be as difficult as the integer factorization problem.

Algorithm 1.2 Basic RSA encryption

INPUT: RSA public key (n, e), plaintext $m \in [0, n-1]$.

OUTPUT: Ciphertext c.

1. Compute $c = m^e \bmod n$.
2. Return(c).

Algorithm 1.3 Basic RSA decryption

INPUT: RSA public key (n, e), RSA private key d, ciphertext c.

OUTPUT: Plaintext m.

1. Compute $m = c^d \bmod n$.
2. Return(m).

RSA signature scheme

The RSA signing and verifying procedures are shown in Algorithms 1.4 and 1.5. The signer of a message m first computes its message digest $h = H(m)$ using a cryptographic hash function H, where h serves as a short fingerprint of m. Then, the signer uses his private key d to compute the eth root s of h modulo n: $s = h^d \bmod n$. Note that $s^e \equiv h \pmod{n}$ from expression (1.1). The signer transmits the message m and its signature s to a verifying party. This party then recomputes the message digest $h = H(m)$, recovers a message digest $h' = s^e \bmod n$ from s, and accepts the signature as being valid for m provided that $h = h'$. The security relies on the inability of a forger (who does not know the private key d) to compute eth roots modulo n.

Algorithm 1.4 Basic RSA signature generation

INPUT: RSA public key (n, e), RSA private key d, message m.
OUTPUT: Signature s.
1. Compute $h = H(m)$ where H is a hash function.
2. Compute $s = h^d \bmod n$.
3. Return(s).

Algorithm 1.5 Basic RSA signature verification

INPUT: RSA public key (n, e), message m, signature s.
OUTPUT: Acceptance or rejection of the signature.
1. Compute $h = H(m)$.
2. Compute $h' = s^e \bmod n$.
3. If $h = h'$ then return("Accept the signature");
   Else return("Reject the signature").

The computationally expensive step in any RSA operation is the modular exponentiation, e.g., computing $m^e \bmod n$ in encryption and $c^d \bmod n$ in decryption. In order to increase the efficiency of encryption and signature verification, one can select a small encryption exponent e; in practice, $e = 3$ or $e = 2^{16} + 1$ is commonly chosen. The decryption exponent d is of the same bitlength as n. Thus, RSA encryption and signature verification with small exponent e are significantly faster than RSA decryption and signature generation.

1.2.2 Discrete logarithm systems

The first discrete logarithm (DL) system was the key agreement protocol proposed by Diffie and Hellman in 1976. In 1984, ElGamal described DL public-key encryption and signature schemes. Since then, many variants of these schemes have been proposed. Here we present the basic ElGamal public-key encryption scheme and the Digital Signature Algorithm (DSA).

DL key generation

In discrete logarithm systems, a key pair is associated with a set of public domain parameters (p, q, g). Here, p is a prime, q is a prime divisor of $p - 1$, and $g \in [1, p - 1]$ has order q (i.e., $t = q$ is the smallest positive integer satisfying $g^t \equiv 1 \pmod{p}$). A private key is an integer x that is selected uniformly at random from the interval $[1, q - 1]$ (this operation is denoted $x \in_R [1, q - 1]$), and the corresponding public key is $y = g^x \bmod p$. The problem of determining x given domain parameters (p, q, g) and y is the *discrete logarithm problem* (DLP). We summarize the DL domain parameter generation and key pair generation procedures in Algorithms 1.6 and 1.7, respectively.

Algorithm 1.6 DL domain parameter generation

INPUT: Security parameters l, t.
OUTPUT: DL domain parameters (p, q, g).
  1. Select a t-bit prime q and an l-bit prime p such that q divides $p - 1$.
  2. Select an element g of order q:
     2.1 Select arbitrary $h \in [1, p - 1]$ and compute $g = h^{(p-1)/q} \bmod p$.
     2.2 If $g = 1$ then go to step 2.1.
  3. Return(p, q, g).

Algorithm 1.7 DL key pair generation

INPUT: DL domain parameters (p, q, g).
OUTPUT: Public key y and private key x.
  1. Select $x \in_R [1, q - 1]$.
  2. Compute $y = g^x \bmod p$.
  3. Return(y, x).

DL encryption scheme

We present the encryption and decryption procedures for the (basic) ElGamal public-key encryption scheme as Algorithms 1.8 and 1.9, respectively. If y is the intended recipient's public key, then a plaintext m is encrypted by multiplying it by $y^k \bmod p$ where k is randomly selected by the sender. The sender transmits this product $c_2 = my^k \bmod p$ and also $c_1 = g^k \bmod p$ to the recipient who uses her private key to compute

$$c_1^x \equiv g^{kx} \equiv y^k \pmod{p}$$

and divides c_2 by this quantity to recover m. An eavesdropper who wishes to recover m needs to calculate $y^k \bmod p$. This task of computing $y^k \bmod p$ from the domain parameters (p, q, g), y, and $c_1 = g^k \bmod p$ is called the *Diffie-Hellman problem* (DHP).

The DHP is assumed (and has been proven in some cases) to be as difficult as the discrete logarithm problem.

Algorithm 1.8 Basic ElGamal encryption

INPUT: DL domain parameters (p, q, g), public key y, plaintext $m \in [0, p-1]$.
OUTPUT: Ciphertext (c_1, c_2).
1. Select $k \in_R [1, q-1]$.
2. Compute $c_1 = g^k \bmod p$.
3. Compute $c_2 = m \cdot y^k \bmod p$.
4. Return(c_1, c_2).

Algorithm 1.9 Basic ElGamal decryption

INPUT: DL domain parameters (p, q, g), private key x, ciphertext (c_1, c_2).
OUTPUT: Plaintext m.
1. Compute $m = c_2 \cdot c_1^{-x} \bmod p$.
2. Return(m).

DL signature scheme

The Digital Signature Algorithm (DSA) was proposed in 1991 by the U.S. National Institute of Standards and Technology (NIST) and was specified in a U.S. Government Federal Information Processing Standard (FIPS 186) called the Digital Signature Standard (DSS). We summarize the signing and verifying procedures in Algorithms 1.10 and 1.11, respectively.

An entity A with private key x signs a message by selecting a random integer k from the interval $[1, q-1]$, and computing $T = g^k \bmod p$, $r = T \bmod q$ and

$$s = k^{-1}(h + xr) \bmod q \qquad (1.2)$$

where $h = H(m)$ is the message digest. A's signature on m is the pair (r, s). To verify the signature, an entity must check that (r, s) satisfies equation (1.2). Since the verifier knows neither A's private key x nor k, this equation cannot be directly verified. Note, however, that equation (1.2) is equivalent to

$$k \equiv s^{-1}(h + xr) \pmod{q}. \qquad (1.3)$$

Raising g to both sides of (1.3) yields the equivalent congruence

$$T \equiv g^{hs^{-1}} y^{rs^{-1}} \pmod{p}.$$

The verifier can therefore compute T and then check that $r = T \bmod q$.

Algorithm 1.10 DSA signature generation

INPUT: DL domain parameters (p, q, g), private key x, message m.
OUTPUT: Signature (r, s).
1. Select $k \in_R [1, q-1]$.
2. Compute $T = g^k \bmod p$.
3. Compute $r = T \bmod q$. If $r = 0$ then go to step 1.
4. Compute $h = H(m)$.
5. Compute $s = k^{-1}(h + xr) \bmod q$. If $s = 0$ then go to step 1.
6. Return(r, s).

Algorithm 1.11 DSA signature verification

INPUT: DL domain parameters (p, q, g), public key y, message m, signature (r, s).
OUTPUT: Acceptance or rejection of the signature.
1. Verify that r and s are integers in the interval $[1, q-1]$. If any verification fails then return("Reject the signature").
2. Compute $h = H(m)$.
3. Compute $w = s^{-1} \bmod q$.
4. Compute $u_1 = hw \bmod q$ and $u_2 = rw \bmod q$.
5. Compute $T = g^{u_1} y^{u_2} \bmod p$.
6. Compute $r' = T \bmod q$.
7. If $r = r'$ then return("Accept the signature");
   Else return("Reject the signature").

1.2.3 Elliptic curve systems

The discrete logarithm systems presented in §1.2.2 can be described in the abstract setting of a finite cyclic group. We introduce some elementary concepts from group theory and explain this generalization. We then look at elliptic curve groups and show how they can be used to implement discrete logarithm systems.

Groups

An *abelian group* $(G, *)$ consists of a set G with a binary operation $* : G \times G \to G$ satisfying the following properties:
   (i) *(Associativity)* $a * (b * c) = (a * b) * c$ for all $a, b, c \in G$.
  (ii) *(Existence of an identity)* There exists an element $e \in G$ such that $a * e = e * a = a$ for all $a \in G$.
 (iii) *(Existence of inverses)* For each $a \in G$, there exists an element $b \in G$, called the *inverse* of a, such that $a * b = b * a = e$.
  (iv) *(Commutativity)* $a * b = b * a$ for all $a, b \in G$.

The group operation is usually called addition $(+)$ or multiplication $(\cdot)$. In the first instance, the group is called an *additive* group, the (additive) identity element is usually denoted by 0, and the (additive) inverse of a is denoted by $-a$. In the second instance, the group is called a *multiplicative* group, the (multiplicative) identity element is usually denoted by 1, and the (multiplicative) inverse of a is denoted by a^{-1}. The group is *finite* if G is a finite set, in which case the number of elements in G is called the *order* of G.

For example, let p be a prime number, and let $\mathbb{F}_p = \{0, 1, 2, \ldots, p-1\}$ denote the set of integers modulo p. Then $(\mathbb{F}_p, +)$, where the operation $+$ is defined to be addition of integers modulo p, is a finite additive group of order p with (additive) identity element 0. Also, $(\mathbb{F}_p^*, \cdot)$, where $\mathbb{F}_p^*$ denotes the nonzero elements in $\mathbb{F}_p$ and the operation $\cdot$ is defined to be multiplication of integers modulo p, is a finite multiplicative group of order $p-1$ with (multiplicative) identity element 1. The triple $(\mathbb{F}_p, +, \cdot)$ is a *finite field* (cf. §2.1), denoted more succinctly as $\mathbb{F}_p$.

Now, if G is a finite multiplicative group of order n and $g \in G$, then the smallest positive integer t such that $g^t = 1$ is called the *order* of g; such a t always exists and is a divisor of n. The set $\langle g \rangle = \{g^i : 0 \le i \le t-1\}$ of all powers of g is itself a group under the same operation as G, and is called the *cyclic subgroup of G generated by g*. Analogous statements are true if G is written additively. In that instance, the order of $g \in G$ is the smallest positive divisor t of n such that $tg = 0$, and $\langle g \rangle = \{ig : 0 \le i \le t-1\}$. Here, tg denotes the element obtained by adding t copies of g. If G has an element g of order n, then G is said to be a *cyclic group* and g is called a *generator* of G.

For example, with the DL domain parameters (p, q, g) defined as in §1.2.2, the multiplicative group $(\mathbb{F}_p^*, \cdot)$ is a cyclic group of order $p-1$. Furthermore, $\langle g \rangle$ is a cyclic subgroup of order q.

Generalized discrete logarithm problem

Suppose now that $(G, \cdot)$ is a multiplicative cyclic group of order n with generator g. Then we can describe the discrete logarithm systems presented in §1.2.2 in the setting of G. For instance, the domain parameters are g and n, the private key is an integer x selected randomly from the interval $[1, n-1]$, and the public key is $y = g^x$. The problem of determining x given g, n and y is the *discrete logarithm problem in G*.

In order for a discrete logarithm system based on G to be efficient, fast algorithms should be known for computing the group operation. For security, the discrete logarithm problem in G should be intractable.

Now, any two cyclic groups of the same order n are essentially the same; that is, they have the same structure even though the elements may be written differently. The different representations of group elements can result in algorithms of varying speeds for computing the group operation and for solving the discrete logarithm problem.

The most popular groups for implementing discrete logarithm systems are the cyclic subgroups of the multiplicative group of a finite field (discussed in §1.2.2), and cyclic subgroups of elliptic curve groups which we introduce next.

Elliptic curve groups

Let p be a prime number, and let $\mathbb{F}_p$ denote the field of integers modulo p. An *elliptic curve* E over $\mathbb{F}_p$ is defined by an equation of the form

$$y^2 = x^3 + ax + b, \tag{1.4}$$

where $a, b \in \mathbb{F}_p$ satisfy $4a^3 + 27b^2 \not\equiv 0 \pmod{p}$. A pair (x, y), where $x, y \in \mathbb{F}_p$, is a *point* on the curve if (x, y) satisfies the equation (1.4). The *point at infinity*, denoted by ∞, is also said to be on the curve. The set of all the points on E is denoted by $E(\mathbb{F}_p)$. For example, if E is an elliptic curve over $\mathbb{F}_7$ with defining equation

$$y^2 = x^3 + 2x + 4,$$

then the points on E are

$$E(\mathbb{F}_7) = \{\infty, (0,2), (0,5), (1,0), (2,3), (2,4), (3,3), (3,4), (6,1), (6,6)\}.$$

Now, there is a well-known method for adding two elliptic curve points (x_1, y_1) and (x_2, y_2) to produce a third point on the elliptic curve (see §3.1). The addition rule requires a few arithmetic operations (addition, subtraction, multiplication and inversion) in $\mathbb{F}_p$ with the coordinates x_1, y_1, x_2, y_2. With this addition rule, the set of points $E(\mathbb{F}_p)$ forms an (additive) abelian group with ∞ serving as the identity element. Cyclic subgroups of such elliptic curve groups can now be used to implement discrete logarithm systems.

We next illustrate the ideas behind elliptic curve cryptography by describing an elliptic curve analogue of the DL encryption scheme that was introduced in §1.2.2. Such elliptic curve systems, and also the elliptic curve analogue of the DSA signature scheme, are extensively studied in Chapter 4.

Elliptic curve key generation

Let E be an elliptic curve defined over a finite field $\mathbb{F}_p$. Let P be a point in $E(\mathbb{F}_p)$, and suppose that P has prime order n. Then the cyclic subgroup of $E(\mathbb{F}_p)$ generated by P is

$$\langle P \rangle = \{\infty, P, 2P, 3P, \ldots, (n-1)P\}.$$

The prime p, the equation of the elliptic curve E, and the point P and its order n, are the public domain parameters. A private key is an integer d that is selected uniformly at random from the interval $[1, n-1]$, and the corresponding public key is $Q = dP$.

The problem of determining d given the domain parameters and Q is the *elliptic curve discrete logarithm problem* (ECDLP).

Algorithm 1.12 Elliptic curve key pair generation

INPUT: Elliptic curve domain parameters (p, E, P, n).
OUTPUT: Public key Q and private key d.
    1. Select $d \in_R [1, n-1]$.
    2. Compute $Q = dP$.
    3. Return(Q, d).

Elliptic curve encryption scheme

We present the encryption and decryption procedures for the elliptic curve analogue of the basic ElGamal encryption scheme as Algorithms 1.13 and 1.14, respectively. A plaintext m is first represented as a point M, and then encrypted by adding it to kQ where k is a randomly selected integer, and Q is the intended recipient's public key. The sender transmits the points $C_1 = kP$ and $C_2 = M + kQ$ to the recipient who uses her private key d to compute

$$dC_1 = d(kP) = k(dP) = kQ,$$

and thereafter recovers $M = C_2 - kQ$. An eavesdropper who wishes to recover M needs to compute kQ. This task of computing kQ from the domain parameters, Q, and $C_1 = kP$, is the elliptic curve analogue of the Diffie-Hellman problem.

Algorithm 1.13 Basic ElGamal elliptic curve encryption

INPUT: Elliptic curve domain parameters (p, E, P, n), public key Q, plaintext m.
OUTPUT: Ciphertext (C_1, C_2).
    1. Represent the message m as a point M in $E(\mathbb{F}_p)$.
    2. Select $k \in_R [1, n-1]$.
    3. Compute $C_1 = kP$.
    4. Compute $C_2 = M + kQ$.
    5. Return(C_1, C_2).

Algorithm 1.14 Basic ElGamal elliptic curve decryption

INPUT: Domain parameters (p, E, P, n), private key d, ciphertext (C_1, C_2).
OUTPUT: Plaintext m.
    1. Compute $M = C_2 - dC_1$, and extract m from M.
    2. Return(m).

1.3 Why elliptic curve cryptography?

There are several criteria that need to be considered when selecting a family of public-key schemes for a specific application. The principal ones are:

1. *Functionality.* Does the public-key family provide the desired capabilities?

2. *Security.* What assurances are available that the protocols are secure?

3. *Performance.* For the desired level of security, do the protocols meet performance objectives?

Other factors that may influence a decision include the existence of best-practice standards developed by accredited standards organizations, the availability of commercial cryptographic products, patent coverage, and the extent of existing deployments.

The RSA, DL and EC families introduced in §1.2 all provide the basic functionality expected of public-key cryptography—encryption, signatures, and key agreement. Over the years, researchers have developed techniques for designing and proving the security of RSA, DL and EC protocols under reasonable assumptions. The fundamental security issue that remains is the hardness of the underlying mathematical problem that is necessary for the security of all protocols in a public-key family—the integer factorization problem for RSA systems, the discrete logarithm problem for DL systems, and the elliptic curve discrete logarithm problem for EC systems. The perceived hardness of these problems directly impacts performance since it dictates the sizes of the domain and key parameters. That in turn affects the performance of the underlying arithmetic operations.

In the remainder of this section, we summarize the state-of-the-art in algorithms for solving the integer factorization, discrete logarithm, and elliptic curve discrete logarithm problems. We then give estimates of parameter sizes providing equivalent levels of security for RSA, DL and EC systems. These comparisons illustrate the appeal of elliptic curve cryptography especially for applications that have high security requirements.

We begin with an introduction to some relevant concepts from algorithm analysis.

Measuring the efficiency of algorithms

The *efficiency* of an algorithm is measured by the scarce resources it consumes. Typically the measure used is time, but sometimes other measures such as space and number of processors are also considered. It is reasonable to expect that an algorithm consumes greater resources for larger inputs, and the efficiency of an algorithm is therefore described as a function of the input size. Here, the *size* is defined to be the number of bits needed to represent the input using a reasonable encoding. For example, an algorithm for factoring an integer n has input size $l = \lfloor \log_2 n \rfloor + 1$ bits.

Expressions for the running time of an algorithm are most useful if they are independent of any particular platform used to implement the algorithm. This is achieved by estimating the number of elementary operations (e.g., bit operations) executed. The (worst-case) *running time* of an algorithm is an upper bound, expressed as a function of the input size, on the number of elementary steps executed by the algorithm. For example, the method of trial division which factors an integer n by checking all possible factors up to $\sqrt{n}$ has a running time of approximately $\sqrt{n} \approx 2^{l/2}$ division steps.

It is often difficult to derive exact expressions for the running time of an algorithm. In these situations, it is convenient to use "big-O" notation. If f and g are two positive real-valued functions defined on the positive integers, then we write $f = O(g)$ when there exist positive constants c and L such that $f(l) \le cg(l)$ for all $l \ge L$. Informally, this means that, asymptotically, $f(l)$ grows no faster than $g(l)$ to within a constant multiple. Also useful is the "little-o" notation. We write $f = o(g)$ if for any positive constant c there exists a constant L such that $f(l) \le cg(l)$ for $l \ge L$. Informally, this means that $f(l)$ becomes insignificant relative to $g(l)$ for large values of l.

The accepted notion of an *efficient* algorithm is one whose running time is bounded by a polynomial in the input size.

Definition 1.15 Let A be an algorithm whose input has bitlength l.

(i) A is a *polynomial-time* algorithm if its running time is $O(l^c)$ for some constant $c > 0$.

(ii) A is an *exponential-time* algorithm if its running time is not of the form $O(l^c)$ for any $c > 0$.

(iii) A is a *subexponential-time* algorithm if its running time is $O(2^{o(l)})$, and A is not a polynomial-time algorithm.

(iv) A is a *fully-exponential-time* algorithm if its running time is not of the form $O(2^{o(l)})$.

It should be noted that a subexponential-time algorithm is also an exponential-time algorithm and, in particular, is not a polynomial-time algorithm. However, the running time of a subexponential-time algorithm does grow slower than that of a fully-exponential-time algorithm. Subexponential functions commonly arise when analyzing the running times of algorithms for factoring integers and finding discrete logarithms.

Example 1.16 (*subexponential-time algorithm*) Let A be an algorithm whose input is an integer n or a small set of integers modulo n (so the input size is $O(\log_2 n)$). If the running time of A is of the form

$$L_n[\alpha, c] = O\left(e^{(c+o(1))(\log n)^\alpha (\log \log n)^{1-\alpha}}\right)$$

where c is a positive constant and α is a constant satisfying $0 < \alpha < 1$, then A is a subexponential-time algorithm. Observe that if $\alpha = 0$ then $L_n[0, c]$ is a polynomial expression in $\log_2 n$ (so A is a polynomial-time algorithm), while if $\alpha = 1$ then $L_n[1, c]$ is fully-exponential expression in $\log_2 n$ (so A is a fully-exponential-time algorithm). Thus the parameter α is a good benchmark of how close a subexponential-time algorithm is to being efficient (polynomial-time) or inefficient (fully-exponential-time).

Solving integer factorization and discrete logarithm problems

We briefly survey the state-in-the-art in algorithms for the integer factorization, discrete logarithm, and elliptic curve discrete logarithm problems.

Algorithms for the integer factorization problem Recall that an instance of the integer factorization problem is an integer n that is the product of two $l/2$-bit primes; the input size is $O(l)$ bits. The fastest algorithm known for factoring such n is the *Number Field Sieve* (NFS) which has a subexponential expected running time of

$$L_n[\frac{1}{3}, 1.923]. \tag{1.5}$$

The NFS has two stages: a *sieving stage* where certain relations are collected, and a *matrix stage* where a large sparse system of linear equations is solved. The sieving stage is easy to parallelize, and can be executed on a collection of workstations on the Internet. However, in order for the sieving to be efficient, each workstation should have a large amount of main memory. The matrix stage is not so easy to parallelize, since the individual processors frequently need to communicate with one another. This stage is more effectively executed on a single massively parallel machine, than on a loosely coupled network of workstations.

As of 2003, the largest RSA modulus factored with the NFS was a 530-bit (160-decimal digit) number.

Algorithms for the discrete logarithm problem Recall that the discrete logarithm problem has parameters p and q where p is an l-bit prime and q is a t-bit prime divisor of $p - 1$; the input size is $O(l)$ bits. The fastest algorithms known for solving the discrete logarithm problem are the *Number Field Sieve* (NFS) which has a subexponential expected running time of

$$L_p[\frac{1}{3}, 1.923], \tag{1.6}$$

and *Pollard's rho algorithm* which has an expected running time of

$$\sqrt{\frac{\pi q}{2}}. \tag{1.7}$$

The comments made above for the NFS for integer factorization also apply to the NFS for computing discrete logarithms. Pollard's rho algorithm can be easily parallelized so that the individual processors do not have to communicate with each other and only occasionally communicate with a central processor. In addition, the algorithm has only very small storage and main memory requirements.

The method of choice for solving a given instance of the DLP depends on the sizes of the parameters p and q, which in turn determine which of the expressions (1.6) and (1.7) represents the smaller computational effort. In practice, DL parameters are selected so that the expected running times in expressions (1.6) and (1.7) are roughly equal.

As of 2003, the largest instance of the DLP solved with the NFS is for a 397-bit (120-decimal digit) prime p.

Algorithms for the elliptic curve discrete logarithm problem Recall that the ECDLP asks for the integer $d \in [1, n-1]$ such that $Q = dP$, where n is a t-bit prime, P is a point of order n on an elliptic curve defined over a finite field $\mathbb{F}_p$, and $Q \in \langle P \rangle$. If we assume that $n \approx p$, as is usually the case in practice, then the input size is $O(t)$ bits. The fastest algorithm known for solving the ECDLP is *Pollard's rho algorithm* (cf. §4.1) which has an expected running time of

$$\frac{\sqrt{\pi n}}{2}. \tag{1.8}$$

The comments above concerning Pollard's rho algorithm for solving the ordinary discrete logarithm problem also apply to solving the ECDLP.

As of 2003, the largest ECDLP instance solved with Pollard's rho algorithm is for an elliptic curve over a 109-bit prime field.

Key size comparisons

Estimates are given for parameter sizes providing comparable levels of security for RSA, DL, and EC systems, under the assumption that the algorithms mentioned above are indeed the best ones that exist for the integer factorization, discrete logarithm, and elliptic curve discrete logarithm problems. Thus, we do not account for fundamental breakthroughs in the future such as the discovery of significantly faster algorithms or the building of a large-scale quantum computer.[3]

If time is the only measure used for the efficiency of an algorithm, then the parameter sizes providing equivalent security levels for RSA, DL and EC systems can be derived using the running times in expressions (1.5), (1.6), (1.7) and (1.8). The parameter sizes, also called *key sizes*, that provide equivalent security levels for RSA, DL and EC systems as an 80-, 112-, 128-, 192- and 256-bit symmetric-key encryption scheme are listed in Table 1.1. By a *security level* of k bits we mean that the best algorithm known for breaking the system takes approximately 2^k steps. These five specific security levels were selected because they represent the amount of work required to perform an exhaustive key search on the symmetric-key encryption schemes SKIPJACK, Triple-DES, AES-Small, AES-Medium, and AES-Large, respectively.

The key size comparisons in Table 1.1 are somewhat unsatisfactory in that they are based only on the time required for the NFS and Pollard's rho algorithms. In particular, the NFS has several limiting factors including the amount of memory required for

---

[3]Efficient algorithms are known for solving the integer factorization, discrete logarithm, and elliptic curve discrete logarithm problems on quantum computers (see the notes on page 196). However, it is still unknown whether large-scale quantum computers can actually be built.

	Security level (bits)				
	80 (SKIPJACK)	112 (Triple-DES)	128 (AES-Small)	192 (AES-Medium)	256 (AES-Large)
DL parameter q EC parameter n	160	224	256	384	512
RSA modulus n DL modulus p	1024	2048	3072	8192	15360

Table 1.1. RSA, DL and EC key sizes for equivalent security levels. Bitlengths are given for the DL parameter q and the EC parameter n, and the RSA modulus n and the DL modulus p, respectively.

the sieving stage, the size of the matrix, and the difficulty in parallelizing the matrix stage, while these factors are not present in the analysis of Pollard's rho algorithm. It is possible to provide *cost-equivalent* key sizes that take into account the full cost of the algorithms—that is, both the running time as well as the cost to build or otherwise acquire the necessary hardware. However, such costs are difficult to estimate with a reasonable degree of precision. Moreover, recent work has shown that the full cost of the sieving and matrix stages can be significantly reduced by building customized hardware. It therefore seems prudent to take a conservative approach and only use time as the measure of efficiency for the NFS and Pollard's rho algorithms.

The comparisons in Table 1.1 demonstrate that smaller parameters can be used in elliptic curve cryptography (ECC) than with RSA and DL systems at a given security level. The difference in parameter sizes is especially pronounced for higher security levels. The advantages that can be gained from smaller parameters include speed (faster computations) and smaller keys and certificates. In particular, private-key operations (such as signature generation and decryption) for ECC are many times more efficient than RSA and DL private-key operations. Public-key operations (such as signature verification and encryption) for ECC are many times more efficient than for DL systems. Public-key operations for RSA are expected to be somewhat faster than for ECC if a small encryption exponent e (such as $e = 3$ or $e = 2^{16} + 1$) is selected for RSA. The advantages offered by ECC can be important in environments where processing power, storage, bandwidth, or power consumption is constrained.

1.4 Roadmap

Before implementing an elliptic curve system, several selections have to be made concerning the finite field, elliptic curve, and cryptographic protocol:

1. a finite field, a representation for the field elements, and algorithms for performing field arithmetic;

2. an elliptic curve, a representation for the elliptic curve points, and algorithms for performing elliptic curve arithmetic; and

3. a protocol, and algorithms for performing protocol arithmetic.

There are many factors that can influence the choices made. All of these must be considered simultaneously in order to arrive at the best solution for a particular application. Relevant factors include security considerations, application platform (software or hardware), constraints of the particular computing environment (e.g., processing speed, code size (ROM), memory size (RAM), gate count, power consumption), and constraints of the particular communications environment (e.g., bandwidth, response time).

Not surprisingly, it is difficult, if not impossible, to decide on a single "best" set of choices. For example, the optimal choices for a workstation application can be quite different from the optimal choices for a smart card application. The purpose of this book is to provide security practitioners with a comprehensive account of the various implementation and security considerations for elliptic curve cryptography, so that informed decisions of the most suitable options can be made for particular applications.

The remainder of the book is organized as follows. Chapter 2 gives a brief introduction to finite fields. It then presents algorithms that are well-suited for software implementation of the arithmetic operations in three kinds of finite fields—prime fields, binary fields and optimal extension fields.

Chapter 3 provides a brief introduction to elliptic curves, and presents different methods for representing points and for performing elliptic curve arithmetic. Also considered are techniques for accelerating the arithmetic on Koblitz curves and other elliptic curves admitting efficiently-computable endomorphisms.

Chapter 4 describes elliptic curve protocols for digital signatures, public-key encryption and key establishment, and considers the generation and validation of domain parameters and key pairs. The state-of-the-art in algorithms for solving the elliptic curve discrete logarithm problem are surveyed.

Chapter 5 considers selected engineering aspects of implementing elliptic curve cryptography in software and hardware. Also examined are side-channel attacks where an adversary exploits information leaked by cryptographic devices, including electromagnetic radiation, power consumption, and error messages.

The appendices present some information that may be useful to implementors. Appendix A presents specific examples of elliptic curve domain parameters that are suitable for cryptographic use. Appendix B summarizes the important standards that describe elliptic curve mechanisms. Appendix C lists selected software tools that are available for performing relevant number-theoretic calculations.

1.5 Notes and further references

§1.1

Popular books on modern cryptography include those of Schneier [409], Menezes, van Oorschot and Vanstone [319], Stinson [454], and Ferguson and Schneier [136]. These books describe the basic symmetric-key and public-key mechanisms outlined in §1.1 including symmetric-key encryption schemes, MAC algorithms, public-key encryption schemes, and digital signature schemes. Practical considerations with deploying public-key cryptography on a large scale are discussed in the books of Ford and Baum [145], Adams and Lloyd [2], and Housley and Polk [200].

§1.2

The notion of public-key cryptography was introduced by Diffie and Hellman [121] and independently by Merkle [321]. A lucid account of its early history and development is given by Diffie [120]; for a popular narrative, see Levy's book [290]. Diffie and Hellman presented their key agreement algorithm using exponentiation in the multiplicative group of the integers modulo a prime, and described public-key encryption and digital signature schemes using generic trapdoor one-way functions. The first concrete realization of a public-key encryption scheme was the knapsack scheme of Merkle and Hellman [322]. This scheme, and its many variants that have been proposed, have been shown to be insecure.

The RSA public-key encryption and signature schemes are due to Rivest, Shamir and Adleman [391].

ElGamal [131] was the first to propose public-key encryption and signature schemes based on the hardness of the discrete logarithm problem. The Digital Signature Algorithm, specified in FIPS 186 [139], was invented by Kravitz [268]. Smith and Skinner [443], Gong and Harn [176], and Lenstra and Verheul [283] showed, respectively, how the elements of the subgroup of order $p + 1$ of $\mathbb{F}_{p^2}^*$, the subgroup of order $p^2 + p + 1$ of $\mathbb{F}_{p^3}^*$, and the subgroup of order $p^2 - p + 1$ of $\mathbb{F}_{p^6}^*$, can be compactly represented. In their systems, more commonly known as LUC, GH, and XTR, respectively, subgroup elements have representations that are smaller than the representations of field elements by factors of 2, 1.5 and 3, respectively.

Koblitz [250] and Miller [325] in 1985 independently proposed using the group of points on an elliptic curve defined over a finite field to devise discrete logarithm cryptographic schemes. Two books devoted to the study of elliptic curve cryptography are those of Menezes [313] and Blake, Seroussi and Smart [49] published in 1993 and 1999, respectively. The books by Enge [132] and Washington [474] focus on the mathematics relevant to elliptic curve cryptography.

Other applications of elliptic curves include the integer factorization algorithm of Lenstra [285] which is notable for its ability to quickly find any small prime factors of an integer, the primality proving algorithm of Goldwasser and Kilian [173], and the pseudorandom bit generators proposed by Kaliski [233]. Koyama, Maurer, Okamoto and Vanstone [267] showed how elliptic curves defined over the integers modulo a composite integer n could be used to design RSA-like cryptographic schemes where the order of the elliptic curve group is the trapdoor. The hardness of factoring n is necessary for these schemes to be secure, and hence n should be the same bitlength as the modulus used in RSA systems. The work of several people including Kurosawa, Okada and Tsujii [273], Pinch [374], Kaliski [236] and Bleichenbacher [52] has shown that these elliptic curve analogues offer no significant advantages over their RSA counterparts.

There have been many other proposals for using finite groups in discrete logarithm cryptographic schemes. These include the group of units of the integers modulo a composite integer by McCurley [310], the jacobian of a hyperelliptic curve over a finite field by Koblitz [251], the jacobian of a superelliptic curve over a finite field by Galbraith, Paulus and Smart [157], and the class group of an imaginary quadratic number field by Buchmann and Williams [80]. Buchmann and Williams [81] (see also Scheidler, Buchmann and Williams [405]) showed how a real quadratic number field which yields a structure that is 'almost' a group can be used to design discrete logarithm schemes. Analogous structures for real quadratic congruence function fields were studied by Scheidler, Stein and Williams [406], and Müller, Vanstone and Zuccherato [336].

§1.3
The number field sieve (NFS) for factoring integers was first proposed by Pollard [380], and is described in the book edited by Lenstra and Lenstra [280]. Cavallar et al. [87] report on their factorization using the NFS of a 512-bit RSA modulus.

Pollard's rho algorithm is due to Pollard [379]. The number field sieve (NFS) for computing discrete logarithms in prime fields was proposed by Gordon [178] and improved by Schirokauer [408]. Joux and Lercier [228] discuss further improvements that were used in their computation in 2001 of discrete logarithms in a 397-bit (120-decimal digit) prime field. The fastest algorithm for computing discrete logarithms in binary fields is due to Coppersmith [102]. The algorithm was implemented by Thomé [460] who succeeded in 2001 in computing logarithms in the 607-bit field $\mathbb{F}_{2^{607}}$.

The Certicom ECCp-109 challenge [88] was solved in 2002 by a team of contributors led by Chris Monico. The method used was the parallelized version of Pollard's rho algorithm as proposed by van Oorschot and Wiener [463]. The ECCp-109 challenge asked for the solution of an ECDLP instance in an elliptic curve defined over a 109-bit prime field. The effort took 549 days and had contributions from over 10,000 workstations on the Internet.

The equivalent key sizes for ECC and DSA parameters in Table 1.1 are from FIPS 186-2 [140] and NIST Special Publication 800-56 [342]. These comparisons are generally in agreement with those of Lenstra and Verheul [284] and Lenstra [279], who also consider cost-equivalent key sizes. Customized hardware designs for lowering the full cost of the matrix stage were proposed and analyzed by Bernstein [41], Wiener [481], and Lenstra, Shamir, Tomlinson and Tromer [282]. Customized hardware designs for lowering the full cost of sieving were proposed by Shamir [421] (see also Lenstra and Shamir [281]), Geiselmann and Steinwandt [169], and Shamir and Tromer [423]. Shamir and Tromer [423] estimate that the sieving stage for a 1024-bit RSA modulus can be completed in less than a year by a machine that would cost about US $10 million to build, and that the matrix stage is easier.

§1.4
Readers can stay abreast of the latest developments in elliptic curve cryptography and related areas by studying the proceedings of the annual cryptography conferences including ASIACRYPT, CRYPTO, EUROCRYPT, INDOCRYPT, the Workshop on Cryptographic Hardware and Embedded Systems (CHES), the International Workshop on Practice and Theory in Public Key Cryptography (PKC), and the biennial Algorithmic Number Theory Symposium (ANTS). The proceedings of all these conferences are published by Springer-Verlag in their *Lecture Notes in Computer Science* series, and are conveniently available online at http://link.springer.de/link/service/series/0558/. Another important repository for the latest research articles in cryptography is the Cryptology ePrint Archive website at http://eprint.iacr.org/.

CHAPTER 2

Finite Field Arithmetic

The efficient implementation of finite field arithmetic is an important prerequisite in elliptic curve systems because curve operations are performed using arithmetic operations in the underlying field. §2.1 provides an informal introduction to the theory of finite fields. Three kinds of fields that are especially amenable for the efficient implementation of elliptic curve systems are prime fields, binary fields, and optimal extension fields. Efficient algorithms for software implementation of addition, subtraction, multiplication and inversion in these fields are discussed at length in §2.2, §2.3, and §2.4, respectively. Hardware implementation is considered in §5.2 and chapter notes and references are provided in §2.5.

2.1 Introduction to finite fields

Fields are abstractions of familiar number systems (such as the rational numbers $\mathbb{Q}$, the real numbers $\mathbb{R}$, and the complex numbers $\mathbb{C}$) and their essential properties. They consist of a set $\mathbb{F}$ together with two operations, addition (denoted by $+$) and multiplication (denoted by $\cdot$), that satisfy the usual arithmetic properties:

  (i) $(\mathbb{F}, +)$ is an abelian group with (additive) identity denoted by 0.

  (ii) $(\mathbb{F} \setminus \{0\}, \cdot)$ is an abelian group with (multiplicative) identity denoted by 1.

  (iii) The distributive law holds: $(a + b) \cdot c = a \cdot c + b \cdot c$ for all $a, b, c \in \mathbb{F}$.

If the set $\mathbb{F}$ is finite, then the field is said to be *finite*.

    This section presents basic facts about finite fields. Other properties will be presented throughout the book as needed.

Field operations

A field $\mathbb{F}$ is equipped with two operations, addition and multiplication. *Subtraction* of field elements is defined in terms of addition: for $a, b \in \mathbb{F}$, $a - b = a + (-b)$ where $-b$ is the unique element in $\mathbb{F}$ such that $b + (-b) = 0$ ($-b$ is called the *negative* of b). Similarly, *division* of field elements is defined in terms of multiplication: for $a, b \in \mathbb{F}$ with $b \neq 0$, $a/b = a \cdot b^{-1}$ where b^{-1} is the unique element in $\mathbb{F}$ such that $b \cdot b^{-1} = 1$. (b^{-1} is called the *inverse* of b.)

Existence and uniqueness

The *order* of a finite field is the number of elements in the field. There exists a finite field $\mathbb{F}$ of order q if and only if q is a prime power, i.e., $q = p^m$ where p is a prime number called the *characteristic* of $\mathbb{F}$, and m is a positive integer. If $m = 1$, then $\mathbb{F}$ is called a *prime field*. If $m \geq 2$, then $\mathbb{F}$ is called an *extension field*. For any prime power q, there is essentially only one finite field of order q; informally, this means that any two finite fields of order q are structurally the same except that the labeling used to represent the field elements may be different (cf. Example 2.3). We say that any two finite fields of order q are *isomorphic* and denote such a field by $\mathbb{F}_q$.

Prime fields

Let p be a prime number. The integers modulo p, consisting of the integers $\{0, 1, 2, \ldots, p - 1\}$ with addition and multiplication performed modulo p, is a finite field of order p. We shall denote this field by $\mathbb{F}_p$ and call p the *modulus* of $\mathbb{F}_p$. For any integer a, $a \bmod p$ shall denote the unique integer remainder r, $0 \leq r \leq p - 1$, obtained upon dividing a by p; this operation is called *reduction modulo p*.

Example 2.1 (*prime field $\mathbb{F}_{29}$*) The elements of $\mathbb{F}_{29}$ are $\{0, 1, 2, \ldots, 28\}$. The following are some examples of arithmetic operations in $\mathbb{F}_{29}$.

  (i) Addition: $17 + 20 = 8$ since $37 \bmod 29 = 8$.

 (ii) Subtraction: $17 - 20 = 26$ since $-3 \bmod 29 = 26$.

(iii) Multiplication: $17 \cdot 20 = 21$ since $340 \bmod 29 = 21$.

 (iv) Inversion: $17^{-1} = 12$ since $17 \cdot 12 \bmod 29 = 1$.

Binary fields

Finite fields of order 2^m are called *binary fields* or *characteristic-two finite fields*. One way to construct $\mathbb{F}_{2^m}$ is to use a *polynomial basis representation*. Here, the elements of $\mathbb{F}_{2^m}$ are the binary polynomials (polynomials whose coefficients are in the field $\mathbb{F}_2 = \{0, 1\}$) of degree at most $m - 1$:

$$\mathbb{F}_{2^m} = \{a_{m-1}z^{m-1} + a_{m-2}z^{m-2} + \cdots + a_2 z^2 + a_1 z + a_0 \, : \, a_i \in \{0, 1\}\}.$$

An irreducible binary polynomial $f(z)$ of degree m is chosen (such a polynomial exists for any m and can be efficiently found; see §A.1). Irreducibility of $f(z)$ means that $f(z)$ cannot be factored as a product of binary polynomials each of degree less than m. Addition of field elements is the usual addition of polynomials, with coefficient arithmetic performed modulo 2. Multiplication of field elements is performed modulo the *reduction polynomial* $f(z)$. For any binary polynomial $a(z)$, $a(z) \bmod f(z)$ shall denote the unique remainder polynomial $r(z)$ of degree less than m obtained upon long division of $a(z)$ by $f(z)$; this operation is called *reduction modulo* $f(z)$.

Example 2.2 (*binary field* $\mathbb{F}_{2^4}$) The elements of $\mathbb{F}_{2^4}$ are the 16 binary polynomials of degree at most 3:

0	z^2	z^3	z^3+z^2
1	z^2+1	z^3+1	z^3+z^2+1
z	z^2+z	z^3+z	z^3+z^2+z
$z+1$	z^2+z+1	z^3+z+1	z^3+z^2+z+1.

The following are some examples of arithmetic operations in $\mathbb{F}_{2^4}$ with reduction polynomial $f(z) = z^4 + z + 1$.

(i) Addition: $(z^3 + z^2 + 1) + (z^2 + z + 1) = z^3 + z$.

(ii) Subtraction: $(z^3 + z^2 + 1) - (z^2 + z + 1) = z^3 + z$. (Note that since $-1 = 1$ in $\mathbb{F}_2$, we have $-a = a$ for all $a \in \mathbb{F}_{2^m}$.)

(iii) Multiplication: $(z^3 + z^2 + 1) \cdot (z^2 + z + 1) = z^2 + 1$ since

$$(z^3 + z^2 + 1) \cdot (z^2 + z + 1) = z^5 + z + 1$$

and

$$(z^5 + z + 1) \bmod (z^4 + z + 1) = z^2 + 1.$$

(iv) Inversion: $(z^3 + z^2 + 1)^{-1} = z^2$ since $(z^3 + z^2 + 1) \cdot z^2 \bmod (z^4 + z + 1) = 1$.

Example 2.3 (*isomorphic fields*) There are three irreducible binary polynomials of degree 4, namely $f_1(z) = z^4 + z + 1$, $f_2(z) = z^4 + z^3 + 1$ and $f_3(z) = z^4 + z^3 + z^2 + z + 1$. Each of these reduction polynomials can be used to construct the field $\mathbb{F}_{2^4}$; let's call the resulting fields K_1, K_2 and K_3. The field elements of K_1, K_2 and K_3 are the same 16 binary polynomials of degree at most 3. Superficially, these fields appear to be different, e.g., $z^3 \cdot z = z + 1$ in K_1, $z^3 \cdot z = z^3 + 1$ in K_2, and $z^3 \cdot z = z^3 + z^2 + z + 1$ in K_3. However, all fields of a given order are isomorphic—that is, the differences are only in the labeling of the elements. An isomorphism between K_1 and K_2 may be constructed by finding $c \in K_2$ such that $f_1(c) \equiv 0 \pmod{f_2}$ and then extending $z \mapsto c$ to an isomorphism $\varphi : K_1 \to K_2$; the choices for c are $z^2 + z$, $z^2 + z + 1$, $z^3 + z^2$, and $z^3 + z^2 + 1$.

Extension fields

The polynomial basis representation for binary fields can be generalized to all extension fields as follows. Let p be a prime and $m \geq 2$. Let $\mathbb{F}_p[z]$ denote the set of all polynomials in the variable z with coefficients from $\mathbb{F}_p$. Let $f(z)$, the *reduction polynomial*, be an irreducible polynomial of degree m in $\mathbb{F}_p[z]$—such a polynomial exists for any p and m and can be efficiently found (see §A.1). Irreducibility of $f(z)$ means that $f(z)$ cannot be factored as a product of polynomials in $\mathbb{F}_p[z]$ each of degree less than m. The elements of $\mathbb{F}_{p^m}$ are the polynomials in $\mathbb{F}_p[z]$ of degree at most $m-1$:

$$\mathbb{F}_{p^m} = \{a_{m-1}z^{m-1} + a_{m-2}z^{m-2} + \cdots + a_2z^2 + a_1z + a_0 \ : \ a_i \in \mathbb{F}_p\}.$$

Addition of field elements is the usual addition of polynomials, with coefficient arithmetic performed in $\mathbb{F}_p$. Multiplication of field elements is performed modulo the polynomial $f(z)$.

Example 2.4 (*an extension field*) Let $p = 251$ and $m = 5$. The polynomial $f(z) = z^5 + z^4 + 12z^3 + 9z^2 + 7$ is irreducible in $\mathbb{F}_{251}[z]$ and thus can serve as reduction polynomial for the construction of $\mathbb{F}_{251^5}$, the finite field of order 251^5. The elements of $\mathbb{F}_{251^5}$ are the polynomials in $\mathbb{F}_{251}[z]$ of degree at most 4.

The following are some examples of arithmetic operations in $\mathbb{F}_{251^5}$. Let $a = 123z^4 + 76z^2 + 7z + 4$ and $b = 196z^4 + 12z^3 + 225z^2 + 76$.

   (i) Addition: $a + b = 68z^4 + 12z^3 + 50z^2 + 7z + 80$.

   (ii) Subtraction: $a - b = 178z^4 + 239z^3 + 102z^2 + 7z + 179$.

   (iii) Multiplication: $a \cdot b = 117z^4 + 151z^3 + 117z^2 + 182z + 217$.

   (iv) Inversion: $a^{-1} = 109z^4 + 111z^3 + 250z^2 + 98z + 85$.

Subfields of a finite field

A subset k of a field K is a *subfield* of K if k is itself a field with respect to the operations of K. In this instance, K is said to be an *extension field* of k. The subfields of a finite field can be easily characterized. A finite field $\mathbb{F}_{p^m}$ has precisely one subfield of order p^l for each positive divisor l of m; the elements of this subfield are the elements $a \in \mathbb{F}_{p^m}$ satisfying $a^{p^l} = a$. Conversely, every subfield of $\mathbb{F}_{p^m}$ has order p^l for some positive divisor l of m.

Bases of a finite field

The finite field $\mathbb{F}_{q^n}$ can be viewed as a vector space over its subfield $\mathbb{F}_q$. Here, vectors are elements of $\mathbb{F}_{q^n}$, scalars are elements of $\mathbb{F}_q$, vector addition is the addition operation in $\mathbb{F}_{q^n}$, and scalar multiplication is the multiplication in $\mathbb{F}_{q^n}$ of $\mathbb{F}_q$-elements with $\mathbb{F}_{q^n}$-elements. The vector space has dimension n and has many bases.

If $B = \{b_1, b_2, \ldots, b_n\}$ is a basis, then $a \in \mathbb{F}_{q^n}$ can be uniquely represented by an n-tuple $(a_1, a_2, \ldots, a_n)$ of $\mathbb{F}_q$-elements where $a = a_1 b_1 + a_2 b_2 + \cdots + a_n b_n$. For example, in the polynomial basis representation of the field $\mathbb{F}_{p^m}$ described above, $\mathbb{F}_{p^m}$ is an m-dimensional vector space over $\mathbb{F}_p$ and $\{z^{m-1}, z^{m-2}, \ldots, z^2, z, 1\}$ is a basis for $\mathbb{F}_{p^m}$ over $\mathbb{F}_p$.

Multiplicative group of a finite field

The nonzero elements of a finite field $\mathbb{F}_q$, denoted $\mathbb{F}_q^*$, form a cyclic group under multiplication. Hence there exist elements $b \in \mathbb{F}_q^*$ called *generators* such that

$$\mathbb{F}_q^* = \{b^i : 0 \le i \le q - 2\}.$$

The *order* of $a \in \mathbb{F}_q^*$ is the smallest positive integer t such that $a^t = 1$. Since $\mathbb{F}_q^*$ is a cyclic group, it follows that t is a divisor of $q - 1$.

2.2 Prime field arithmetic

This section presents algorithms for performing arithmetic in the prime field $\mathbb{F}_p$. Algorithms for arbitrary primes p are presented in §2.2.1–§2.2.5. The reduction step can be accelerated considerably when the modulus p has a special form. Efficient reduction algorithms for the NIST primes such as $p = 2^{192} - 2^{64} - 1$ are considered in §2.2.6.

The algorithms presented here are well suited for software implementation. We assume that the implementation platform has a W-bit architecture where W is a multiple of 8. Workstations are commonly 64- or 32-bit architectures. Low-power or inexpensive components may have smaller W, for example, some embedded systems are 16-bit and smartcards may have $W = 8$. The bits of a W-bit word U are numbered from 0 to $W - 1$, with the rightmost bit of U designated as bit 0.

The elements of $\mathbb{F}_p$ are the integers from 0 to $p - 1$. Let $m = \lceil \log_2 p \rceil$ be the bitlength of p, and $t = \lceil m/W \rceil$ be its wordlength. Figure 2.1 illustrates the case where the binary representation of a field element a is stored in an array $A = (A[t - 1], \ldots, A[2], A[1], A[0])$ of t W-bit words, where the rightmost bit of $A[0]$ is the least significant bit.

$A[t-1]$	$\cdots$	$A[2]$	$A[1]$	$A[0]$

Figure 2.1. Representation of $a \in \mathbb{F}_p$ as an array A of W-bit words. As an integer, $a = 2^{(t-1)W} A[t-1] + \cdots + 2^{2W} A[2] + 2^W A[1] + A[0]$.

Hardware characteristics may favour approaches different from those of the algorithms and field element representation presented here. §5.1.1 examines possible bottlenecks in multiplication due to constraints on hardware integer multipliers and the cost of propagating carries. §5.1.2 briefly discusses the use of floating-point hardware commonly found on workstations, which can give substantial improvement in multiplication times (and uses a different field element representation). Similarly, single-instruction multiple-data (SIMD) registers on some processors can be employed; see §5.1.3. Selected timings for field operations appear in §5.1.5.

2.2.1 *Addition and subtraction*

Algorithms for field addition and subtraction are given in terms of corresponding algorithms for multi-word integers. The following notation and terminology is used. An assignment of the form "$(\varepsilon, z) \leftarrow w$" for an integer w is understood to mean

$$z \leftarrow w \bmod 2^W, \text{ and}$$

$$\varepsilon \leftarrow 0 \text{ if } w \in [0, 2^W), \text{ otherwise } \varepsilon \leftarrow 1.$$

If $w = x + y + \varepsilon'$ for $x, y \in [0, 2^W)$ and $\varepsilon' \in \{0, 1\}$, then $w = \varepsilon 2^W + z$ and ε is called the *carry bit* from single-word addition (with $\varepsilon = 1$ if and only if $z < x + \varepsilon'$). Algorithm 2.5 performs addition of multi-word integers.

Algorithm 2.5 Multiprecision addition

INPUT: Integers $a, b \in [0, 2^{Wt})$.
OUTPUT: (ε, c) where $c = a + b \bmod 2^{Wt}$ and ε is the carry bit.
   1. $(\varepsilon, C[0]) \leftarrow A[0] + B[0]$.
   2. For i from 1 to $t - 1$ do
      2.1 $(\varepsilon, C[i]) \leftarrow A[i] + B[i] + \varepsilon$.
   3. Return(ε, c).

On processors that handle the carry as part of the instruction set, there need not be any explicit check for carry. Multi-word subtraction (Algorithm 2.6) is similar to addition, with the carry bit often called a "borrow" in this context.

Algorithm 2.6 Multiprecision subtraction

INPUT: Integers $a, b \in [0, 2^{Wt})$.
OUTPUT: (ε, c) where $c = a - b \bmod 2^{Wt}$ and ε is the borrow.
   1. $(\varepsilon, C[0]) \leftarrow A[0] - B[0]$.
   2. For i from 1 to $t - 1$ do
      2.1 $(\varepsilon, C[i]) \leftarrow A[i] - B[i] - \varepsilon$.
   3. Return(ε, c).

Modular addition $((x + y) \bmod p)$ and subtraction $((x - y) \bmod p)$ are adapted directly from the corresponding algorithms above, with an additional step for reduction modulo p.

Algorithm 2.7 Addition in $\mathbb{F}_p$

INPUT: Modulus p, and integers $a, b \in [0, p - 1]$.
OUTPUT: $c = (a + b) \bmod p$.
1. Use Algorithm 2.5 to obtain (ε, c) where $c = a + b \bmod 2^{Wt}$ and ε is the carry bit.
2. If $\varepsilon = 1$, then subtract p from $c = (C[t - 1], \ldots, C[2], C[1], C[0])$;
   Else if $c \geq p$ then $c \leftarrow c - p$.
3. Return(c).

Algorithm 2.8 Subtraction in $\mathbb{F}_p$

INPUT: Modulus p, and integers $a, b \in [0, p - 1]$.
OUTPUT: $c = (a - b) \bmod p$.
1. Use Algorithm 2.6 to obtain (ε, c) where $c = a - b \bmod 2^{Wt}$ and ε is the borrow.
2. If $\varepsilon = 1$, then add p to $c = (C[t - 1], \ldots, C[2], C[1], C[0])$.
3. Return(c).

2.2.2 Integer multiplication

Field multiplication of $a, b \in \mathbb{F}_p$ can be accomplished by first multiplying a and b as integers, and then reducing the result modulo p. Algorithms 2.9 and 2.10 are elementary integer multiplication routines which illustrate basic operand scanning and product scanning methods, respectively. In both algorithms, (UV) denotes a $(2W)$-bit quantity obtained by concatenation of W-bit words U and V.

Algorithm 2.9 Integer multiplication (operand scanning form)

INPUT: Integers $a, b \in [0, p - 1]$.
OUTPUT: $c = a \cdot b$.
1. Set $C[i] \leftarrow 0$ for $0 \leq i \leq t - 1$.
2. For i from 0 to $t - 1$ do
   2.1 $U \leftarrow 0$.
   2.2 For j from 0 to $t - 1$ do:
       $(UV) \leftarrow C[i + j] + A[i] \cdot B[j] + U$.
       $C[i + j] \leftarrow V$.
   2.3 $C[i + t] \leftarrow U$.
3. Return(c).

The calculation $C[i + j] + A[i] \cdot B[j] + U$ at step 2.2 is called the *inner product operation*. Since the operands are W-bit values, the inner product is bounded by $2(2^W - 1) + (2^W - 1)^2 = 2^{2W} - 1$ and can be represented by (UV).

Algorithm 2.10 is arranged so that the product $c = ab$ is calculated right-to-left. As in the preceding algorithm, a $(2W)$-bit product of W-bit operands is required. The values R_0, R_1, R_2, U, and V are W-bit words.

Algorithm 2.10 Integer multiplication (product scanning form)

INPUT: Integers $a, b \in [0, p-1]$.
OUTPUT: $c = a \cdot b$.
  1. $R_0 \leftarrow 0,\ R_1 \leftarrow 0,\ R_2 \leftarrow 0$.
  2. For k from 0 to $2t - 2$ do
      2.1 For each element of $\{(i, j) \mid i + j = k,\ 0 \le i, j \le t - 1\}$ do
          $(UV) \leftarrow A[i] \cdot B[j]$.
          $(\varepsilon, R_0) \leftarrow R_0 + V$.
          $(\varepsilon, R_1) \leftarrow R_1 + U + \varepsilon$.
          $R_2 \leftarrow R_2 + \varepsilon$.
      2.2 $C[k] \leftarrow R_0,\ R_0 \leftarrow R_1,\ R_1 \leftarrow R_2,\ R_2 \leftarrow 0$.
  3. $C[2t - 1] \leftarrow R_0$.
  4. Return(c).

Note 2.11 (*implementing Algorithms 2.9 and 2.10*) Algorithms 2.9 and 2.10 are written in a form motivated by the case where a W-bit architecture has a multiplication operation giving a $2W$-bit result (e.g., the Intel Pentium or Sun SPARC). A common exception is illustrated by the 64-bit Sun UltraSPARC, where the multiplier produces the lower 64 bits of the product of 64-bit inputs. One variation of these algorithms splits a and b into $(W/2)$-bit half-words, but accumulates in W-bit registers. See also §5.1.3 for an example concerning a 32-bit architecture which has some 64-bit operations.

Karatsuba-Ofman multiplication

Algorithms 2.9 and 2.10 take $O(n^2)$ bit operations for multiplying two n-bit integers. A divide-and-conquer algorithm due to Karatsuba and Ofman reduces the complexity to $O(n^{\log_2 3})$. Suppose that $n = 2l$ and $x = x_1 2^l + x_0$ and $y = y_1 2^l + y_0$ are $2l$-bit integers. Then

$$xy = (x_1 2^l + x_0)(y_1 2^l + y_0)$$
$$= x_1 \cdot y_1 2^{2l} + [(x_0 + x_1) \cdot (y_0 + y_1) - x_1 y_1 - x_0 \cdot y_0]2^l + x_0 y_0$$

and xy can be computed by performing three multiplications of l-bit integers (as opposed to one multiplication with $2l$-bit integers) along with two additions and two subtractions.[1] For large values of l, the cost of the additions and subtractions is insignificant relative to the cost of the multiplications. The procedure may be applied recursively to the intermediate values, terminating at some threshold (possibly the word size of the machine) where a classical or other method is employed.

For integers of modest size, the overhead in Karatsuba-Ofman may be significant. Implementations may deviate from the traditional description in order to reduce the shifting required (for multiplications by 2^l and 2^{2l}) and make more efficient use of word-oriented operations. For example, it may be more effective to split on word boundaries, and the split at a given stage may be into more than two fragments.

Example 2.12 (*Karatsuba-Ofman methods*) Consider multiplication of 224-bit values x and y, on a machine with word size $W = 32$. Two possible depth-2 approaches are indicated in Figure 2.2. The split in Figure 2.2(a) is perhaps mathematically more elegant

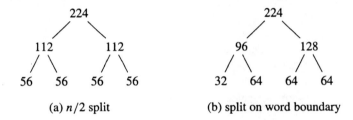

(a) $n/2$ split   (b) split on word boundary

Figure 2.2. Depth-2 splits for 224-bit integers. The product xy using (a) has three 112×112 multiplications, each performed using three 56×56 multiplications. Using (b), xy has a 96×96 (split as a 32×32 and two 64×64) and two 128×128 multiplications (each generating three 64×64 multiplies).

and may have more reusable code compared with that in Figure 2.2(b). However, more shifting will be required (since the splits are not on word boundaries). If multiplication of 56-bit quantities (perhaps by another application of Karatsuba-Ofman) has approximately the same cost as multiplication of 64-bit values, then the split has under-utilized the hardware capabilities since the cost is nine 64-bit multiplications versus one 32-bit and eight 64-bit multiplications in (b). On the other hand, the split on word boundaries in Figure 2.2(b) has more complicated cross term calculations, since there may be carry to an additional word. For example, the cross terms at depth 2 are of the form

$$(x_0 + x_1)(y_0 + y_1) - x_1 y_1 - x_0 y_0$$

where $x_0 + x_1$ and $y_0 + y_1$ are 57-bit in (a) and 65-bit in (b). Split (b) costs somewhat more here, although $(x_0 + x_1)(y_0 + y_1)$ can be managed as a 64×64 mulitply followed by two possible additions corresponding to the high bits.

---

[1] The cross term can be written $(x_0 - x_1)(y_1 - y_0) + x_0 y_0 + x_1 y_1$ which may be useful on some platforms or if it is known a priori that $x_0 \geq x_1$ and $y_0 \leq y_1$.

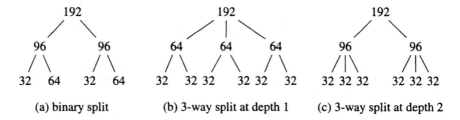

   (a) binary split   (b) 3-way split at depth 1   (c) 3-way split at depth 2

Figure 2.3. Depth-2 splits for 192-bit integers. The product xy using (a) has three 96×96 multiplications. Each is performed with a 32×32 and two 64×64 (each requiring three 32×32) multiplications, for a total of 21 multiplications of size 32×32. Using (b) or (c), only 18 multiplications of size 32×32 are required.

As a second illustration, consider Karatsuba-Ofman applied to 192-bit integers, again with $W = 32$. Three possible depth-2 approaches are given in Figure 2.3. In terms of 32×32 multiplications, the split in Figure 2.3(a) will require 21, while (b) and (c) use 18. The basic idea is that multiplication of $3l$-bit integers $x = x_2 2^{2l} + x_1 2^l + x_0$ and $y = y_2 2^{2l} + y_1 2^l + y_0$ can be done as

$$
\begin{aligned}
xy &= (x_2 2^{2l} + x_1 2^l + x_0) \cdot (y_2 2^{2l} + y_1 2^l + y_0) \\
&= x_2 y_2 2^{4l} + (x_2 y_1 + x_1 y_2) 2^{3l} + (x_2 y_0 + x_0 y_2 + x_1 y_1) 2^{2l} \\
&\quad + (x_1 y_0 + x_0 y_1) 2^l + x_0 y_0 \\
&= x_2 \cdot y_2 2^{4l} + [(x_2 + x_1) \cdot (y_2 + y_1) - x_2 y_2 - x_1 \cdot y_1] 2^{3l} \\
&\quad + [(x_2 + x_0) \cdot (y_2 + y_0) - x_2 y_2 - x_0 \cdot y_0 + x_1 y_1] 2^{2l} \\
&\quad + [(x_1 + x_0) \cdot (y_1 + y_0) - x_1 y_1 - x_0 y_0] 2^l + x_0 y_0
\end{aligned}
$$

for a total of six multiplications of l-bit integers.

The performance of field multiplication is fundamental to mechanisms based on elliptic curves. Constraints on hardware integer multipliers and the cost of carry propagation can result in significant bottlenecks in direct implementations of Algorithms 2.9 and 2.10. As outlined in the introductory paragraphs of §2.2, Chapter 5 discusses alternative strategies applicable in some environments.

2.2.3 Integer squaring

Field squaring of $a \in \mathbb{F}_p$ can be accomplished by first squaring a as an integer, and then reducing the result modulo p. A straightforward modification of Algorithm 2.10 gives the following algorithm for integer squaring, reducing the number of required single-precision multiplications by roughly half. In step 2.1, a $(2W + 1)$-bit result (ε, UV) is obtained from multiplication of the $(2W)$-bit quantity (UV) by 2.

Algorithm 2.13 Integer squaring

INPUT: Integer $a \in [0, p-1]$.
OUTPUT: $c = a^2$.

1. $R_0 \leftarrow 0$, $R_1 \leftarrow 0$, $R_2 \leftarrow 0$.
2. For k from 0 to $2t - 2$ do
    2.1 For each element of $\{(i, j) \mid i + j = k, \ 0 \le i \le j \le t - 1\}$ do
        $(UV) \leftarrow A[i] \cdot A[j]$.
        If $(i < j)$ then do: $(\varepsilon, UV) \leftarrow (UV) \cdot 2$, $R_2 \leftarrow R_2 + \varepsilon$.
        $(\varepsilon, R_0) \leftarrow R_0 + V$.
        $(\varepsilon, R_1) \leftarrow R_1 + U + \varepsilon$.
        $R_2 \leftarrow R_2 + \varepsilon$.
    2.2 $C[k] \leftarrow R_0$, $R_0 \leftarrow R_1$, $R_1 \leftarrow R_2$, $R_2 \leftarrow 0$.
3. $C[2t - 1] \leftarrow R_0$.
4. Return(c).

The multiplication by 2 in step 2.1 may be implemented as two single-precision shift-through-carry (if available) or as two single-precision additions with carry. The step can be rewritten so that each output word $C[k]$ requires at most one multiplication by 2, at the cost of two additional accumulators and an associated accumulation step.

2.2.4 Reduction

For moduli p that are not of special form, the reduction $z \bmod p$ can be an expensive part of modular multiplication. Since the performance of elliptic curve schemes depends heavily on the speed of field multiplication, there is considerable incentive to select moduli, such as the NIST-recommended primes of §2.2.6, that permit fast reduction. In this section, we present only the reduction method of Barrett and an overview of Montgomery multiplication.

The methods of Barrett and Montgomery are similar in that expensive divisions in classical reduction methods are replaced by less-expensive operations. Barrett reduction can be regarded as a direct replacement for classical methods; however, an expensive modulus-dependent calculation is required, and hence the method is applicable when many reductions are performed with a single modulus. Montgomery's method, on the other hand, requires transformations of the data. The technique can be effective when the cost of the input and output conversions is offset by savings in many intermediate multiplications, as occurs in modular exponentiation.

Note that some modular operations are typically required in a larger framework such as the signature schemes of §4.4, and the moduli involved need not be of special form. In these instances, Barrett reduction may be an appropriate method.

Barrett reduction

Barrett reduction (Algorithm 2.14) finds $z \bmod p$ for given positive integers z and p. In contrast to the algorithms presented in §2.2.6, Barrett reduction does not exploit any special form of the modulus p. The quotient $\lfloor z/p \rfloor$ is estimated using less-expensive operations involving powers of a suitably-chosen base b (e.g., $b = 2^L$ for some L which may depend on the modulus but not on z). A modulus-dependent quantity $\lfloor b^{2k}/p \rfloor$ must be calculated, making the algorithm suitable for the case that many reductions are performed with a single modulus.

Algorithm 2.14 Barrett reduction

INPUT: p, $b \geq 3$, $k = \lfloor \log_b p \rfloor + 1$, $0 \leq z < b^{2k}$, and $\mu = \lfloor b^{2k}/p \rfloor$.
OUTPUT: $z \bmod p$.
    1. $\widehat{q} \leftarrow \lfloor \lfloor z/b^{k-1} \rfloor \cdot \mu / b^{k+1} \rfloor$.
    2. $r \leftarrow (z \bmod b^{k+1}) - (\widehat{q} \cdot p \bmod b^{k+1})$.
    3. If $r < 0$ then $r \leftarrow r + b^{k+1}$.
    4. While $r \geq p$ do: $r \leftarrow r - p$.
    5. Return(r).

Note 2.15 (*correctness of Algorithm 2.14*) Let $q = \lfloor z/p \rfloor$; then $r = z \bmod p = z - qp$. Step 1 of the algorithm calculates an estimate $\widehat{q}$ to q since

$$\frac{z}{p} = \frac{z}{b^{k-1}} \cdot \frac{b^{2k}}{p} \cdot \frac{1}{b^{k+1}}.$$

Note that

$$0 \leq \widehat{q} = \left\lfloor \frac{\left\lfloor \frac{z}{b^{k-1}} \right\rfloor \cdot \mu}{b^{k+1}} \right\rfloor \leq \left\lfloor \frac{z}{p} \right\rfloor = q.$$

The following argument shows that $q - 2 \leq \widehat{q} \leq q$; that is, $\widehat{q}$ is a good estimate for q. Define

$$\alpha = \frac{z}{b^{k-1}} - \left\lfloor \frac{z}{b^{k-1}} \right\rfloor, \quad \beta = \frac{b^{2k}}{p} - \left\lfloor \frac{b^{2k}}{p} \right\rfloor.$$

Then $0 \leq \alpha, \beta < 1$ and

$$q = \left\lfloor \frac{\left(\left\lfloor \frac{z}{b^{k-1}} \right\rfloor + \alpha \right) \left(\left\lfloor \frac{b^{2k}}{p} \right\rfloor + \beta \right)}{b^{k+1}} \right\rfloor$$

$$\leq \left\lfloor \frac{\left\lfloor \frac{z}{b^{k-1}} \right\rfloor \cdot \mu}{b^{k+1}} + \frac{\left\lfloor \frac{z}{b^{k-1}} \right\rfloor + \left\lfloor \frac{b^{2k}}{p} \right\rfloor + 1}{b^{k+1}} \right\rfloor.$$

Since $z < b^{2k}$ and $p \geq b^{k-1}$, it follows that

$$\left\lfloor \frac{z}{b^{k-1}} \right\rfloor + \left\lfloor \frac{b^{2k}}{p} \right\rfloor + 1 \leq (b^{k+1} - 1) + b^{k+1} + 1 = 2b^{k+1}$$

and

$$q \leq \left\lfloor \frac{\left\lfloor \frac{z}{b^{k-1}} \right\rfloor \cdot \mu}{b^{k+1}} + 2 \right\rfloor = \widehat{q} + 2.$$

The value r calculated in step 2 necessarily satisfies $r \equiv z - \widehat{q}p \pmod{b^{k+1}}$ with $|r| < b^{k+1}$. Hence $0 \leq r < b^{k+1}$ and $r = z - \widehat{q}p \bmod b^{k+1}$ after step 3. Now, since $0 \leq z - qp < p$, we have

$$0 \leq z - \widehat{q}p \leq z - (q-2)p < 3p.$$

Since $b \geq 3$ and $p < b^k$, we have $3p < b^{k+1}$. Thus $0 \leq z - \widehat{q}p < b^{k+1}$, and so $r = z - \widehat{q}p$ after step 3. Hence, at most two subtractions at step 4 are required to obtain $0 \leq r < p$, and then $r = z \bmod p$.

Note 2.16 (*computational considerations for Algorithm 2.14*)

(i) A natural choice for the base is $b = 2^L$ where L is near the word size of the processor.

(ii) Other than the calculation of μ (which is done once per modulus), the divisions required are simple shifts of the base-b representation.

(iii) Let $z' = \lfloor z/b^{k-1} \rfloor$. Note that z' and μ have at most $k + 1$ base-b digits. The calculation of $\widehat{q}$ in step 1 discards the $k + 1$ least-significant digits of the product $z'\mu$. Given the base-b representations $z' = \sum z'_i b^i$ and $\mu = \sum \mu_j b^j$, write

$$z'\mu = \sum_{l=0}^{2k} \underbrace{\left(\sum_{i+j=l} z'_i \mu_j \right)}_{w_l} b^l$$

where w_l may exceed $b - 1$. If $b \geq k - 1$, then $\sum_{l=0}^{k-2} w_l b^l < b^{k+1}$ and hence

$$0 \leq \frac{z'\mu}{b^{k+1}} - \sum_{l=k-1}^{2k} \frac{w_l b^l}{b^{k+1}} = \sum_{l=0}^{k-2} \frac{w_l b^l}{b^{k+1}} < 1.$$

It follows that $\left\lfloor \sum_{l=k-1}^{2k} w_l b^l / b^{k+1} \right\rfloor$ underestimates $\widehat{q}$ by at most 1 if $b \geq k - 1$. At most $\binom{k+2}{2} + k = (k^2 + 5k + 2)/2$ single-precision multiplications (i.e., multiplications of values less than b) are required to find this estimate for $\widehat{q}$.

(iv) Only the $k + 1$ least significant digits of $\widehat{q} \cdot p$ are required at step 2. Since $p < b^k$, the $k + 1$ digits can be obtained with $\binom{k+1}{2} + k$ single-precision multiplications.

Montgomery multiplication

As with Barrett reduction, the strategy in Montgomery's method is to replace division in classical reduction algorithms with less-expensive operations. The method is not efficient for a single modular multiplication, but can be used effectively in computations such as modular exponentiation where many multiplications are performed for given input. For this section, we give only an overview (for more details, see §2.5).

Let $R > p$ with $\gcd(R, p) = 1$. Montgomery reduction produces $zR^{-1} \bmod p$ for an input $z < pR$. We consider the case that p is odd, so that $R = 2^{Wt}$ may be selected and division by R is relatively inexpensive. If $p' = -p^{-1} \bmod R$, then $c = zR^{-1} \bmod p$ may be obtained via

$$c \leftarrow (z + (zp' \bmod R)p)/R,$$
$$\text{if } c \geq p \text{ then } c \leftarrow c - p,$$

with $t(t+1)$ single-precision multiplications (and no divisions).

Given $x \in [0, p)$, let $\tilde{x} = xR \bmod p$. Note that $(\tilde{x}\tilde{y})R^{-1} \bmod p = (xy)R \bmod p$; that is, Montgomery reduction can be used in a multiplication method on representatives $\tilde{x}$. We define the Montgomery product of $\tilde{x}$ and $\tilde{y}$ to be

$$\text{Mont}(\tilde{x}, \tilde{y}) = \tilde{x}\tilde{y}R^{-1} \bmod p = xyR \bmod p. \tag{2.1}$$

A single modular multiplication cannot afford the expensive transformations $x \mapsto \tilde{x} = xR \bmod p$ and $\tilde{x} \mapsto \tilde{x}R^{-1} \bmod p = x$; however, the transformations are performed only once when used as part of a larger calculation such as modular exponentiation, as illustrated in Algorithm 2.17.

Algorithm 2.17 Montgomery exponentiation (basic)

INPUT: Odd modulus p, $R = 2^{Wt}$, $p' = -p^{-1} \bmod R$, $x \in [0, p)$, $e = (e_l, \ldots, e_0)_2$.
OUTPUT: $x^e \bmod p$.
    1. $\tilde{x} \leftarrow xR \bmod p$, $A \leftarrow R \bmod p$.
    2. For i from l downto 0 do
        2.1 $A \leftarrow \text{Mont}(A, A)$.
        2.2 If $e_i = 1$ then $A \leftarrow \text{Mont}(A, \tilde{x})$.
    3. Return($\text{Mont}(A, 1)$).

As a rough comparison, Montgomery reduction requires $t(t+1)$ single-precision multiplications, while Barrett (with $b = 2^W$) uses $t(t+4)+1$, and hence Montgomery methods are expected to be superior in calculations such as general modular exponentiation. Both methods are expected to be much slower than the direct reduction techniques of §2.2.6 for moduli of special form.

Montgomery arithmetic can be used to accelerate modular inversion methods that use repeated multiplication, where a^{-1} is obtained as $a^{p-2} \bmod p$ (since $a^{p-1} \equiv 1$ (mod p) if $\gcd(a, p) = 1$). Elliptic curve point multiplication (§3.3) can benefit from Montgomery arithmetic, where the Montgomery inverse discussed in §2.2.5 may also be of interest.

2.2.5 Inversion

Recall that the inverse of a nonzero element $a \in \mathbb{F}_p$, denoted $a^{-1} \bmod p$ or simply a^{-1} if the field is understood from context, is the unique element $x \in \mathbb{F}_p$ such that $ax = 1$ in $\mathbb{F}_p$, i.e., $ax \equiv 1$ (mod p). Inverses can be efficiently computed by the extended Euclidean algorithm for integers.

The extended Euclidean algorithm for integers

Let a and b be integers, not both 0. The *greatest common divisor (gcd)* of a and b, denoted $\gcd(a, b)$, is the largest integer d that divides both a and b. Efficient algorithms for computing $\gcd(a, b)$ exploit the following simple result.

Theorem 2.18 Let a and b be positive integers. Then $\gcd(a, b) = \gcd(b - ca, a)$ for all integers c.

In the classical Euclidean algorithm for computing the gcd of positive integers a and b where $b \geq a$, b is divided by a to obtain a quotient q and a remainder r satisfying $b = qa + r$ and $0 \leq r < a$. By Theorem 2.18, $\gcd(a, b) = \gcd(r, a)$. Thus, the problem of determining $\gcd(a, b)$ is reduced to that of computing $\gcd(r, a)$ where the arguments (r, a) are smaller than the original arguments (a, b). This process is repeated until one of the arguments is 0, and the result is then immediately obtained since $\gcd(0, d) = d$. The algorithm must terminate since the non-negative remainders are strictly decreasing. Moreover, it is efficient because the number of division steps can be shown to be at most $2k$ where k is the bitlength of a.

The Euclidean algorithm can be extended to find integers x and y such that $ax + by = d$ where $d = \gcd(a, b)$. Algorithm 2.19 maintains the invariants

$$ ax_1 + by_1 = u, \quad ax_2 + by_2 = v, \quad u \leq v. $$

The algorithm terminates when $u = 0$, in which case $v = \gcd(a, b)$ and $x = x_2$, $y = y_2$ satisfy $ax + by = d$.

Algorithm 2.19 Extended Euclidean algorithm for integers

INPUT: Positive integers a and b with $a \leq b$.
OUTPUT: $d = \gcd(a, b)$ and integers x, y satisfying $ax + by = d$.
1. $u \leftarrow a, v \leftarrow b$.
2. $x_1 \leftarrow 1, y_1 \leftarrow 0, x_2 \leftarrow 0, y_2 \leftarrow 1$.
3. While $u \neq 0$ do
   3.1 $q \leftarrow \lfloor v/u \rfloor, r \leftarrow v - qu, x \leftarrow x_2 - qx_1, y \leftarrow y_2 - qy_1$.
   3.2 $v \leftarrow u, u \leftarrow r, x_2 \leftarrow x_1, x_1 \leftarrow x, y_2 \leftarrow y_1, y_1 \leftarrow y$.
4. $d \leftarrow v, x \leftarrow x_2, y \leftarrow y_2$.
5. Return(d, x, y).

Suppose now that p is prime and $a \in [1, p-1]$, and hence $\gcd(a, p) = 1$. If Algorithm 2.19 is executed with inputs (a, p), the last nonzero remainder r encountered in step 3.1 is $r = 1$. Subsequent to this occurrence, the integers u, x_1 and y_1 as updated in step 3.2 satisfy $ax_1 + py_1 = u$ with $u = 1$. Hence $ax_1 \equiv 1 \pmod{p}$ and so $a^{-1} = x_1 \bmod p$. Note that y_1 and y_2 are not needed for the determination of x_1. These observations lead to Algorithm 2.20 for inversion in $\mathbb{F}_p$.

Algorithm 2.20 Inversion in $\mathbb{F}_p$ using the extended Euclidean algorithm

---

INPUT: Prime p and $a \in [1, p-1]$.
OUTPUT: $a^{-1} \bmod p$.
1. $u \leftarrow a, v \leftarrow p$.
2. $x_1 \leftarrow 1, x_2 \leftarrow 0$.
3. While $u \neq 1$ do
   3.1 $q \leftarrow \lfloor v/u \rfloor, r \leftarrow v - qu, x \leftarrow x_2 - qx_1$.
   3.2 $v \leftarrow u, u \leftarrow r, x_2 \leftarrow x_1, x_1 \leftarrow x$.
4. Return($x_1 \bmod p$).

Binary inversion algorithm

A drawback of Algorithm 2.20 is the requirement for computationally expensive division operations in step 3.1. The binary inversion algorithm replaces the divisions with cheaper shifts (divisions by 2) and subtractions. The algorithm is an extended version of the binary gcd algorithm which is presented next.

Before each iteration of step 3.1 of Algorithm 2.21, at most one of u and v is odd. Thus the divisions by 2 in steps 3.1 and 3.2 do not change the value of $\gcd(u, v)$. In each iteration, after steps 3.1 and 3.2, both u and v are odd and hence exactly one of u and v will be even at the end of step 3.3. Thus, each iteration of step 3 reduces the bitlength of either u or v by at least one. It follows that the total number of iterations of step 3 is at most $2k$ where k is the maximum of the bitlengths of a and b.

Algorithm 2.21 Binary gcd algorithm

INPUT: Positive integers a and b.

OUTPUT: $\gcd(a, b)$.

    1. $u \leftarrow a, v \leftarrow b, e \leftarrow 1$.

    2. While both u and v are even do: $u \leftarrow u/2, v \leftarrow v/2, e \leftarrow 2e$.

    3. While $u \neq 0$ do

        3.1 While u is even do: $u \leftarrow u/2$.

        3.2 While v is even do: $v \leftarrow v/2$.

        3.3 If $u \geq v$ then $u \leftarrow u - v$; else $v \leftarrow v - u$.

    4. Return($e \cdot v$).

Algorithm 2.22 computes $a^{-1} \bmod p$ by finding an integer x such that $ax + py = 1$. The algorithm maintains the invariants

$$ax_1 + py_1 = u, \quad ax_2 + py_2 = v$$

where y_1 and y_2 are not explicitly computed. The algorithm terminates when $u = 1$ or $v = 1$. In the former case, $ax_1 + py_1 = 1$ and hence $a^{-1} = x_1 \bmod p$. In the latter case, $ax_2 + py_2 = 1$ and $a^{-1} = x_2 \bmod p$.

Algorithm 2.22 Binary algorithm for inversion in $\mathbb{F}_p$

INPUT: Prime p and $a \in [1, p-1]$.

OUTPUT: $a^{-1} \bmod p$.

    1. $u \leftarrow a, v \leftarrow p$.

    2. $x_1 \leftarrow 1, x_2 \leftarrow 0$.

    3. While ($u \neq 1$ and $v \neq 1$) do

        3.1 While u is even do

            $u \leftarrow u/2$.

            If x_1 is even then $x_1 \leftarrow x_1/2$; else $x_1 \leftarrow (x_1 + p)/2$.

        3.2 While v is even do

            $v \leftarrow v/2$.

            If x_2 is even then $x_2 \leftarrow x_2/2$; else $x_2 \leftarrow (x_2 + p)/2$.

        3.3 If $u \geq v$ then: $u \leftarrow u - v, x_1 \leftarrow x_1 - x_2$;

            Else: $v \leftarrow v - u, x_2 \leftarrow x_2 - x_1$.

    4. If $u = 1$ then return($x_1 \bmod p$); else return($x_2 \bmod p$).

A division algorithm producing $b/a = ba^{-1} \bmod p$ can be obtained directly from the binary algorithm by changing the initialization condition $x_1 \leftarrow 1$ to $x_1 \leftarrow b$. The running times are expected to be the same, since x_1 in the inversion algorithm is expected to be full-length after a few iterations. Division algorithms are discussed in more detail for binary fields (§2.3) where the lower cost of inversion relative to multiplication makes division especially attractive.

Algorithm 2.22 can be converted to a two-stage inversion method that first finds $a^{-1}2^k \bmod p$ for some integer $k \geq 0$ and then solves for a^{-1}. This alternative is similar to the almost inverse method (Algorithm 2.50) for inversion in binary fields, and permits some optimizations not available in a direct implementation of Algorithm 2.22. The basic method is outlined in the context of the Montgomery inverse below, where the strategy is particularly appropriate.

Montgomery inversion

As outlined in §2.2.4, the basic strategy in Montgomery's method is to replace modular reduction $z \bmod p$ by a less-expensive operation $zR^{-1} \bmod p$ for a suitably chosen R. Montgomery arithmetic can be regarded as operating on representatives $\tilde{x} = xR \bmod p$, and is applicable in calculations such as modular exponentiation where the required initial and final conversions $x \mapsto \tilde{x}$ and $\tilde{x} \mapsto \tilde{x}R^{-1} \bmod p = x$ are an insignificant portion of the overall computation.

Let $p > 2$ be an odd (but possibly composite) integer, and define $n = \lceil \log_2 p \rceil$. The *Montgomery inverse* of an integer a with $\gcd(a, p) = 1$ is $a^{-1}2^n \bmod p$. Algorithm 2.23 is a modification of the binary algorithm (Algorithm 2.22), and computes $a^{-1}2^k \bmod p$ for some integer $k \in [n, 2n]$.

Algorithm 2.23 Partial Montgomery inversion in $\mathbb{F}_p$

INPUT: Odd integer $p > 2$, $a \in [1, p-1]$, and $n = \lceil \log_2 p \rceil$.
OUTPUT: Either "not invertible" or (x, k) where $n \leq k \leq 2n$ and $x = a^{-1}2^k \bmod p$.
  1. $u \leftarrow a, v \leftarrow p, x_1 \leftarrow 1, x_2 \leftarrow 0, k \leftarrow 0$.
  2. While $v > 0$ do
      2.1 If v is even then $v \leftarrow v/2, x_1 \leftarrow 2x_1$;
            else if u is even then $u \leftarrow u/2, x_2 \leftarrow 2x_2$;
            else if $v \geq u$ then $v \leftarrow (v-u)/2, x_2 \leftarrow x_2 + x_1, x_1 \leftarrow 2x_1$;
            else $u \leftarrow (u-v)/2, x_1 \leftarrow x_2 + x_1, x_2 \leftarrow 2x_2$.
      2.2 $k \leftarrow k+1$.
  3. If $u \neq 1$ then return("not invertible").
  4. If $x_1 > p$ then $x_1 \leftarrow x_1 - p$.
  5. Return(x_1, k).

For invertible a, the Montgomery inverse $a^{-1}2^n \bmod p$ may be obtained from the output (x, k) by $k - n$ repeated divisions of the form:

$$\text{if } x \text{ is even then } x \leftarrow x/2; \text{ else } x \leftarrow (x+p)/2. \tag{2.2}$$

Compared with the binary method (Algorithm 2.22) for producing the ordinary inverse, Algorithm 2.23 has simpler updating of the variables x_1 and x_2, although $k - n$ of the more expensive updates occur in (2.2).

Note 2.24 (*correctness of and implementation considerations for Algorithm 2.23*)

(i) In addition to $\gcd(u, v) = \gcd(a, p)$, the invariants

$$ax_1 \equiv u2^k \pmod{p} \quad \text{and} \quad ax_2 \equiv -v2^k \pmod{p}$$

are maintained. If $\gcd(a, p) = 1$, then $u = 1$ and $x_1 \equiv a^{-1}2^k \pmod{p}$ at the last iteration of step 2.

(ii) Until the last iteration, the conditions

$$p = vx_1 + ux_2, \quad x_1 \geq 1, \quad v \geq 1, \quad 0 \leq u \leq a,$$

hold, and hence $x_1, v \in [1, p]$. At the last iteration, $x_1 \leftarrow 2x_1 \leq 2p$; if $\gcd(a, p) = 1$, then necessarily $x_1 < 2p$ and step 4 ensures $x_1 < p$. Unlike Algorithm 2.22, the variables x_1 and x_2 grow slowly, possibly allowing some implementation optimizations.

(iii) Each iteration of step 2 reduces the product uv by at least half and the sum $u + v$ by at most half. Initially $u + v = a + p$ and $uv = ap$, and $u = v = 1$ before the final iteration. Hence $(a + p)/2 \leq 2^{k-1} \leq ap$, and it follows that $2^{n-2} < 2^{k-1} < 2^{2n}$ and $n \leq k \leq 2n$.

Montgomery arithmetic commonly selects $R = 2^{Wt} \geq 2^n$ for efficiency and uses representatives $\tilde{x} = xR \bmod p$. The Montgomery product $\text{Mont}(\tilde{x}, \tilde{y})$ of $\tilde{x}$ and $\tilde{y}$ is as defined in (2.1). The second stage (2.2) can be modified to use Montgomery multiplication to produce $a^{-1} \bmod p$ or $a^{-1}R \bmod p$ (rather than $a^{-1}2^n \bmod p$) from a, or to calculate $a^{-1}R \bmod p$ when Algorithm 2.23 is presented with $\tilde{a}$ rather than a. Algorithm 2.25 is applicable in elliptic curve point multiplication (§3.3) if Montgomery arithmetic is used with affine coordinates.

Algorithm 2.25 Montgomery inversion in $\mathbb{F}_p$

INPUT: Odd integer $p > 2$, $n = \lceil \log_2 p \rceil$, $R^2 \bmod p$, and $\tilde{a} = aR \bmod p$ with $\gcd(a, p) = 1$.

OUTPUT: $a^{-1}R \bmod p$.

1. Use Algorithm 2.23 to find (x, k) where $x = \tilde{a}^{-1}2^k \bmod p$ and $n \leq k \leq 2n$.
2. If $k < Wt$ then
    2.1 $x \leftarrow \text{Mont}(x, R^2) = a^{-1}2^k \bmod p$.
    2.2 $k \leftarrow k + Wt$.   {Now, $k > Wt$.}
3. $x \leftarrow \text{Mont}(x, R^2) = a^{-1}2^k \bmod p$.
4. $x \leftarrow \text{Mont}(x, 2^{2Wt-k}) = a^{-1}R \bmod p$.
5. Return(x).

The value $a^{-1}R \equiv R^2/(aR) \pmod{p}$ may also be obtained by a division algorithm variant of Algorithm 2.22 with inputs $R^2 \bmod p$ and $\tilde{a}$. However, Algorithm 2.25 may have implementation advantages, and the Montgomery multiplications required are expected to be relatively inexpensive compared to the cost of inversion.

Simultaneous inversion

Field inversion tends to be expensive relative to multiplication. If inverses are required for several elements, then the method of simultaneous inversion finds the inverses with a single inversion and approximately three multiplications per element. The method is based on the observation that $1/x = y(1/xy)$ and $1/y = x(1/xy)$, which is generalized in Algorithm 2.26 to k elements.

Algorithm 2.26 Simultaneous inversion

INPUT: Prime p and nonzero elements $a_1, \ldots, a_k$ in $\mathbb{F}_p$

OUTPUT: Field elements $a_1^{-1}, \ldots, a_k^{-1}$, where $a_i a_i^{-1} \equiv 1 \pmod{p}$.

    1. $c_1 \leftarrow a_1$.

    2. For i from 2 to k do: $c_i \leftarrow c_{i-1} a_i \bmod p$.

    3. $u \leftarrow c_k^{-1} \bmod p$.

    4. For i from k downto 2 do

        4.1 $a_i^{-1} \leftarrow u c_{i-1} \bmod p$.

        4.2 $u \leftarrow u a_i \bmod p$.

    5. $a_1^{-1} \leftarrow u$.

    6. Return($a_1^{-1}, \ldots, a_k^{-1}$).

For k elements, the algorithm requires one inversion and $3(k-1)$ multiplications, along with k elements of temporary storage. Although the algorithm is presented in the context of prime fields, the technique can be adapted to other fields and is superior to k separate inversions whenever the cost of an inversion is higher than that of three multiplications.

2.2.6 NIST primes

The FIPS 186-2 standard recommends elliptic curves over the five prime fields with moduli:

$$p_{192} = 2^{192} - 2^{64} - 1$$
$$p_{224} = 2^{224} - 2^{96} + 1$$
$$p_{256} = 2^{256} - 2^{224} + 2^{192} + 2^{96} - 1$$
$$p_{384} = 2^{384} - 2^{128} - 2^{96} + 2^{32} - 1$$
$$p_{521} = 2^{521} - 1.$$

These primes have the property that they can be written as the sum or difference of a small number of powers of 2. Furthermore, except for p_{521}, the powers appearing in these expressions are all multiples of 32. These properties yield reduction algorithms that are especially fast on machines with wordsize 32.

For example, consider $p = p_{192} = 2^{192} - 2^{64} - 1$, and let c be an integer with $0 \leq c < p^2$. Let

$$c = c_5 2^{320} + c_4 2^{256} + c_3 2^{192} + c_2 2^{128} + c_1 2^{64} + c_0 \qquad (2.3)$$

be the base-2^{64} representation of c, where each $c_i \in [0, 2^{64} - 1]$. We can then reduce the higher powers of 2 in (2.3) using the congruences

$$2^{192} \equiv 2^{64} + 1 \pmod{p}$$
$$2^{256} \equiv 2^{128} + 2^{64} \pmod{p}$$
$$2^{320} \equiv 2^{128} + 2^{64} + 1 \pmod{p}.$$

We thus obtain

$$\begin{aligned}
c \equiv \quad & c_5 2^{128} + c_5 2^{64} + c_5 \\
+ & c_4 2^{128} + c_4 2^{64} \\
+ & \qquad\quad c_3 2^{64} + c_3 \\
+ & c_2 2^{128} + c_1 2^{64} + c_0 \pmod{p}.
\end{aligned}$$

Hence, c modulo p can be obtained by adding the four 192-bit integers $c_5 2^{128} + c_5 2^{64} + c_5$, $c_4 2^{128} + c_4 2^{64}$, $c_3 2^{64} + c_3$ and $c_2 2^{128} + c_1 2^{64} + c_0$, and repeatedly subtracting p until the result is less than p.

Algorithm 2.27 Fast reduction modulo $p_{192} = 2^{192} - 2^{64} - 1$

INPUT: An integer $c = (c_5, c_4, c_3, c_2, c_1, c_0)$ in base 2^{64} with $0 \leq c < p_{192}^2$.
OUTPUT: $c \bmod p_{192}$.
    1. Define 192-bit integers:
       $s_1 = (c_2, c_1, c_0)$, $s_2 = (0, c_3, c_3)$,
       $s_3 = (c_4, c_4, 0)$, $s_4 = (c_5, c_5, c_5)$.
    2. Return($s_1 + s_2 + s_3 + s_4 \bmod p_{192}$).

Algorithm 2.28 Fast reduction modulo $p_{224} = 2^{224} - 2^{96} + 1$

INPUT: An integer $c = (c_{13}, \ldots, c_2, c_1, c_0)$ in base 2^{32} with $0 \leq c < p_{224}^2$.
OUTPUT: $c \bmod p_{224}$.
    1. Define 224-bit integers:
       $s_1 = (c_6, c_5, c_4, c_3, c_2, c_1, c_0)$, $s_2 = (c_{10}, c_9, c_8, c_7, 0, 0, 0)$,
       $s_3 = (0, c_{13}, c_{12}, c_{11}, 0, 0, 0)$, $s_4 = (c_{13}, c_{12}, c_{11}, c_{10}, c_9, c_8, c_7)$,
       $s_5 = (0, 0, 0, 0, c_{13}, c_{12}, c_{11})$.
    2. Return($s_1 + s_2 + s_3 - s_4 - s_5 \bmod p_{224}$).

Algorithm 2.29 Fast reduction modulo $p_{256} = 2^{256} - 2^{224} + 2^{192} + 2^{96} - 1$

INPUT: An integer $c = (c_{15}, \ldots, c_2, c_1, c_0)$ in base 2^{32} with $0 \le c < p_{256}^2$.

OUTPUT: $c \bmod p_{256}$.

    1. Define 256-bit integers:

$$s_1 = (c_7, c_6, c_5, c_4, c_3, c_2, c_1, c_0),$$
$$s_2 = (c_{15}, c_{14}, c_{13}, c_{12}, c_{11}, 0, 0, 0),$$
$$s_3 = (0, c_{15}, c_{14}, c_{13}, c_{12}, 0, 0, 0),$$
$$s_4 = (c_{15}, c_{14}, 0, 0, 0, c_{10}, c_9, c_8),$$
$$s_5 = (c_8, c_{13}, c_{15}, c_{14}, c_{13}, c_{11}, c_{10}, c_9),$$
$$s_6 = (c_{10}, c_8, 0, 0, 0, c_{13}, c_{12}, c_{11}),$$
$$s_7 = (c_{11}, c_9, 0, 0, c_{15}, c_{14}, c_{13}, c_{12}),$$
$$s_8 = (c_{12}, 0, c_{10}, c_9, c_8, c_{15}, c_{14}, c_{13}),$$
$$s_9 = (c_{13}, 0, c_{11}, c_{10}, c_9, 0, c_{15}, c_{14}).$$

    2. Return($s_1 + 2s_2 + 2s_3 + s_4 + s_5 - s_6 - s_7 - s_8 - s_9 \bmod p_{256}$).

Algorithm 2.30 Fast reduction modulo $p_{384} = 2^{384} - 2^{128} - 2^{96} + 2^{32} - 1$

INPUT: An integer $c = (c_{23}, \ldots, c_2, c_1, c_0)$ in base 2^{32} with $0 \le c < p_{384}^2$.

OUTPUT: $c \bmod p_{384}$.

    1. Define 384-bit integers:

$$s_1 = (c_{11}, c_{10}, c_9, c_8, c_7, c_6, c_5, c_4, c_3, c_2, c_1, c_0),$$
$$s_2 = (0, 0, 0, 0, 0, c_{23}, c_{22}, c_{21}, 0, 0, 0, 0),$$
$$s_3 = (c_{23}, c_{22}, c_{21}, c_{20}, c_{19}, c_{18}, c_{17}, c_{16}, c_{15}, c_{14}, c_{13}, c_{12}),$$
$$s_4 = (c_{20}, c_{19}, c_{18}, c_{17}, c_{16}, c_{15}, c_{14}, c_{13}, c_{12}, c_{23}, c_{22}, c_{21}),$$
$$s_5 = (c_{19}, c_{18}, c_{17}, c_{16}, c_{15}, c_{14}, c_{13}, c_{12}, c_{20}, 0, c_{23}, 0),$$
$$s_6 = (0, 0, 0, 0, c_{23}, c_{22}, c_{21}, c_{20}, 0, 0, 0, 0),$$
$$s_7 = (0, 0, 0, 0, 0, 0, c_{23}, c_{22}, c_{21}, 0, 0, c_{20}),$$
$$s_8 = (c_{22}, c_{21}, c_{20}, c_{19}, c_{18}, c_{17}, c_{16}, c_{15}, c_{14}, c_{13}, c_{12}, c_{23}),$$
$$s_9 = (0, 0, 0, 0, 0, 0, 0, c_{23}, c_{22}, c_{21}, c_{20}, 0),$$
$$s_{10} = (0, 0, 0, 0, 0, 0, 0, c_{23}, c_{23}, 0, 0, 0).$$

    2. Return($s_1 + 2s_2 + s_3 + s_4 + s_5 + s_6 + s_7 - s_8 - s_9 - s_{10} \bmod p_{384}$).

Algorithm 2.31 Fast reduction modulo $p_{521} = 2^{521} - 1$

INPUT: An integer $c = (c_{1041}, \ldots, c_2, c_1, c_0)$ in base 2 with $0 \le c < p_{521}^2$.

OUTPUT: $c \bmod p_{521}$.

    1. Define 521-bit integers:

$$s_1 = (c_{1041}, \ldots, c_{523}, c_{522}, c_{521}),$$
$$s_2 = (c_{520}, \ldots, c_2, c_1, c_0).$$

    2. Return($s_1 + s_2 \bmod p_{521}$).

2.3   Binary field arithmetic

This section presents algorithms that are suitable for performing binary field arithmetic in software. Chapter 5 includes additional material on use of single-instruction multiple-data (SIMD) registers found on some processors (§5.1.3), and on design considerations for hardware implementation (§5.2.2). Selected timings for field operations appear in §5.1.5.

We assume that the implementation platform has a W-bit architecture where W is a multiple of 8. The bits of a W-bit word U are numbered from 0 to $W-1$, with the rightmost bit of U designated as bit 0. The following standard notation is used to denote operations on words U and V:

$U \oplus V$	bitwise exclusive-or
$U \, \& \, V$	bitwise AND
$U \gg i$	right shift of U by i positions with the i high-order bits set to 0
$U \ll i$	left shift of U by i positions with the i low-order bits set to 0.

Let $f(z)$ be an irreducible binary polynomial of degree m, and write $f(z) = z^m + r(z)$. The elements of $\mathbb{F}_{2^m}$ are the binary polynomials of degree at most $m-1$. Addition of field elements is the usual addition of binary polynomials. Multiplication is performed modulo $f(z)$. A field element $a(z) = a_{m-1}z^{m-1} + \cdots + a_2z^2 + a_1z + a_0$ is associated with the binary vector $a = (a_{m-1}, \ldots, a_2, a_1, a_0)$ of length m. Let $t = \lceil m/W \rceil$, and let $s = Wt - m$. In software, a may be stored in an array of t W-bit words: $A = (A[t-1], \ldots, A[2], A[1], A[0])$, where the rightmost bit of $A[0]$ is a_0, and the leftmost s bits of $A[t-1]$ are unused (always set to 0).

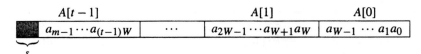

Figure 2.4. Representation of $a \in \mathbb{F}_{2^m}$ as an array A of W-bit words. The $s = tW - m$ highest order bits of $A[t-1]$ remain unused.

2.3.1   Addition

Addition of field elements is performed bitwise, thus requiring only t word operations.

Algorithm 2.32 Addition in $\mathbb{F}_{2^m}$

INPUT: Binary polynomials $a(z)$ and $b(z)$ of degrees at most $m-1$.
OUTPUT: $c(z) = a(z) + b(z)$.
   1. For i from 0 to $t-1$ do
      1.1 $C[i] \leftarrow A[i] \oplus B[i]$.
   2. Return(c).

2.3.2 Multiplication

The shift-and-add method (Algorithm 2.33) for field multiplication is based on the observation that

$$a(z) \cdot b(z) = a_{m-1}z^{m-1}b(z) + \cdots + a_2 z^2 b(z) + a_1 z b(z) + a_0 b(z).$$

Iteration i in the algorithm computes $z^i b(z) \bmod f(z)$ and adds the result to the accumulator c if $a_i = 1$. If $b(z) = b_{m-1}z^{m-1} + \cdots + b_2 z^2 + b_1 z + b_0$, then

$$
\begin{aligned}
b(z) \cdot z &= b_{m-1}z^m + b_{m-2}z^{m-1} + \cdots + b_2 z^3 + b_1 z^2 + b_0 z \\
&\equiv b_{m-1}r(z) + (b_{m-2}z^{m-1} + \cdots + b_2 z^3 + b_1 z^2 + b_0 z) \pmod{f(z)}.
\end{aligned}
$$

Thus $b(z) \cdot z \bmod f(z)$ can be computed by a left-shift of the vector representation of $b(z)$, followed by addition of $r(z)$ to $b(z)$ if the high order bit b_{m-1} is 1.

Algorithm 2.33 Right-to-left shift-and-add field multiplication in $\mathbb{F}_{2^m}$

INPUT: Binary polynomials $a(z)$ and $b(z)$ of degree at most $m - 1$.
OUTPUT: $c(z) = a(z) \cdot b(z) \bmod f(z)$.
  1. If $a_0 = 1$ then $c \leftarrow b$; else $c \leftarrow 0$.
  2. For i from 1 to $m - 1$ do
     2.1 $b \leftarrow b \cdot z \bmod f(z)$.
     2.2 If $a_i = 1$ then $c \leftarrow c + b$.
  3. Return(c).

While Algorithm 2.33 is well-suited for hardware where a vector shift can be performed in one clock cycle, the large number of word shifts make it less desirable for software implementation. We next consider faster methods for field multiplication which first multiply the field elements as polynomials (§2.3.3 and §2.3.4), and then reduce the result modulo $f(z)$ (§2.3.5).

2.3.3 Polynomial multiplication

The *right-to-left comb method* (Algorithm 2.34) for polynomial multiplication is based on the observation that if $b(z) \cdot z^k$ has been computed for some $k \in [0, W - 1]$, then $b(z) \cdot z^{Wj+k}$ can be easily obtained by appending j zero words to the right of the vector representation of $b(z) \cdot z^k$. Algorithm 2.34 processes the bits of the words of A from right to left, as shown in Figure 2.5 when the parameters are $m = 163$, $W = 32$. The following notation is used: if $C = (C[n], \ldots, C[2], C[1], C[0])$ is an array, then $C\{j\}$ denotes the truncated array $(C[n], \ldots, C[j + 1], C[j])$.

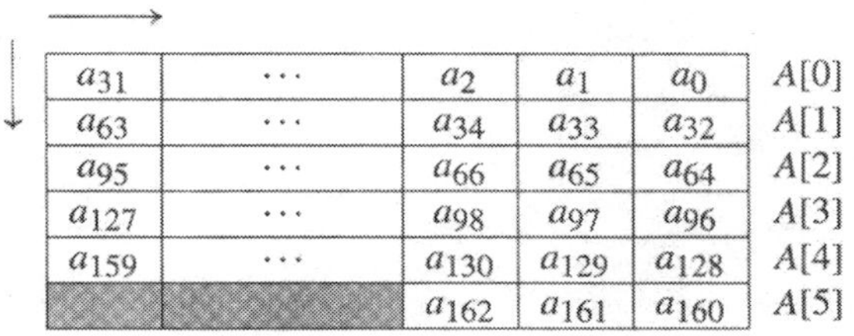

Figure 2.5. The right-to-left comb method (Algorithm 2.34) processes the columns of the exponent array for a right-to-left. The bits in a column are processed from top to bottom. Example parameters are $W = 32$ and $m = 163$.

Algorithm 2.34 Right-to-left comb method for polynomial multiplication

---

INPUT: Binary polynomials $a(z)$ and $b(z)$ of degree at most $m - 1$.
OUTPUT: $c(z) = a(z) \cdot b(z)$.
1. $C \leftarrow 0$.
2. For k from 0 to $W - 1$ do
    2.1 For j from 0 to $t - 1$ do
        If the kth bit of $A[j]$ is 1 then add B to $C\{j\}$.
    2.2 If $k \neq (W - 1)$ then $B \leftarrow B \cdot z$.
3. Return(C).

The left-to-right comb method for polynomial multiplication processes the bits of a from left to right as follows:

$$a(z) \cdot b(z) = \Big(\cdots \big((a_{m-1}b(z)z + a_{m-2}b(z))z + a_{m-3}b(z)\big)z + \cdots + a_1 b(z)\Big)z + a_0 b(z).$$

Algorithm 2.35 is a modification of this method where the bits of the words of A are processed from left to right. This is illustrated in Figure 2.6 when $m = 163$, $W = 32$ are the parameters.

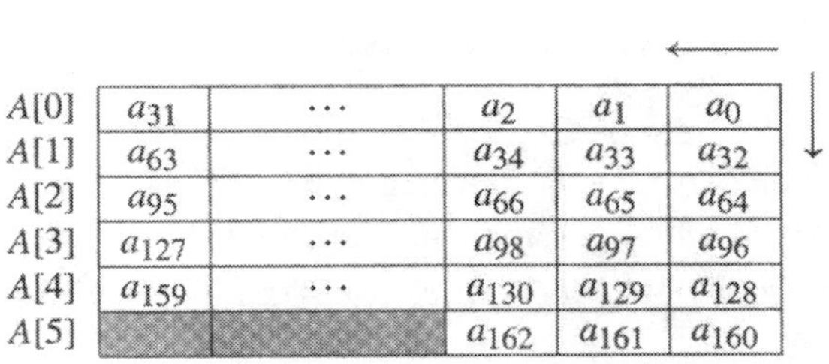

Figure 2.6. The left-to-right comb method (Algorithm 2.35) processes the columns of the exponent array for a left-to-right. The bits in a column are processed from top to bottom. Example parameters are $W = 32$ and $m = 163$.

Algorithm 2.35 Left-to-right comb method for polynomial multiplication

---

INPUT: Binary polynomials $a(z)$ and $b(z)$ of degree at most $m - 1$.
OUTPUT: $c(z) = a(z) \cdot b(z)$.

1. $C \leftarrow 0$.
2. For k from $W - 1$ downto 0 do
   2.1 For j from 0 to $t - 1$ do
             If the kth bit of $A[j]$ is 1 then add B to $C\{j\}$.
   2.2 If $k \neq 0$ then $C \leftarrow C \cdot z$.
3. Return(C).

Algorithms 2.34 and 2.35 are both faster than Algorithm 2.33 since there are fewer vector shifts (multiplications by z). Algorithm 2.34 is faster than Algorithm 2.35 since the vector shifts in the former involve the t-word array B (which can grow to size $t + 1$), while the vector shifts in the latter involve the $2t$-word array C.

Algorithm 2.35 can be accelerated considerably at the expense of some storage overhead by first computing $u(z) \cdot b(z)$ for all polynomials $u(z)$ of degree less than w, and then processing the bits of $A[j]$ w at a time. The modified method is presented as Algorithm 2.36. The order in which the bits of a are processed is shown in Figure 2.7 when the parameters are $M = 163$, $W = 32$, $w = 4$.

Algorithm 2.36 Left-to-right comb method with windows of width w

---

INPUT: Binary polynomials $a(z)$ and $b(z)$ of degree at most $m - 1$.
OUTPUT: $c(z) = a(z) \cdot b(z)$.

1. Compute $B_u = u(z) \cdot b(z)$ for all polynomials $u(z)$ of degree at most $w - 1$.
2. $C \leftarrow 0$.
3. For k from $(W/w) - 1$ downto 0 do
   3.1 For j from 0 to $t - 1$ do
             Let $u = (u_{w-1}, \ldots, u_1, u_0)$, where u_i is bit $(wk + i)$ of $A[j]$.
             Add B_u to $C\{j\}$.
   3.2 If $k \neq 0$ then $C \leftarrow C \cdot z^w$.
4. Return(C).

As written, Algorithm 2.36 performs polynomial multiplication—modular reduction for field multiplication is performed separately. In some situations, it may be advantageous to include the reduction polynomial f as an input to the algorithm. Step 1 may then be modified to calculate $ub \bmod f$, which may allow optimizations in step 3.

Note 2.37 (*enhancements to Algorithm 2.36*) Depending on processor characteristics, one potentially useful variation of Algorithm 2.36 exchanges shifts for additions and table lookups. Precomputation is split into l tables; for simplicity, we assume $l \mid w$. Table i, $0 \leq i < l$, consists of values $B_{v,i} = v(z)z^{iw/l}b(z)$ for all polynomials v of degree

a_{31}	a_{30}	a_{29}	a_{28}	$\cdots$	a_3	a_2	a_1	a_0	$A[0]$
a_{63}	a_{62}	a_{61}	a_{60}	$\cdots$	a_{35}	a_{34}	a_{33}	a_{32}	$A[1]$
a_{95}	a_{94}	a_{93}	a_{92}	$\cdots$	a_{67}	a_{66}	a_{65}	a_{64}	$A[2]$
a_{127}	a_{126}	a_{125}	a_{124}	$\cdots$	a_{99}	a_{98}	a_{97}	a_{96}	$A[3]$
a_{159}	a_{158}	a_{157}	a_{156}	$\cdots$	a_{131}	a_{130}	a_{129}	a_{128}	$A[4]$
						a_{162}	a_{161}	a_{160}	$A[5]$

$\longleftarrow w \longrightarrow$ $\longleftarrow w \longrightarrow$

Figure 2.7. *Algorithm 2.36 processes columns of the exponent array for a left-to-right. The entries within a width w column are processed from top to bottom. Example parameters are $W = 32$, $m = 163$, and $w = 4$.*

less than w/l. Step 3.1 of Algorithm 2.36 is modified to calculate $B_u = \sum_{i=0}^{l-1} B_{u^i,i}$ where $u = (u_{w-1}, \ldots, u_0) = (u^{l-1}, \ldots, u^0)$ and u^i has w/l bits. As an example, Algorithm 2.36 with $w = 4$ has 16 elements of precomputation. The modified algorithm with parameters $w = 8$ and $l = 4$ has the same amount of precomputation (four tables of four points each). Compared with the original algorithm, there are fewer iterations at step 3 (and hence fewer shifts at step 3.2); however, step 3.1 is more expensive.

The comb methods are due to López and Dahab, and are based on the observation that the exponentiation methods of Lim and Lee can be adapted for use in binary fields. §3.3.2 discusses Lim-Lee methods in more detail in the context of elliptic curve point multiplication; see Note 3.47.

Karatsuba-Ofman multiplication

The divide-and-conquer method of Karatsuba-Ofman outlined in §2.2.2 can be directly adapted for the polynomial case. For example,

$$a(z)b(z) = (A_1 z^l + A_0)(B_1 z^l + B_0)$$
$$= A_1 B_1 z^{2l} + [(A_1 + A_0)(B_1 + B_0) + A_1 B_1 + A_0 B_0] z^l + A_0 B_0$$

where $l = \lceil m/2 \rceil$ and the coefficients A_0, A_1, B_0, B_1 are binary polynomials in z of degree less than l. The process may be repeated, using table-lookup or other methods at some threshold. The overhead, however, is often sufficient to render such strategies inferior to Algorithm 2.36 for m of practical interest.

Note 2.38 (*implementing polynomial multiplication*) Algorithm 2.36 appears to be among the fastest in practice for binary fields of interest in elliptic curve methods, provided that the hardware characteristics are targeted reasonably accurately. The code produced by various C compilers can differ dramatically in performance, and compilers can be sensitive to the precise form in which the algorithm is written.

The contribution by Sun Microsystems Laboratories (SML) to the OpenSSL project in 2002 provides a case study of the compromises chosen in practice. OpenSSL is widely used to provide cryptographic services for the Apache web server and the OpenSSH secure shell communication tool. SML's contribution must be understood in context: OpenSSL is a public and collaborative effort—it is likely that Sun's proprietary code has significant enhancements.

To keep the code size relatively small, SML implemented a fairly generic polynomial multiplication method. Karatsuba-Ofman is used, but only on multiplication of 2-word quantities rather than recursive application. At the lowest level of multiplication of 1-word quantities, a simplified Algorithm 2.36 is applied (with $w = 2$, $w = 3$, and $w = 4$ on 16-bit, 32-bit, and 64-bit platforms, respectively). As expected, the result tends to be much slower than the fastest versions of Algorithm 2.36. In our tests on Sun SPARC and Intel P6-family hardware, the Karatsuba-Ofman method implemented is less efficient than use of Algorithm 2.36 at the 2-word stage. However, the contribution from SML may be a better compromise in OpenSSL if the same code is used across platforms and compilers.

2.3.4 *Polynomial squaring*

Since squaring a binary polynomial is a linear operation, it is much faster than multiplying two arbitrary polynomials; i.e., if $a(z) = a_{m-1}z^{m-1} + \cdots + a_2z^2 + a_1z + a_0$, then

$$a(z)^2 = a_{m-1}z^{2m-2} + \cdots + a_2z^4 + a_1z^2 + a_0.$$

The binary representation of $a(z)^2$ is obtained by inserting a 0 bit between consecutive bits of the binary representation of $a(z)$ as shown in Figure 2.8. To facilitate this process, a table T of size 512 bytes can be precomputed for converting 8-bit polynomials into their expanded 16-bit counterparts. Algorithm 2.39 describes this procedure for the parameter $W = 32$.

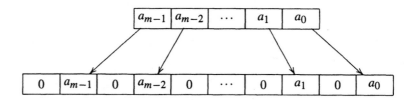

Figure 2.8. Squaring a binary polynomial $a(z) = a_{m-1}z^{m-1} + \cdots + a_2z^2 + a_1z + a_0$.

Algorithm 2.39 Polynomial squaring (with wordlength $W = 32$)

INPUT: A binary polynomial $a(z)$ of degree at most $m - 1$.
OUTPUT: $c(z) = a(z)^2$.
  1. *Precomputation.* For each byte $d = (d_7, \ldots, d_1, d_0)$, compute the 16-bit quantity
     $T(d) = (0, d_7, \ldots, 0, d_1, 0, d_0)$.
  2. For i from 0 to $t - 1$ do
     2.1 Let $A[i] = (u_3, u_2, u_1, u_0)$ where each u_j is a byte.
     2.2 $C[2i] \leftarrow (T(u_1), T(u_0)), \ C[2i + 1] \leftarrow (T(u_3), T(u_2))$.
  3. Return(c).

2.3.5 Reduction

We now discuss techniques for reducing a binary polynomial $c(z)$ obtained by multiplying two binary polynomials of degree $\leq m - 1$, or by squaring a binary polynomial of degree $\leq m - 1$. Such polynomials $c(z)$ have degree at most $2m - 2$.

Arbitrary reduction polynomials

Recall that $f(z) = z^m + r(z)$, where $r(z)$ is a binary polynomial of degree at most $m - 1$. Algorithm 2.40 reduces $c(z)$ modulo $f(z)$ one bit at a time, starting with the leftmost bit. It is based on the observation that

$$c(z) = c_{2m-2}z^{2m-2} + \cdots + c_m z^m + c_{m-1}z^{m-1} + \cdots + c_1 z + c_0$$
$$\equiv (c_{2m-2}z^{m-2} + \cdots + c_m)r(z) + c_{m-1}z^{m-1} + \cdots + c_1 z + c_0 \pmod{f(z)}.$$

The reduction is accelerated by precomputing the polynomials $z^k r(z), 0 \leq k \leq W - 1$. If $r(z)$ is a low-degree polynomial, or if $f(z)$ is a trinomial, then the space requirements are smaller, and furthermore the additions involving $z^k r(z)$ in step 2.1 are faster. The following notation is used: if $C = (C[n], \ldots, C[2], C[1], C[0])$ is an array, then $C\{j\}$ denotes the truncated array $(C[n], \ldots, C[j + 1], C[j])$.

Algorithm 2.40 Modular reduction (one bit at a time)

INPUT: A binary polynomial $c(z)$ of degree at most $2m - 2$.
OUTPUT: $c(z) \bmod f(z)$.
  1. *Precomputation.* Compute $u_k(z) = z^k r(z), 0 \leq k \leq W - 1$.
  2. For i from $2m - 2$ downto m do
     2.1 If $c_i = 1$ then
              Let $j = \lfloor (i - m)/W \rfloor$ and $k = (i - m) - Wj$.
              Add $u_k(z)$ to $C\{j\}$.
  3. Return($C[t - 1], \ldots, C[1], C[0]$).

If $f(z)$ is a trinomial, or a pentanomial with middle terms close to each other, then reduction of $c(z)$ modulo $f(z)$ can be efficiently performed one word at a time. For example, suppose $m = 163$ and $W = 32$ (so $t = 6$), and consider reducing the word $C[9]$ of $c(z)$ modulo $f(z) = z^{163} + z^7 + z^6 + z^3 + 1$. The word $C[9]$ represents the polynomial $c_{319}z^{319} + \cdots + c_{289}z^{289} + c_{288}z^{288}$. We have

$$z^{288} \equiv z^{132} + z^{131} + z^{128} + z^{125} \pmod{f(z)},$$
$$z^{289} \equiv z^{133} + z^{132} + z^{129} + z^{126} \pmod{f(z)},$$
$$\vdots$$
$$z^{319} \equiv z^{163} + z^{162} + z^{159} + z^{156} \pmod{f(z)}.$$

By considering the four columns on the right side of the above congruences, we see that reduction of $C[9]$ can be performed by adding $C[9]$ four times to C, with the rightmost bit of $C[9]$ added to bits 132, 131, 128 and 125 of C; this is illustrated in Figure 2.9.

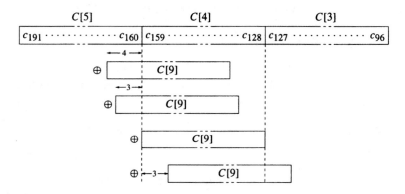

Figure 2.9. *Reducing the 32-bit word $C[9]$ modulo $f(z) = z^{163} + z^7 + z^6 + z^3 + 1$.*

NIST reduction polynomials

We next present algorithms for fast reduction modulo the following reduction polynomials recommended by NIST in the FIPS 186-2 standard:

$$f(z) = z^{163} + z^7 + z^6 + z^3 + 1$$
$$f(z) = z^{233} + z^{74} + 1$$
$$f(z) = z^{283} + z^{12} + z^7 + z^5 + 1$$
$$f(z) = z^{409} + z^{87} + 1$$
$$f(z) = z^{571} + z^{10} + z^5 + z^2 + 1.$$

These algorithms, which assume a wordlength $W = 32$, are based on ideas similar to those leading to Figure 2.9. They are faster than Algorithm 2.40 and furthermore have no storage overhead.

Algorithm 2.41 Fast reduction modulo $f(z) = z^{163} + z^7 + z^6 + z^3 + 1$ (with $W = 32$)

INPUT: A binary polynomial $c(z)$ of degree at most 324.
OUTPUT: $c(z) \bmod f(z)$.

1. For i from 10 downto 6 do   {Reduce $C[i]z^{32i}$ modulo $f(z)$}
    1.1 $T \leftarrow C[i]$.
    1.2 $C[i-6] \leftarrow C[i-6] \oplus (T \ll 29)$.
    1.3 $C[i-5] \leftarrow C[i-5] \oplus (T \ll 4) \oplus (T \ll 3) \oplus T \oplus (T \gg 3)$.
    1.4 $C[i-4] \leftarrow C[i-4] \oplus (T \gg 28) \oplus (T \gg 29)$.
2. $T \leftarrow C[5] \gg 3$.   {Extract bits 3–31 of $C[5]$}
3. $C[0] \leftarrow C[0] \oplus (T \ll 7) \oplus (T \ll 6) \oplus (T \ll 3) \oplus T$.
4. $C[1] \leftarrow C[1] \oplus (T \gg 25) \oplus (T \gg 26)$.
5. $C[5] \leftarrow C[5] \, \& \, 0x7$.   {Clear the reduced bits of $C[5]$}
6. Return $(C[5], C[4], C[3], C[2], C[1], C[0])$.

Algorithm 2.42 Fast reduction modulo $f(z) = z^{233} + z^{74} + 1$ (with $W = 32$)

INPUT: A binary polynomial $c(z)$ of degree at most 464.
OUTPUT: $c(z) \bmod f(z)$.

1. For i from 15 downto 8 do   {Reduce $C[i]z^{32i}$ modulo $f(z)$}
    1.1 $T \leftarrow C[i]$.
    1.2 $C[i-8] \leftarrow C[i-8] \oplus (T \ll 23)$.
    1.3 $C[i-7] \leftarrow C[i-7] \oplus (T \gg 9)$.
    1.4 $C[i-5] \leftarrow C[i-5] \oplus (T \ll 1)$.
    1.5 $C[i-4] \leftarrow C[i-4] \oplus (T \gg 31)$.
2. $T \leftarrow C[7] \gg 9$.   {Extract bits 9–31 of $C[7]$}
3. $C[0] \leftarrow C[0] \oplus T$.
4. $C[2] \leftarrow C[2] \oplus (T \ll 10)$.
5. $C[3] \leftarrow C[3] \oplus (T \gg 22)$.
6. $C[7] \leftarrow C[7] \, \& \, 0x1FF$.   {Clear the reduced bits of $C[7]$}
7. Return $(C[7], C[6], C[5], C[4], C[3], C[2], C[1], C[0])$.

Algorithm 2.43 Fast reduction modulo $f(z) = z^{283} + z^{12} + z^7 + z^5 + 1$ (with $W = 32$)

INPUT: A binary polynomial $c(z)$ of degree at most 564.
OUTPUT: $c(z) \bmod f(z)$.

1. For i from 17 downto 9 do   {Reduce $C[i]z^{32i}$ modulo $f(z)$}
    1.1 $T \leftarrow C[i]$.
    1.2 $C[i - 9] \leftarrow C[i - 9] \oplus (T \ll 5) \oplus (T \ll 10) \oplus (T \ll 12) \oplus (T \ll 17)$.
    1.3 $C[i - 8] \leftarrow C[i - 8] \oplus (T \gg 27) \oplus (T \gg 22) \oplus (T \gg 20) \oplus (T \gg 15)$.
2. $T \leftarrow C[8] \gg 27$.   {Extract bits 27–31 of $C[8]$}
3. $C[0] \leftarrow C[0] \oplus T \oplus (T \ll 5) \oplus (T \ll 7) \oplus (T \ll 12)$.
4. $C[8] \leftarrow C[8] \,\&\, \text{0x7FFFFFF}$.   {Clear the reduced bits of $C[8]$}
5. Return $(C[8], C[7], C[6], C[5], C[4], C[3], C[2], C[1], C[0])$.

Algorithm 2.44 Fast reduction modulo $f(z) = z^{409} + z^{87} + 1$ (with $W = 32$)

INPUT: A binary polynomial $c(z)$ of degree at most 816.
OUTPUT: $c(z) \bmod f(z)$.

1. For i from 25 downto 13 do   {Reduce $C[i]z^{32i}$ modulo $f(z)$}
    1.1 $T \leftarrow C[i]$.
    1.2 $C[i - 13] \leftarrow C[i - 13] \oplus (T \ll 7)$.
    1.3 $C[i - 12] \leftarrow C[i - 12] \oplus (T \gg 25)$.
    1.4 $C[i - 11] \leftarrow C[i - 11] \oplus (T \ll 30)$.
    1.5 $C[i - 10] \leftarrow C[i - 10] \oplus (T \gg 2)$.
2. $T \leftarrow C[12] \gg 25$.   {Extract bits 25–31 of $C[12]$}
3. $C[0] \leftarrow C[0] \oplus T$.
4. $C[2] \leftarrow C[2] \oplus (T_{¡¡}23)$.
5. $C[12] \leftarrow C[12] \,\&\, \text{0x1FFFFFF}$.   {Clear the reduced bits of $C[12]$}
6. Return $(C[12], C[11], \ldots, C[1], C[0])$.

Algorithm 2.45 Fast reduction modulo $f(z) = z^{571} + z^{10} + z^5 + z^2 + 1$ (with $W = 32$)

INPUT: A binary polynomial $c(z)$ of degree at most 1140.
OUTPUT: $c(z) \bmod f(z)$.

1. For i from 35 downto 18 do   {Reduce $C[i]z^{32i}$ modulo $f(z)$}
    1.1 $T \leftarrow C[i]$.
    1.2 $C[i - 18] \leftarrow C[i - 18] \oplus (T \ll 5) \oplus (T \ll 7) \oplus (T \ll 10) \oplus (T \ll 15)$.
    1.3 $C[i - 17] \leftarrow C[i - 17] \oplus (T \gg 27) \oplus (T \gg 25) \oplus (T \gg 22) \oplus (T \gg 17)$.
2. $T \leftarrow C[17] \gg 27$.   {Extract bits 27–31 of $C[17]$}
3. $C[0] \leftarrow C[0] \oplus T \oplus (T \ll 2) \oplus (T \ll 5) \oplus (T \ll 10)$.
4. $C[17] \leftarrow C[17] \,\&\, \text{0x7FFFFFF}$.   {Clear the reduced bits of $C[17]$}
5. Return $(C[17], C[16], \ldots, C[1], C[0])$.

2.3.6 Inversion and division

In this subsection, we simplify the notation and denote binary polynomials $a(z)$ by a. Recall that the inverse of a nonzero element $a \in \mathbb{F}_{2^m}$ is the unique element $g \in \mathbb{F}_{2^m}$ such that $ag = 1$ in $\mathbb{F}_{2^m}$, that is, $ag \equiv 1 \pmod{f}$. This inverse element is denoted a^{-1} mod f or simply a^{-1} if the reduction polynomial f is understood from context. Inverses can be efficiently computed by the extended Euclidean algorithm for polynomials.

The extended Euclidean algorithm for polynomials

Let a and b be binary polynomials, not both 0. The *greatest common divisor (gcd)* of a and b, denoted $\gcd(a, b)$, is the binary polynomial d of highest degree that divides both a and b. Efficient algorithms for computing $\gcd(a, b)$ exploit the following polynomial analogue of Theorem 2.18.

Theorem 2.46 Let a and b be binary polynomials. Then $\gcd(a, b) = \gcd(b - ca, a)$ for all binary polynomials c.

In the classical Euclidean algorithm for computing the gcd of binary polynomials a and b, where $\deg(b) \geq \deg(a)$, b is divided by a to obtain a quotient q and a remainder r satisfying $b = qa + r$ and $\deg(r) < \deg(a)$. By Theorem 2.46, $\gcd(a, b) = \gcd(r, a)$. Thus, the problem of determining $\gcd(a, b)$ is reduced to that of computing $\gcd(r, a)$ where the arguments (r, a) have lower degrees than the degrees of the original arguments (a, b). This process is repeated until one of the arguments is zero—the result is then immediately obtained since $\gcd(0, d) = d$. The algorithm must terminate since the degrees of the remainders are strictly decreasing. Moreover, it is efficient because the number of (long) divisions is at most k where $k = \deg(a)$.

In a variant of the classical Euclidean algorithm, only one step of each long division is performed. That is, if $\deg(b) \geq \deg(a)$ and $j = \deg(b) - \deg(a)$, then one computes $r = b + z^j a$. By Theorem 2.46, $\gcd(a, b) = \gcd(r, a)$. This process is repeated until a zero remainder is encountered. Since $\deg(r) < \deg(b)$, the number of (partial) division steps is at most $2k$ where $k = \max\{\deg(a), \deg(b)\}$.

The Euclidean algorithm can be extended to find binary polynomials g and h satisfying $ag + bh = d$ where $d = \gcd(a, b)$. Algorithm 2.47 maintains the invariants

$$ag_1 + bh_1 = u$$
$$ag_2 + bh_2 = v.$$

The algorithm terminates when $u = 0$, in which case $v = \gcd(a, b)$ and $ag_2 + bh_2 = d$.

Algorithm 2.47 Extended Euclidean algorithm for binary polynomials

---

INPUT: Nonzero binary polynomials a and b with $\deg(a) \le \deg(b)$.
OUTPUT: $d = \gcd(a, b)$ and binary polynomials g, h satisfying $ag + bh = d$.

    1. $u \leftarrow a, v \leftarrow b$.
    2. $g_1 \leftarrow 1, g_2 \leftarrow 0, h_1 \leftarrow 0, h_2 \leftarrow 1$.
    3. While $u \ne 0$ do
        3.1 $j \leftarrow \deg(u) - \deg(v)$.
        3.2 If $j < 0$ then: $u \leftrightarrow v, g_1 \leftrightarrow g_2, h_1 \leftrightarrow h_2, j \leftarrow -j$.
        3.3 $u \leftarrow u + z^j v$.
        3.4 $g_1 \leftarrow g_1 + z^j g_2, h_1 \leftarrow h_1 + z^j h_2$.
    4. $d \leftarrow v, g \leftarrow g_2, h \leftarrow h_2$.
    5. Return(d, g, h).

Suppose now that f is an irreducible binary polynomial of degree m and the nonzero polynomial a has degree at most $m - 1$ (hence $\gcd(a, f) = 1$). If Algorithm 2.47 is executed with inputs a and f, the last nonzero u encountered in step 3.3 is $u = 1$. After this occurrence, the polynomials g_1 and h_1, as updated in step 3.4, satisfy $ag_1 + fh_1 = 1$. Hence $ag_1 \equiv 1 \pmod{f}$ and so $a^{-1} = g_1$. Note that h_1 and h_2 are not needed for the determination of g_1. These observations lead to Algorithm 2.48 for inversion in $\mathbb{F}_{2^m}$.

Algorithm 2.48 Inversion in $\mathbb{F}_{2^m}$ using the extended Euclidean algorithm

---

INPUT: A nonzero binary polynomial a of degree at most $m - 1$.
OUTPUT: $a^{-1} \bmod f$.

    1. $u \leftarrow a, v \leftarrow f$.
    2. $g_1 \leftarrow 1, g_2 \leftarrow 0$.
    3. While $u \ne 1$ do
        3.1 $j \leftarrow \deg(u) - \deg(v)$.
        3.2 If $j < 0$ then: $u \leftrightarrow v, g_1 \leftrightarrow g_2, j \leftarrow -j$.
        3.3 $u \leftarrow u + z^j v$.
        3.4 $g_1 \leftarrow g_1 + z^j g_2$.
    4. Return(g_1).

Binary inversion algorithm

Algorithm 2.49 is the polynomial analogue of the binary algorithm for inversion in $\mathbb{F}_p$ (Algorithm 2.22). In contrast to Algorithm 2.48 where the bits of u and v are cleared from left to right (high degree terms to low degree terms), the bits of u and v in Algorithm 2.49 are cleared from right to left.

Algorithm 2.49 Binary algorithm for inversion in $\mathbb{F}_{2^m}$

INPUT: A nonzero binary polynomial a of degree at most $m - 1$.

OUTPUT: $a^{-1} \bmod f$.

1. $u \leftarrow a, v \leftarrow f$.
2. $g_1 \leftarrow 1, g_2 \leftarrow 0$.
3. While $(u \neq 1 \text{ and } v \neq 1)$ do

    3.1 While z divides u do

    $\quad\quad u \leftarrow u/z$.

    $\quad\quad$ If z divides g_1 then $g_1 \leftarrow g_1/z$; else $g_1 \leftarrow (g_1 + f)/z$.

    3.2 While z divides v do

    $\quad\quad v \leftarrow v/z$.

    $\quad\quad$ If z divides g_2 then $g_2 \leftarrow g_2/z$; else $g_2 \leftarrow (g_2 + f)/z$.

    3.3 If $\deg(u) > \deg(v)$ then: $u \leftarrow u + v, g_1 \leftarrow g_1 + g_2$;

    $\quad\quad$ Else: $v \leftarrow v + u, g_2 \leftarrow g_2 + g_1$.
4. If $u = 1$ then return(g_1); else return(g_2).

The expression involving degree calculations in step 3.3 may be replaced by a simpler comparison on the binary representations of the polynomials. This differs from Algorithm 2.48, where explicit degree calculations are required in step 3.1.

Almost inverse algorithm

The almost inverse algorithm (Algorithm 2.50) is a modification of the binary inversion algorithm (Algorithm 2.49) in which a polynomial g and a positive integer k are first computed satisfying

$$ag \equiv z^k \quad (\bmod f).$$

A reduction is then applied to obtain

$$a^{-1} = z^{-k} g \bmod f.$$

The invariants maintained are

$$ag_1 + fh_1 = z^k u$$
$$ag_2 + fh_2 = z^k v$$

for some h_1, h_2 that are not explicitly calculated.

Algorithm 2.50 Almost Inverse Algorithm for inversion in $\mathbb{F}_{2^m}$

INPUT: A nonzero binary polynomial a of degree at most $m - 1$.
OUTPUT: $a^{-1} \bmod f$.
  1. $u \leftarrow a, v \leftarrow f$.
  2. $g_1 \leftarrow 1, g_2 \leftarrow 0, k \leftarrow 0$.
  3. While ($u \neq 1$ and $v \neq 1$) do
        3.1 While z divides u do
                $u \leftarrow u/z, g_2 \leftarrow z \cdot g_2, k \leftarrow k + 1$.
        3.2 While z divides v do
                $v \leftarrow v/z, g_1 \leftarrow z \cdot g_1, k \leftarrow k + 1$.
        3.3 If $\deg(u) > \deg(v)$ then: $u \leftarrow u + v, g_1 \leftarrow g_1 + g_2$.
              Else: $v \leftarrow v + u, g_2 \leftarrow g_2 + g_1$.
  4. If $u = 1$ then $g \leftarrow g_1$; else $g \leftarrow g_2$.
  5. Return($z^{-k} g \bmod f$).

The reduction in step 5 can be performed as follows. Let $l = \min\{i \geq 1 \mid f_i = 1\}$, where $f(z) = f_m z^m + \cdots + f_1 z + f_0$. Let S be the polynomial formed by the l rightmost bits of g. Then $Sf + g$ is divisible by z^l and $T = (Sf + g)/z^l$ has degree less than m; thus $T = gz^{-l} \bmod f$. This process can be repeated to finally obtain $gz^{-k} \bmod f$. The reduction polynomial f is said to be *suitable* if l is above some threshold (which may depend on the implementation; e.g., $l \geq W$ is desirable with W-bit words), since then less effort is required in the reduction step.

Steps 3.1–3.2 are simpler than those in Algorithm 2.49. In addition, the g_1 and g_2 appearing in these algorithms grow more slowly in almost inverse. Thus one can expect Algorithm 2.50 to outperform Algorithm 2.49 if the reduction polynomial is suitable, and conversely. As with the binary algorithm, the conditional involving degree calculations may be replaced with a simpler comparison.

Division

The binary inversion algorithm (Algorithm 2.49) can be easily modified to perform division $b/a = ba^{-1}$. In cases where the ratio I/M of inversion to multiplication costs is small, this could be especially significant in elliptic curve schemes, since an elliptic curve point operation in affine coordinates (see §3.1.2) could use division rather than an inversion and multiplication.

Division based on the binary algorithm To obtain b/a, Algorithm 2.49 is modified at step 2, replacing $g_1 \leftarrow 1$ with $g_1 \leftarrow b$. The associated invariants are

$$ag_1 + fh_1 = ub$$
$$ag_2 + fh_2 = vb.$$

On termination with $u = 1$, it follows that $g_1 = ba^{-1}$. The division algorithm is expected to have the same running time as the binary algorithm, since g_1 in Algorithm 2.49 goes to full-length in a few iterations at step 3.1 (i.e., the difference in initialization of g_1 does not contribute significantly to the time for division versus inversion).

If the binary algorithm is the inversion method of choice, then affine point operations would benefit from use of division, since the cost of a point double or addition changes from $I + 2M$ to $I + M$. (I and M denote the time to perform an inversion and a multiplication, respectively.) If I/M is small, then this represents a significant improvement. For example, if I/M is 3, then use of a division algorithm variant of Algorithm 2.49 provides a 20% reduction in the time to perform an affine point double or addition. However, if $I/M > 7$, then the savings is less than 12%. Unless I/M is very small, it is likely that schemes are used which reduce the number of inversions required (e.g., halving and projective coordinates), so that point multiplication involves relatively few field inversions, diluting any savings from use of a division algorithm.

Division based on the extended Euclidean algorithm   Algorithm 2.48 can be transformed to a division algorithm in a similar fashion. However, the change in the initialization step may have significant impact on implementation of a division algorithm variant. There are two performance issues: tracking of the lengths of variables, and implementing the addition to g_1 at step 3.4.

In Algorithm 2.48, it is relatively easy to track the lengths of u and v efficiently (the lengths shrink), and, moreover, it is also possible to track the lengths of g_1 and g_2. However, the change in initialization for division means that g_1 goes to full-length immediately, and optimizations based on shorter lengths disappear.

The second performance issue concerns the addition to g_1 at step 3.4. An implementation may assume that ordinary polynomial addition with no reduction may be performed; that is, the degrees of g_1 and g_2 never exceed $m - 1$. In adapting for division, step 3.4 may be less-efficiently implemented, since g_1 is full-length on initialization.

Division based on the almost inverse algorithm   Although Algorithm 2.50 is similar to the binary algorithm, the ability to efficiently track the lengths of g_1 and g_2 (in addition to the lengths of u and v) may be an implementation advantage of Algorithm 2.50 over Algorithm 2.49 (provided that the reduction polynomial f is suitable). As with Algorithm 2.48, this advantage is lost in a division algorithm variant.

It should be noted that efficient tracking of the lengths of g_1 and g_2 (in addition to the lengths of u and v) in Algorithm 2.50 may involve significant code expansion (perhaps t^2 fragments rather than the t fragments in the binary algorithm). If the expansion cannot be tolerated (because of application constraints or platform characteristics), then almost inverse may not be preferable to the other inversion algorithms (even if the reduction polynomial is suitable).

2.4 *Optimal extension field arithmetic*

Preceding sections discussed arithmetic for fields $\mathbb{F}_{p^m}$ in the case that $p = 2$ (binary fields) and $m = 1$ (prime fields). As noted on page 28, the polynomial basis representation in the binary field case can be generalized to all extension fields $\mathbb{F}_{p^m}$, with coefficient arithmetic performed in $\mathbb{F}_p$.

For hardware implementations, binary fields are attractive since the operations involve only shifts and bitwise addition modulo 2. The simplicity is also attractive for software implementations on general-purpose processors; however the field multiplication is essentially a few bits at a time and can be much slower than prime field arithmetic if a hardware integer multiplier is available. On the other hand, the arithmetic in prime fields can be more difficult to implement efficiently, due in part to the propagation of carry bits.

The general idea in optimal extension fields is to select p, m, and the reduction polynomial to more closely match the underlying hardware characteristics. In particular, the value of p may be selected to fit in a single word, simplifying the handling of carry (since coefficients are single-word).

Definition 2.51 An *optimal extension field* (OEF) is a finite field $\mathbb{F}_{p^m}$ such that:

1. $p = 2^n - c$ for some integers n and c with $\log_2 |c| \le n/2$; and
2. an irreducible polynomial $f(z) = z^m - \omega$ in $\mathbb{F}_p[z]$ exists.

If $c \in \{\pm 1\}$, then the OEF is said to be of *Type I* (p is a Mersenne prime if $c = 1$); if $\omega = 2$, the OEF is said to be of *Type II*.

Type I OEFs have especially simple arithmetic in the subfield $\mathbb{F}_p$, while Type II OEFs allow simplifications in the $\mathbb{F}_{p^m}$ extension field arithmetic. Examples of OEFs are given in Table 2.1.

p	f	parameters				Type
$2^7 + 3$	$z^{13} - 5$	$n = 7,$	$c = -3,$	$m = 13,$	$\omega = 5$	—
$2^{13} - 1$	$z^{13} - 2$	$n = 13,$	$c = 1,$	$m = 13,$	$\omega = 2$	I, II
$2^{31} - 19$	$z^6 - 2$	$n = 31,$	$c = 19,$	$m = 6,$	$\omega = 2$	II
$2^{31} - 1$	$z^6 - 7$	$n = 31,$	$c = 1,$	$m = 6,$	$\omega = 7$	I
$2^{32} - 5$	$z^5 - 2$	$n = 32,$	$c = 5,$	$m = 5,$	$\omega = 2$	II
$2^{57} - 13$	$z^3 - 2$	$n = 57,$	$c = 13,$	$m = 3,$	$\omega = 2$	II
$2^{61} - 1$	$z^3 - 37$	$n = 61,$	$c = 1,$	$m = 3,$	$\omega = 37$	I
$2^{89} - 1$	$z^2 - 3$	$n = 89,$	$c = 1,$	$m = 2,$	$\omega = 3$	I

Table 2.1. OEF example parameters. Here, $p = 2^n - c$ is prime, and $f(z) = z^m - \omega \in \mathbb{F}_p[z]$ is irreducible over $\mathbb{F}_p$. The field is $\mathbb{F}_{p^m} = \mathbb{F}_p[z]/(f)$ of order approximately 2^{mn}.

The following results can be used to determine if a given polynomial $f(z) = z^m - \omega$ is irreducible in $\mathbb{F}_p[z]$.

Theorem 2.52 Let $m \geq 2$ be an integer and $\omega \in \mathbb{F}_p^*$. Then the binomial $f(z) = z^m - \omega$ is irreducible in $\mathbb{F}_p[z]$ if and only if the following two conditions are satisfied:

(i) each prime factor of m divides the order e of ω in $\mathbb{F}_p^*$, but not $(p-1)/e$;

(ii) $p \equiv 1 \pmod 4$ if $m \equiv 0 \pmod 4$.

If the order of ω as an element of $\mathbb{F}_p^*$ is $p-1$, then ω is said to be *primitive*. It is easily verified that conditions (i) and (ii) of Theorem 2.52 are satisfied if ω is primitive and $m \mid (p-1)$.

Corollary 2.53 If ω is a primitive element of $\mathbb{F}_p^*$ and $m \mid (p-1)$, then $z^m - \omega$ is irreducible in $\mathbb{F}_p[z]$.

Elements of $\mathbb{F}_{p^m}$ are polynomials

$$a(z) = a_{m-1}z^{m-1} + \cdots + a_2 z^2 + a_1 z + a_0$$

where the coefficients a_i are elements of $\mathbb{F}_p$. We next present algorithms for performing arithmetic operations in OEFs. Selected timings for field operations appear in §5.1.5.

2.4.1 Addition and subtraction

If $a(z) = \sum_{i=0}^{m-1} a_i z^i$ and $b(z) = \sum_{i=0}^{m-1} b_i z^i$ are elements of $\mathbb{F}_{p^m}$, then

$$a(z) + b(z) = \sum_{i=0}^{m-1} c_i z^i,$$

where $c_i = (a_i + b_i) \bmod p$; that is, p is subtracted whenever $a_i + b_i \geq p$. Subtraction of elements of $\mathbb{F}_{p^m}$ is done similarly.

2.4.2 Multiplication and reduction

Multiplication of elements $a, b \in \mathbb{F}_{p^m}$ can be done by ordinary polynomial multiplication in $\mathbb{Z}[z]$ (i.e., multiplication of polynomials having integer coefficients), along with coefficient reductions in $\mathbb{F}_p$ and a reduction by the polynomial f. This multiplication takes the form

$$c(z) = a(z)b(z) = \left(\sum_{i=0}^{m-1} a_i z^i \right) \left(\sum_{j=0}^{m-1} b_j z^j \right)$$

$$\equiv \sum_{k=0}^{2m-2} c_k z^k \equiv c_{m-1} z^{m-1} + \sum_{k=0}^{m-2} (c_k + \omega c_{k+m}) z^k \pmod{f(z)}$$

where

$$c_k = \sum_{i+j=k} a_i b_j \bmod p.$$

Karatsuba-Ofman techniques may be applied to reduce the number of $\mathbb{F}_p$ multiplications. For example,

$$\begin{aligned}a(z)b(z) &= (A_1 z^l + A_0)(B_1 z^l + B_0) \\ &= A_1 B_1 z^{2l} + [(A_1 + A_0)(B_1 + B_0) - A_1 B_1 - A_0 B_0] z^l + A_0 B_0\end{aligned}$$

where $l = \lceil m/2 \rceil$ and the coefficients A_0, A_1, B_0, B_1 are polynomials in $\mathbb{F}_p[z]$ of degree less than l. The process may be repeated, although for small values of m it may be advantageous to consider splits other than binary. The analogous case for prime fields was discussed in §2.2.2.

Reduction in $\mathbb{F}_p$

The most straightforward implementation performs reductions in $\mathbb{F}_p$ for every addition and multiplication encountered during the calculation of each c_k. The restriction $\log_2 |c| \le n/2$ means that reduction in the subfield $\mathbb{F}_p$ requires only a few simple operations. Algorithm 2.54 performs reduction of base-B numbers, using only shifts, additions, and single-precision multiplications.

Algorithm 2.54 Reduction modulo $M = B^n - c$

INPUT: A base B, positive integer x, and modulus $M = B^n - c$ where c is an l-digit base-B positive integer for some $l < n$.

OUTPUT: $x \bmod M$.

    1. $q_0 \leftarrow \lfloor x/B^n \rfloor$, $r_0 \leftarrow x - q_0 B^n$. $\{x = q_0 B^n + r_0 \text{ with } r_0 < B^n\}$

    2. $r \leftarrow r_0$, $i \leftarrow 0$.

    3. While $q_i > 0$ do

        3.1 $q_{i+1} \leftarrow \lfloor q_i c / B^n \rfloor$. $\{q_i c = q_{i+1} B^n + r_{i+1} \text{ with } r_{i+1} < B^n\}$

        3.2 $r_{i+1} \leftarrow q_i c - q_{i+1} B^n$.

        3.3 $i \leftarrow i + 1$, $r \leftarrow r + r_i$.

    4. While $r \ge M$ do: $r \leftarrow r - M$.

    5. Return(r).

Note 2.55 (*implementation details for Algorithm 2.54*)

   (i) If $l \le n/2$ and x has at most $2n$ base-B digits, Algorithm 2.54 executes step 3.1 at most twice (i.e., there are at most two multiplications by c).

  (ii) As an alternative, the quotient and remainder may be folded into x at each stage. Steps 1–4 are replaced with the following.

    1. While $x \geq B^n$
       1.1 Write $x = vB^n + u$ with $u < B^n$.
       1.2 $x \leftarrow cv + u$.
    2. If $x \geq M$ then $x \leftarrow x - M$.

(iii) Algorithm 2.54 can be modified to handle the case $M = B^n + c$ for some positive integer $c < B^{n-1}$: in step 3.3, replace $r \leftarrow r + r_i$ with $r \leftarrow r + (-1)^i r_i$, and modify step 4 to also process the case $r < 0$.

For OEFs, Algorithm 2.54 with $B = 2$ may be applied, requiring at most two multiplications by c in the case that $x < 2^{2n}$. When $c = 1$ (a type I OEF) and $x \leq (p-1)^2$, the reduction is given by:

$$\text{write } x = 2^n v + u; \quad x \leftarrow v + u; \quad \text{if } x \geq p \text{ then } x \leftarrow x - p.$$

Type I OEFs are attractive in the sense that $\mathbb{F}_p$ multiplication (with reduction) can be done with a single multiplication and a few other operations. However, the reductions modulo p are likely to contribute a significant amount to the cost of multiplication in $\mathbb{F}_{p^m}$, and it may be more efficient to employ a direct multiply-and-accumulate strategy to decrease the number of reductions.

Accumulation and reduction

The number of $\mathbb{F}_p$ reductions performed in finding the product $c(z) = a(z)b(z)$ in $\mathbb{F}_{p^m}$ can be decreased by accumulation strategies on the coefficients of $c(z)$. Since $f(z) = z^m - \omega$, the product can be written

$$c(z) = a(z)b(z) \equiv \sum_{k=0}^{2m-2} c_k z^k \equiv \sum_{k=0}^{m-1} c_k z^k + \omega \sum_{k=m}^{2m-2} c_k z^{k-m}$$

$$\equiv \sum_{k=0}^{m-1} \underbrace{\left(\sum_{i=0}^{k} a_i b_{k-i} + \omega \sum_{i=k+1}^{m-1} a_i b_{k+m-i} \right)}_{c_k'} z^k \pmod{f(z)}.$$

If the coefficient c_k' is calculated as an expression in $\mathbb{Z}$ (i.e., as an integer without reduction modulo p), then $c_k' \bmod p$ may be performed with a single reduction (rather than m reductions). The penalty incurred is the multiple-word operations (additions and multiplication by ω) required in accumulating the terms of c_k'.

In comparison with the straightforward reduce-on-every-operation strategy, it should be noted that complete reduction on each $\mathbb{F}_p$ operation may not be necessary; for example, it may suffice to reduce the result to a value which fits in a single word. However, frequent reduction (to a single word or value less than 2^n) is likely to be expensive, especially if a "carry" or comparison must be processed.

Depending on the value of p, the multiply-and-accumulate strategy employs two or three registers for the accumulation (under the assumption that p fits in a register). The arithmetic resembles that commonly used in prime-field implementations, and multiplication cost in $\mathbb{F}_{p^m}$ is expected to be comparable to that in a prime field $\mathbb{F}_q$ where $q \approx p^m$ and which admits fast reduction (e.g., the NIST-recommended primes in §2.2.6).

For the reduction c_k' mod p, note that

$$c_k' \le (p-1)^2 + \omega(m-1)(p-1)^2 = (p-1)^2(1 + \omega(m-1)).$$

If $p = 2^n - c$ is such that

$$\log_2(1 + \omega(m-1)) + 2\log_2|c| \le n, \tag{2.4}$$

then reduction can be done with at most two multiplications by c. As an example, if $p = 2^{28} - 165$ and $f(z) = z^6 - 2$, then

$$\log_2(1 + \omega(m-1)) + 2\log_2|c| = \log_2 11 + 2\log_2 165 < n = 28$$

and condition (2.4) is satisfied.

If accumulation is in a series of registers each of size W bits, then selecting $p = 2^n - c$ with $n < W$ allows several terms to be accumulated in two registers (rather than spilling into a third register or requiring a partial reduction). The example with $p = 2^{28} - 165$ is attractive in this sense if $W = 32$. However, this strategy competes with optimal use of the integer multiply, and hence may not be effective if it requires use of a larger m to obtain a field of sufficient size.

Example 2.56 (*accumulation strategies*) Consider the OEF defined by $p = 2^{31} - 1$ and $f(z) = z^6 - 7$, on a machine with wordsize $W = 32$. Since this is a Type I OEF, subfield reduction is especially simple, and a combination of partial reduction with accumulation may be effective in finding c_k' mod p. Although reduction into a single register after each operation may be prohibitively expensive, an accumulation into two registers (with some partial reductions) or into three registers can be employed.

Suppose the accumulator consists of two registers. A partial reduction may be performed on each term of the form $a_i b_j$ by writing $a_i b_j = 2^{32}v + u$ and then $2v + u$ is added to the accumulator. Similarly, the accumulator itself could be partially reduced after the addition of a product $a_i b_j$.

If the accumulator is three words, then the partial reductions are unnecessary, and a portion of the accumulation involves only two registers. On the other hand, the multiplication by $\omega = 7$ and the final reduction are slightly more complicated than in the two-register approach.

The multiply-and-accumulate strategies also apply to field squaring in $\mathbb{F}_{p^m}$. Squaring requires a total of $m + \binom{m}{2} = m(m+1)/2$ integer multiplications (and possibly $m-1$ multiplications by ω). The cost of the $\mathbb{F}_p$ reductions depends on the method; in particular, if only a single reduction is used in finding c_k', then the number of reductions is the same as for general multiplication.

2.4.3 *Inversion*

Inversion of $a \in \mathbb{F}_{p^m}$, $a \neq 0$, finds a polynomial $a^{-1} \in \mathbb{F}_{p^m}$ such that $aa^{-1} \equiv 1$ (mod f). Variants of the Euclidean Algorithm have been proposed for use with OEFs. However, the action of the Frobenius map along with the special form of f can be used to obtain an inversion method that is among the fastest. The method is also relatively simple to implement efficiently once field multiplication is written, since only a few multiplications are needed to reduce inversion in $\mathbb{F}_{p^m}$ to inversion in the subfield $\mathbb{F}_p$.

Algorithm 2.59 computes

$$a^{-1} = (a^r)^{-1} a^{r-1} \bmod f \tag{2.5}$$

where

$$r = \frac{p^m - 1}{p - 1} = p^{m-1} + \cdots + p^2 + p + 1.$$

Since $(a^r)^{p-1} \equiv 1$ (mod p^m), it follows that $a^r \in \mathbb{F}_p$. Hence a suitable algorithm may be applied for inversion in $\mathbb{F}_p$ in order to compute the term $(a^r)^{-1}$ in (2.5).

Efficient calculation of $a^{r-1} = a^{p^{m-1} + \cdots + p}$ in (2.5) is performed by using properties of the *Frobenius map* $\varphi : \mathbb{F}_{p^m} \to \mathbb{F}_{p^m}$ defined by $\varphi(a) = a^p$. Elements of $\mathbb{F}_p$ are fixed by this map. Hence, if $a = a_{m-1} z^{m-1} + \cdots + a_2 z^2 + a_1 z + a_0$, then

$$\varphi^i : a \mapsto a_{m-1} z^{(m-1)p^i} + \cdots + a_1 z^{p^i} + a_0 \bmod f.$$

To reduce the powers of z modulo f, write a given nonnegative integer e as $e = qm + r$, where $q = \lfloor e/m \rfloor$ and $r = e \bmod m$. Since $f(z) = z^m - \omega$, it follows that

$$z^e = z^{qm+r} \equiv \omega^q z^r \pmod{f(z)}.$$

Notice that $\varphi^i(a)$ is somewhat simpler to evaluate if $p \equiv 1$ (mod m). By Theorem 2.52, every prime factor of m divides $p - 1$. Necessarily, if m is square free, the condition $p \equiv 1$ (mod m) holds. The results are collected in the following theorem.

Theorem 2.57 (*action of Frobenius map iterates*) Given an OEF with $p = 2^n - c$ and $f(z) = z^m - \omega$, let the Frobenius map on $\mathbb{F}_{p^m}$ be given by $\varphi : a \mapsto a^p \bmod f$.

(i) The ith iterate of φ is the map

$$\varphi^i : a \mapsto \sum_{j=0}^{m-1} a_j \omega^{\lfloor jp^i/m \rfloor} z^{jp^i \bmod m}.$$

(ii) If m is square-free, then $p \equiv 1$ (mod m) and hence $jp^i \bmod m = j$ for all $0 \le j \le m - 1$.

The values $z^e \equiv \omega^{\lfloor e/m \rfloor} z^{e \bmod m}$ (mod $f(z)$) may be precomputed for $e = jp^i$ of interest, in which case $\varphi^i(a)$ may be evaluated with only $m - 1$ multiplications in $\mathbb{F}_p$. Use of an addition chain then efficiently finds a^{r-1} in equation (2.5) using a few field multiplications and applications of φ^i.

Example 2.58 (*calculating a^{r-1}*) The OEF defined by $p = 2^{31} - 1$ and $f(z) = z^6 - 7$ has $r - 1 = p^5 + p^4 + \cdots + p$. We may calculate a^{r-1} using the sequence indicated in Table 2.2 (an addition-chain-like method) for $m = 6$. Evaluation of φ and φ^2 uses the precomputed values in Table 2.3 obtained from Theorem 2.57.

$m = 3$	$m = 5$	$m = 6$
$T \leftarrow a^p$	$T_1 \leftarrow a^p$	$T_1 \leftarrow a^p$
$T \leftarrow Ta = a^{p+1}$	$T_1 \leftarrow T_1 a = a^{p+1}$	$T_2 \leftarrow T_1 a = a^{p+1}$
$a^{r-1} \leftarrow T^p = a^{p^2+p}$	$T_2 \leftarrow T_1^{p^2} = a^{p^3+p^2}$	$T_3 \leftarrow T_2^{p^2} = a^{p^3+p^2}$
	$T_1 \leftarrow T_1 T_2 = a^{p^3+p^2+p+1}$	$T_2 \leftarrow T_3 T_2 = a^{p^3+p^2+p+1}$
	$a^{r-1} \leftarrow T_1^p$	$T_2 \leftarrow T_2^{p^2} = a^{p^5+p^4+p^3+p^2}$
		$a^{r-1} \leftarrow T_2 T_1$
Cost: $1M + 2\varphi$	Cost: $2M + 3\varphi$	Cost: $3M + 3\varphi$

Table 2.2. *Computation of a^{r-1} for $r = \frac{p^m-1}{p-1}$, $m \in \{3, 5, 6\}$. The final row indicates the cost in $\mathbb{F}_{p^m}$ multiplications (M) and applications of an iterate of the Frobenius map (φ).*

$z^{jp} \equiv \omega^{\lfloor jp/m \rfloor} z^j$ (mod f)	$z^{jp^2} \equiv \omega^{\lfloor jp^2/m \rfloor} z^j$ (mod f)
$z^p \equiv 1513477736z$	$z^{p^2} \equiv 1513477735z$
$z^{2p} \equiv 1513477735z^2$	$z^{2p^2} \equiv 634005911z^2$
$z^{3p} \equiv 2147483646z^3 \equiv -1z^3$	$z^{3p^2} \equiv 1z^3$
$z^{4p} \equiv 634005911z^4$	$z^{4p^2} \equiv 1513477735z^4$
$z^{5p} \equiv 634005912z^5$	$z^{5p^2} \equiv 634005911z^5$

Table 2.3. *Precomputation for evaluating φ^i, $i \in \{1, 2\}$, in the case $p = 2^{31} - 1$ and $f(z) = z^6 - 7$ (cf. Example 2.58). If $a = a_5 z^5 + \cdots + a_1 z + a_0 \in \mathbb{F}_{p^6}$, then $\varphi^i(a) = a^{p^i} \equiv \sum_{j=0}^{5} a_j \omega^{\lfloor jp^i/m \rfloor} z^j$ (mod f).*

In general, if $w(x)$ is the Hamming weight of the integer x, then a^{r-1} can be calculated with

$$t_1(m) = \lfloor \log_2(m - 1) \rfloor + w(m - 1) - 1$$

multiplications in $\mathbb{F}_{p^m}$, and

$$t_2(m) = \begin{cases} t_1(m) + 1, & m \text{ odd}, \\ j = \lfloor \log_2(m-1) \rfloor + 1, & m = 2^j \text{ for some } j, \\ \lfloor \log_2(m-1) \rfloor + w(m) - 1, & \text{otherwise}, \end{cases}$$

applications of Frobenius map iterates. Since $t_2(m) \leq t_1(m) + 1$, the time for calculating a^{r-1} with $m > 2$ is dominated by the multiplications in $\mathbb{F}_{p^m}$ (each of which is much more expensive than the $m - 1$ multiplications in $\mathbb{F}_p$ needed for evaluation of φ^i).

Algorithm 2.59 OEF inversion

INPUT: $a \in \mathbb{F}_{p^m}$, $a \neq 0$.
OUTPUT: The element $a^{-1} \in \mathbb{F}_{p^m}$ such that $aa^{-1} \equiv 1 \pmod{f}$.
1. Use an addition-chain approach to find a^{r-1}, where $r = (p^m - 1)/(p - 1)$.
2. $c \leftarrow a^r = a^{r-1}a \in \mathbb{F}_p$.
3. Obtain c^{-1} such that $cc^{-1} \equiv 1 \pmod{p}$ via an inversion algorithm in $\mathbb{F}_p$.
4. Return($c^{-1}a^{r-1}$).

Note 2.60 (*implementation details for Algorithm 2.59*)

(i) The element c in step 2 of Algorithm 2.59 belongs to $\mathbb{F}_p$. Hence, only arithmetic contributing to the constant term of $a^{r-1}a$ need be performed (requiring m multiplications of elements in $\mathbb{F}_p$ and a multiplication by ω).

(ii) Since $c^{-1} \in \mathbb{F}_p$, the multiplication in step 4 requires only m $\mathbb{F}_p$-multiplications.

(iii) The running time is dominated by the $t_1(m)$ multiplications in $\mathbb{F}_{p^m}$ in finding a^{r-1}, and the cost of the subfield inversion in step 3.

The ratio I/M of field inversion cost to multiplication cost is of fundamental interest. When $m = 6$, Algorithm 2.59 will require significantly more time than the $t_1(6) = 3$ multiplications involved in finding a^{r-1}, since the time for subfield inversion (step 3) will be substantial. However, on general-purpose processors, the ratio is expected to be much smaller than the corresponding ratio in a prime field $\mathbb{F}_q$ where $q \approx p^m$.

2.5 *Notes and further references*

§2.1
For an introduction to the theory of finite fields, see the books of Koblitz [254] and McEliece [311]. A more comprehensive treatment is given by Lidl and Niederreiter [292].

§2.2

Menezes, van Oorshot, and Vanstone [319] concisely cover algorithms for ordinary and modular integer arithmetic of practical interest in cryptography. Knuth [249] is a standard reference. Koç [258] describes several (modular) multiplication methods, including classical and Karatsuba-Ofman, a method which interleaves multiplication with reduction, and Montgomery multiplication.

The decision to base multiplication on operand scanning (Algorithm 2.9) or product scanning (Algorithm 2.10) is platform dependent. Generally speaking, Algorithm 2.9 has more memory accesses, while Algorithm 2.10 has more complex control code unless loops are unrolled. Comba [101] compares the methods in detail for 16-bit Intel 80286 processors, and the unrolled product-scanning versions were apparently the inspiration for the "comba" routines in OpenSSL.

Scott [416] discusses multiplication methods on three 32-bit Intel IA-32 processors (the 80486, Pentium, and Pentium Pro), and provides experimental results for modular exponentiation with multiplication based on operand scanning, product scanning (Comba's method), Karatsuba-Ofman with product scanning, and floating-point hardware. Multiplication with features introduced on newer IA-32 processors is discussed in §5.1.3. On the Motorola digital signal processor 56000, Dussé and Kaliski [127] note that extraction of U in the inner loop of Algorithm 2.9 is relatively expensive. The processor has a 56-bit accumulator but only signed multiplication of 24-bit quantities, and the product scanning approach in Montgomery multiplication is reportedly significantly faster.

The multiplication method of Karatsuba-Ofman is due to Karatsuba and Ofman [239]. For integers of relatively small size, the savings in multiplications is often insufficient in Karatsuba-Ofman variants to make the methods competitive with optimized versions of classical algorithms. Knuth [249] and Koç [258] cover Karatsuba-Ofman in more detail.

Barrett reduction (Algorithm 2.14) is due to Barrett [29]. Bosselaers, Govaerts, and Vandewalle [66] provide descriptions and comparative results for classical reduction and the reduction methods of Barrett and Montgomery. If the transformations and precomputation are excluded, their results indicate that the methods are fairly similar in cost, with Montgomery reduction fastest and classical reduction likely to be slightly slower than Barrett reduction. These operation count comparisons are supported by implementation results on an Intel 80386 in portable C. De Win, Mister, Preneel and Wiener [111] report that the difference between Montgomery and Barrett reduction was negligible in their implementation on an Intel Pentium Pro of field arithmetic in $\mathbb{F}_p$ for a 192-bit prime p.

Montgomery reduction is due to Montgomery [330]. Koç, Acar, and Kaliski [260] analyze five Montgomery multiplication algorithms. The methods were identified as having a separate reduction phase or reduction integrated with multiplication, and according to the general form of the multiplication as operand-scanning or product-scanning. Among the algorithms tested, they conclude that a "coarsely integrated operand scanning" method (where a reduction step follows a multiplication step at each index of an outer loop through one of the operands) is simplest and probably best for general-purpose processors. Koç and Acar [259] extend Montgomery multiplication to binary fields.

The binary gcd algorithm (Algorithm 2.21) is due to Stein [451], and is analyzed by Knuth [249]. Bach and Shallit [23] provide a comprehensive analysis of several gcd algorithms. The binary algorithm for inversion (Algorithm 2.22) is adapted from the corresponding extended gcd algorithm.

Lehmer [278] proposed a variant of the classical Euclidean algorithm which replaces most of the expensive multiple-precision divisions by single-precision operations. The algorithm is examined in detail by Knuth [249], and a slight modification is analyzed by Sorenson [450]. Durand [126] provides concise coverage of inversion algorithms adapted from the extended versions of the Euclidean, binary gcd, and Lehmer algorithms, along with timings for RSA and elliptic curve point multiplication on 32-bit RISC processors (for smartcards) from SGS-Thomson. On these processors, Lehmer's method showed significant advantages, and in fact produced point multiplication times faster than was obtained with projective coordinates.

Algorithm 2.23 for the partial Montgomery inverse is due to Kaliski [234]. De Win, Mister, Preneel and Wiener [111] report that an inversion method based on this algorithm was superior to variations of the extended Euclidean algorithm (Algorithm 2.19) in their tests on an Intel Pentium Pro, although details are not provided. The generalization in Algorithm 2.25 is due to Savas and Koç [403]; a similar algorithm is provided for finding the usual inverse.

Simultaneous inversion (Algorithm 2.26) is attributed to Montgomery [331], where the technique was suggested for accelerating the elliptic curve method (ECM) of factoring. Cohen [99, Algorithm 10.3.4] gives an extended version of Algorithm 2.26, presented in the context of ECM.

The NIST primes (§2.2.6) are given in the Federal Information Processing Standards (FIPS) publication 186-2 [140] on the Digital Signature Standard, as part of the recommended elliptic curves for US Government use. Solinas [445] discusses generalizations of Mersenne numbers $2^k - 1$ that permit fast reduction (without division); the NIST primes are special cases.

§2.3

Algorithms 2.35 and 2.36 for polynomial multiplication are due to López and Dahab [301]. Their work expands on "comb" exponentiation methods of Lim and Lee [295]. Operation count comparisons and implementation results (on Intel family and Sun UltraSPARC processors) suggest that Algorithm 2.36 will be significantly faster than

Algorithm 2.34 at relatively modest storage requirements. The multiple-table variants in Note 2.37 are essentially described by López and Dahab [301, Remark 2].

The OpenSSL contribution by Sun Microsystems Laboratories mentioned in Note 2.38 is authored by Sheueling Chang Shantz and Douglas Stebila. Our notes are based in part on OpenSSL-0.9.8 snapshots. A significant enchancement is discussed by Weimerskirch, Stebila, and Chang Shantz [478]. Appendix C has a few notes on the OpenSSL library.

The NIST reduction polynomials (§2.3.5) are given in the Federal Information Processing Standards (FIPS) publication 186-2 [140] on the Digital Signature Standard, as part of the recommended elliptic curves for US Government use.

The binary algorithm for inversion (Algorithm 2.49) is the polynomial analogue of Algorithm 2.22. The almost inverse algorithm (Algorithm 2.50) is due to Schroeppel, Orman, O'Malley, and Spatscheck [415]; a similar algorithm (Algorithm 2.23) in the context of Montgomery inversion was described by Kaliski [234].

Algorithms for field division were described by Goodman and Chandrakasan [177], Chang Shantz [90], Durand [126], and Schroeppel [412]. Inversion and division algorithm implementations are especially sensitive to compiler differences and processor characteristics, and rough operation count analysis can be misleading. Fong, Hankerson, López and Menezes [144] discuss inversion and division algorithm considerations and provide comparative timings for selected compilers on the Intel Pentium III and Sun UltraSPARC.

In a *normal basis* representation, elements of $\mathbb{F}_{2^m}$ are expressed in terms of a basis of the form $\{\beta, \beta^2, \beta^{2^2}, \ldots, \beta^{2^{m-1}}\}$. One advantage of normal bases is that squaring of a field element is a simple rotation of its vector representation. Mullin, Onyszchuk, Vanstone and Wilson [337] introduced the concept of an *optimal normal basis* in order to reduce the hardware complexity of multiplying field elements in $\mathbb{F}_{2^m}$ whose elements are represented using a normal basis. Hardware implementations of the arithmetic in $\mathbb{F}_{2^m}$ using optimal normal bases are described by Agnew, Mullin, Onyszchuk and Vanstone [6] and Sunar and Koç [456].

Normal bases of low complexity, also known as *Gaussian normal bases*, were further studied by Ash, Blake and Vanstone [19]. Gaussian normal bases are explicitly described in the ANSI X9.62 standard [14] for the ECDSA. Experience has shown that optimal normal bases do not have any significant advantages over polynomial bases for hardware implementation. Moreover, field multiplication in software for normal basis representations is very slow in comparison to multiplication with a polynomial basis; see Reyhani-Masoleh and Hasan [390] and Ning and Yin [348].

§2.4

Optimal extension fields were introduced by Bailey and Paar [25, 26]. Theorem 2.52 is from Lidl and Niederreiter [292, Theorem 3.75]. Theorem 2.57 corrects [26, Corollary

2]. The OEF construction algorithm of [26] has a minor flaw in the test for irreducibility, leading to a few incorrect entries in their table of Type II OEFs (e.g, $z^{25} - 2$ is not irreducible when $p = 2^8 - 5$). The inversion method of §2.4.3 given by Bailey and Paar is based on Itoh and Tsujii [217]; see also [183].

Lim and Hwang [293] give thorough coverage to various optimization strategies and provide useful benchmark timings on Intel and DEC processors. Their operation count analysis favours a Euclidean algorithm variant over Algorithm 2.59 for inversion. However, rough operation counts at this level often fail to capture processor or compiler characteristics adequately, and in subsequent work [294] they note that Algorithm 2.59 appears to be significantly faster in implementation on Intel Pentium II and DEC Alpha processors. Chung, Sim, and Lee [97] note that the count for the number of required Frobenius-map applications in inversion given in [26] is not necessarily minimal. A revised formula is given, along with inversion algorithm comparisons and implementation results for a low-power Samsung CalmRISC 8-bit processor with a math coprocessor.

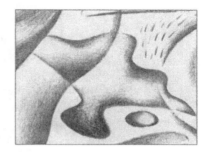

CHAPTER 3

Elliptic Curve Arithmetic

Cryptographic mechanisms based on elliptic curves depend on arithmetic involving the points of the curve. As noted in Chapter 2, curve arithmetic is defined in terms of underlying field operations, the efficiency of which is essential. Efficient curve operations are likewise crucial to performance.

Figure 3.1 illustrates module framework required for a protocol such as the Elliptic Curve Digital Signature Algorithm (ECDSA, discussed in §4.4.1). The curve arithmetic not only is built on field operations, but in some cases also relies on big number and modular arithmetic (e.g., τ-adic operations if Koblitz curves are used; see §3.4). ECDSA uses a hash function and certain modular operations, but the computationally-expensive steps involve curve operations.

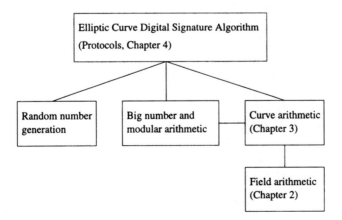

Figure 3.1. ECDSA support modules.

§3.1 provides an introduction to elliptic curves. The group operations of addition and doubling for the points on an elliptic curve are given, along with fundamental structure and other properties. §3.2 presents projective-coordinate representations (and associated point addition and doubling algorithms), of principal interest when field inversion is expensive relative to field multiplication. §3.3 discusses strategies for point multiplication, the operation which dominates the execution time of schemes based on elliptic curves.

The methods in §3.4, §3.5, and §3.6 are related in the sense that they all exploit endomorphisms of the elliptic curve to reduce the cost of doubling in point multiplication. §3.4 discusses the special Koblitz curves, which allow point doubling for curves over $\mathbb{F}_2$ to be replaced by inexpensive field squaring operations. §3.5 examines a broader class of elliptic curves which admit endomorphisms that can be used efficiently to reduce the number of doublings in point multiplication. Strategies in §3.6 for elliptic curves over binary fields replace most point doublings by a potentially faster halving operation. §3.7 contains operation count comparisons for selected point multiplication methods. §3.8 concludes with chapter notes and references.

3.1 Introduction to elliptic curves

Definition 3.1 An *elliptic curve E over a field K* is defined by an equation

$$E : y^2 + a_1 xy + a_3 y = x^3 + a_2 x^2 + a_4 x + a_6 \tag{3.1}$$

where $a_1, a_2, a_3, a_4, a_6 \in K$ and $\Delta \neq 0$, where Δ is the *discriminant* of E and is defined as follows:

$$\left. \begin{aligned} \Delta &= -d_2^2 d_8 - 8 d_4^3 - 27 d_6^2 + 9 d_2 d_4 d_6 \\ d_2 &= a_1^2 + 4 a_2 \\ d_4 &= 2 a_4 + a_1 a_3 \\ d_6 &= a_3^2 + 4 a_6 \\ d_8 &= a_1^2 a_6 + 4 a_2 a_6 - a_1 a_3 a_4 + a_2 a_3^2 - a_4^2. \end{aligned} \right\} \tag{3.2}$$

If L is any extension field of K, then the set of *L-rational points* on E is

$$E(L) = \{(x, y) \in L \times L : y^2 + a_1 xy + a_3 y - x^3 - a_2 x^2 - a_4 x - a_6 = 0\} \cup \{\infty\}$$

where ∞ is the *point at infinity*.

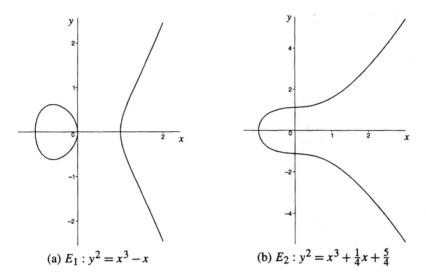

(a) $E_1 : y^2 = x^3 - x$

(b) $E_2 : y^2 = x^3 + \frac{1}{4}x + \frac{5}{4}$

Figure 3.2. Elliptic curves over $\mathbb{R}$.

Remark 3.2 (*comments on Definition 3.1*)

  (i) Equation (3.1) is called a *Weierstrass equation*.

 (ii) We say that E is *defined over K* because the coefficients a_1, a_2, a_3, a_4, a_6 of its defining equation are elements of K. We sometimes write E/K to emphasize that E is defined over K, and K is called the *underlying field*. Note that if E is defined over K, then E is also defined over any extension field of K.

(iii) The condition $\Delta \neq 0$ ensures that the elliptic curve is "smooth", that is, there are no points at which the curve has two or more distinct tangent lines.

(iv) The point ∞ is the only point on the line at infinity that satisfies the projective form of the Weierstrass equation (see §3.2).

 (v) The *L-rational points* on E are the points (x, y) that satisfy the equation of the curve and whose coordinates x and y belong to L. The point at infinity is considered an L-rational point for all extension fields L of K.

Example 3.3 (*elliptic curves over* $\mathbb{R}$) Consider the elliptic curves

$$E_1 : y^2 = x^3 - x$$
$$E_2 : y^2 = x^3 + \frac{1}{4}x + \frac{5}{4}$$

defined over the field $\mathbb{R}$ of real numbers. The points $E_1(\mathbb{R}) \setminus \{\infty\}$ and $E_2(\mathbb{R}) \setminus \{\infty\}$ are graphed in Figure 3.2.

3.1.1 Simplified Weierstrass equations

Definition 3.4 Two elliptic curves E_1 and E_2 defined over K and given by the Weierstrass equations

$$E_1 : y^2 + a_1 xy + a_3 y = x^3 + a_2 x^2 + a_4 x + a_6$$

$$E_2 : y^2 + \overline{a}_1 xy + \overline{a}_3 y = x^3 + \overline{a}_2 x^2 + \overline{a}_4 x + \overline{a}_6$$

are said to be *isomorphic over K* if there exist $u, r, s, t \in K, u \neq 0$, such that the change of variables

$$(x, y) \rightarrow (u^2 x + r, u^3 y + u^2 sx + t) \tag{3.3}$$

transforms equation E_1 into equation E_2. The transformation (3.3) is called an *admissible change of variables*.

A Weierstrass equation

$$E : y^2 + a_1 xy + a_3 y = x^3 + a_2 x^2 + a_4 x + a_6$$

defined over K can be simplified considerably by applying admissible changes of variables. The simplified equations will be used throughout the remainder of this book. We consider separately the cases where the underlying field K has characteristic different from 2 and 3, or has characteristic equal to 2 or 3.

1. If the characteristic of K is not equal to 2 or 3, then the admissible change of variables

$$(x, y) \rightarrow \left(\frac{x - 3a_1^2 - 12a_2}{36}, \frac{y - 3a_1 x}{216} - \frac{a_1^3 + 4a_1 a_2 - 12a_3}{24} \right)$$

   transforms E to the curve
$$y^2 = x^3 + ax + b \tag{3.4}$$
   where $a, b \in K$. The discriminant of this curve is $\Delta = -16(4a^3 + 27b^2)$.

2. If the characteristic of K is 2, then there are two cases to consider. If $a_1 \neq 0$, then the admissible change of variables

$$(x, y) \rightarrow \left(a_1^2 x + \frac{a_3}{a_1}, a_1^3 y + \frac{a_1^2 a_4 + a_3^2}{a_1^3} \right)$$

   transforms E to the curve
$$y^2 + xy = x^3 + ax^2 + b \tag{3.5}$$
   where $a, b \in K$. Such a curve is said to be *non-supersingular* (cf. Definition 3.10) and has discriminant $\Delta = b$. If $a_1 = 0$, then the admissible change of variables

$$(x, y) \rightarrow (x + a_2, y)$$

transforms E to the curve

$$y^2 + cy = x^3 + ax + b \tag{3.6}$$

where $a, b, c \in K$. Such a curve is said to be *supersingular* (cf. Definition 3.10) and has discriminant $\Delta = c^4$.

3. If the characteristic of K is 3, then there are two cases to consider. If $a_1^2 \neq -a_2$, then the admissible change of variables

$$(x, y) \to \left(x + \frac{d_4}{d_2}, y + a_1 x + a_1 \frac{d_4}{d_2} + a_3 \right),$$

where $d_2 = a_1^2 + a_2$ and $d_4 = a_4 - a_1 a_3$, transforms E to the curve

$$y^2 = x^3 + ax^2 + b \tag{3.7}$$

where $a, b \in K$. Such a curve is said to be *non-supersingular* and has discriminant $\Delta = -a^3 b$. If $a_1^2 = -a_2$, then the admissible change of variables

$$(x, y) \to (x, y + a_1 x + a_3)$$

transforms E to the curve

$$y^2 = x^3 + ax + b \tag{3.8}$$

where $a, b \in K$. Such a curve is said to be *supersingular* and has discriminant $\Delta = -a^3$.

3.1.2 Group law

Let E be an elliptic curve defined over the field K. There is a *chord-and-tangent rule* for adding two points in $E(K)$ to give a third point in $E(K)$. Together with this addition operation, the set of points $E(K)$ forms an abelian group with ∞ serving as its identity. It is this group that is used in the construction of elliptic curve cryptographic systems.

The addition rule is best explained geometrically. Let $P = (x_1, y_1)$ and $Q = (x_2, y_2)$ be two distinct points on an elliptic curve E. Then the *sum* R, of P and Q, is defined as follows. First draw a line through P and Q; this line intersects the elliptic curve at a third point. Then R is the reflection of this point about the x-axis. This is depicted in Figure 3.3(a).

The *double* R, of P, is defined as follows. First draw the tangent line to the elliptic curve at P. This line intersects the elliptic curve at a second point. Then R is the reflection of this point about the x-axis. This is depicted in Figure 3.3(b).

Algebraic formulas for the group law can be derived from the geometric description. These formulas are presented next for elliptic curves E of the simplified Weierstrass form (3.4) in affine coordinates when the characteristic of the underlying field K is not 2 or 3 (e.g., $K = \mathbb{F}_p$ where $p > 3$ is a prime), for non-supersingular elliptic curves E of the form (3.5) over $K = \mathbb{F}_{2^m}$, and for supersingular elliptic curves E of the form (3.6) over $K = \mathbb{F}_{2^m}$.

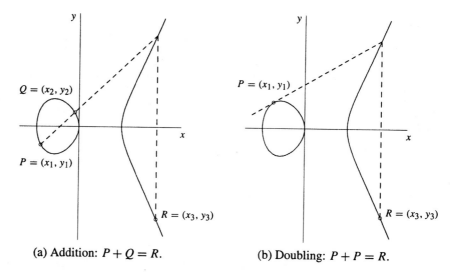

(a) Addition: $P + Q = R$.   (b) Doubling: $P + P = R$.

Figure 3.3. *Geometric addition and doubling of elliptic curve points.*

Group law for $E/K : y^2 = x^3 + ax + b$, char$(K) \neq 2, 3$

1. *Identity.* $P + \infty = \infty + P = P$ for all $P \in E(K)$.

2. *Negatives.* If $P = (x, y) \in E(K)$, then $(x, y) + (x, -y) = \infty$. The point $(x, -y)$ is denoted by $-P$ and is called the *negative* of P; note that $-P$ is indeed a point in $E(K)$. Also, $-\infty = \infty$.

3. *Point addition.* Let $P = (x_1, y_1) \in E(K)$ and $Q = (x_2, y_2) \in E(K)$, where $P \neq \pm Q$. Then $P + Q = (x_3, y_3)$, where

$$x_3 = \left(\frac{y_2 - y_1}{x_2 - x_1} \right)^2 - x_1 - x_2 \quad \text{and} \quad y_3 = \left(\frac{y_2 - y_1}{x_2 - x_1} \right)(x_1 - x_3) - y_1.$$

4. *Point doubling.* Let $P = (x_1, y_1) \in E(K)$, where $P \neq -P$. Then $2P = (x_3, y_3)$, where

$$x_3 = \left(\frac{3x_1^2 + a}{2y_1} \right)^2 - 2x_1 \quad \text{and} \quad y_3 = \left(\frac{3x_1^2 + a}{2y_1} \right)(x_1 - x_3) - y_1.$$

Example 3.5 (*elliptic curve over the prime field* $\mathbb{F}_{29}$) Let $p = 29$, $a = 4$, and $b = 20$, and consider the elliptic curve

$$E : y^2 = x^3 + 4x + 20$$

defined over $\mathbb{F}_{29}$. Note that $\Delta = -16(4a^3 + 27b^2) = -176896 \not\equiv 0 \pmod{29}$, so E is indeed an elliptic curve. The points in $E(\mathbb{F}_{29})$ are the following:

∞	(2, 6)	(4, 19)	(8, 10)	(13, 23)	(16, 2)	(19, 16)	(27, 2)
(0, 7)	(2, 23)	(5, 7)	(8, 19)	(14, 6)	(16, 27)	(20, 3)	(27, 27)
(0, 22)	(3, 1)	(5, 22)	(10, 4)	(14, 23)	(17, 10)	(20, 26)	
(1, 5)	(3, 28)	(6, 12)	(10, 25)	(15, 2)	(17, 19)	(24, 7)	
(1, 24)	(4, 10)	(6, 17)	(13, 6)	(15, 27)	(19, 13)	(24, 22)	

Examples of elliptic curve addition are $(5, 22) + (16, 27) = (13, 6)$, and $2(5, 22) = (14, 6)$.

Group law for non-supersingular $E/\mathbb{F}_{2^m} : y^2 + xy = x^3 + ax^2 + b$

1. *Identity.* $P + \infty = \infty + P = P$ for all $P \in E(\mathbb{F}_{2^m})$.

2. *Negatives.* If $P = (x, y) \in E(\mathbb{F}_{2^m})$, then $(x, y) + (x, x + y) = \infty$. The point $(x, x + y)$ is denoted by $-P$ and is called the *negative* of P; note that $-P$ is indeed a point in $E(\mathbb{F}_{2^m})$. Also, $-\infty = \infty$.

3. *Point addition.* Let $P = (x_1, y_1) \in E(\mathbb{F}_{2^m})$ and $Q = (x_2, y_2) \in E(\mathbb{F}_{2^m})$, where $P \neq \pm Q$. Then $P + Q = (x_3, y_3)$, where

$$x_3 = \lambda^2 + \lambda + x_1 + x_2 + a \quad \text{and} \quad y_3 = \lambda(x_1 + x_3) + x_3 + y_1$$

with $\lambda = (y_1 + y_2)/(x_1 + x_2)$.

4. *Point doubling.* Let $P = (x_1, y_1) \in E(\mathbb{F}_{2^m})$, where $P \neq -P$. Then $2P = (x_3, y_3)$, where

$$x_3 = \lambda^2 + \lambda + a = x_1^2 + \frac{b}{x_1^2} \quad \text{and} \quad y_3 = x_1^2 + \lambda x_3 + x_3$$

with $\lambda = x_1 + y_1/x_1$.

Example 3.6 (*non-supersingular elliptic curve over* $\mathbb{F}_{2^4}$) Consider the finite field $\mathbb{F}_{2^4}$ as represented by the reduction polynomial $f(z) = z^4 + z + 1$ (cf. Example 2.2). An element $a_3 z^3 + a_2 z^2 + a_1 z + a_0 \in \mathbb{F}_{2^4}$ is represented by the bit string $(a_3 a_2 a_1 a_0)$ of length 4; for example, (0101) represents $z^2 + 1$. Let $a = z^3$, $b = z^3 + 1$, and consider the non-supersingular elliptic curve

$$E : y^2 + xy = x^3 + z^3 x^2 + (z^3 + 1)$$

defined over $\mathbb{F}_{2^4}$. The points in $E(\mathbb{F}_{2^4})$ are the following:

∞	(0011, 1100)	(1000, 0001)	(1100, 0000)
(0000, 1011)	(0011, 1111)	(1000, 1001)	(1100, 1100)
(0001, 0000)	(0101, 0000)	(1001, 0110)	(1111, 0100)
(0001, 0001)	(0101, 0101)	(1001, 1111)	(1111, 1011)
(0010, 1101)	(0111, 1011)	(1011, 0010)	
(0010, 1111)	(0111, 1100)	(1011, 1001)	

Examples of elliptic curve addition are $(0010, 1111) + (1100, 1100) = (0001, 0001)$, and $2(0010, 1111) = (1011, 0010)$.

Group law for supersingular $E/\mathbb{F}_{2^m} : y^2 + cy = x^3 + ax + b$

1. *Identity.* $P + \infty = \infty + P = P$ for all $P \in E(\mathbb{F}_{2^m})$.

2. *Negatives.* If $P = (x, y) \in E(\mathbb{F}_{2^m})$, then $(x, y) + (x, y + c) = \infty$. The point $(x, y + c)$ is denoted by $-P$ and is called the *negative* of P; note that $-P$ is indeed a point in $E(\mathbb{F}_{2^m})$. Also, $-\infty = \infty$.

3. *Point addition.* Let $P = (x_1, y_1) \in E(\mathbb{F}_{2^m})$ and $Q = (x_2, y_2) \in E(\mathbb{F}_{2^m})$, where $P \neq \pm Q$. Then $P + Q = (x_3, y_3)$, where

$$x_3 = \left(\frac{y_1 + y_2}{x_1 + x_2}\right)^2 + x_1 + x_2 \quad \text{and} \quad y_3 = \left(\frac{y_1 + y_2}{x_1 + x_2}\right)(x_1 + x_3) + y_1 + c.$$

4. *Point doubling.* Let $P = (x_1, y_1) \in E(\mathbb{F}_{2^m})$, where $P \neq -P$. Then $2P = (x_3, y_3)$, where

$$x_3 = \left(\frac{x_1^2 + a}{c}\right)^2 \quad \text{and} \quad y_3 = \left(\frac{x_1^2 + a}{c}\right)(x_1 + x_3) + y_1 + c.$$

3.1.3 Group order

Let E be an elliptic curve defined over $\mathbb{F}_q$. The number of points in $E(\mathbb{F}_q)$, denoted $\#E(\mathbb{F}_q)$, is called the *order* of E over $\mathbb{F}_q$. Since the Weierstrass equation (3.1) has at most two solutions for each $x \in \mathbb{F}_q$, we know that $\#E(\mathbb{F}_q) \in [1, 2q + 1]$. Hasse's theorem provides tighter bounds for $\#E(\mathbb{F}_q)$.

Theorem 3.7 (*Hasse*) Let E be an elliptic curve defined over $\mathbb{F}_q$. Then

$$q + 1 - 2\sqrt{q} \leq \#E(\mathbb{F}_q) \leq q + 1 + 2\sqrt{q}.$$

The interval $[q + 1 - 2\sqrt{q}, q + 1 + 2\sqrt{q}]$ is called the *Hasse interval*. An alternate formulation of Hasse's theorem is the following: if E is defined over $\mathbb{F}_q$, then $\#E(\mathbb{F}_q) = q + 1 - t$ where $|t| \leq 2\sqrt{q}$; t is called the *trace* of E over $\mathbb{F}_q$. Since $2\sqrt{q}$ is small relative to q, we have $\#E(\mathbb{F}_q) \approx q$.

The next result determines the possible values for $\#E(\mathbb{F}_q)$ as E ranges over all elliptic curves defined over $\mathbb{F}_q$.

Theorem 3.8 (*admissible orders of elliptic curves*) Let $q = p^m$ where p is the characteristic of $\mathbb{F}_q$. There exists an elliptic curve E defined over $\mathbb{F}_q$ with $\#E(\mathbb{F}_q) = q + 1 - t$ if and only if one of the following conditions holds:

(i) $t \not\equiv 0 \pmod{p}$ and $t^2 \leq 4q$.

(ii) m is odd and either (a) $t = 0$; or (b) $t^2 = 2q$ and $p = 2$; or (c) $t^2 = 3q$ and $p = 3$.

(iii) m is even and either (a) $t^2 = 4q$; or (b) $t^2 = q$ and $p \not\equiv 1 \pmod{3}$; or (c) $t = 0$ and $p \not\equiv 1 \pmod 4$.

A consequence of Theorem 3.8 is that for any prime p and integer t satisfying $|t| \leq 2\sqrt{p}$, there exists an elliptic curve E over $\mathbb{F}_p$ with $\#E(\mathbb{F}_p) = p + 1 - t$. This is illustrated in Example 3.9.

Example 3.9 (*orders of elliptic curves over $\mathbb{F}_{37}$*) Let $p = 37$. Table 3.1 lists, for each integer n in the Hasse interval $[37 + 1 - 2\sqrt{37}, 37 + 1 + 2\sqrt{37}]$, the coefficients (a, b) of an elliptic curve $E : y^2 = x^3 + ax + b$ defined over $\mathbb{F}_{37}$ with $\#E(\mathbb{F}_{37}) = n$.

n	(a,b)	n	(a,b)	n	(a,b)	n	(a,b)	n	(a,b)
26	(5,0)	31	(2,8)	36	(1,0)	41	(1,16)	46	(1,11)
27	(0,9)	32	(3,6)	37	(0,5)	42	(1,9)	47	(3,15)
28	(0,6)	33	(1,13)	38	(1,5)	43	(2,9)	48	(0,1)
29	(1,12)	34	(1,18)	39	(0,3)	44	(1,7)	49	(0,2)
30	(2,2)	35	(1,8)	40	(1,2)	45	(2,14)	50	(2,0)

Table 3.1. *The admissible orders* $n = \#E(\mathbb{F}_{37})$ *of elliptic curves* $E : y^2 = x^3 + ax + b$ *defined over* $\mathbb{F}_{37}$.

The order $\#E(\mathbb{F}_q)$ can be used to define supersingularity of an elliptic curve.

Definition 3.10 Let p be the characteristic of $\mathbb{F}_q$. An elliptic curve E defined over $\mathbb{F}_q$ is *supersingular* if p divides t, where t is the trace. If p does not divide t, then E is *non-supersingular*.

If E is an elliptic curve defined over $\mathbb{F}_q$, then E is also defined over any extension $\mathbb{F}_{q^n}$ of $\mathbb{F}_q$. The group $E(\mathbb{F}_q)$ of $\mathbb{F}_q$-rational points is a subgroup of the group $E(\mathbb{F}_{q^n})$ of $\mathbb{F}_{q^n}$-rational points and hence $\#E(\mathbb{F}_q)$ divides $\#E(\mathbb{F}_{q^n})$. If $\#E(\mathbb{F}_q)$ is known, then $\#E(\mathbb{F}_{q^n})$ can be efficiently determined by the following result.

Theorem 3.11 Let E be an elliptic curve defined over $\mathbb{F}_q$, and let $\#E(\mathbb{F}_q) = q + 1 - t$. Then $\#E(\mathbb{F}_{q^n}) = q^n + 1 - V_n$ for all $n \geq 2$, where $\{V_n\}$ is the sequence defined recursively by $V_0 = 2$, $V_1 = t$, and $V_n = V_1 V_{n-1} - q V_{n-2}$ for $n \geq 2$.

3.1.4 Group structure

Theorem 3.12 describes the group structure of $E(\mathbb{F}_q)$. We use $\mathbb{Z}_n$ to denote a cyclic group of order n.

Theorem 3.12 (*group structure of an elliptic curve*) Let E be an elliptic curve defined over $\mathbb{F}_q$. Then $E(\mathbb{F}_q)$ is isomorphic to $\mathbb{Z}_{n_1} \oplus \mathbb{Z}_{n_2}$ where n_1 and n_2 are uniquely determined positive integers such that n_2 divides both n_1 and $q - 1$.

Note that $\#E(\mathbb{F}_q) = n_1 n_2$. If $n_2 = 1$, then $E(\mathbb{F}_q)$ is a cyclic group. If $n_2 > 1$, then $E(\mathbb{F}_q)$ is said to have *rank 2*. If n_2 is a small integer (e.g., $n = 2, 3$ or 4), we sometimes say that $E(\mathbb{F}_q)$ is *almost cyclic*. Since n_2 divides both n_1 and $q - 1$, one expects that $E(\mathbb{F}_q)$ is cyclic or almost cyclic for most elliptic curves E over $\mathbb{F}_q$.

Example 3.13 (*group structure*) The elliptic curve $E : y^2 = x^3 + 4x + 20$ defined over $\mathbb{F}_{29}$ (cf. Example 3.5) has $\#E(\mathbb{F}_{29}) = 37$. Since 37 is prime, $E(\mathbb{F}_{29})$ is a cyclic group and any point in $E(\mathbb{F}_{29})$ except for ∞ is a generator of $E(\mathbb{F}_{29})$. The following shows that the multiples of the point $P = (1, 5)$ generate all the points in $E(\mathbb{F}_{29})$.

$0P = \infty$	$8P = (8, 10)$	$16P = (0, 22)$	$24P = (16, 2)$	$32P = (6, 17)$
$1P = (1, 5)$	$9P = (14, 23)$	$17P = (27, 2)$	$25P = (19, 16)$	$33P = (15, 2)$
$2P = (4, 19)$	$10P = (13, 23)$	$18P = (2, 23)$	$26P = (10, 4)$	$34P = (20, 26)$
$3P = (20, 3)$	$11P = (10, 25)$	$19P = (2, 6)$	$27P = (13, 6)$	$35P = (4, 10)$
$4P = (15, 27)$	$12P = (19, 13)$	$20P = (27, 27)$	$28P = (14, 6)$	$36P = (1, 24)$
$5P = (6, 12)$	$13P = (16, 27)$	$21P = (0, 7)$	$29P = (8, 19)$	
$6P = (17, 19)$	$14P = (5, 22)$	$22P = (3, 28)$	$30P = (24, 7)$	
$7P = (24, 22)$	$15P = (3, 1)$	$23P = (5, 7)$	$31P = (17, 10)$	

Example 3.14 (*group structure*) Consider $\mathbb{F}_{2^4}$ as represented by the reduction polynomial $f(z) = z^4 + z + 1$. The elliptic curve $E : y^2 + xy = x^3 + z^3 x^2 + (z^3 + 1)$ defined over $\mathbb{F}_{2^4}$ has $\#E(\mathbb{F}_{2^4}) = 22$ (cf. Example 3.6). Since 22 does not have any repeated factors, $E(\mathbb{F}_{2^4})$ is cyclic. The point $P = (z^3, 1) = (1000, 0001)$ has order 11; its multiples are shown below.

$0P = \infty$	$3P = (1100, 0000)$	$6P = (1011, 1001)$	$9P = (1001, 0110)$
$1P = (1000, 0001)$	$4P = (1111, 1011)$	$7P = (1111, 0100)$	$10P = (1000, 1001)$
$2P = (1001, 1111)$	$5P = (1011, 0010)$	$8P = (1100, 1100)$	

3.1.5 Isomorphism classes

Recall the definition of isomorphic elliptic curves (Definition 3.4). The relation of isomorphism is an equivalence relation on the set of elliptic curves defined over a finite field K. If two elliptic curves E_1 and E_2 are isomorphic over K, then their groups $E_1(K)$ and $E_2(K)$ of K-rational points are also isomorphic. However, the converse is not true (cf. Examples 3.16 and 3.17). We present some results on the isomorphism classes of elliptic curves defined over finite fields of characteristic not equal to 2 or 3, and for non-supersingular elliptic curves defined over binary fields.

Theorem 3.15 (*isomorphism classes of elliptic curves*) Let $K = \mathbb{F}_q$ be a finite field with $\mathrm{char}(K) \neq 2, 3$.

(i) The elliptic curves

$$E_1 : y^2 = x^3 + ax + b \tag{3.9}$$

$$E_2 : y^2 = x^3 + \bar{a}x + \bar{b} \tag{3.10}$$

defined over K are isomorphic over K if and only if there exists $u \in K^*$ such that $u^4\bar{a} = a$ and $u^6\bar{b} = b$. If such a u exists, then the admissible change of variables

$$(x, y) \rightarrow (u^2x, u^3y)$$

transforms equation (3.9) into equation (3.10).

(ii) The number of isomorphism classes of elliptic curves over K is $2q + 6$, $2q + 2$, $2q + 4$, $2q$, for $q \equiv 1, 5, 7, 11 \pmod{12}$ respectively.

Example 3.16 (*isomorphism classes of elliptic curves over* $\mathbb{F}_5$) Table 3.2 lists the 12 isomorphism classes of elliptic curves over $\mathbb{F}_5$. Note that if the groups $E_1(\mathbb{F}_q)$ and $E_2(\mathbb{F}_q)$ of $\mathbb{F}_q$-rational points are isomorphic, then this does not imply that the elliptic curves E_1 and E_2 are isomorphic over $\mathbb{F}_q$. For example, the elliptic curves $E_1 : y^2 = x^3 + 1$ and $E_2 : y^2 = x^3 + 2$ are not isomorphic over $\mathbb{F}_5$, but $E_1(\mathbb{F}_5)$ and $E_2(\mathbb{F}_5)$ both have order 6 and therefore both groups are isomorphic to $\mathbb{Z}_6$.

Isomorphism class	$\#E(\mathbb{F}_5)$	Group structure of $E(\mathbb{F}_5)$
$\{y^2 = x^3 + 1,\ y^2 = x^3 + 4\}$	6	$\mathbb{Z}_6$
$\{y^2 = x^3 + 2,\ y^2 = x^3 + 3\}$	6	$\mathbb{Z}_6$
$\{y^3 = x^3 + x\}$	4	$\mathbb{Z}_2 \oplus \mathbb{Z}_2$
$\{y^3 = x^3 + 2x\}$	2	$\mathbb{Z}_2$
$\{y^3 = x^3 + 3x\}$	10	$\mathbb{Z}_{10}$
$\{y^3 = x^3 + 4x\}$	8	$\mathbb{Z}_4 \oplus \mathbb{Z}_2$
$\{y^2 = x^3 + x + 1,\ y^2 = x^3 + x + 4\}$	9	$\mathbb{Z}_9$
$\{y^2 = x^3 + x + 2,\ y^2 = x^3 + x + 3\}$	4	$\mathbb{Z}_4$
$\{y^2 = x^3 + 2x + 1,\ y^2 = x^3 + 2x + 4\}$	7	$\mathbb{Z}_7$
$\{y^2 = x^3 + 3x + 2,\ y^2 = x^3 + 3x + 3\}$	5	$\mathbb{Z}_5$
$\{y^2 = x^3 + 4x + 1,\ y^2 = x^3 + 4x + 4\}$	8	$\mathbb{Z}_8$
$\{y^2 = x^3 + 4x + 2,\ y^2 = x^3 + 4x + 3\}$	3	$\mathbb{Z}_3$

Table 3.2. Isomorphism classes of elliptic curves E over $\mathbb{F}_5$.

Example 3.17 Let $p = 73$. It is easy to verify using Theorem 3.15 that the elliptic curves

$$E_1 : y^2 = x^3 + 25x$$

$$E_2 : y^2 = x^3 + 53x + 55$$

defined over $\mathbb{F}_p$ are not isomorphic over $\mathbb{F}_p$. However, the groups $E_1(\mathbb{F}_{p^m})$ and $E_2(\mathbb{F}_{p^m})$ of $\mathbb{F}_{p^m}$-rational points are isomorphic for every $m \geq 1$.

Theorem 3.18 (*isomorphism classes of elliptic curves over a binary field*)   Let $K = \mathbb{F}_{2^m}$ be a binary field.

(i) The non-supersingular elliptic curves

$$E_1 : y^2 + xy = x^3 + ax^2 + b \tag{3.11}$$

$$E_2 : y^2 + xy = x^3 + \bar{a}x^2 + \bar{b} \tag{3.12}$$

defined over K are isomorphic over K if and only if $b = \bar{b}$ and $\text{Tr}(a) = \text{Tr}(\bar{a})$, where Tr is the trace function (see Definition 3.78). If these conditions are satisfied, then there exists $s \in \mathbb{F}_{2^m}$ such that $\bar{a} = s^2 + s + a$, and the admissible change of variables

$$(x, y) \rightarrow (x, y + sx)$$

transforms equation (3.11) into equation (3.12).

(ii) The number of isomorphism classes of non-supersingular elliptic curves over K is $2^{m+1} - 2$. Let $\gamma \in \mathbb{F}_{2^m}$ satisfy $\text{Tr}(\gamma) = 1$. A set of representatives of the isomorphism classes is

$$\{y^2 + xy = x^3 + ax^2 + b \mid a \in \{0, \gamma\},\ b \in \mathbb{F}_{2^m}^*\}.$$

(iii) The order $\#E(\mathbb{F}_{2^m})$ of the non-supersingular elliptic curve $E : y^2 + xy = x^3 + \gamma x^2 + b$ is divisible by 2. If $\text{Tr}(\gamma) = 0$, then $\#E(\mathbb{F}_{2^m})$ is divisible by 4.

3.2   Point representation and the group law

Formulas for adding two elliptic points were presented in §3.1 for the elliptic curves $y^2 = x^3 + ax + b$ defined over a field K of characteristic that is neither 2 nor 3, and for $y^2 + xy = x^3 + ax^2 + b$ defined over a binary field K. For both curves, the formulas for point addition (i.e., adding two distinct finite points that are not negatives of each other) and point doubling require a field inversion and several field multiplications. If inversion in K is significantly more expensive than multiplication, then it may be advantageous to represent points using projective coordinates.

3.2.1   Projective coordinates

Let K be a field, and let c and d be positive integers. One can define an equivalence relation $\sim$ on the set $K^3 \backslash \{(0, 0, 0)\}$ of nonzero triples over K by

$$(X_1, Y_1, Z_1) \sim (X_2, Y_2, Z_2) \text{ if } X_1 = \lambda^c X_2, Y_1 = \lambda^d Y_2, Z_1 = \lambda Z_2 \text{ for some } \lambda \in K^*.$$

The equivalence class containing $(X, Y, Z) \in K^3 \backslash \{(0, 0, 0)\}$ is

$$(X : Y : Z) = \{(\lambda^c X, \lambda^d Y, \lambda Z) : \lambda \in K^*\}.$$

$(X : Y : Z)$ is called a *projective point*, and (X, Y, Z) is called a *representative* of $(X : Y : Z)$. The set of all projective points is denoted by $\mathbb{P}(K)$. Notice that if $(X', Y', Z') \in (X : Y : Z)$ then $(X' : Y' : Z') = (X : Y : Z)$; that is, any element of an equivalence class can serve as its representative. In particular, if $Z \neq 0$, then $(X/Z^c, Y/Z^d, 1)$ is a representative of the projective point $(X : Y : Z)$, and in fact is the only representative with Z-coordinate equal to 1. Thus we have a 1-1 correspondence between the set of projective points

$$\mathbb{P}(K)^* = \{(X : Y : Z) : X, Y, Z \in K, Z \neq 0\}$$

and the set of *affine points*

$$\mathbb{A}(K) = \{(x, y) : x, y \in K\}.$$

The set of projective points

$$\mathbb{P}(K)^0 = \{(X : Y : Z) : X, Y, Z \in K, Z = 0\}$$

is called the *line at infinity* since its points do not correspond to any of the affine points.

The *projective form* of Weierstrass equation (3.1) of an elliptic curve E defined over K is obtained by replacing x by X/Z^c and y by Y/Z^d, and clearing denominators. Now, if $(X, Y, Z) \in K^3 \backslash \{(0, 0, 0)\}$ satisfies the projective equation then so does any $(X', Y', Z') \in (X : Y : Z)$. Therefore it makes sense to say that the projective point $(X : Y : Z)$ lies on E. We thus have a 1-1 correspondence between the affine points in $\mathbb{A}(K)$ that lie on E and the projective points in $\mathbb{P}(K)^*$ that lie on E. The projective points in $\mathbb{P}(K)^0$ which lie on E are the *points at infinity* on E.

Example 3.19 (*standard projective coordinates*) Let $c = 1$ and $d = 1$. Then the projective form of the Weierstrass equation

$$E : y^2 + a_1 xy + a_3 y = x^3 + a_2 x^2 + a_4 x + a_6$$

defined over K is

$$Y^2 Z + a_1 XYZ + a_3 YZ^2 = X^3 + a_2 X^2 Z + a_4 XZ^2 + a_6 Z^3.$$

The only point on the line at infinity that also lies on E is $(0 : 1 : 0)$. This projective point corresponds to the point ∞ in Definition 3.1.

Formulas that do not involve field inversions for adding and doubling points in projective coordinates can be derived by first converting the points to affine coordinates, then using the formulas from §3.1 to add the affine points, and finally clearing denominators. Also of use in point multiplication methods (see §3.3) is the addition of two points in *mixed coordinates*—where the two points are given in different coordinate systems.

Example 3.20 (*addition formulas using Jacobian coordinates*) Let $c = 2$ and $d = 3$. The projective point $(X : Y : Z)$, $Z \neq 0$, corresponds to the affine point $(X/Z^2, Y/Z^3)$. The projective form of the Weierstrass equation

$$E : y^2 = x^3 + ax + b$$

defined over K is

$$Y^2 = X^3 + aXZ^4 + bZ^6.$$

The point at infinity ∞ corresponds to $(1 : 1 : 0)$, while the negative of $(X : Y : Z)$ is $(X : -Y : Z)$.

Point doubling. Let $P = (X_1 : Y_1 : Z_1) \in E$, and suppose that $P \neq -P$. Since $P = (X_1/Z_1^2 : Y_1/Z_1^3 : 1)$, we can use the doubling formula for E in affine coordinates to compute $2P = (X_3' : Y_3' : 1)$, obtaining

$$X_3' = \left(\frac{3\frac{X_1^2}{Z_1^4} + a}{2\frac{Y_1}{Z_1^3}} \right)^2 - 2\frac{X_1}{Z_1^2} = \frac{(3X_1^2 + aZ_1^4)^2 - 8X_1Y_1^2}{4Y_1^2Z_1^2}$$

and

$$Y_3' = \left(\frac{3\frac{X_1^2}{Z_1^4} + a}{2\frac{Y_1}{Z_1^3}} \right) \left(\frac{X_1}{Z_1^2} - X_3' \right) - \frac{Y_1}{Z_1^3} = \frac{3X_1^2 + aZ_1^4}{2Y_1Z_1} \left(\frac{X_1}{Z_1^2} - X_3' \right) - \frac{Y_1}{Z_1^3}.$$

To eliminate denominators in the expressions for X_3' and Y_3', we set $X_3 = X_3' \cdot Z_3^2$ and $Y_3 = Y_3' \cdot Z_3^3$ where $Z_3 = 2Y_1Z_1$, and obtain the following formulas for computing $2P = (X_3 : Y_3 : Z_3)$ in Jacobian coordinates:

$$\left. \begin{aligned} X_3 &= (3X_1^2 + aZ_1^4)^2 - 8X_1Y_1^2 \\ Y_3 &= (3X_1^2 + aZ_1^4)(4X_1Y_1^2 - X_3) - 8Y_1^4 \\ Z_3 &= 2Y_1Z_1. \end{aligned} \right\} \tag{3.13}$$

By storing some intermediate elements, X_3, Y_3 and Z_3 can be computed using six field squarings and four field multiplications as follows:

$$A \leftarrow Y_1^2, \quad B \leftarrow 4X_1 \cdot A, \quad C \leftarrow 8A^2, \quad D \leftarrow 3X_1^2 + a \cdot Z_1^4,$$
$$X_3 \leftarrow D^2 - 2B, \quad Y_3 \leftarrow D \cdot (B - X_3) - C, \quad Z_3 \leftarrow 2Y_1 \cdot Z_1.$$

Point addition using mixed Jacobian-affine coordinates. Let $P = (X_1 : Y_1 : Z_1) \in E$, $Z_1 \neq 0$, and $Q = (X_2 : Y_2 : 1)$, and suppose that $P \neq \pm Q$. Since $P = (X_1/Z_1^2 : Y_1/Z_1^3 :$

1), we can use the addition formula for E in affine coordinates to compute $P + Q = (X_3' : Y_3' : 1)$, obtaining

$$X_3' = \left(\frac{Y_2 - \frac{Y_1}{Z_1^3}}{X_2 - \frac{X_1}{Z_1^2}}\right)^2 - \frac{X_1}{Z_1^2} - X_2 = \left(\frac{Y_2 Z_1^3 - Y_1}{(X_2 Z_1^2 - X_1) Z_1}\right)^2 - \frac{X_1}{Z_1^2} - X_2$$

and

$$Y_3' = \left(\frac{Y_2 - \frac{Y_1}{Z_1^3}}{X_2 - \frac{X_1}{Z_1^2}}\right)\left(\frac{X_1}{Z_1^2} - X_3'\right) - \frac{Y_1}{Z_1^3} = \left(\frac{Y_2 Z_1^3 - Y_1}{(X_2 Z_1^2 - X_1) Z_1}\right)\left(\frac{X_1}{Z_1^2} - X_3'\right) - \frac{Y_1}{Z_1^3}.$$

To eliminate denominators in the expressions for X_3' and Y_3', we set $X_3 = X_3' \cdot Z_3^2$ and $Y_3 = Y_3' \cdot Z_3^3$ where $Z_3 = (X_2 Z_1^2 - X_1) Z_1$, and obtain the following formulas for computing $P + Q = (X_3 : Y_3 : Z_3)$ in Jacobian coordinates:

$$\left. \begin{aligned} X_3 &= (Y_2 Z_1^3 - Y_1)^2 - (X_2 Z_1^2 - X_1)^2 (X_1 + X_2 Z_1^2) \\ Y_3 &= (Y_2 Z_1^3 - Y_1)(X_1 (X_2 Z_1^2 - X_1)^2 - X_3) - Y_1 (X_2 Z_1^2 - X_1)^3 \\ Z_3 &= (X_2 Z_1^2 - X_1) Z_1. \end{aligned} \right\} \qquad (3.14)$$

By storing some intermediate elements, X_3, Y_3 and Z_3 can be computed using three field squarings and eight field multiplications as follows:

$$A \leftarrow Z_1^2, \quad B \leftarrow Z_1 \cdot A, \quad C \leftarrow X_2 \cdot A, \quad D \leftarrow Y_2 \cdot B, \quad E \leftarrow C - X_1,$$

$$F \leftarrow D - Y_1, \quad G \leftarrow E^2, \quad H \leftarrow G \cdot E, \quad I \leftarrow X_1 \cdot G,$$

$$X_3 \leftarrow F^2 - (H + 2I), \quad Y_3 \leftarrow F \cdot (I - X_3) - Y_1 \cdot H, \quad Z_3 \leftarrow Z_1 \cdot E.$$

3.2.2 The elliptic curve $y^2 = x^3 + ax + b$

This subsection considers coordinate systems and addition formulas for the elliptic curve $E : y^2 = x^3 + ax + b$ defined over a field K whose characteristic is neither 2 nor 3. Several types of projective coordinates have been proposed.

1. *Standard projective coordinates.* Here $c = 1$ and $d = 1$. The projective point $(X : Y : Z)$, $Z \neq 0$, corresponds to the affine point $(X/Z, Y/Z)$. The projective equation of the elliptic curve is

$$Y^2 Z = X^3 + a X Z^2 + b Z^3.$$

The point at infinity ∞ corresponds to $(0 : 1 : 0)$, while the negative of $(X : Y : Z)$ is $(X : -Y : Z)$.

2. *Jacobian projective coordinates.* Here $c = 2$ and $d = 3$. The projective point $(X : Y : Z)$, $Z \neq 0$, corresponds to the affine point $(X/Z^2, Y/Z^3)$. The projective equation of the elliptic curve is

$$Y^2 = X^3 + aXZ^4 + bZ^6.$$

The point at infinity ∞ corresponds to $(1 : 1 : 0)$, while the negative of $(X : Y : Z)$ is $(X : -Y : Z)$. Doubling and addition formulas were derived in Example 3.20. If $a = -3$, the expression $3X_1^2 + aZ_1^4$ that occurs in the doubling formula (3.13) can be computed using only one field multiplication and one field squaring since

$$3X_1^2 - 3Z_1^4 = 3(X_1 - Z_1^2) \cdot (X_1 + Z_1^2).$$

Henceforth, we shall assume that the elliptic curve $y^2 = x^3 + ax + b$ has $a = -3$. Theorem 3.15 confirms that the selection is without much loss of generality. Point doubling can be further accelerated by using the fact that $2Y_1$ appears several times in (3.13) and trading multiplications by 4 and 8 for divisions by 2. The revised doubling formulas are:

$$A \leftarrow 3(X_1 - Z_1^2) \cdot (X_1 + Z_1^2), \quad B \leftarrow 2Y_1, \quad Z_3 \leftarrow B \cdot Z_1, \quad C \leftarrow B^2,$$
$$D \leftarrow C \cdot X_1, \quad X_3 \leftarrow A^2 - 2D, \quad Y_3 \leftarrow (D - X_3) \cdot A - C^2/2.$$

The point doubling and point addition procedures for the case $a = -3$ are given in Algorithms 3.21 and 3.22 where an effort was made to minimize the number of temporary variables T_i. The algorithms are written in terms of basic field operations; however, specialized routines consisting of integrated basic operations may be advantageous (see §5.1.2 for a concrete example when floating-point hardware is used).

3. *Chudnovsky coordinates.* Here the Jacobian point $(X : Y : Z)$ is represented as $(X : Y : Z : Z^2 : Z^3)$. The redundancy in this representation is beneficial in some point multiplication methods where additions are performed in projective coordinates.

Algorithm 3.21 Point doubling ($y^2 = x^3 - 3x + b$, Jacobian coordinates)

INPUT: $P = (X_1 : Y_1 : Z_1)$ in Jacobian coordinates on $E/K : y^2 = x^3 - 3x + b$.
OUTPUT: $2P = (X_3 : Y_3 : Z_3)$ in Jacobian coordinates.

  1. If $P = \infty$ then return(∞).
  2. $T_1 \leftarrow Z_1^2$. $\{T_1 \leftarrow Z_1^2\}$
  3. $T_2 \leftarrow X_1 - T_1$. $\{T_2 \leftarrow X_1 - Z_1^2\}$
  4. $T_1 \leftarrow X_1 + T_1$. $\{T_1 \leftarrow X_1 + Z_1^2\}$
  5. $T_2 \leftarrow T_2 \cdot T_1$. $\{T_2 \leftarrow X_1^2 - Z_1^4\}$
  6. $T_2 \leftarrow 3T_2$. $\{T_2 \leftarrow A = 3(X_1 - Z_1^2)(X_1 + Z_1^2)\}$
  7. $Y_3 \leftarrow 2Y_1$. $\{Y_3 \leftarrow B = 2Y_1\}$
  8. $Z_3 \leftarrow Y_3 \cdot Z_1$. $\{Z_3 \leftarrow BZ_1\}$
  9. $Y_3 \leftarrow Y_3^2$. $\{Y_3 \leftarrow C = B^2\}$
10. $T_3 \leftarrow Y_3 \cdot X_1$. $\{T_3 \leftarrow D = CX_1\}$
11. $Y_3 \leftarrow Y_3^2$. $\{Y_3 \leftarrow C^2\}$
12. $Y_3 \leftarrow Y_3/2$. $\{Y_3 \leftarrow C^2/2\}$
13. $X_3 \leftarrow T_2^2$. $\{X_3 \leftarrow A^2\}$
14. $T_1 \leftarrow 2T_3$. $\{T_1 \leftarrow 2D\}$
15. $X_3 \leftarrow X_3 - T_1$. $\{X_3 \leftarrow A^2 - 2D\}$
16. $T_1 \leftarrow T_3 - X_3$. $\{T_1 \leftarrow D - X_3\}$
17. $T_1 \leftarrow T_1 \cdot T_2$. $\{T_1 \leftarrow (D - X_3)A\}$
18. $Y_3 \leftarrow T_1 - Y_3$. $\{Y_3 \leftarrow (D - X_3)A - C^2/2\}$
19. Return($X_3 : Y_3 : Z_3$).

Algorithm 3.22 Point addition ($y^2 = x^3 - 3x + b$, affine-Jacobian coordinates)

INPUT: $P = (X_1 : Y_1 : Z_1)$ in Jacobian coordinates, $Q = (x_2, y_2)$ in affine coordinates
    on $E/K : y^2 = x^3 - 3x + b$.
OUTPUT: $P + Q = (X_3 : Y_3 : Z_3)$ in Jacobian coordinates.

  1. If $Q = \infty$ then return($X_1 : Y_1 : Z_1$).
  2. If $P = \infty$ then return($x_2 : y_2 : 1$).
  3. $T_1 \leftarrow Z_1^2$. $\{T_1 \leftarrow A = Z_1^2\}$
  4. $T_2 \leftarrow T_1 \cdot Z_1$. $\{T_2 \leftarrow B = Z_1 A\}$
  5. $T_1 \leftarrow T_1 \cdot x_2$. $\{T_1 \leftarrow C = X_2 A\}$
  6. $T_2 \leftarrow T_2 \cdot y_2$. $\{T_2 \leftarrow D = Y_2 B\}$
  7. $T_1 \leftarrow T_1 - X_1$. $\{T_1 \leftarrow E = C - X_1\}$
  8. $T_2 \leftarrow T_2 - Y_1$. $\{T_2 \leftarrow F = D - Y_1\}$
  9. If $T_1 = 0$ then
     9.1 If $T_2 = 0$ then use Algorithm 3.21 to compute
          $(X_3 : Y_3 : Z_3) = 2(x_2 : y_2 : 1)$ and return($X_3 : Y_3 : Z_3$).
     9.2 Else return(∞).
10. $Z_3 \leftarrow Z_1 \cdot T_1$. $\{Z_3 \leftarrow Z_1 E\}$

11. $T_3 \leftarrow T_1^2$. $\{T_3 \leftarrow G = E^2\}$
12. $T_4 \leftarrow T_3 \cdot T_1$. $\{T_4 \leftarrow H = E^3\}$
13. $T_3 \leftarrow T_3 \cdot X_1$. $\{T_3 \leftarrow I = X_1 G\}$
14. $T_1 \leftarrow 2T_3$. $\{T_1 \leftarrow 2I\}$
15. $X_3 \leftarrow T_2^2$. $\{X_3 \leftarrow F^2\}$
16. $X_3 \leftarrow X_3 - T_1$. $\{X_3 \leftarrow F^2 - 2I\}$
17. $X_3 \leftarrow X_3 - T_4$. $\{X_3 \leftarrow F^2 - (H + 2I)\}$
18. $T_3 \leftarrow T_3 - X_3$. $\{T_3 \leftarrow I - X_3\}$
19. $T_3 \leftarrow T_3 \cdot T_2$. $\{T_3 \leftarrow F(I - X_3)\}$
20. $T_4 \leftarrow T_4 \cdot Y_1$. $\{T_4 \leftarrow Y_1 H\}$
21. $Y_3 \leftarrow T_3 - T_4$. $\{Y_3 \leftarrow F(I - X_3) - Y_1 H\}$
22. Return($X_3 : Y_3 : Z_3$).

The field operation counts for point addition and doubling in various coordinate systems are listed in Table 3.3. The notation $C_1 + C_2 \to C_3$ means that the points to be added are in C_1 coordinates and C_2 coordinates, while their sum is expressed in C_3 coordinates; for example, $J + A \to J$ is an addition of points in Jacobian and affine coordinates, with result in Jacobian coordinates. We see that Jacobian coordinates yield the fastest point doubling, while mixed Jacobian-affine coordinates yield the fastest point addition. Also useful in some point multiplication algorithms (see Note 3.43) are mixed Jacobian-Chudnovsky coordinates and mixed Chudnovsky-affine coordinates for point addition.

Doubling		General addition		Mixed coordinates	
$2A \to A$	$1I, 2M, 2S$	$A + A \to A$	$1I, 2M, 1S$	$J + A \to J$	$8M, 3S$
$2P \to P$	$7M, 3S$	$P + P \to P$	$12M, 2S$	$J + C \to J$	$11M, 3S$
$2J \to J$	$4M, 4S$	$J + J \to J$	$12M, 4S$	$C + A \to C$	$8M, 3S$
$2C \to C$	$5M, 4S$	$C + C \to C$	$11M, 3S$		

Table 3.3. *Operation counts for point addition and doubling on* $y^2 = x^3 - 3x + b$. $A = affine$, $P = standard projective$, $J = Jacobian$, $C = Chudnovsky$, $I = inversion$, $M = multiplication$, $S = squaring$.

Repeated doublings

If consecutive point doublings are to be performed, then Algorithm 3.23 may be slightly faster than repeated use of the doubling formula. By working with $2Y$ until the final step, only one division by 2 is required. A field addition in the loop is eliminated by calculating $3(X - Z^2)(X + Z^2)$ as $3(X^2 - W)$, where $W = Z^4$ is computed at the first doubling and then updated according to $W \leftarrow WY^4$ before each subsequent doubling.

Algorithm 3.23 Repeated point doubling ($y^2=x^3-3x+b$, Jacobian coordinates)

INPUT: $P = (X : Y : Z)$ in Jacobian coordinates on $E/K : y^2 = x^3 - 3x + b$, and an integer $m > 0$.

OUTPUT: $2^m P$ in Jacobian coordinates.

   1. If $P = \infty$ then return(P).

   2. $Y \leftarrow 2Y$, $W \leftarrow Z^4$.

   3. While $m > 0$ do:

      3.1 $A \leftarrow 3(X^2 - W)$, $B \leftarrow XY^2$.

      3.2 $X \leftarrow A^2 - 2B$, $Z \leftarrow ZY$.

      3.3 $m \leftarrow m - 1$. If $m > 0$ then $W \leftarrow WY^4$.

      3.4 $Y \leftarrow 2A(B - X) - Y^4$.

   4. Return($X, Y/2, Z$).

In m consecutive doublings, Algorithm 3.23 trades $m - 1$ field additions, $m - 1$ divisions by two, and a multiplication for two field squarings (in comparison with repeated applications of Algorithm 3.21). The strategy can be adapted to the case where $a \neq -3$, saving two field squarings in each of $m - 1$ doublings.

3.2.3 The elliptic curve $y^2 + xy = x^3 + ax^2 + b$

This subsection considers coordinate systems and addition formulas for the non-supersingular elliptic curve $E : y^2 + xy = x^3 + ax^2 + b$ defined over a binary field K. Several types of projective coordinates have been proposed.

1. *Standard projective coordinates.* Here $c = 1$ and $d = 1$. The projective point $(X : Y : Z)$, $Z \neq 0$, corresponds to the affine point $(X/Z, Y/Z)$. The projective equation of the elliptic curve is

$$Y^2Z + XYZ = X^3 + aX^2Z + bZ^3.$$

   The point at infinity ∞ corresponds to $(0 : 1 : 0)$, while the negative of $(X : Y : Z)$ is $(X : X + Y : Z)$.

2. *Jacobian projective coordinates.* Here $c = 2$ and $d = 3$. The projective point $(X : Y : Z)$, $Z \neq 0$, corresponds to the affine point $(X/Z^2, Y/Z^3)$. The projective equation of the elliptic curve is

$$Y^2 + XYZ = X^3 + aX^2Z^2 + bZ^6.$$

   The point at infinity ∞ corresponds to $(1 : 1 : 0)$, while the negative of $(X : Y : Z)$ is $(X : X + Y : Z)$.

3. *López-Dahab (LD) projective coordinates.* Here $c = 1$ and $d = 2$. The projective point $(X : Y : Z)$, $Z \neq 0$, corresponds to the affine point $(X/Z, Y/Z^2)$. The

projective equation of the elliptic curve is

$$Y^2 + XYZ = X^3 Z + aX^2 Z^2 + bZ^4.$$

The point at infinity ∞ corresponds to $(1 : 0 : 0)$, while the negative of $(X : Y : Z)$ is $(X : X + Y : Z)$. Formulas for computing the double $(X_3 : Y_3 : Z_3)$ of $(X_1 : Y_1 : Z_1)$ are

$$Z_3 \leftarrow X_1^2 \cdot Z_1^2, \quad X_3 \leftarrow X_1^4 + b \cdot Z_1^4, \quad Y_3 \leftarrow bZ_1^4 \cdot Z_3 + X_3 \cdot (aZ_3 + Y_1^2 + bZ_1^4).$$

Formulas for computing the sum $(X_3 : Y_3 : Z_3)$ of $(X_1 : Y_1 : Z_1)$ and $(X_2 : Y_2 : 1)$ are

$$A \leftarrow Y_2 \cdot Z_1^2 + Y_1, \quad B \leftarrow X_2 \cdot Z_1 + X_1, \quad C \leftarrow Z_1 \cdot B, \quad D \leftarrow B^2 \cdot (C + aZ_1^2),$$
$$Z_3 \leftarrow C^2, \quad E \leftarrow A \cdot C, \quad X_3 \leftarrow A^2 + D + E, \quad F \leftarrow X_3 + X_2 \cdot Z_3,$$
$$G \leftarrow (X_2 + Y_2) \cdot Z_3^2, \quad Y_3 \leftarrow (E + Z_3) \cdot F + G.$$

The point doubling and point addition procedures when $a \in \{0, 1\}$ are given in Algorithms 3.24 and 3.25 where an effort was made to minimize the number of temporary variables T_i. Theorem 3.18(ii) confirms that the restriction $a \in \{0, 1\}$ is without much loss of generality.

Algorithm 3.24 Point doubling ($y^2 + xy = x^3 + ax^2 + b$, $a \in \{0, 1\}$, LD coordinates)

INPUT: $P = (X_1 : Y_1 : Z_1)$ in LD coordinates on $E/K : y^2 + xy = x^3 + ax^2 + b$.
OUTPUT: $2P = (X_3 : Y_3 : Z_3)$ in LD coordinates.

1. If $P = \infty$ then return(∞).
2. $T_1 \leftarrow Z_1^2$. $\qquad\qquad\qquad \{T_1 \leftarrow Z_1^2\}$
3. $T_2 \leftarrow X_1^2$. $\qquad\qquad\qquad \{T_2 \leftarrow X_1^2\}$
4. $Z_3 \leftarrow T_1 \cdot T_2$. $\qquad\qquad\quad \{Z_3 \leftarrow X_1^2 Z_1^2\}$
5. $X_3 \leftarrow T_2^2$. $\qquad\qquad\qquad \{X_3 \leftarrow X_1^4\}$
6. $T_1 \leftarrow T_1^2$. $\qquad\qquad\qquad \{T_1 \leftarrow Z_1^4\}$
7. $T_2 \leftarrow T_1 \cdot b$. $\qquad\qquad\quad \{T_2 \leftarrow bZ_1^4\}$
8. $X_3 \leftarrow X_3 + T_2$. $\qquad\qquad \{X_3 \leftarrow X_1^4 + bZ_1^4\}$
9. $T_1 \leftarrow Y_1^2$. $\qquad\qquad\qquad \{T_1 \leftarrow Y_1^2\}$
10. If $a = 1$ then $T_1 \leftarrow T_1 + Z_3$. $\quad \{T_1 \leftarrow aZ_3 + Y_1^2\}$
11. $T_1 \leftarrow T_1 + T_2$. $\qquad\qquad \{T_1 \leftarrow aZ_3 + Y_1^2 + bZ_1^4\}$
12. $Y_3 \leftarrow X_3 \cdot T_1$. $\qquad\qquad \{Y_3 \leftarrow X_3(aZ_3 + Y_1^2 + bZ_1^4)\}$
13. $T_1 \leftarrow T_2 \cdot Z_3$. $\qquad\qquad \{T_1 \leftarrow bZ_1^4 Z_3\}$
14. $Y_3 \leftarrow Y_3 + T_1$. $\qquad\qquad \{Y_3 \leftarrow bZ_1^4 Z_3 + X_3(aZ_3 + Y_1^2 + bZ_1^4)\}$
15. Return($X_3 : Y_3 : Z_3$).

Algorithm 3.25 Point addition ($y^2+xy=x^3+ax^2+b$, $a\in\{0, 1\}$, LD-affine coordinates)

INPUT: $P = (X_1 : Y_1 : Z_1)$ in LD coordinates, $Q = (x_2, y_2)$ in affine coordinates on
$E/K : y^2 + xy = x^3 + ax^2 + b$.

OUTPUT: $P + Q = (X_3 : Y_3 : Z_3)$ in LD coordinates.

1. If $Q = \infty$ then return(P).
2. If $P = \infty$ then return($x_2 : y_2 : 1$).
3. $T_1 \leftarrow Z_1 \cdot x_2$. $\{T_1 \leftarrow X_2Z_1\}$
4. $T_2 \leftarrow Z_1^2$. $\{T_2 \leftarrow Z_1^2\}$
5. $X_3 \leftarrow X_1 + T_1$. $\{X_3 \leftarrow B = X_2Z_1 + X_1\}$
6. $T_1 \leftarrow Z_1 \cdot X_3$. $\{T_1 \leftarrow C = Z_1 B\}$
7. $T_3 \leftarrow T_2 \cdot y_2$. $\{T_3 \leftarrow Y_2Z_1^2\}$
8. $Y_3 \leftarrow Y_1 + T_3$. $\{Y_3 \leftarrow A = Y_2Z_1^2 + Y_1\}$
9. If $X_3 = 0$ then
    9.1 If $Y_3 = 0$ then use Algorithm 3.24 to compute
        $(X_3 : Y_3 : Z_3) = 2(x_2 : y_2 : 1)$ and return($X_3 : Y_3 : Z_3$).
    9.2 Else return(∞).
10. $Z_3 \leftarrow T_1^2$. $\{Z_3 \leftarrow C^2\}$
11. $T_3 \leftarrow T_1 \cdot Y_3$. $\{T_3 \leftarrow E = AC\}$
12. If $a = 1$ then $T_1 \leftarrow T_1 + T_2$. $\{T_1 \leftarrow C + aZ_1^2\}$
13. $T_2 \leftarrow X_3^2$. $\{T_2 \leftarrow B^2\}$
14. $X_3 \leftarrow T_2 \cdot T_1$. $\{X_3 \leftarrow D = B^2(C + aZ_1^2)\}$
15. $T_2 \leftarrow Y_3^2$. $\{T_2 \leftarrow A^2\}$
16. $X_3 \leftarrow X_3 + T_2$. $\{X_3 \leftarrow A^2 + D\}$
17. $X_3 \leftarrow X_3 + T_3$. $\{X_3 \leftarrow A^2 + D + E\}$
18. $T_2 \leftarrow x_2 \cdot Z_3$. $\{T_2 \leftarrow X_2Z_3\}$
19. $T_2 \leftarrow T_2 + X_3$. $\{T_2 \leftarrow F = X_3 + X_2Z_3\}$
20. $T_1 \leftarrow Z_3^2$. $\{T_1 \leftarrow Z_3^2\}$
21. $T_3 \leftarrow T_3 + Z_3$. $\{T_3 \leftarrow E + Z_3\}$
22. $Y_3 \leftarrow T_3 \cdot T_2$. $\{Y_3 \leftarrow (E + Z_3)F\}$
23. $T_2 \leftarrow x_2 + y_2$. $\{T_2 \leftarrow X_2 + Y_2\}$
24. $T_3 \leftarrow T_1 \cdot T_2$. $\{T_3 \leftarrow G = (X_2 + Y_2)Z_3^2\}$
25. $Y_3 \leftarrow Y_3 + T_3$. $\{Y_3 \leftarrow (E + Z_3)F + G\}$
26. Return($X_3 : Y_3 : Z_3$).

The field operation counts for point addition and doubling in various coordinate systems are listed in Table 3.4.

3.3 *Point multiplication*

This section considers methods for computing kP, where k is an integer and P is a point on an elliptic curve E defined over a field $\mathbb{F}_q$. This operation is called *point mul-*

Coordinate system	General addition	General addition (mixed coordinates)	Doubling
Affine	$V+M$	—	$V+M$
Standard projective	$13M$	$12M$	$7M$
Jacobian projective	$14M$	$10M$	$5M$
López-Dahab projective	$14M$	$8M$	$4M$

Table 3.4. *Operation counts for point addition and doubling on* $y^2 + xy = x^3 + ax^2 + b$. M = *multiplication*, V = *division (see §2.3.6).*

tiplication or *scalar multiplication*, and dominates the execution time of elliptic curve cryptographic schemes (see Chapter 4). The techniques presented do not exploit any special structure of the curve. Point multiplication methods that take advantage of efficiently computable endomorphisms on some special curves are considered in §3.4, §3.5, and §3.6. §3.3.1 covers the case where P is not known a priori. In instances where P is fixed, for example in ECDSA signature generation (see §4.4.1), point multiplication algorithms can exploit precomputed data that depends only on P (and not on k); algorithms of this kind are presented in §3.3.2. Efficient techniques for computing $kP + lQ$ are considered in §3.3.3. This operation, called *multiple point multiplication*, dominates the execution time of some elliptic curve cryptographic schemes such as ECDSA signature verification (see §4.4.1).

We will assume that $\#E(\mathbb{F}_q) = nh$ where n is prime and h is small (so $n \approx q$), P and Q have order n, and multipliers such as k are randomly selected integers from the interval $[1, n-1]$. The binary representation of k is denoted $(k_{t-1}, \ldots, k_2, k_1, k_0)_2$, where $t \approx m = \lceil \log_2 q \rceil$.

3.3.1 Unknown point

Algorithms 3.26 and 3.27 are the additive versions of the basic repeated-square-and-multiply methods for exponentiation. Algorithm 3.26 processes the bits of k from right to left, while Algorithm 3.27 processes the bits from left to right.

Algorithm 3.26 Right-to-left binary method for point multiplication

INPUT: $k = (k_{t-1}, \ldots, k_1, k_0)_2$, $P \in E(\mathbb{F}_q)$.
OUTPUT: kP.
1. $Q \leftarrow \infty$.
2. For i from 0 to $t-1$ do
    2.1 If $k_i = 1$ then $Q \leftarrow Q + P$.
    2.2 $P \leftarrow 2P$.
3. Return(Q).

Algorithm 3.27 Left-to-right binary method for point multiplication

---

INPUT: $k = (k_{t-1}, \ldots, k_1, k_0)_2$, $P \in E(\mathbb{F}_q)$.
OUTPUT: kP.

1. $Q \leftarrow \infty$.
2. For i from $t - 1$ downto 0 do
   2.1 $Q \leftarrow 2Q$.
   2.2 If $k_i = 1$ then $Q \leftarrow Q + P$.
3. Return(Q).

The expected number of ones in the binary representation of k is $t/2 \approx m/2$, whence the expected running time of Algorithm 3.27 is approximately $m/2$ point additions and m point doublings, denoted

$$\frac{m}{2}A + mD. \tag{3.15}$$

Let M denote a field multiplication, S a field squaring, and I a field inversion. If affine coordinates (see §3.1.2) are used, then the running time expressed in terms of field operations is

$$2.5mS + 3mM + 1.5mI \tag{3.16}$$

if $\mathbb{F}_q$ has characteristic > 3, and

$$3mM + 1.5mI \tag{3.17}$$

if $\mathbb{F}_q$ is a binary field.

Suppose that $\mathbb{F}_q$ has characteristic > 3. If mixed coordinates (see §3.2.2) are used, then Q is stored in Jacobian coordinates, while P is stored in affine coordinates. Thus the doubling in step 2.1 can be performed using Algorithm 3.21, while the addition in step 2.2 can be performed using Algorithm 3.22. The field operation count of Algorithm 3.27 is then

$$8mM + 5.5mS + (1I + 3M + 1S) \tag{3.18}$$

(one inversion, three multiplications and one squaring are required to convert back to affine coordinates).

Suppose now that $\mathbb{F}_q$ is a binary field. If mixed coordinates (see §3.2.3) are used, then Q is stored in LD projective coordinates, while P can be stored in affine coordinates. Thus the doubling in step 2.1 can be performed using Algorithm 3.24, and the addition in step 2.2 can be performed using Algorithm 3.25. The field operation count of Algorithm 3.27 is then

$$8.5mM + (2M + 1I) \tag{3.19}$$

(one inversion and two multiplications are required to convert back to affine coordinates).

Non-adjacent form (NAF)

If $P = (x, y) \in E(\mathbb{F}_q)$ then $-P = (x, x + y)$ if $\mathbb{F}_q$ is a binary field, and $-P = (x, -y)$ if $\mathbb{F}_q$ has characteristic > 3. Thus subtraction of points on an elliptic curve is just as efficient as addition. This motivates using a *signed digit representation* $k = \sum_{i=0}^{l-1} k_i 2^i$, where $k_i \in \{0, \pm 1\}$. A particularly useful signed digit representation is the *non-adjacent form* (NAF).

Definition 3.28 A *non-adjacent form* (NAF) of a positive integer k is an expression $k = \sum_{i=0}^{l-1} k_i 2^i$ where $k_i \in \{0, \pm 1\}$, $k_{l-1} \neq 0$, and no two consecutive digits k_i are nonzero. The *length* of the NAF is l.

Theorem 3.29 (*properties of NAFs*) Let k be a positive integer.

  (i) k has a unique NAF denoted NAF(k).

  (ii) NAF(k) has the fewest nonzero digits of any signed digit representation of k.

  (iii) The length of NAF(k) is at most one more than the length of the binary representation of k.

  (iv) If the length of NAF(k) is l, then $2^l/3 < k < 2^{l+1}/3$.

  (v) The average density of nonzero digits among all NAFs of length l is approximately $1/3$.

NAF(k) can be efficiently computed using Algorithm 3.30. The digits of NAF(k) are generated by repeatedly dividing k by 2, allowing remainders of 0 or ± 1. If k is odd, then the remainder $r \in \{-1, 1\}$ is chosen so that the quotient $(k - r)/2$ is even—this ensures that the next NAF digit is 0.

Algorithm 3.30 Computing the NAF of a positive integer

INPUT: A positive integer k.
OUTPUT: NAF(k).
  1. $i \leftarrow 0$.
  2. While $k \geq 1$ do
      2.1 If k is odd then: $k_i \leftarrow 2 - (k \bmod 4)$, $k \leftarrow k - k_i$;
      2.2 Else: $k_i \leftarrow 0$.
      2.3 $k \leftarrow k/2$, $i \leftarrow i + 1$.
  3. Return($k_{i-1}, k_{i-2}, \ldots, k_1, k_0$).

Algorithm 3.31 modifies the left-to-right binary method for point multiplication (Algorithm 3.27) by using NAF(k) instead of the binary representation of k. It follows from (iii) and (v) of Theorem 3.29 that the expected running time of Algorithm 3.31 is approximately

$$\frac{m}{3} A + m D. \tag{3.20}$$

Algorithm 3.31 Binary NAF method for point multiplication

INPUT: Positive integer k, $P \in E(\mathbb{F}_q)$.

OUTPUT: kP.

1. Use Algorithm 3.30 to compute $\text{NAF}(k) = \sum_{i=0}^{l-1} k_i 2^i$.
2. $Q \leftarrow \infty$.
3. For i from $l-1$ downto 0 do
   3.1 $Q \leftarrow 2Q$.
   3.2 If $k_i = 1$ then $Q \leftarrow Q + P$.
   3.3 If $k_i = -1$ then $Q \leftarrow Q - P$.
4. Return(Q).

Window methods

If some extra memory is available, the running time of Algorithm 3.31 can be decreased by using a window method which processes w digits of k at a time.

Definition 3.32 Let $w \geq 2$ be a positive integer. A *width-w NAF* of a positive integer k is an expression $k = \sum_{i=0}^{l-1} k_i 2^i$ where each nonzero coefficient k_i is odd, $|k_i| < 2^{w-1}$, $k_{l-1} \neq 0$, and at most one of any w consecutive digits is nonzero. The *length* of the width-w NAF is l.

Theorem 3.33 (*properties of width-w NAFs*) Let k be a positive integer.

   (i) k has a unique width-w NAF denoted $\text{NAF}_w(k)$.

  (ii) $\text{NAF}_2(k) = \text{NAF}(k)$.

 (iii) The length of $\text{NAF}_w(k)$ is at most one more than the length of the binary representation of k.

 (iv) The average density of nonzero digits among all width-w NAFs of length l is approximately $1/(w+1)$.

Example 3.34 (*width-w NAFs*) Let $k = 1122334455$. We denote a negative integer $-c$ by $\bar{c}$. The binary representation of k and the width-w NAFs of k for $2 \leq w \leq 6$ are:

$$
\begin{array}{ll}
(k)_2 = & 1\ 0\ 0\ 0 \quad 0\ 1\ 0\ 1\ 1 \quad 1\ 0\ 0\ 1\ 0\ 1 \quad 0\ 1\ 1\ 0\ 1\ 1\ 0\ 1\ 1\ 1\ 1\ 0\ 1\ 1\ 1 \\
\text{NAF}_2(k) = & 1\ 0\ 0\ 0 \quad 1\ 0\ \bar{1}\ 0\ 0 \quad \bar{1}\ 0\ 1\ 0\ \bar{1}\ 0 \quad \bar{1}\ 0\ 0\ 0\ \bar{1}\ 0\ 0\ \bar{1}\ 0\ 0\ 0\ 0\ \bar{1}\ 0\ 0\ \bar{1} \\
\text{NAF}_3(k) = & 1\ 0\ 0\ 0 \quad 0\ 0\ 3\ 0\ 0 \quad \bar{1}\ 0\ 0\ 1\ 0\ 0 \quad 3\ 0\ 0\ 0\ \bar{1}\ 0\ 0\ \bar{1}\ 0\ 0\ 0\ 0\ \bar{1}\ 0\ 0\ \bar{1} \\
\text{NAF}_4(k) = & 1\ 0\ 0\ 0 \quad 0\ 1\ 0\ 0\ 0 \quad 7\ 0\ 0\ 0\ 0\ 5 \quad 0\ 0\ 0\ 7\ 0\ 0\ 0\ 7\ 0\ 0\ 0\ \bar{1}\ 0\ 0\ 0\ 7 \\
\text{NAF}_5(k) = & 1\ 0\ 0\ 0\ 0 \quad \bar{15}\ 0\ 0\ 0\ 0 \quad \bar{9}\ 0\ 0\ 0\ 0\ 0\ 11\ 0\ 0\ 0\ 0\ 0\ 0\ \bar{9}\ 0\ 0\ 0\ 0\ 0\ 0\ 0\ \bar{9} \\
\text{NAF}_6(k) = & 1\ 0\ 0\ 0 \quad 0\ 0\ 0\ 0\ 0 \quad 23\ 0\ 0\ 0\ 0\ 0\ 11\ 0\ 0\ 0\ 0\ 0\ 0\ \bar{9}\ 0\ 0\ 0\ 0\ 0\ 0\ 0\ \bar{9}
\end{array}
$$

$\text{NAF}_w(k)$ can be efficiently computed using Algorithm 3.35, where $k \bmod 2^w$ denotes the integer u satisfying $u \equiv k \pmod{2^w}$ and $-2^{w-1} \leq u < 2^{w-1}$. The digits of $\text{NAF}_w(k)$ are obtained by repeatedly dividing k by 2, allowing remainders r in $[-2^{w-1}, 2^{w-1} - 1]$. If k is odd and the remainder $r = k \bmod s\, 2^w$ is chosen, then $(k - r)/2$ will be divisible by 2^{w-1}, ensuring that the next $w - 1$ digits are zero.

Algorithm 3.35 Computing the width-w NAF of a positive integer

---

INPUT: Window width w, positive integer k.
OUTPUT: $\text{NAF}_w(k)$.
   1. $i \leftarrow 0$.
   2. While $k \geq 1$ do
      2.1 If k is odd then: $k_i \leftarrow k \bmod s\, 2^w$, $k \leftarrow k - k_i$;
      2.2 Else: $k_i \leftarrow 0$.
      2.3 $k \leftarrow k/2$, $i \leftarrow i + 1$.
   3. Return$(k_{i-1}, k_{i-2}, \ldots, k_1, k_0)$.

Algorithm 3.36 generalizes the binary NAF method (Algorithm 3.31) by using $\text{NAF}_w(k)$ instead of $\text{NAF}(k)$. If follows from (iii) and (iv) of Theorem 3.33 that the expected running time of Algorithm 3.36 is approximately

$$\left[1D + (2^{w-2} - 1)A \right] + \left[\frac{m}{w+1} A + mD \right]. \tag{3.21}$$

Algorithm 3.36 Window NAF method for point multiplication

INPUT: Window width w, positive integer k, $P \in E(\mathbb{F}_q)$.
OUTPUT: kP.
   1. Use Algorithm 3.35 to compute $\text{NAF}_w(k) = \sum_{i=0}^{l-1} k_i 2^i$,
   2. Compute $P_i = iP$ for $i \in \{1, 3, 5, \ldots, 2^{w-1} - 1\}$.
   3. $Q \leftarrow \infty$.
   4. For i from $l - 1$ downto 0 do
      4.1 $Q \leftarrow 2Q$.
      4.2 If $k_i \neq 0$ then:
           If $k_i > 0$ then $Q \leftarrow Q + P_{k_i}$;
           Else $Q \leftarrow Q - P_{-k_i}$.
   5. Return(Q).

Note 3.37 (*selection of coordinates*) The number of field inversions required can be reduced by use of projective coordinates for the accumulator Q. If inversion is sufficiently expensive relative to field multiplication, then projective coordinates may also be effective for P_i. Chudnovsky coordinates (§3.2.2) for curves over prime fields eliminate inversions in precomputation at the cost of less-efficient Jacobian-Chudnovsky mixed additions in the evaluation phase.

The window NAF method employs a "sliding window" in the sense that Algorithm 3.35 has a width-w window, moving right-to-left, skipping consecutive zero entries after a nonzero digit k_i is processed. As an alternative, a sliding window can be used on the NAF of k, leading to Algorithm 3.38. The window (which has width at most w) moves left-to-right over the digits in NAF(k), with placement so that the value in the window is odd (to reduce the required precomputation).

Algorithm 3.38 Sliding window method for point multiplication

---

INPUT: Window width w, positive integer k, $P \in E(\mathbb{F}_q)$.
OUTPUT: kP.
1. Use Algorithm 3.30 to compute NAF(k) $= \sum_{i=0}^{l-1} k_i 2^i$.
2. Compute $P_i = iP$ for $i \in \{1, 3, \ldots, 2(2^w - (-1)^w)/3 - 1\}$.
3. $Q \leftarrow \infty$, $i \leftarrow l - 1$.
4. While $i \geq 0$ do
   4.1 If $k_i = 0$ then $t \leftarrow 1$, $u \leftarrow 0$;
   4.2 Else: find the largest $t \leq w$ such that $u \leftarrow (k_i, \ldots, k_{i-t+1})$ is odd.
   4.3 $Q \leftarrow 2^t Q$.
   4.4 If $u > 0$ then $Q \leftarrow Q + P_u$; else if $u < 0$ then $Q \leftarrow Q - P_{-u}$.
   4.5 $i \leftarrow i - t$.
5. Return(Q).

The average length of a run of zeros between windows in the sliding window method is

$$v(w) = \frac{4}{3} - \frac{(-1)^w}{3 \cdot 2^{w-2}}.$$

It follows that the expected running time of Algorithm 3.38 is approximately

$$\left[1D + \left(\frac{2^w - (-1)^w}{3} - 1 \right) A \right] + \frac{m}{w + v(w)} A + mD. \tag{3.22}$$

Note 3.39 (*comparing sliding window and window NAF methods*) For a given w, the sliding window method allows larger values in a window compared with those appearing in a width-w NAF. This translates to a higher cost for precomputation (roughly $2^w/3$ in step 2 of Algorithm 3.38 versus $2^w/4$ point operations in step 2 of Algorithm 3.36) in the sliding window method, but fewer point operations in the main loop ($m/(w + v(w))$ versus $m/(w + 1)$). If the comparison is on point operations, then the window NAF method will usually result in fewer point additions (when the optimum w is selected for each method) for m of interest. To make a more precise comparison, the coordinate representations (driven by the cost of field inversion versus multiplication) must be considered.

As an example, consider the NIST binary curves and suppose that the inverse to multiplication ratio is $I/M = 8$. Affine coordinates are used in precomputation, while the

	points		$m = 163$		$m = 233$		$m = 283$		$m = 409$		$m = 571$	
w	WN	SW	WN	SW	WN	SW	WN	SW	WN	SW	WN	SW
2	1	1	442	442	626	626	762	762	1098	1098	1530	1530
3	2	3	340	318	484	438	580	526	836	750	1156	1038
4	4	5	296	298	408	402	488	474	688	666	952	914
5	8	11	296	310	384	398	456	462	624	622	840	822
6	16	21	344	386	424	458	480	514	624	650	808	834

Table 3.5. *Point addition cost in sliding versus window NAF methods, when $I/M = 8$. "points" denotes the number the points stored in the precomputation stage. "WN" denotes the window NAF method (Algorithm 3.36). "SW" denotes the sliding window method (Algorithm 3.38).*

main loop uses mixed projective-affine additions. Table 3.5 shows the expected cost of point additions in each method. Note that there will also be m point doublings with each method, so the difference in times for point multiplication will be even smaller than Table 3.5 suggests. If there are constraints on the number of points that can be stored at the precomputation phase, then the difference in precomputation may decide the best method. For example, if only three points can be stored, then the sliding window method will be preferred, while storage for four points will favour the window NAF method. The differences are fairly small however; in the example, use of $w = 3$ (two and three points of precomputation, respectively) for both methods will favour sliding window, but gives only 7–10% reduction in point addition cost over window NAF.

Montgomery's method

Algorithm 3.40 for non-supersingular elliptic curves $y^2 + xy = x^3 + ax^2 + b$ over binary fields is due to López and Dahab, and is based on an idea of Montgomery. Let $Q_1 = (x_1, y_1)$ and $Q_2 = (x_2, y_2)$ with $Q_1 \neq \pm Q_2$. Let $Q_1 + Q_2 = (x_3, y_3)$ and $Q_1 - Q_2 = (x_4, y_4)$. Then using the addition formulas (see §3.1.2), it can be verified that

$$x_3 = x_4 + \frac{x_2}{x_1 + x_2} + \left(\frac{x_2}{x_1 + x_2}\right)^2. \tag{3.23}$$

Thus, the x-coordinate of $Q_1 + Q_2$ can be computed from the x-coordinates of Q_1, Q_2 and $Q_1 - Q_2$. Iteration j of Algorithm 3.40 for determining kP computes the x-coordinates only of $T_j = [lP, (l+1)P]$, where l is the integer represented by the j leftmost bits of k. Then $T_{j+1} = [2lP, (2l+1)P]$ or $[(2l+1)P, (2l+2)P]$ if the $(j+1)$st leftmost bit of k is 0 or 1, respectively, as illustrated in Figure 3.4. Each iteration requires one doubling and one addition using (3.23). After the last iteration, having computed the x-coordinates of $kP = (x_1, y_1)$ and $(k+1)P = (x_2, y_2)$, the y-coordinate of kP can be recovered as:

$$y_1 = x^{-1}(x_1 + x)[(x_1 + x)(x_2 + x) + x^2 + y] + y. \tag{3.24}$$

$$\underbrace{(k_{t-1}k_{t-2}\cdots k_{t-j}}_{\downarrow}\underbrace{k_{t-(j+1)}}_{\downarrow}k_{t-(j+2)}\cdots k_1 k_0)_2 P$$

$$[lP, (l+1)P] \rightarrow \boxed{\begin{array}{ll} [2lP, lP+(l+1)P], & \text{if } k_{t-(j+1)} = 0 \\ [lP+(l+1)P, 2(l+1)P], & \text{if } k_{t-(j+1)} = 1 \end{array}}$$

Figure 3.4. *One iteration in Montgomery point multiplication. After j iterations, the x-coordinates of lP and $(l+1)P$ are known for $l = (k_{t-1}\cdots k_{t-j})_2$. Iteration $j+1$ requires a doubling and an addition to find the x-coordinates of $l'P$ and $(l'+1)P$ for $l' = (k_{t-1}\cdots k_{t-(j+1)})_2$.*

Equation (3.24) is derived using the addition formula for computing the x-coordinate x_2 of $(k+1)P$ from $kP = (x_1, y_1)$ and $P = (x, y)$.

Algorithm 3.40 is presented using standard projective coordinates (see §3.2.1); only the X- and Z-coordinates of points are computed in steps 1 and 2. The approximate running time is

$$6mM + (1I + 10M). \tag{3.25}$$

One advantage of Algorithm 3.40 is that it does not have any extra storage requirements. Another advantage is that the same operations are performed in every iteration of the main loop, thereby potentially increasing resistance to timing attacks and power analysis attacks (cf. §5.3).

Algorithm 3.40 Montgomery point multiplication (for elliptic curves over $\mathbb{F}_{2^m}$)

INPUT: $k = (k_{t-1}, \ldots, k_1, k_0)_2$ with $k_{t-1} = 1$, $P = (x, y) \in E(\mathbb{F}_{2^m})$.
OUTPUT: kP.
1. $X_1 \leftarrow x$, $Z_1 \leftarrow 1$, $X_2 \leftarrow x^4 + b$, $Z_2 \leftarrow x^2$. {Compute $(P, 2P)$}
2. For i from $t - 2$ downto 0 do
   2.1 If $k_i = 1$ then
   $\quad\quad T \leftarrow Z_1$, $Z_1 \leftarrow (X_1 Z_2 + X_2 Z_1)^2$, $X_1 \leftarrow x Z_1 + X_1 X_2 T Z_2$.
   $\quad\quad T \leftarrow X_2$, $X_2 \leftarrow X_2^4 + b Z_2^4$, $Z_2 \leftarrow T^2 Z_2^2$.
   2.2 Else
   $\quad\quad T \leftarrow Z_2$, $Z_2 \leftarrow (X_1 Z_2 + X_2 Z_1)^2$, $X_2 \leftarrow x Z_2 + X_1 X_2 Z_1 T$.
   $\quad\quad T \leftarrow X_1$, $X_1 \leftarrow X_1^4 + b Z_1^4$, $Z_1 \leftarrow T^2 Z_1^2$.
3. $x_3 \leftarrow X_1/Z_1$.
4. $y_3 \leftarrow (x + X_1/Z_1)[(X_1 + xZ_1)(X_2 + xZ_2) + (x^2 + y)(Z_1 Z_2)](xZ_1 Z_2)^{-1} + y$.
5. Return(x_3, y_3).

3.3.2 Fixed point

If the point P is fixed and some storage is available, then the point multiplication operation kP can be accelerated by precomputing some data that depends only on P.

For example, if the points $2P, 2^2 P, \ldots, 2^{t-1}P$ are precomputed, then the right-to-left binary method (Algorithm 3.26) has expected running time $(m/2)A$ (all doublings are eliminated).[1]

Fixed-base windowing methods

Brickell, Gordon, McCurley and Wilson proposed the following refinement to the simple method of precomputing every multiple $2^i P$. Let $(K_{d-1}, \ldots, K_1, K_0)_{2^w}$ be the base-2^w representation of k, where $d = \lceil t/w \rceil$, and let $Q_j = \sum_{i:K_i=j} 2^{wi} P$ for each j, $1 \le j \le 2^w - 1$. Then

$$kP = \sum_{i=0}^{d-1} K_i (2^{wi} P) = \sum_{j=1}^{2^w-1} \left(j \sum_{i:K_i=j} 2^{wi} P \right) = \sum_{j=1}^{2^w-1} j Q_j$$

$$= Q_{2^w-1} + (Q_{2^w-1} + Q_{2^w-2}) + \cdots + (Q_{2^w-1} + Q_{2^w-2} + \cdots + Q_1).$$

Algorithm 3.41 is based on this observation. Its expected running time is approximately

$$(2^w + d - 3)A \qquad\qquad (3.26)$$

where $d = \lceil t/w \rceil$ and $t \approx m$.

Algorithm 3.41 Fixed-base windowing method for point multiplication

---

INPUT: Window width w, $d = \lceil t/w \rceil$, $k = (K_{d-1}, \ldots, K_1, K_0)_{2^w}$, $P \in E(\mathbb{F}_q)$.
OUTPUT: kP.
1. *Precomputation.* Compute $P_i = 2^{wi} P$, $0 \le i \le d - 1$.
2. $A \leftarrow \infty$, $B \leftarrow \infty$.
3. For j from $2^w - 1$ downto 1 do
   3.1 For each i for which $K_i = j$ do: $B \leftarrow B + P_i$.   {Add Q_j to B}
   3.2 $A \leftarrow A + B$.
4. Return(A).

Algorithm 3.42 modifies Algorithm 3.41 by using NAF(k) instead of the binary representation of k. In Algorithm 3.42, NAF(k) is divided into $\{0, \pm 1\}$-strings K_i each of the same length w:

$$\text{NAF}(k) = K_{d-1} \| \cdots \| K_1 \| K_0.$$

Since each K_i is in non-adjacent form, it represents an integer in the interval $[-I, I]$ where $I = (2^{w+1} - 2)/3$ if w is even, and $I = (2^{w+1} - 1)/3$ if w is odd. The expected running time of Algorithm 3.42 is approximately

$$\left(\frac{2^{w+1}}{3} + d - 2 \right) A \qquad\qquad (3.27)$$

where $d = \lceil (t+1)/w \rceil$.

---

[1]Recall the following notation: t is the bitlength of k, and $m = \lceil \log_2 q \rceil$. Also, we assume that $t \approx m$.

Algorithm 3.42 Fixed-base NAF windowing method for point multiplication

---

INPUT: Window width w, positive integer k, $P \in E(\mathbb{F}_q)$.

OUTPUT: kP.

1. *Precomputation.* Compute $P_i = 2^{wi} P$, $0 \le i \le \lceil (t+1)/w \rceil$.
2. Use Algorithm 3.30 to compute $\text{NAF}(k) = \sum_{i=0}^{l-1} k_i 2^i$.
3. $d \leftarrow \lceil l/w \rceil$.
4. By padding $\text{NAF}(k)$ on the left with 0s if necessary, write $(k_{l-1}, \ldots, k_1, k_0) = K_{d-1} \| \cdots \| K_1 \| K_0$ where each K_i is a $\{0, \pm 1\}$-string of length d.
5. If w is even then $I \leftarrow (2^{w+1} - 2)/3$; else $I \leftarrow (2^{w+1} - 1)/3$.
6. $A \leftarrow \infty$, $B \leftarrow \infty$.
7. For j from I downto 1 do
    7.1 For each i for which $K_i = j$ do: $B \leftarrow B + P_i$. {Add Q_j to B}
    7.2 For each i for which $K_i = -j$ do: $B \leftarrow B - P_i$. {Add $-Q_j$ to B}
    7.3 $A \leftarrow A + B$.
8. Return(A).

Note 3.43 (*selection of coordinates*) If field inversion is sufficiently expensive, then projective coordinates will be preferred for one or both of the accumulators A and B in Algorithms 3.41 and 3.42. In the case of curves over prime fields, Table 3.3 shows that Chudnovsky coordinates for B and Jacobian coordinates for A is the preferred selection if projective coordinates are used, in which case Algorithm 3.42 has mixed Chudnovsky-affine additions at steps 7.1 and 7.2, and mixed Jacobian-Chudnovsky addition at step 7.3.

Fixed-base comb methods

Let $d = \lceil t/w \rceil$. In the fixed-base comb method (Algorithm 3.44), the binary representation of k is first padded on the left with $dw - t$ 0s, and is then divided into w bit strings each of the same length d so that

$$k = K^{w-1} \| \cdots \| K^1 \| K^0.$$

The bit strings K^j are written as rows of an *exponent array*

$$
\begin{bmatrix} K^0 \\ \vdots \\ K^{w'} \\ \vdots \\ K^{w-1} \end{bmatrix}
=
\begin{bmatrix} K^0_{d-1} & \cdots & K^0_0 \\ \vdots & & \vdots \\ K^{w'}_{d-1} & \cdots & K^{w'}_0 \\ \vdots & & \vdots \\ K^{w-1}_{d-1} & \cdots & K^{w-1}_0 \end{bmatrix}
=
\begin{bmatrix} k_{d-1} & \cdots & k_0 \\ \vdots & & \vdots \\ k_{(w'+1)d-1} & \cdots & k_{w'd} \\ \vdots & & \vdots \\ k_{wd-1} & \cdots & k_{(w-1)d} \end{bmatrix}
$$

whose columns are then processed one at a time. In order to accelerate the computation, the points

$$[a_{w-1}, \ldots, a_2, a_1, a_0]P = a_{w-1}2^{(w-1)d}P + \cdots + a_2 2^{2d}P + a_1 2^d P + a_0 P$$

are precomputed for all possible bit strings $(a_{w-1}, \ldots, a_1, a_0)$.

Algorithm 3.44 Fixed-base comb method for point multiplication

---

INPUT: Window width w, $d = \lceil t/w \rceil$, $k = (k_{t-1}, \ldots, k_1, k_0)_2$, $P \in E(\mathbb{F}_q)$.
OUTPUT: kP.
  1. *Precomputation.* Compute $[a_{w-1}, \ldots, a_1, a_0]P$ for all bit strings $(a_{w-1}, \ldots, a_1, a_0)$ of length w.
  2. By padding k on the left with 0s if necessary, write $k = K^{w-1} \| \cdots \| K^1 \| K^0$, where each K^j is a bit string of length d. Let K_i^j denote the ith bit of K^j.
  3. $Q \leftarrow \infty$.
  4. For i from $d - 1$ downto 0 do
     4.1 $Q \leftarrow 2Q$.
     4.2 $Q \leftarrow Q + [K_i^{w-1}, \ldots, K_i^1, K_i^0]P$.
  5. Return(Q).

The expected running time of Algorithm 3.44 is

$$\left(\frac{2^w - 1}{2^w} d - 1 \right) A + (d - 1)D. \tag{3.28}$$

For $w > 2$, Algorithm 3.44 has approximately the same number of point additions as point doubles in the main loop. Figure 3.5 illustrates the use of a second table of precomputation in Algorithm 3.45, leading to roughly half as many point doubles as point additions.

Algorithm 3.45 Fixed-base comb method (with two tables) for point multiplication

---

INPUT: Window width w, $d = \lceil t/w \rceil$, $e = \lceil d/2 \rceil$, $k = (k_{t-1}, \ldots, k_0)_2$, $P \in E(\mathbb{F}_q)$.
OUTPUT: kP.
  1. *Precomputation.* Compute $[a_{w-1}, \ldots, a_1, a_0]P$ and $2^e[a_{w-1}, \ldots, a_1, a_0]P$ for all bit strings $(a_{w-1}, \ldots, a_1, a_0)$ of length w.
  2. By padding k on the left with 0s if necessary, write $k = K^{w-1} \| \cdots \| K^1 \| K^0$, where each K^j is a bit string of length d. Let K_i^j denote the ith bit of K^j.
  3. $Q \leftarrow \infty$.
  4. For i from $e - 1$ downto 0 do
     4.1 $Q \leftarrow 2Q$.
     4.2 $Q \leftarrow Q + [K_i^{w-1}, \ldots, K_i^1, K_i^0]P + 2^e[K_{i+e}^{w-1}, \ldots, K_{i+e}^1, K_{i+e}^0]P$.
  5. Return(Q).

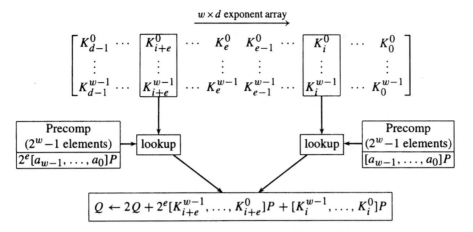

Figure 3.5. One iteration in Algorithm 3.45. The $w \times d$ exponent array is processed left-to-right in $e = \lceil d/2 \rceil$ iterations to find kP. Precomputation finds $[a_{w-1}, \ldots, a_0]P$ and $2^e[a_{w-1}, \ldots, a_0]P$ for all w-bit values $(a_{w-1}, \ldots, a_0)$, where $[a_{w-1}, \ldots, a_0] = a_{w-1}2^{(w-1)d} + \cdots + a_1 2^d + a_0$.

The expected running time of Algorithm 3.45 is approximately

$$\left(\frac{2^w - 1}{2^w} 2e - 1 \right) A + (e - 1)D. \tag{3.29}$$

For a fixed w, Algorithm 3.45 requires twice as much storage for precomputation as Algorithm 3.44. For a given amount of precomputation, Algorithm 3.45 is expected to outperform Algorithm 3.44 whenever

$$\frac{2^{w-1}(w - 2)}{2^w - w - 1} \geq \frac{A}{D},$$

where w is the window width used in Algorithm 3.44 (and hence width $w - 1$ is used with Algorithm 3.45). As an example, LD coordinates in the binary field case give $A/D \approx 2$, requiring (roughly) $w \geq 6$ in Algorithm 3.44 in order for the two-table method to be superior. For the NIST curves over prime fields, $A/D \approx 1.4$ with Jacobian coordinates and $S = .8M$, requiring $w \geq 4$.

Note 3.46 (*Algorithm 3.45 with simultaneous addition*) If storage for an additional e points (which depend on k) can be tolerated, then the values

$$T_i \leftarrow [K_i^{w-1}, \ldots, K_i^1, K_i^0]P + 2^e[K_{i+e}^{w-1}, \ldots, K_{i+e}^1, K_{i+e}^0]P, \quad 0 \leq i < e,$$

at step 4.2 of Algorithm 3.45 can be determined in a (data-dependent) precomputation phase. The strategy calculates the points T_i in affine coordinates, using the method of simultaneous inversion (Algorithm 2.26) to replace an expected $e' = (1 - 1/2^w)^2 e$ field inverses with one inverse and $3(e' - 1)$ field multiplications.

If Q is maintained in projective coordinates, then e' mixed-coordinate additions at step 4.2 are replaced by e' simultaneous additions in the new precomputation phase. With the coordinates discussed in §3.2, this translates into the following approximate field operation counts.

e' additions in $E(\mathbb{F}_{2^m})$		e' additions in $E(\mathbb{F}_{p^m})$, $p > 3$	
mixed-coordinate	simultaneous	mixed-coordinate	simultaneous
$8e'M$	$I + (5e' - 3)M$	$8e'M + 3e'S$	$I + (5e' - 3)M + e'S$

For curves of practical interest from §3.2 over fields where I/M is expected to be small (e.g., binary fields and OEFs), a roughly 15% reduction in point multiplication time is predicted.

Note 3.47 (*comb methods*) Algorithms 3.44 and 3.45 are special cases of exponentiation methods due to Lim and Lee. For given parameters w and v, a t-bit integer k is written as an exponent array of $w \times d$ bits where $d = \lceil t/w \rceil$, as illustrated in Figure 3.6. A typical entry $K_{v'}^{w'}$ consists of the $e = \lceil d/v \rceil$ bits of k given by $K_{v'}^{w'} = (k_{l+e-1}, \ldots, k_{l+1}, k_l)$ where $l = dw' + ev'$ (with zeros replacing some entries if $v' = v - 1$ and $v \nmid d$).

$$
w \left\{
\begin{array}{ccccccc}
K_{v-1}^0 & \cdots & (K_{v',e-1}^0, \ldots, K_{v',0}^0) & \cdots & K_0^0 \\
\vdots & & \vdots & & \vdots \\
K_{v-1}^{w'} & \cdots & (K_{v',e-1}^{w'}, \ldots, K_{v',0}^{w'}) & \cdots & K_0^{w'} \\
\vdots & & \vdots & & \vdots \\
K_{v-1}^{w-1} & \cdots & \underbrace{(K_{v',e-1}^{w-1}, \ldots, K_{v',0}^{w-1})} & \cdots & K_0^{w-1}
\end{array}
\right.
$$

$$\underbrace{\phantom{(K_{v',e-1}^{w-1}, \ldots, K_{v',0}^{w-1})}}_{e = \lceil d/v \rceil \text{ bits}}$$

$$\underbrace{\phantom{K_{v-1}^0 \cdots (K_{v',e-1}^0, \ldots, K_{v',0}^0) \cdots K_0^0}}_{d = \lceil t/w \rceil \text{ bits}}$$

Figure 3.6. The exponent array in Lim-Lee combing methods. Given parameters w and v, a t-bit integer k is written as a $w \times d$ bit array for $d = \lceil t/w \rceil$. Entries $K_{v'}^{w'}$ have $e = \lceil d/v \rceil$ bits.

If $K^{w'}$ denotes the integer formed from the bits in row w', then

$$
kP = \sum_{w'=0}^{w-1} K^{w'} 2^{dw'} P = \sum_{w'=0}^{w-1} \left(\sum_{v'=0}^{v-1} K_{v'}^{w'} 2^{ev'} \right) 2^{dw'} P
$$

$$
= \sum_{w'=0}^{w-1} \sum_{v'=0}^{v-1} \left(\sum_{e'=0}^{e-1} K_{v',e'}^{w'} 2^{e'} \right) 2^{ev'} 2^{dw'} P
$$

$$
= \sum_{e'=0}^{e-1} 2^{e'} \sum_{v'=0}^{v-1} \left(2^{ev'} \underbrace{\sum_{w'=0}^{w-1} K_{v',e'}^{w'} 2^{dw'} P}_{P[v'][K_{v',e'}]} \right)
$$

where $v(2^w - 1)$ points $P[v'][u]$ for $v' \in [0, v-1]$ and $u \in [1, 2^w - 1]$ are precomputed. A point multiplication algorithm based on this method is expected to require approximately $e - 1 \approx \frac{t}{wv} - 1$ point doublings and $(\frac{t}{w} - 1)\frac{2^w - 1}{2^w}$ point additions. Algorithms 3.44 and 3.45 are the cases $v = 1$ and $v = 2$, respectively.

3.3.3 Multiple point multiplication

One method to potentially speed the computation of $kP + lQ$ is simultaneous multiple point multiplication (Algorithm 3.48), also known as *Shamir's trick*. If k and l are t-bit numbers, then their binary representations are written in a $2 \times t$ matrix known as the *exponent array*. Given width w, the values $iP + jQ$ are calculated for $0 \le i, j < 2^w$. At each of $\lceil t/w \rceil$ steps, the accumulator receives w doublings and an addition from the table of values $iP + jQ$ determined by the contents of a $2 \times w$ window passed over the exponent array; see Figure 3.7.

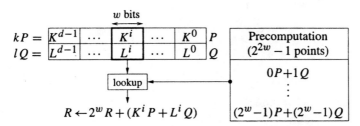

Figure 3.7. Simultaneous point multiplication accumulation step.

Algorithm 3.48 has an expected running time of approximately

$$\left[(3 \cdot 2^{2(w-1)} - 2^{w-1} - 1)A + (2^{2(w-1)} - 2^{w-1})D\right] + \left[\left(\frac{2^{2w} - 1}{2^{2w}}d - 1\right)A + (d-1)wD\right],$$
(3.30)

and requires storage for $2^{2w} - 1$ points.

Algorithm 3.48 Simultaneous multiple point multiplication

INPUT: Window width w, $k = (k_{t-1}, \ldots, k_0)_2$, $l = (l_{t-1}, \ldots, l_0)_2$, $P, Q \in E(\mathbb{F}_q)$.
OUTPUT: $kP + lQ$.
1. Compute $iP + jQ$ for all $i, j \in [0, 2^w - 1]$.
2. Write $k = (K^{d-1}, \ldots, K^1, K^0)$ and $l = (L^{d-1}, \ldots, L^1, L^0)$ where each K^i, L^i is a bitstring of length w, and $d = \lceil t/w \rceil$.
3. $R \leftarrow \infty$.
4. For i from $d - 1$ downto 0 do
   4.1 $R \leftarrow 2^w R$.
   4.2 $R \leftarrow R + (K^i P + L^i Q)$.
5. Return(R).

Algorithm 3.48 can be improved by use of a sliding window. At each step, place-ment of a window of width at most w is such that the right-most column is nonzero. Precomputation storage is reduced by $2^{2(w-1)} - 1$ points. The improved algorithm is expected to have $t/(w + (1/3))$ point additions in the evaluation stage, a savings of approximately 9% (in evaluation stage additions) compared with Algorithm 3.48 for $w \in \{2, 3\}$.

Joint sparse form

If k and l are each written in NAF form, then the expected number of zero columns in the exponent array increases, so that the expected number of additions in the evaluation stage of a suitably modified Algorithm 3.48 (processing one column at a time) is $5t/9$. The expected number of zero columns can be increased by choosing signed binary expansions of k and l jointly. The *joint sparse form (JSF)* exponent array of positive integers k and l is characterized by the following properties.

1. At least one of any three consecutive columns is zero.

2. Consecutive terms in a row do not have opposite signs.

3. If $k_{j+1}k_j \neq 0$ then $l_{j+1} \neq 0$ and $l_j = 0$. If $l_{j+1}l_j \neq 0$ then $k_{j+1} \neq 0$ and $k_j = 0$.

The representation has minimal weight among all joint signed binary expansions, where the weight is defined to be the number of nonzero columns.

Example 3.49 (*joint sparse form*) The following table gives exponent arrays for $k = 53$ and $l = 102$.

	binary	NAF	joint sparse form
$k = 53$	0 1 1 0 1 0 1	0 1 0 −1 0 1 0 1	1 0 0 −1 0 −1 −1
$l = 102$	1 1 0 0 1 1 0	1 0 −1 0 1 0 −1 0	1 1 0 1 0 −1 0
weight	6	8	5

If Algorithm 3.48 is modified to use JSF, processing a single column in each itera-tion, then $t/2$ additions (rather than $5t/9$ using NAFs) are required in the evaluation stage. Algorithm 3.50 finds the joint sparse form for integers k^1 and k^2. Although it is written in terms of integer operations, in fact only simple bit arithmetic is required; for example, evaluation modulo 8 means that three bits must be examined, and $\lfloor k^i/2 \rfloor$ discards the rightmost bit.

Algorithm 3.50 Joint sparse form

INPUT: Nonnegative integers k^1 and k^2, not both zero.
OUTPUT: JSF(k^2, k^1), the joint sparse form of k^1 and k^2.
  1. $l \leftarrow 0$, $d_1 \leftarrow 0$, $d_2 \leftarrow 0$.
  2. While $(k^1 + d_1 > 0$ or $k^2 + d_2 > 0)$ do
      2.1 $\ell_1 \leftarrow d_1 + k^1$, $\ell_2 \leftarrow d_2 + k^2$.
      2.2 For i from 1 to 2 do
              If ℓ_i is even then $u \leftarrow 0$;
              Else
                    $u \leftarrow \ell_i \bmod 4$.
                    If $\ell_i \equiv \pm 3 \pmod 8$ and $\ell_{3-i} \equiv 2 \pmod 4$ then $u \leftarrow -u$.
              $k_l^i \leftarrow u$.
      2.3 For i from 1 to 2 do
              If $2d_i = 1 + k_l^i$ then $d_i \leftarrow 1 - d_i$.
              $k^i \leftarrow \lfloor k^i / 2 \rfloor$.
      2.4 $l \leftarrow l + 1$.
  3. Return JSF$(k^2, k^1) = \begin{pmatrix} k_{l-1}^1, \ldots, k_0^1 \\ k_{l-1}^2, \ldots, k_0^2 \end{pmatrix}$.

Interleaving

The simultaneous and comb methods process multiple point multiplications using precomputation involving combinations of the points. Roughly speaking, if each precomputed value involves only a single point, then the associated method is known as *interleaving*.

In the calculation of $\sum k^j P_j$ for points P_j and integers k^j, interleaving allows different methods to be used for each $k^j P_j$, provided that the doubling step can be done jointly. For example, width-w NAF methods with different widths can be used, or some point multiplications may be done by comb methods. However, the cost of the doubling is determined by the maximum number of doublings required in the methods for $k^j P_j$, and hence the benefits of a comb method may be lost in interleaving.

Algorithm 3.51 is an interleaving method for computing $\sum_{j=1}^{v} k^j P_j$, where a width-w_j NAF is used on k^j. Points $i P_j$ for odd $i < 2^{w_j - 1}$ are calculated in a precomputation phase. The expansions $\mathrm{NAF}_{w_j}(k^j)$ are processed jointly, left to right, with a single doubling of the accumulator at each stage; Figure 3.8 illustrates the case $v = 2$. The algorithm has an expected running time of approximately

$$\left[|\{j : w_j > 2\}| D + \sum_{j=1}^{v} (2^{w_j - 2} - 1) A \right] + \left[\max_{1 \le j \le v} l_j D + \sum_{j=1}^{v} \frac{l_j}{w_j + 1} A \right] \qquad (3.31)$$

where l_j denotes the length of $\mathrm{NAF}_{w_j}(k^j)$, and requires storage for $\sum_{j=1}^{v} 2^{w_j - 2}$ points.

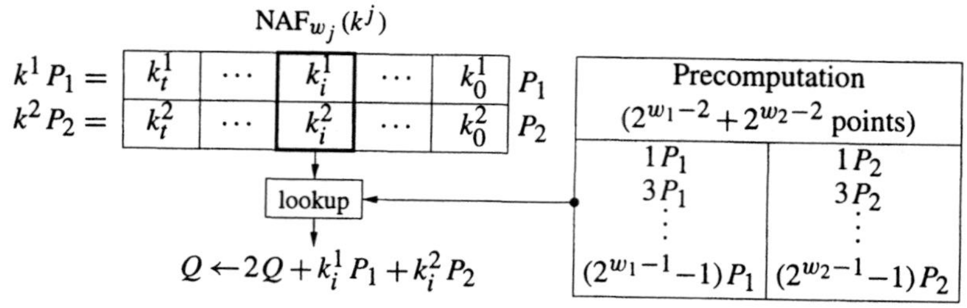

Figure 3.8. *Computing $k^1 P_1 + k^2 P_2$ using interleaving with NAFs. The point multiplication accumulation step is shown for the case $v = 2$ points. Scalar k^j is written in width-w_j NAF form.*

Algorithm 3.51 Interleaving with NAFs

INPUT: v, integers k^j, widths w_j and points P_j, $1 \le j \le v$.
OUTPUT: $\sum_{j=1}^{v} k^j P_j$

1. Compute $i P_j$ for $i \in \{1, 3, \dots, 2^{w_j-1} - 1\}$, $1 \le j \le v$.
2. Use Algorithm 3.30 to compute $\mathrm{NAF}_{w_j}(k^j) = \sum_{i=0}^{l_j-1} k_i^j 2^i$, $1 \le j \le v$.
3. Let $l = \max\{l_j : 1 \le j \le v\}$.
4. Define $k_i^j = 0$ for $l_j \le i < l$, $1 \le j \le v$.
5. $Q \leftarrow \infty$.
6. For i from $l-1$ downto 0 do
   6.1 $Q \leftarrow 2Q$.
   6.2 For j from 1 to v do
      If $k_i^j \ne 0$ then
         If $k_i^j > 0$ then $Q \leftarrow Q + k_i^j P_j$;
         Else $Q \leftarrow Q - k_i^j P_j$.
7. Return(Q).

Note 3.52 (*comparison with simultaneous methods*) Consider the calculation of $kP + lQ$, where k and l are approximately the same bitlength. The simultaneous sliding and interleaving methods require essentially the same number of point doublings regardless of the window widths. For a given w, simultaneous sliding requires $3 \cdot 2^{2(w-1)}$ points of storage, and approximately $t/(w + (1/3))$ point additions in the evaluation stage, while interleaving with width $2w + 1$ on k and width $2w$ on l requires the same amount of storage, but only $(4w + 3)t/(4w^2 + 5w + 2) < t/(w + (1/2))$ additions in evaluation. Interleaving may also be preferable at the precomputation phase, since operations involving a known point P may be done in advance (encouraging the use of a wider width for $\mathrm{NAF}_w(k)$), in contrast to the joint computations required in the simultaneous method. Table 3.6 compares operation counts for computing $kP + lQ$ in the case that P (but not Q) is known in advance.

In the case that storage for precomputation is limited to four points (including P and Q), interleaving with width-3 NAFs or use of the JSF give essentially the same performance, with interleaving requiring one or two more point doublings at the precomputation stage. Table 3.6 gives some comparative results for small window sizes.

method	w	storage	additions	doubles
Alg 3.48	1	3	$1 + 3t/4 \approx 1 + .75t$	t
Alg 3.48	2	15	$9 + 15t/32 \approx 9 + .47t$	$2 + t$
Alg 3.48 with sliding	2	12	$9 + 3t/7 \approx 9 + .43t$	$2 + t$
Alg 3.48 with NAF		4	$2 + 5t/9 \approx 2 + .56t$	t
Alg 3.48 with JSF		4	$2 + t/2 \approx 2 + .5t$	t
interleave with 3-NAF	3, 3	2+2	$1 + t/2 \approx 1 + .5t$	$1 + t$
interleave with 5-NAF & 4-NAF	5, 4	8+4	$3 + 11t/30 \approx 3 + .37t$	$1 + t$

Table 3.6. Approximate operation counts for computing $kP + lQ$, where k and l are t-bit integers. The precomputation involving only P is excluded.

Interleaving can be considered as an alternative to the comb method (Algorithm 3.44) for computing kP. In this case, the exponent array for k is processed using interleaving (Algorithm 3.51), with k^j given by $k = \sum_{j=1}^{w} k^j 2^{(j-1)d}$ and points P_j given by $P_j = 2^{(j-1)d} P$, $1 \le j \le w$, where d is defined in Algorithm 3.44. Table 3.7 compares the comb and interleaving methods for fixed storage.

method	rows	storage	additions	doubles
comb	2	3	$3t/8 \approx .38t$	$t/2$
interleave (3, 3)	2	4	$t/4 \approx .25t$	$t/2$
comb	4	15	$15t/64 \approx .23t$	$t/4$
comb (two-table)	3	14	$7t/24 \approx .29t$	$t/6$
interleave (4, 4, 4, 4)	4	16	$t/4 \approx .25t$	$t/4$
interleave (4, 4, 4, 3, 3)	5	16	$11t/50 \approx .22t$	$t/5$
comb	5	31	$31t/160 \approx .19t$	$t/5$
comb (two-table)	4	30	$15t/64 \approx .23t$	$t/8$
interleave (5, 5, 5, 4, 4)	5	32	$9t/50 \approx .18t$	$t/5$
interleave (5, 5, 4, 4, 4, 4)	6	32	$17t/90 \approx .19t$	$t/6$

Table 3.7. Approximate operation counts in comb and interleaving methods for computing kP, P known in advance. The bitlength of k is denoted by t. The interleaving methods list the widths used on each row in calculating the NAF.

3.4 Koblitz curves

Koblitz curves, also known as *anomalous binary curves*, are elliptic curves defined over $\mathbb{F}_2$. The primary advantage of these curves is that point multiplication algorithms can be devised that do not use any point doublings. The material in this section is closely based on the detailed paper by Solinas [446] which contains proofs of facts and analyses of algorithms presented.

Definition 3.53 *Koblitz curves* are the following elliptic curves defined over $\mathbb{F}_2$:

$$E_0 : y^2 + xy = x^3 + 1$$
$$E_1 : y^2 + xy = x^3 + x^2 + 1.$$

In cryptographic protocols, one uses the group $E_0(\mathbb{F}_{2^m})$ or $E_1(\mathbb{F}_{2^m})$ of $\mathbb{F}_{2^m}$-rational points for some extension field $\mathbb{F}_{2^m}$. Let $a \in \{0, 1\}$. For each proper divisor l of m, $E_a(\mathbb{F}_{2^l})$ is a subgroup of $E_a(\mathbb{F}_{2^m})$ and hence $\#E_a(\mathbb{F}_{2^l})$ divides $\#E_a(\mathbb{F}_{2^m})$. In particular, since $\#E_0(\mathbb{F}_2) = 4$ and $\#E_1(\mathbb{F}_2) = 2$, $\#E_0(\mathbb{F}_{2^m})$ is a multiple of 4 and $\#E_1(\mathbb{F}_{2^m})$ is a multiple of 2.

Definition 3.54 A Koblitz curve E_a has *almost-prime* group order over $\mathbb{F}_{2^m}$ if $\#E_a(\mathbb{F}_{2^m}) = hn$ where n is prime and

$$h = \begin{cases} 4 & \text{if } a = 0 \\ 2 & \text{if } a = 1. \end{cases}$$

h is called the *cofactor*.

We shall assume throughout the remainder of this section that E_a is a Koblitz curve with almost-prime group order $\#E_a(\mathbb{F}_{2^m})$. Observe that $\#E_a(\mathbb{F}_{2^m})$ can only be almost prime if m is a prime number. The group orders $\#E_a(\mathbb{F}_{2^m})$ can be efficiently computed using Theorem 3.11. Table 3.8 lists the extension degrees $m \in [100, 600]$, and Koblitz curves E_a for which $\#E_a(\mathbb{F}_{2^m})$ is almost prime.

3.4.1   The Frobenius map and the ring $\mathbb{Z}[\tau]$

Definition 3.55 Let E_a be a Koblitz curve. The *Frobenius map* $\tau : E_a(\mathbb{F}_{2^m}) \to E_a(\mathbb{F}_{2^m})$ is defined by

$$\tau(\infty) = \infty, \quad \tau(x, y) = (x^2, y^2).$$

The Frobenius map can be efficiently computed since squaring in $\mathbb{F}_{2^m}$ is relatively inexpensive (see §2.3.4). It is known that

$$(\tau^2 + 2)P = \mu\tau(P) \text{ for all } P \in E_a(\mathbb{F}_{2^m}),$$

m	Curve	Prime factorization of $\#E_a(\mathbb{F}_{2^m})$
101	E_1	$2 \cdot 1267650600228230886142808508011$
103	E_0	$2^2 \cdot 2535301200456459535862530067069$
107	E_0	$2^2 \cdot 405648192073033356043634890037809$
107	E_1	$2 \cdot 811296384146066921828510322212511$
109	E_1	$2 \cdot 3245185536584267014874486564614617$
113	E_1	$2 \cdot 5192296858534827627896703833467507$
131	E_0	$2^2 \cdot 680564733841876926932320129493409985129$
163	E_1	$2 \cdot 5846006549323611672814741753598448348329118574063$
233	E_0	$2^2 \cdot 3450873173395281893717377931138512760570940988862252126\backslash$ 328087024741343
239	E_0	$2^2 \cdot 2208558830972980411979121875928648149482165613217098488\backslash$ 87480219215362213
277	E_0	$2^2 \cdot 6070840288205403346623318458823496583257511049878650876\backslash$ $48841755618916221650646650683$
283	E_0	$2^2 \cdot 3885337784451458141838923813647037813284811733793061324\backslash$ $29587499752981582970442260387$3
283	E_1	$2 \cdot 7770675568902916283677847627294075626569631244830993521\backslash$ $4227492828516026222328227776$63
311	E_1	$2 \cdot 2085924839766513752338888384931203236916703635071711166\backslash$ $73989121858491635472665429482533830218$3
331	E_1	$2 \cdot 2187250724783011924372502227117621365353169430893227643\backslash$ $44701030671135871258677658859434350525561430$3
347	E_1	$2 \cdot 1433436634993794694756763059563804337997853118230175657\backslash$ $2853742030724076380332577411549372319390025702931$1
349	E_0	$2^2 \cdot 2866873269987589389513526119127608675995706236460351478\backslash$ $840674433541530787625118990359606515490187750443$23
359	E_1	$2 \cdot 5871356456934583069723701491973342568439206372270799668\backslash$ $11081824609485917244124494882365172478748165648998663$
409	E_0	$2^2 \cdot 3305279843951242994759576540163855199142023414821406096\backslash$ $4232439502288071128924919105067325845777745801409636659\backslash$ 0617731358671
571	E_0	$2^2 \cdot 1932268761508629172347675945465993672149463664853217499\backslash$ $3286176257257595711447802122681339785227067118347067128\backslash$ $0082535146127367497406661731192968242161709250355573368\backslash$ 5276673

Table 3.8. Koblitz curves E_a with almost-prime group order $\#E_a(\mathbb{F}_{2^m})$ and $m \in [100, 600]$.

where $\mu = (-1)^{1-a}$ and $\tau^l(P)$ denotes the l-fold application of τ to P. Hence the Frobenius map can be regarded as a complex number τ satisfying

$$\tau^2 + 2 = \mu\tau; \tag{3.32}$$

we choose $\tau = (\mu + \sqrt{-7})/2$. Let $\mathbb{Z}[\tau]$ denote the ring of polynomials in τ with integer coefficients. It now makes sense to multiply points in $E_a(\mathbb{F}_{2^m})$ by elements of the ring $\mathbb{Z}[\tau]$: if $u_{l-1}\tau^{l-1} + \cdots + u_1\tau + u_0 \in \mathbb{Z}[\tau]$ and $P \in E_a(\mathbb{F}_{2^m})$, then

$$(u_{l-1}\tau^{l-1} + \cdots + u_1\tau + u_0)P = u_{l-1}\tau^{l-1}(P) + \cdots + u_1\tau(P) + u_0 P. \tag{3.33}$$

The strategy for developing an efficient point multiplication algorithm for Koblitz curves is to find, for a given integer k, a "nice" expression of the form $k = \sum_{i=0}^{l-1} u_i\tau^i$, and then use (3.33) to compute kP. Here, "nice" means that l is relatively small and the nonzero digits u_i are small (e.g., ± 1) and sparse.

Since $\tau^2 = \mu\tau - 2$, every element α in $\mathbb{Z}[\tau]$ can be expressed in canonical form $\alpha = a_0 + a_1\tau$ where $a_0, a_1 \in \mathbb{Z}$.

Definition 3.56 The *norm* of $\alpha = a_0 + a_1\tau \in \mathbb{Z}[\tau]$ is the (integer) product of α and its complex conjugate. Explicitly,

$$N(a_0 + a_1\tau) = a_0^2 + \mu a_0 a_1 + 2a_1^2.$$

Theorem 3.57 (*properties of the norm function*)

  (i) $N(\alpha) \geq 0$ for all $\alpha \in \mathbb{Z}[\tau]$ with equality if and only if $\alpha = 0$.

 (ii) 1 and -1 are the only elements of $\mathbb{Z}[\tau]$ having norm 1.

(iii) $N(\tau) = 2$ and $N(\tau - 1) = h$.

 (iv) $N(\tau^m - 1) = \#E_a(\mathbb{F}_{2^m})$ and $N((\tau^m - 1)/(\tau - 1)) = n$.

  (v) The norm function is multiplicative; that is, $N(\alpha_1\alpha_2) = N(\alpha_1)N(\alpha_2)$ for all $\alpha_1, \alpha_2 \in \mathbb{Z}[\tau]$.

 (vi) $\mathbb{Z}[\tau]$ is a Euclidean domain with respect to the norm function. That is, for any $\alpha, \beta \in \mathbb{Z}[\tau]$ with $\beta \neq 0$, there exist $\kappa, \rho \in \mathbb{Z}[\tau]$ (not necessarily unique) such that $\alpha = \kappa\beta + \rho$ and $N(\rho) < N(\beta)$.

τ-adic non-adjacent form (TNAF)

It follows from Theorem 3.57 that any positive integer k can be written in the form $k = \sum_{i=0}^{l-1} u_i\tau^i$ where each $u_i \in \{0, \pm 1\}$. Such a τ-*adic representation* can be obtained by repeatedly dividing k by τ; the digits u_i are the remainders of the division steps. This procedure is analogous to the derivation of the binary representation of k by repeated division by 2. In order to decrease the number of point additions in (3.33), it is desirable to obtain a τ-adic representation for k that has a small number of nonzero digits. This can be achieved by using the τ-adic NAF, which can be viewed as a τ-adic analogue of the ordinary NAF (Definition 3.28).

Definition 3.58 A τ-*adic NAF* or *TNAF* of a nonzero element $\kappa \in \mathbb{Z}[\tau]$ is an expression $\kappa = \sum_{i=0}^{l-1} u_i \tau^i$ where each $u_i \in \{0, \pm 1\}$, $u_{l-1} \neq 0$, and no two consecutive digits u_i are nonzero. The *length* of the TNAF is l.

Theorem 3.59 (*properties of TNAFs*) Let $\kappa \in \mathbb{Z}[\tau]$, $\kappa \neq 0$.

(i) κ has a unique TNAF denoted $\text{TNAF}(\kappa)$.

(ii) If the length $l(\kappa)$ of $\text{TNAF}(\kappa)$ is greater than 30, then

$$\log_2(N(\kappa)) - 0.55 < l(\kappa) < \log_2(N(\kappa)) + 3.52.$$

(iii) The average density of nonzero digits among all TNAFs of length l is approximately $1/3$.

$\text{TNAF}(\kappa)$ can be efficiently computed using Algorithm 3.61, which can be viewed as a τ-adic analogue of Algorithm 3.30. The digits of $\text{TNAF}(\kappa)$ are generated by repeatedly dividing κ by τ, allowing remainders of 0 or ± 1. If κ is not divisible by τ, then the remainder $r \in \{-1, 1\}$ is chosen so that the quotient $(\kappa - r)/\tau$ is divisible by τ, ensuring that the next TNAF digit is 0. Division of $\alpha \in \mathbb{Z}[\tau]$ by τ and τ^2 is easily accomplished using the following result.

Theorem 3.60 (*division by τ and τ^2 in $\mathbb{Z}[\tau]$*) Let $\alpha = r_0 + r_1 \tau \in \mathbb{Z}[\tau]$.

(i) α is divisible by τ if and only if r_0 is even. If r_0 is even, then

$$\alpha/\tau = (r_1 + \mu r_0/2) - (r_0/2)\tau.$$

(ii) α is divisible by τ^2 if and only if $r_0 \equiv 2r_1 \pmod 4$.

Algorithm 3.61 Computing the TNAF of an element in $\mathbb{Z}[\tau]$

INPUT: $\kappa = r_0 + r_1 \tau \in \mathbb{Z}[\tau]$.
OUTPUT: $\text{TNAF}(\kappa)$.
  1. $i \leftarrow 0$.
  2. While $r_0 \neq 0$ or $r_1 \neq 0$ do
     2.1 If r_0 is odd then: $u_i \leftarrow 2 - (r_0 - 2r_1 \bmod 4)$, $r_0 \leftarrow r_0 - u_i$;
     2.2 Else: $u_i \leftarrow 0$.
     2.3 $t \leftarrow r_0$, $r_0 \leftarrow r_1 + \mu r_0/2$, $r_1 \leftarrow -t/2$, $i \leftarrow i + 1$.
  3. Return$(u_{i-1}, u_{i-2}, \ldots, u_1, u_0)$.

To compute kP, one can find $\text{TNAF}(k)$ using Algorithm 3.61 and then use (3.33). By Theorem 3.59(ii), the length of $\text{TNAF}(k)$ is approximately $\log_2(N(k)) = 2\log_2 k$, which is twice the length of $\text{NAF}(k)$. To circumvent the problem of a long TNAF, notice that if $\gamma \equiv k \pmod{\tau^m - 1}$ then $kP = \gamma P$ for all $P \in E_a(\mathbb{F}_{2^m})$. This follows because

$$(\tau^m - 1)(P) = \tau^m(P) - P = P - P = \infty.$$

It can also be shown that if $\rho \equiv k \pmod{\delta}$ where $\delta = (\tau^m - 1)/(\tau - 1)$, then $kP = \rho P$ for all points P of order n in $E_a(\mathbb{F}_{2^m})$. The strategy now is to find $\rho \in \mathbb{Z}[\tau]$ of as small norm as possible with $\rho \equiv k \pmod{\delta}$, and then use $\text{TNAF}(\rho)$ to compute ρP. Algorithm 3.62 finds, for any $\alpha, \beta \in \mathbb{Z}[\tau]$ with $\beta \neq 0$, a quotient $\kappa \in \mathbb{Z}[\tau]$ and a remainder $\rho \in \mathbb{Z}[\tau]$ with $\alpha = \kappa\beta + \rho$ and $N(\rho)$ as small as possible. It uses, as a subroutine, Algorithm 3.63 for finding an element of $\mathbb{Z}[\tau]$ that is "close" to a given complex number $\lambda_0 + \lambda_1 \tau$ with $\lambda_0, \lambda_1 \in \mathbb{Q}$.

Algorithm 3.62 Division in $\mathbb{Z}[\tau]$

INPUT: $\alpha = a_0 + a_1 \tau \in \mathbb{Z}[\tau]$, $\beta = b_0 + b_1 \tau \in \mathbb{Z}[\tau]$ with $\beta \neq 0$.
OUTPUT: $\kappa = q_0 + q_1 \tau$, $\rho = r_0 + r_1 \tau \in \mathbb{Z}[\tau]$ with $\alpha = \kappa\beta + \rho$ and $N(\rho) \leq \frac{4}{7}N(\beta)$.
  1. $g_0 \leftarrow a_0 b_0 + \mu a_0 b_1 + 2a_1 b_1$,
  2. $g_1 \leftarrow a_1 b_0 - a_0 b_1$.
  3. $N \leftarrow b_0^2 + \mu b_0 b_1 + 2b_1^2$.
  4. $\lambda_0 \leftarrow g_0/N$, $\lambda_1 \leftarrow g_1/N$.
  5. Use Algorithm 3.63 to compute $(q_0, q_1) \leftarrow \text{Round}(\lambda_0, \lambda_1)$.
  6. $r_0 \leftarrow a_0 - b_0 q_0 + 2b_1 q_1$,
  7. $r_1 \leftarrow a_1 - b_1 q_0 - b_0 q_1 - \mu b_1 q_1$.
  8. $\kappa \leftarrow q_0 + q_1 \tau$,
  9. $\rho \leftarrow r_0 + r_1 \tau$.
 10. Return(κ, ρ).

Algorithm 3.63 Rounding off in $\mathbb{Z}[\tau]$

INPUT: Rational numbers λ_0 and λ_1.
OUTPUT: Integers q_0, q_1 such that $q_0 + q_1 \tau$ is close to complex number $\lambda_0 + \lambda_1 \tau$.
  1. For i from 0 to 1 do
     1.1 $f_i \leftarrow \lfloor \lambda_i + \frac{1}{2} \rfloor$, $\eta_i \leftarrow \lambda_i - f_i$, $h_i \leftarrow 0$.
  2. $\eta \leftarrow 2\eta_0 + \mu\eta_1$.
  3. If $\eta \geq 1$ then
     3.1 If $\eta_0 - 3\mu\eta_1 < -1$ then $h_1 \leftarrow \mu$; else $h_0 \leftarrow 1$.
    Else
     3.2 If $\eta_0 + 4\mu\eta_1 \geq 2$ then $h_1 \leftarrow \mu$.
  4. If $\eta < -1$ then
     4.1 If $\eta_0 - 3\mu\eta_1 \geq 1$ then $h_1 \leftarrow -\mu$; else $h_0 \leftarrow -1$.
    Else
     4.2 If $\eta_0 + 4\mu\eta_1 < -2$ then $h_1 \leftarrow -\mu$.
  5. $q_0 \leftarrow f_0 + h_0$, $q_1 \leftarrow f_1 + h_1$.
  6. Return(q_0, q_1).

Definition 3.64 Let $\alpha, \beta \in \mathbb{Z}[\tau]$ with $\beta \neq 0$. Then $\alpha \bmod \beta$ is defined to be the output $\rho \in \mathbb{Z}[\tau]$ of Algorithm 3.62.

Algorithm 3.62 for computing $\rho = k \bmod \delta$ is cumbersome to implement on some platforms because it requires two multiprecision integer divisions (in step 4). Algorithm 3.65 computes an element $\rho' \equiv k \pmod{\delta}$ without the expensive multiprecision integer divisions. We write $\rho' = k$ partmod δ. Solinas proved that $l(\rho) \leq m + a$ and if $C \geq 2$ then $l(\rho') \leq m + a + 3$. However, it is still possible that $l(\rho')$ is significantly bigger than $l(\rho)$. This is not a concern in practice since the probability that $\rho' \neq \rho$ is less than $2^{-(C-5)}$—hence selection of a sufficiently large C ensures $\rho' = \rho$ with overwhelming probability.

Algorithm 3.65 Partial reduction modulo $\delta = (\tau^m - 1)/(\tau - 1)$

INPUT: $k \in [1, n-1]$, $C \geq 2$, $s_0 = d_0 + \mu d_1$, $s_1 = -d_1$, where $\delta = d_0 + d_1 \tau$.
OUTPUT: $\rho' = k$ partmod δ.

1. $k' \leftarrow \lfloor k/2^{a-C+(m-9)/2} \rfloor$.
2. $V_m \leftarrow 2^m + 1 - \#E_a(\mathbb{F}_{2^m})$.
3. For i from 0 to 1 do
      3.1 $g' \leftarrow s_i \cdot k'$. $j' \leftarrow V_m \cdot \lfloor g'/2^m \rfloor$.
      3.2 $\lambda_i \leftarrow \lfloor (g' + j')/2^{(m+5)/2} + \frac{1}{2} \rfloor / 2^C$.
4. Use Algorithm 3.63 to compute $(q_0, q_1) \leftarrow \text{Round}(\lambda_0, \lambda_1)$.
5. $r_0 \leftarrow k - (s_0 + \mu s_1)q_0 - 2s_1 q_1$, $r_1 \leftarrow s_1 q_0 - s_0 q_1$.
6. Return$(r_0 + r_1 \tau)$.

3.4.2 Point multiplication

Algorithm 3.66 is an efficient point multiplication method that incorporates the ideas of the preceding subsection. Since the length of TNAF(ρ') is approximately m, and since its density is expected to be about $1/3$, Algorithm 3.66 has an expected running time of approximately

$$\frac{m}{3}A. \tag{3.34}$$

Algorithm 3.66 TNAF method for point multiplication on Koblitz curves

---

INPUT: Integer $k \in [1, n-1]$, $P \in E(\mathbb{F}_{2^m})$ of order n.
OUTPUT: kP.

1. Use Algorithm 3.65 to compute $\rho' = k$ partmod δ.
2. Use Algorithm 3.61 to compute TNAF$(\rho') = \sum_{i=0}^{l-1} u_i \tau^i$.
3. $Q \leftarrow \infty$.
4. For i from $l-1$ downto 0 do
      4.1 $Q \leftarrow \tau Q$.
      4.2 If $u_i = 1$ then $Q \leftarrow Q + P$.
      4.3 If $u_i = -1$ then $Q \leftarrow Q - P$.
5. Return(Q).

Window methods

If some extra memory is available, the running time of Algorithm 3.66 can be decreased by deploying a window method which processes w digits of ρ' at a time. This is achieved by using a width-w TNAF, which can be viewed as a τ-adic analogue of the ordinary width-w NAF (Definition 3.32).

Theorem 3.67 Let $\{U_k\}$ be the integer sequence defined by $U_0 = 0$, $U_1 = 1$, $U_{k+1} = \mu U_k - 2U_{k-1}$ for $k \geq 1$.

(i) $U_k^2 - \mu U_{k-1} U_k + 2U_{k-1}^2 = 2^{k-1}$ for all $k \geq 1$.

(ii) Let $t_k = 2U_{k-1} U_k^{-1} \bmod 2^k$ for $k \geq 1$. (Since U_k is odd for each $k \geq 1$, $U_k^{-1} \bmod 2^k$ does indeed exist.) Then $t_k^2 + 2 \equiv \mu t_k \pmod{2^k}$ for all $k \geq 1$.

From (3.32) and Theorem 3.67(ii), it follows that the map $\phi_w : \mathbb{Z}[\tau] \to \mathbb{Z}_{2^w}$ induced by $\tau \mapsto t_w$ is a surjective ring homomorphism with kernel $\{\alpha \in \mathbb{Z}[\tau] : \tau^w \text{ divides } \alpha\}$. Moreover, a set of distinct representatives of the equivalence classes of $\mathbb{Z}[\tau]$ modulo τ^w is $\{0, \pm 1, \pm 2, \pm 3, \ldots, \pm(2^{w-1} - 1), -2^{w-1}\}$, of which $\{\pm 1, \pm 3, \ldots, \pm(2^{w-1} - 1)\}$ are not divisible by τ.

Definition 3.68 Let $w \geq 2$ be a positive integer. Define $\alpha_i = i \bmod \tau^w$ for $i \in \{1, 3, 5, \ldots, 2^{w-1} - 1\}$. A *width-$w$ TNAF* of a nonzero element $\kappa \in \mathbb{Z}[\tau]$ is an expression $\kappa = \sum_{i=0}^{l-1} u_i \tau^i$ where each $u_i \in \{0, \pm\alpha_1, \pm\alpha_3, \ldots, \pm\alpha_{2^{w-1}-1}\}$, $u_{l-1} \neq 0$, and at most one of any w consecutive digits is nonzero. The *length* of the width-w TNAF is l.

Note that $\text{TNAF}_2(\kappa) = \text{TNAF}(\kappa)$. Tables 3.9 and 3.10 list the α_u's for $a \in \{0, 1\}$ and $3 \leq w \leq 6$. The expressions given for each α_u has at most two terms that involve powers of τ and other α_u's. $\text{TNAF}(\alpha_u) = (u_{l-1}, \ldots, u_1, u_0)$ is understood to mean $\sum_{i=0}^{l-1} u_i \tau^i$. Most of the entries in the last columns of the tables were obtained from the TNAF; a few exceptions were made where use of the TNAF is less efficient. With these expressions, each $\alpha_u P$ can be computed using at most one elliptic curve addition operation.

$\text{TNAF}_w(\rho)$ can be efficiently computed using Algorithm 3.69. In Algorithm 3.69, $k \bmod s \, 2^w$ denotes the integer u satisfying $u \equiv k \pmod{2^w}$ and $-2^{w-1} \leq u < 2^{w-1}$. The digits of $\text{TNAF}_w(\rho)$ are obtained by repeatedly dividing ρ by τ, allowing remainders γ in $\{0, \pm\alpha_1, \pm\alpha_3 \ldots, \pm\alpha_{2^{w-1}-1}\}$. If ρ is not divisible by τ and the remainder chosen is α_u where $u = \phi_w(\rho) \bmod s \, 2^w$, then $(\rho - \alpha_u)/\tau$ will be divisible by τ^{w-1}, ensuring that the next $w - 1$ digits are 0.

w	u	$u \bmod \tau^w$	TNAF($u \bmod \tau^w$)	α_u
3	1	1	(1)	1
	3	$\tau+1$	$(-1,0,-1)$	$\tau+1$
4	1	1	(1)	1
	3	$-\tau-3$	$(1,0,-1)$	τ^2-1
	5	$-\tau-1$	$(1,0,1)$	τ^2+1
	7	$-\tau+1$	$(1,0,0,-1)$	τ^3-1
5	1	1	(1)	1
	3	$-\tau-3$	$(1,0,-1)$	τ^2-1
	5	$-\tau-1$	$(1,0,1)$	τ^2+1
	7	$-\tau+1$	$(1,0,0,-1)$	τ^3-1
	9	$-2\tau-3$	$(1,0,1,0,0,1)$	$\tau^3\alpha_5+1$
	11	$-2\tau-1$	$(-1,0,-1,0,-1)$	$-\tau^2\alpha_5-1$
	13	$-2\tau+1$	$(-1,0,-1,0,1)$	$-\tau^2\alpha_5+1$
	15	$3\tau+1$	$(1,0,0,0,-1)$	$\tau^2\alpha_5-\alpha_5$
6	1	1	(1)	1
	3	3	$(-1,0,0,1,0,-1)$	$\tau^2\alpha_{25}-1$
	5	5	$(-1,0,0,1,0,1)$	$\tau^2\alpha_{25}+1$
	7	$-2\tau-5$	$(1,0,1,0,0,-1)$	$-\tau^3\alpha_{27}-1$
	9	$-2\tau-3$	$(1,0,1,0,0,1)$	$-\tau^3\alpha_{27}+1$
	11	$-2\tau-1$	$(-1,0,-1,0,-1)$	$\tau^2\alpha_{27}-1$
	13	$-2\tau+1$	$(-1,0,-1,0,1)$	$\tau^2\alpha_{27}+1$
	15	$3\tau+1$	$(1,0,0,0,-1)$	$-\tau^2\alpha_{27}+\alpha_{27}$
	17	$3\tau+3$	$(1,0,0,0,1)$	$-\tau^2\alpha_{27}+\alpha_{29}$
	19	$3\tau+5$	$(1,0,0,-1,0,1,0,-1)$	$-\tau^2\alpha_3-1$
	21	$-4\tau-3$	$(-1,0,1,0,1)$	$\tau^2\alpha_{29}+1$
	23	$\tau-3$	$(-1,0,0,-1)$	$-\tau^3-1$
	25	$\tau-1$	$(-1,0,0,1)$	$-\tau^3+1$
	27	$\tau+1$	$(-1,0,-1)$	$-\tau^2-1$
	29	$\tau+3$	$(-1,0,1)$	$-\tau^2+1$
	31	$\tau+5$	$(-1,0,0,0,0,-1)$	$\tau^2\alpha_{25}+\alpha_{27}$

Table 3.9. Expressions for $\alpha_u = u \bmod \tau^w$ for $a=0$ and $3 \le w \le 6$.

w	u	$u \bmod \tau^w$	TNAF($u \bmod \tau^w$)	α_u
3	1	1	(1)	1
	3	$-\tau+1$	$(-1,0,-1)$	$-\tau+1$
4	1	1	(1)	1
	3	$\tau-3$	$(1,0,-1)$	τ^2-1
	5	$\tau-1$	$(1,0,1)$	τ^2+1
	7	$\tau+1$	$(-1,0,0,-1)$	$-\tau^3-1$
5	1	1	(1)	1
	3	$\tau-3$	$(1,0,-1)$	τ^2-1
	5	$\tau-1$	$(1,0,1)$	τ^2+1
	7	$\tau+1$	$(-1,0,0,-1)$	$-\tau^3-1$
	9	$2\tau-3$	$(-1,0,-1,0,0,1)$	$-\tau^3\alpha_5+1$
	11	$2\tau-1$	$(-1,0,-1,0,-1)$	$-\tau^2\alpha_5-1$
	13	$2\tau+1$	$(-1,0,-1,0,1)$	$-\tau^2\alpha_5+1$
	15	$-3\tau+1$	$(1,0,0,0,-1)$	$\tau^2\alpha_5-\alpha_5$
6	1	1	(1)	1
	3	3	$(1,0,0,1,0,-1)$	$\tau^2\alpha_{25}-1$
	5	5	$(1,0,0,1,0,1)$	$\tau^2\alpha_{25}+1$
	7	$2\tau-5$	$(-1,0,-1,0,0,-1)$	$\tau^3\alpha_{27}-1$
	9	$2\tau-3$	$(-1,0,-1,0,0,1)$	$\tau^3\alpha_{27}+1$
	11	$2\tau-1$	$(-1,0,-1,0,-1)$	$\tau^2\alpha_{27}-1$
	13	$2\tau+1$	$(-1,0,-1,0,1)$	$\tau^2\alpha_{27}+1$
	15	$-3\tau+1$	$(1,0,0,0,-1)$	$-\tau^2\alpha_{27}+\alpha_{27}$
	17	$-3\tau+3$	$(1,0,0,0,1)$	$-\tau^2\alpha_{27}+\alpha_{29}$
	19	$-3\tau+5$	$(-1,0,0,-1,0,1,0,-1)$	$-\tau^2\alpha_3-1$
	21	$4\tau-3$	$(-1,0,1,0,1)$	$\tau^2\alpha_{29}+1$
	23	$-\tau-3$	$(1,0,0,-1)$	τ^3-1
	25	$-\tau-1$	$(1,0,0,1)$	τ^3+1
	27	$-\tau+1$	$(-1,0,-1)$	$-\tau^2-1$
	29	$-\tau+3$	$(-1,0,1)$	$-\tau^2+1$
	31	$-\tau+5$	$(1,0,0,0,0,-1)$	$\tau^2\alpha_{25}+\alpha_{27}$

Table 3.10. Expressions for $\alpha_u = u \bmod \tau^w$ for $a = 1$ and $3 \leq w \leq 6$.

Algorithm 3.69 Computing a width-w TNAF of an element in $\mathbb{Z}[\tau]$

INPUT: $w, t_w, \alpha_u = \beta_u + \gamma_u \tau$ for $u \in \{1, 3, 5, \ldots, 2^{w-1} - 1\}$, $\rho = r_0 + r_1 \tau \in \mathbb{Z}[\tau]$.
OUTPUT: $\text{TNAF}_w(\rho)$.

1. $i \leftarrow 0$.
2. While $r_0 \neq 0$ or $r_1 \neq 0$ do
   2.1 If r_0 is odd then
   $\qquad u \leftarrow r_0 + r_1 t_w \text{ mods } 2^w$.
   $\qquad$ If $u > 0$ then $s \leftarrow 1$; else $s \leftarrow -1$, $u \leftarrow -u$.
   $\qquad r_0 \leftarrow r_0 - s\beta_u$, $r_1 \leftarrow r_1 - s\gamma_u$, $u_i \leftarrow s\alpha_u$.
   2.2 Else: $u_i \leftarrow 0$.
   2.3 $t \leftarrow r_0$, $r_0 \leftarrow r_1 + \mu r_0/2$, $r_1 \leftarrow -t/2$, $i \leftarrow i + 1$.
3. Return($u_{i-1}, u_{i-2}, \ldots, u_1, u_0$).

Algorithm 3.70 is an efficient point multiplication algorithm that uses the width-w TNAF. Since the expected length of $\text{TNAF}(\rho')$ is m, and since its density is expected to be about $1/(w+1)$, Algorithm 3.70 has an expected running time of approximately

$$\left(2^{w-2} - 1 + \frac{m}{w+1} \right) A. \tag{3.35}$$

Algorithm 3.70 Window TNAF point multiplication method for Koblitz curves

---

INPUT: Window width w, integer $k \in [1, n-1]$, $P \in E(\mathbb{F}_{2^m})$ of order n.
OUTPUT: kP.

1. Use Algorithm 3.65 to compute $\rho' = k$ partmod δ.
2. Use Algorithm 3.69 to compute $\text{TNAF}_w(\rho') = \sum_{i=0}^{l-1} u_i \tau^i$.
3. Compute $P_u = \alpha_u P$, for $u \in \{1, 3, 5, \ldots, 2^{w-1} - 1\}$.
4. $Q \leftarrow \infty$.
5. For i from $l - 1$ downto 0 do
   5.1 $Q \leftarrow \tau Q$.
   5.2 If $u_i \neq 0$ then:
   $\qquad$ Let u be such that $\alpha_u = u_i$ or $\alpha_{-u} = -u_i$.
   $\qquad$ If $u > 0$ then $Q \leftarrow Q + P_u$;
   $\qquad$ Else $Q \leftarrow Q - P_{-u}$.
6. Return(Q).

3.5 *Curves with efficiently computable endomorphisms*

The Frobenius map (Definition 3.55) is an example of an endomorphism of an elliptic curve. This section presents a general technique for accelerating point multiplication on elliptic curves that have efficiently computable endomorphisms. While the technique does not yield a speedup that is as dramatic as achieved in §3.4 for Koblitz curves (where all the point doublings are replaced by much faster applications of the Frobenius map), it can be used to accelerate point multiplication on a larger class of curves including some elliptic curves over large prime fields. Roughly speaking, if the endomorphism can be computed in no more time than it takes to perform a small number of point doublings, then the technique eliminates about half of all doublings and reduces the point multiplication time by roughly 33%.

Endomorphisms of elliptic curves

Let E be an elliptic curve defined over a field K. The set of all points on E whose coordinates lie in any finite extension of K is also denoted by E. An *endomorphism* ϕ of E over K is a map $\phi : E \to E$ such that $\phi(\infty) = \infty$ and $\phi(P) = (g(P), h(P))$ for all $P \in E$, where g and h are rational functions whose coefficients lie in K. The set of all endomorphisms of E over K forms a ring, called the *endomorphism ring* of E over K. An endomorphism ϕ is also a group homomorphism, that is,

$$\phi(P_1 + P_2) = \phi(P_1) + \phi(P_2) \text{ for all } P_1, P_2 \in E.$$

The *characteristic polynomial* of an endomorphism ϕ is the monic polynomial $f(X)$ of least degree in $\mathbb{Z}[X]$ such that $f(\phi) = 0$, that is, $f(\phi)(P) = \infty$ for all $P \in E$. If E is a non-supersingular elliptic curve, then the characteristic polynomial of ϕ has degree 1 or 2.

Example 3.71 (*endomorphisms of elliptic curves*)

    (i) Let E be an elliptic curve defined over $\mathbb{F}_q$. For each integer m, the *multiplication by m map* $[m] : E \to E$ defined by

$$[m] : P \mapsto mP$$

    is an endomorphism of E defined over $\mathbb{F}_q$. A special case is the *negation* map defined by $P \mapsto -P$. The characteristic polynomial of $[m]$ is $X - m$.

    (ii) Let E be an elliptic curve defined over $\mathbb{F}_q$. Then the q-th power map $\phi : E \to E$ defined by

$$\phi : (x, y) \mapsto (x^q, y^q), \quad \phi : \infty \mapsto \infty$$

    is an endomorphism of E defined over $\mathbb{F}_q$, called the *Frobenius endomorphism*. The characteristic polynomial of ϕ is $X^2 - tX + q$, where $t = q + 1 - \#E(\mathbb{F}_q)$.

    (iii) Let $p \equiv 1 \pmod 4$ be a prime, and consider the elliptic curve

$$E : y^2 = x^3 + ax$$

    defined over $\mathbb{F}_p$. Let $i \in \mathbb{F}_p$ be an element of order 4. Then the map $\phi : E \to E$ defined by

$$\phi : (x, y) \mapsto (-x, iy), \quad \phi : \infty \mapsto \infty$$

is an endomorphism of E defined over $\mathbb{F}_p$. Note that $\phi(P)$ can be computed using only one multiplication. The characteristic polynomial of ϕ is $X^2 + 1$.

(iv) Let $p \equiv 1 \pmod 3$ be a prime, and consider the elliptic curve

$$E : y^2 = x^3 + b$$

defined over $\mathbb{F}_p$. Let $\beta \in \mathbb{F}_p$ be an element of order 3. Then the map $\phi : E \to E$ defined by

$$\phi : (x, y) \mapsto (\beta x, y), \qquad \phi : \infty \mapsto \infty$$

is an endomorphism of E defined over $\mathbb{F}_p$. Note that $\phi(P)$ can be computed using only one multiplication. The characteristic polynomial of ϕ is $X^2 + X + 1$.

Note 3.72 (*integer representation of an endomorphism*) Suppose now that E is an elliptic curve defined over the finite field $\mathbb{F}_q$. Suppose also that $\#E(\mathbb{F}_q)$ is divisible by a prime n, and that n^2 does not divide $\#E(\mathbb{F}_q)$. Then $E(\mathbb{F}_q)$ contains exactly one subgroup of order n; let this subgroup be $\langle P \rangle$ where $P \in E(\mathbb{F}_q)$ has order n. If ϕ is an endomorphism of E defined over $\mathbb{F}_q$, then $\phi(P) \in E(\mathbb{F}_q)$ and hence $\phi(P) \in \langle P \rangle$. Suppose that $\phi(P) \neq \infty$. Then we can write

$$\phi(P) = \lambda P \text{ for some } \lambda \in [1, n-1].$$

In fact λ is a root modulo n of the characteristic polynomial of ϕ.

Example 3.73 (*the elliptic curve P-160*) Consider the elliptic curve

$$E : y^2 = x^3 + 3$$

defined over the 160-bit prime field $\mathbb{F}_p$, where

$$p = 2^{160} - 229233$$
$$= 1461501637330902918203684832716283019655932313743.$$

Since $p \equiv 1 \pmod 3$, the curve is of the type described in Example 3.71(iv). The group of $\mathbb{F}_p$-rational points on E has prime order

$$\#E(\mathbb{F}_p) = n = 1461501637330902918203687013445034429194588307251.$$

An element of order 3 in $\mathbb{F}_p$ is

$$\beta = 771473166210819779552257112796337671037538143582$$

and so the map $\phi : E \to E$ defined by $\phi : \infty \mapsto \infty$ and $\phi : (x, y) \mapsto (\beta x, y)$ is an endomorphism of E defined over $\mathbb{F}_p$. The solution

$$\lambda = 903860042511079968555273866340564498116022318806$$

to the equation $\lambda^2 + \lambda + 1 \equiv 0 \pmod n$ has the property that $\phi(P) = \lambda P$ for all $P \in E(\mathbb{F}_p)$.

Accelerating point multiplication

The strategy for computing kP, where $k \in [0, n-1]$, is the following. First write

$$k = k_1 + k_2\lambda \bmod n \qquad (3.36)$$

where the integers k_1 and k_2 are of approximately half the bitlength of k. Such an expression is called a *balanced length-two representation of k*. Since

$$\begin{aligned} kP &= k_1 P + k_2 \lambda P \\ &= k_1 P + k_2 \phi(P), \end{aligned} \qquad (3.37)$$

kP can be obtained by first computing $\phi(P)$ and then using simultaneous multiple point multiplication (Algorithm 3.48) or interleaving (Algorithm 3.51) to evaluate (3.37). Since k_1 and k_2 are of half the bitlength of k, half of the point doublings are eliminated. The strategy is effective provided that a decomposition (3.36) and $\phi(P)$ can be computed efficiently.

Decomposing a multiplier

We describe one method for obtaining a balanced length-two representation of the multiplier k. For a vector $v = (a, b) \in \mathbb{Z} \times \mathbb{Z}$, define

$$f(v) = a + b\lambda \bmod n.$$

The idea is to first find two vectors, $v_1 = (a_1, b_1)$ and $v_2 = (a_2, b_2)$ in $\mathbb{Z} \times \mathbb{Z}$ such that

1. v_1 and v_2 are linearly independent over $\mathbb{R}$;
2. $f(v_1) = f(v_2) = 0$; and
3. v_1 and v_2 have small Euclidean norm (i.e., $\|v_1\| = \sqrt{a_1^2 + b_1^2} \approx \sqrt{n}$, and similarly for v_2).

Then, by considering $(k, 0)$ as a vector in $\mathbb{Q} \times \mathbb{Q}$, we can use elementary linear algebra to write

$$(k, 0) = \gamma_1 v_1 + \gamma_2 v_2, \text{ where } \gamma_1, \gamma_2 \in \mathbb{Q}.$$

If we let $c_1 = \lfloor \gamma_1 \rceil$ and $c_2 = \lfloor \gamma_2 \rceil$, where $\lfloor x \rceil$ denotes the integer closest to x, then $v = c_1 v_1 + c_2 v_2$ is an integer-valued vector close to $(k, 0)$ such that $f(v) = 0$. Thus the vector $u = (k, 0) - v$ has small norm and satisfies $f(u) = k$. It follows that the components k_1, k_2 of u are small in absolute value and satisfy $k_1 + k_2\lambda \equiv k \pmod{n}$.

The independent short vectors v_1 and v_2 satisfying $f(v_1) = f(v_2) = 0$ can be found by applying the extended Euclidean algorithm (Algorithm 2.19) to n and λ. The algorithm produces a sequences of equations $s_i n + t_i \lambda = r_i$ where $s_0 = 1$, $t_0 = 0$, $r_0 = n$, $s_1 = 0$, $t_1 = 1$, $r_1 = \lambda$. Furthermore, it is easy to show that the remainders r_i are strictly decreasing and non-negative, that $|t_i| < |t_{i+1}|$ for $i \geq 0$, and that $|s_i| < |s_{i+1}|$ and

$r_{i-1}|t_i| + r_i|t_{i-1}| = n$ for $i \geq 1$. Now, let l be the greatest index for which $r_l \geq \sqrt{n}$. Then it can be easily verified that $v_1 = (r_{l+1}, -t_{l+1})$ satisfies $f(v_1) = 0$ and $||v_1|| \leq \sqrt{2n}$, and that $v_2 = (r_l, -t_l)$ (and also $v_2 = (r_{l+2}, -t_{l+2})$) is linearly independent of v_1 and satisfies $f(v_2) = 0$. Heuristically, we would expect v_2 to have small norm. Thus v_1 and v_2 satisfy conditions 1–3 above. For this choice of v_1, v_2, we have $\gamma_1 = b_2 k/n$ and $\gamma_2 = -b_1 k/n$. The method for decomposing k is summarized in Algorithm 3.74.

Algorithm 3.74 Balanced length-two representation of a multiplier

---

INPUT: Integers n, λ, $k \in [0, n-1]$.
OUTPUT: Integers k_1, k_2 such that $k = k_1 + k_2\lambda \mod n$ and $|k_1|, |k_2| \approx \sqrt{n}$.

1. Run the extended Euclidean algorithm (Algorithm 2.19) with inputs n and λ. The algorithm produces a sequence of equations $s_i n + t_i \lambda = r_i$ where $s_0 = 1$, $t_0 = 0$, $r_0 = n$, $s_1 = 0$, $t_1 = 1$, $r_1 = \lambda$, and the remainders r_i and are non-negative and strictly decreasing. Let l be the greatest index for which $r_l \geq \sqrt{n}$.
2. Set $(a_1, b_1) \leftarrow (r_{l+1}, -t_{l+1})$.
3. If $(r_l^2 + t_l^2) \leq (r_{l+2}^2 + t_{l+2}^2)$ then set $(a_2, b_2) \leftarrow (r_l, -t_l)$;
   Else set $(a_2, b_2) \leftarrow (r_{l+2}, -t_{l+2})$.
4. Compute $c_1 = \lfloor b_2 k/n \rceil$ and $c_2 = \lfloor -b_1 k/n \rceil$.
5. Compute $k_1 = k - c_1 a_1 - c_2 a_2$ and $k_2 = -c_1 b_1 - c_2 b_2$.
6. Return(k_1, k_2).

Example 3.75 (*balanced length-two representation of a multiplier k*) Consider the elliptic curve P-160 defined in Example 3.73. In the notation of Algorithm 3.74 we have

$$(r_l, t_l) = (2180728751409538655993509, -1860295391676851199353061)$$
$$(r_{l+1}, t_{l+1}) = (788919430192407951782190, 602889891024722752429129)$$
$$(r_{l+2}, t_{l+2}) = (602889891024722752429129, -1391809321217130704211319)$$
$$(a_1, b_1) = (788919430192407951782190, -602889891024722752429129)$$
$$(a_2, b_2) = (602889891024722752429129, 1391809321217130704211319).$$

Now, let

$$k = 965486288327218559097909069724275579360008398257.$$

We obtain

$$c_1 = 919446671339517233512759, \quad c_2 = 398276613783683332374156$$

and

$$k_1 = -98093723971803846754077, \quad k_2 = 381880690058693066485147.$$

Example 3.76 (*balanced representation for special parameters*) The elliptic curve can be chosen so that the parameters k_1 and k_2 may be obtained with much less effort than that required by Algorithm 3.74. For example, consider the curve

$$E : y^2 = x^3 - 2$$

over $\mathbb{F}_p$, where $p = 2^{390} + 3$ is prime and, as in Example 3.71(iv), satisfies $p \equiv 1 \pmod{3}$. The group of $\mathbb{F}_p$-rational points on E has order

$$\#E(\mathbb{F}_p) = 2^{390} - 2^{195} + 7 = 63n$$

where n is prime. If

$$\lambda = \frac{2^{195} - 2}{3} \quad \text{and} \quad \beta = 2^{389} + 2^{194} + 1,$$

then β is an element of order 3 in $\mathbb{F}_p$, λ satisfies $\lambda^2 + \lambda + 1 \equiv 0 \pmod{n}$, and $\lambda(x, y) = (\beta x, y)$ for all (x, y) in the order-n subgroup of $E(\mathbb{F}_p)$.

Suppose now that $P = (x, y)$ is in the order-n subgroup of $E(\mathbb{F}_p)$, and $k \in [0, n-1]$ is a multiplier. To find a balanced length-two representation of k, write $k = 2^{195}k_2' + k_1'$ for $k_1' < 2^{195}$. Then

$$kP = (2^{195}k_2' + k_1')P = ((3\lambda + 2)k_2' + k_1')P = \underbrace{(2k_2' + k_1')}_{k_1}P + \underbrace{3k_2'}_{k_2}\lambda P$$

$$= k_1(x, y) + k_2(\beta x, y).$$

The method splits a multiplier $k < n$ of approximately 384 bits into k_1 and k_2 where each is approximately half the bitlength of k. Finally, note that the cost of calculating $\beta x = (2^{389} + 2^{194} + 1)x$ is less than a field multiplication.

Point multiplication algorithm

Given an elliptic curve E defined over a finite field $\mathbb{F}_q$ with a suitable endomorphism ϕ, Algorithm 3.77 calculates the point multiplication kP using the decomposition $k = k_1 + k_2\lambda \bmod n$ and interleaving $k_1 P + k_2\phi(P)$. The expected running time is approximately

$$\left[|\{j : w_j > 2\}|D + \sum_{j=1}^{2}(2^{w_j - 2} - 1)A + C_k + C_\phi \right] + \left[D + \sum_{j=1}^{2} \frac{1}{w_j + 1}A \right] \frac{t}{2} \quad (3.38)$$

where t is the bitlength of n, k_j is written with a width-w_j NAF, C_k denotes the cost of the decomposition of k, and C_ϕ is the cost of finding $\phi(P)$. The storage requirement is $2^{w_1-2} + 2^{w_2-2}$ points.

Since v_1 and v_2 do not depend on k, it is possible to precompute estimates for b_1/n and $-b_2/n$ for use in step 4 of Algorithm 3.74. In this case, only steps 4–6 of Algorithm 3.74 must be performed, and hence the cost C_k is insignificant in the overall point multiplication.

Algorithm 3.77 Point multiplication with efficiently computable endomorphisms

---

INPUT: Integer $k \in [1, n-1]$, $P \in E(\mathbb{F}_q)$, window widths w_1 and w_2, and λ.
OUTPUT: kP.
  1. Use Algorithm 3.74 to find k_1 and k_2 such that $k = k_1 + k_2\lambda \bmod n$.
  2. Calculate $P_2 = \phi(P)$, and let $P_1 = P$.
  3. Use Algorithm 3.30 to compute $\text{NAF}_{w_j}(|k_j|) = \sum_{i=0}^{l_j-1} k_{j,i} 2^i$ for $j = 1, 2$.
  4. Let $l = \max\{l_1, l_2\}$ and define $k_{j,i} = 0$ for $l_j \le i < l$, $1 \le j \le 2$.
  5. If $k_j < 0$, then set $k_{j,i} \leftarrow -k_{j,i}$ for $0 \le i < l_j$, $1 \le j \le 2$.
  6. Compute iP_j for $i \in \{1, 3, \ldots, 2^{w_j-1} - 1\}$, $1 \le j \le 2$.
  7. $Q \leftarrow \infty$.
  8. For i from $l - 1$ downto 0 do
     8.1 $Q \leftarrow 2Q$.
     8.2 For j from 1 to 2 do
          If $k_{j,i} \ne 0$ then
               If $k_{j,i} > 0$ then $Q \leftarrow Q + k_{j,i} P_j$;
               Else $Q \leftarrow Q - |k_{j,i}| P_j$.
  9. Return(Q).

3.6 *Point multiplication using halving*

Point multiplication methods based on point halving share strategy with τ-adic methods on Koblitz curves (§3.4) in the sense that point doubling is replaced by a potentially faster operation. As with the efficiently computable endomorphisms in §3.5, the improvement is not as dramatic as that obtained with methods for Koblitz curves, although halving applies to a wider class of curves.

Point halving was proposed independently by E. Knudsen and R. Schroeppel. We restrict our attention to elliptic curves E over binary fields $\mathbb{F}_{2^m}$ defined by the equation

$$y^2 + xy = x^3 + ax^2 + b$$

where $a, b \in \mathbb{F}_{2^m}$, $b \ne 0$. To simplify the exposition, we assume that $\text{Tr}(a) = 1$ (cf. Theorem 3.18).[2] We further assume that m is prime and that the reduction polynomials

---

[2]The algorithms presented in this section can be modified for binary curves with $\text{Tr}(a) = 0$; however, they are more complicated than the case where $\text{Tr}(a) = 1$.

are trinomials or pentanomials. These properties are satisfied by the five random curves over binary fields recommended by NIST in the FIPS 186-2 standard (see §A.2.2).

Let $P = (x, y)$ be a point on E with $P \neq -P$. From §3.1.2, the (affine) coordinates of $Q = 2P = (u, v)$ can be computed as follows:

$$\lambda = x + y/x \tag{3.39}$$

$$u = \lambda^2 + \lambda + a \tag{3.40}$$

$$v = x^2 + u(\lambda + 1). \tag{3.41}$$

Affine point doubling requires one field multiplication and one field division. With projective coordinates and $a \in \{0, 1\}$, point doubling can be done in four field multiplications. *Point halving* is the following operation: given $Q = (u, v)$, compute $P = (x, y)$ such that $Q = 2P$. Since halving is the reverse operation of doubling, the basic idea for halving is to solve (3.40) for λ, (3.41) for x, and finally (3.39) for y.

When $\mathcal{G}$ is a subgroup of odd order n in E, point doubling and point halving are automorphisms of $\mathcal{G}$. Therefore, given a point $Q \in \mathcal{G}$, one can always find a unique point $P \in \mathcal{G}$ such that $Q = 2P$. §3.6.1 and §3.6.2 describe an efficient algorithm for point halving in $\mathcal{G}$. In §3.6.3, point halving is used to obtain efficient *halve-and-add* methods for point multiplication in cryptographic schemes based on elliptic curves over binary fields.

3.6.1 Point halving

The notion of *trace* plays a central role in deriving an efficient algorithm for point halving.

Definition 3.78 The *trace function* on $\mathbb{F}_{2^m}$ is the function $\mathrm{Tr} : \mathbb{F}_{2^m} \to \mathbb{F}_{2^m}$ defined by $\mathrm{Tr}(c) = c + c^2 + c^{2^2} + \cdots + c^{2^{m-1}}$.

Lemma 3.79 (*properties of the trace function*) Let $c, d \in \mathbb{F}_{2^m}$.

  (i) $\mathrm{Tr}(c) = \mathrm{Tr}(c^2) = \mathrm{Tr}(c)^2$; in particular, $\mathrm{Tr}(c) \in \{0, 1\}$.

 (ii) Trace is linear; that is, $\mathrm{Tr}(c + d) = \mathrm{Tr}(c) + \mathrm{Tr}(d)$.

(iii) If $(u, v) \in \mathcal{G}$, then $\mathrm{Tr}(u) = \mathrm{Tr}(a)$.

Property (iii) follows from (3.40) because

$$\mathrm{Tr}(u) = \mathrm{Tr}(\lambda^2 + \lambda + a) = \mathrm{Tr}(\lambda)^2 + \mathrm{Tr}(\lambda) + \mathrm{Tr}(a) = \mathrm{Tr}(a).$$

Given $Q = (u, v) \in \mathcal{G}$, point halving seeks the unique point $P = (x, y) \in \mathcal{G}$ such that $Q = 2P$. The first step of halving is to find $\lambda = x + y/x$ by solving the equation

$$\widehat{\lambda}^2 + \widehat{\lambda} = u + a \tag{3.42}$$

for $\widehat{\lambda}$. An efficient algorithm for solving (3.42) is presented in §3.6.2. Let $\widehat{\lambda}$ denote the solution of (3.42) obtained from this algorithm. It is easily verified that $\lambda \in \{\widehat{\lambda}, \widehat{\lambda}+1\}$. If $\text{Tr}(a) = 1$, the following result can be used to identify λ.

Theorem 3.80 Let $P = (x, y)$, $Q = (u, v) \in \mathcal{G}$ be such that $Q = 2P$, and denote $\lambda = x + y/x$. Let $\widehat{\lambda}$ be a solution to (3.42), and $t = v + u\widehat{\lambda}$. Suppose that $\text{Tr}(a) = 1$. Then $\widehat{\lambda} = \lambda$ if and only if $\text{Tr}(t) = 0$.

Proof: Recall from (3.41) that $x^2 = v + u(\lambda + 1)$. By Lemma 3.79(iii), we get $\text{Tr}(x) = \text{Tr}(a)$ since $P = (x, y) \in \mathcal{G}$. Thus,

$$\text{Tr}(v + u(\lambda + 1)) = \text{Tr}(x^2) = \text{Tr}(x) = \text{Tr}(a) = 1.$$

Hence, if $\widehat{\lambda} = \lambda + 1$, then $\text{Tr}(t) = \text{Tr}(v + u(\lambda + 1)) = 1$ as required. Otherwise, we must have $\widehat{\lambda} = \lambda$, which gives $\text{Tr}(t) = \text{Tr}(v + u\lambda) = \text{Tr}(v + u((\lambda + 1) + 1))$. Since the trace function is linear,

$$\text{Tr}(v + u((\lambda + 1) + 1)) = \text{Tr}(v + u(\lambda + 1)) + \text{Tr}(u) = 1 + \text{Tr}(u) = 0.$$

Hence, we conclude that $\widehat{\lambda} = \lambda$ if and only if $\text{Tr}(t) = 0$. $\square$

Theorem 3.80 suggests a simple algorithm for identifying λ in the case that $\text{Tr}(a) = 1$. We can then solve $x^2 = v + u(\lambda + 1)$ for the unique root x. §3.6.2 presents efficient algorithms for finding traces and square roots in $\mathbb{F}_{2^m}$. Finally, if needed, $y = \lambda x + x^2$ may be recovered with one field multiplication.

Let the λ-*representation* of a point $Q = (u, v)$ be (u, λ_Q), where

$$\lambda_Q = u + \frac{v}{u}.$$

Given the λ-representation of Q as the input to point halving, we may compute t in Theorem 3.80 without converting to affine coordinates since

$$t = v + u\widehat{\lambda} = u\left(u + u + \frac{v}{u}\right) + u\widehat{\lambda} = u(u + \lambda_Q + \widehat{\lambda}).$$

In point multiplication, repeated halvings may be performed directly on the λ-representation of a point, with conversion to affine only when a point addition is required.

Algorithm 3.81 Point halving

INPUT: λ-representation (u, λ_Q) or affine representation (u, v) of $Q \in \mathcal{G}$.
OUTPUT: λ-representation (x, λ_P) of $P = (x, y) \in \mathcal{G}$, where $Q = 2P$.
   1. Find a solution $\widehat{\lambda}$ of $\widehat{\lambda}^2 + \widehat{\lambda} = u + a$.
   2. If the input is in λ-representation, then compute $t = u(u + \lambda_Q + \widehat{\lambda})$; else, compute $t = v + u\widehat{\lambda}$.
   3. If $\text{Tr}(t) = 0$, then $\lambda_P \leftarrow \widehat{\lambda}$, $x \leftarrow \sqrt{t + u}$; else $\lambda_P \leftarrow \widehat{\lambda} + 1$, $x \leftarrow \sqrt{t}$.
   4. Return (x, λ_P).

3.6.2 Performing point halving efficiently

Point halving requires a field multiplication and three main steps: (i) computing the trace of t; (ii) solving the quadratic equation (3.42); and (iii) computing a square root. In a normal basis, field elements are represented in terms of a basis of the form $\{\beta, \beta^2, \ldots, \beta^{2^{m-1}}\}$. The trace of an element $c = \sum c_i \beta^{2^i} = (c_0, c_1, \ldots, c_{m-1})$ is given by $\text{Tr}(c) = \sum c_i$. The square root computation is a left rotation: $\sqrt{c} = (c_1, \ldots, c_{m-1}, c_0)$. Squaring is a right rotation, and $x^2 + x = c$ can be solved bitwise. These operations are expected to be inexpensive relative to field multiplication. However, field multiplication in software for normal basis representations is very slow in comparison to multiplication with a polynomial basis. Conversion between polynomial and normal bases at each halving appears unlikely to give a competitive method, even if significant storage is used. For these reasons, we restrict our discussion to computations in a polynomial basis representation.

Computing the trace

Let $c = \sum_{i=0}^{m-1} c_i z^i \in \mathbb{F}_{2^m}$, with $c_i \in \{0, 1\}$, represented as the vector $c = (c_{m-1}, \ldots, c_0)$. A primitive method for computing $\text{Tr}(c)$ uses the definition of trace, requiring $m - 1$ field squarings and $m - 1$ field additions. A much more efficient method makes use of the property that the trace is linear:

$$\text{Tr}(c) = \text{Tr}\left(\sum_{i=0}^{m-1} c_i z^i\right) = \sum_{i=0}^{m-1} c_i \text{Tr}(z^i).$$

The values $\text{Tr}(z^i)$ may be precomputed, allowing the trace of an element to be found efficiently, especially if $\text{Tr}(z^i) = 0$ for most i.

Example 3.82 (*computing traces of elements in* $\mathbb{F}_{2^{163}}$) Consider $\mathbb{F}_{2^{163}}$ with reduction polynomial $f(z) = z^{163} + z^7 + z^6 + z^3 + 1$. A routine calculation shows that $\text{Tr}(z^i) = 1$ if and only if $i \in \{0, 157\}$. As examples, $\text{Tr}(z^{160} + z^{46}) = 0$, $\text{Tr}(z^{157} + z^{46}) = 1$, and $\text{Tr}(z^{157} + z^{46} + 1) = 0$.

Solving the quadratic equation

The first step of point halving seeks a solution x of a quadratic equation of the form $x^2 + x = c$ over $\mathbb{F}_{2^m}$. The time performance of this step is crucial in obtaining an efficient point halving.

Definition 3.83 Let m be an odd integer. The *half-trace function* $H : \mathbb{F}_{2^m} \to \mathbb{F}_{2^m}$ is defined by

$$H(c) = \sum_{i=0}^{(m-1)/2} c^{2^{2i}}.$$

Lemma 3.84 (*properties of the half-trace function*) Let m be an odd integer.

(i) $H(c+d) = H(c) + H(d)$ for all $c, d \in \mathbb{F}_{2^m}$.

(ii) $H(c)$ is a solution of the equation $x^2 + x = c + \text{Tr}(c)$.

(iii) $H(c) = H(c^2) + c + \text{Tr}(c)$ for all $c \in \mathbb{F}_{2^m}$.

Let $c = \sum_{i=0}^{m-1} c_i z^i \in \mathbb{F}_{2^m}$ with $\text{Tr}(c) = 0$; in particular, $H(c)$ is a solution of $x^2 + x = c$. A simple method for finding $H(c)$ directly from the definition requires $m-1$ squarings and $(m-1)/2$ additions. If storage for $\{H(z^i) : 0 \le i < m\}$ is available, then Lemma 3.84(i) may be applied to obtain

$$H(c) = H\left(\sum_{i=0}^{m-1} c_i z^i\right) = \sum_{i=0}^{m-1} c_i H(z^i).$$

However, this requires storage for m field elements, and the associated method requires an average of $m/2$ field additions.

Lemma 3.84 can be used to significantly reduce the storage required as well as the time needed to solve the quadratic equation. The basic strategy is to write $H(c) = H(c') + s$ where c' has fewer nonzero coefficients than c. For even i, note that

$$H(z^i) = H(z^{i/2}) + z^{i/2} + \text{Tr}(z^i).$$

Algorithm 3.85 is based on this observation, eliminating storage of $H(z^i)$ for all even i. Precomputation builds a table of $(m-1)/2$ field elements $H(z^i)$ for odd i, and the algorithm is expected to have approximately $m/4$ field additions at step 4. The terms involving $\text{Tr}(z^i)$ and $H(1)$ have been discarded, since it suffices to produce a solution $s \in \{H(c), H(c)+1\}$ of $x^2 + x = c$.

Algorithm 3.85 Solve $x^2 + x = c$ (basic version)

INPUT: $c = \sum_{i=0}^{m-1} c_i z^i \in \mathbb{F}_{2^m}$ where m is odd and $\text{Tr}(c) = 0$.
OUTPUT: A solution s of $x^2 + x = c$.
1. Precompute $H(z^i)$ for odd i, $1 \le i \le m-2$.
2. $s \leftarrow 0$.
3. For i from $(m-1)/2$ downto 1 do
   3.1 If $c_{2i} = 1$ then do: $c \leftarrow c + z^i$, $s \leftarrow s + z^i$.
4. $s \leftarrow s + \sum_{i=1}^{(m-1)/2} c_{2i-1} H(z^{2i-1})$.
5. Return(s).

Further improvements are possible by use of Lemma 3.84 together with the reduction polynomial $f(z)$. Let i be odd, and define j and s by

$$m \le 2^j i = m + s < 2m.$$

The basic idea is to apply Lemma 3.84(iii) j times, obtaining

$$H(z^i) = H(z^{2^j i}) + z^{2^{j-1}i} + \cdots + z^{4i} + z^{2i} + z^i + j\operatorname{Tr}(z^i). \qquad (3.43)$$

Let $f(z) = z^m + r(z)$, where $r(z) = z^{b_\ell} + \cdots + z^{b_1} + 1$ and $0 < b_1 < \cdots < b_\ell < m$. Then

$$H(z^{2^j i}) = H(z^s r(z)) = H(z^{s+b_\ell}) + H(z^{s+b_{\ell-1}}) + \cdots + H(z^{s+b_1}) + H(z^s).$$

Thus, storage for $H(z^i)$ may be exchanged for storage of $H(z^{s+e})$ for $e \in \{0, b_1, \ldots, b_\ell\}$ (some of which may be further reduced). The amount of storage reduction is limited by dependencies among elements $H(z^i)$.

If $\deg r < m/2$, the strategy can be applied in an especially straightforward fashion to eliminate some of the storage for $H(z^i)$ in Algorithm 3.85. For $m/2 < i < m - \deg r$,

$$
\begin{aligned}
H(z^i) &= H(z^{2i}) + z^i + \operatorname{Tr}(z^i) \\
&= H(r(z)z^{2i-m}) + z^i + \operatorname{Tr}(z^i) \\
&= H(z^{2i-m+b_\ell} + \cdots + z^{2i-m+b_1} + z^{2i-m}) + z^i + \operatorname{Tr}(z^i).
\end{aligned}
$$

Since $2i - m + \deg r < i$, the reduction may be applied to eliminate storage of $H(z^i)$ for odd i, $m/2 < i < m - \deg r$. If $\deg r$ is small, Algorithm 3.86 requires approximately $m/4$ elements of storage.

Algorithm 3.86 Solve $x^2 + x = c$

INPUT: $c = \sum_{i=0}^{m-1} c_i z^i \in \mathbb{F}_{2^m}$ where m is odd and $\operatorname{Tr}(c) = 0$, and reduction polynomial $f(z) = z^m + r(z)$.

OUTPUT: A solution s of $x^2 + x = c$.

1. Precompute $H(z^i)$ for $i \in I_0 \cup I_1$, where I_0 and I_1 consist of the odd integers in $[1, (m-1)/2]$ and $[m - \deg r, m - 2]$, respectively.
2. $s \leftarrow 0$.
3. For each odd $i \in ((m-1)/2, m - \deg r)$, processed in decreasing order, do:
    3.1 If $c_i = 1$ then do: $c \leftarrow c + z^{2i-m+b_\ell} + \cdots + z^{2i-m}$, $s \leftarrow s + z^i$.
4. For i from $(m-1)/2$ downto 1 do:
    4.1 If $c_{2i} = 1$ then do: $c \leftarrow c + z^i$, $s \leftarrow s + z^i$.
5. $s \leftarrow s + \sum_{i \in I_0 \cup I_1} c_i H(z^i)$.
6. Return(s).

The technique may also reduce the time required for solving the quadratic equation, since the cost of reducing each $H(z^i)$ may be less than the cost of adding a precomputed value of $H(z^i)$ to the accumulator. Elimination of the even terms (step 4) can be implemented efficiently. Processing odd terms (as in step 3) is more involved, but will be less expensive than a field addition if only a few words must be updated.

Example 3.87 (*Algorithm 3.86 for the field* $\mathbb{F}_{2^{163}}$) Consider $\mathbb{F}_{2^{163}}$ with reduction polynomial $f(z) = z^{163} + z^7 + z^6 + z^3 + 1$. Step 3 of Algorithm 3.86 begins with $i = 155$. By Lemma 3.84,

$$
\begin{aligned}
H(z^{155}) &= H(z^{310}) + z^{155} + \mathrm{Tr}(z^{155}) \\
&= H(z^{147}z^{163}) + z^{155} \\
&= H(z^{147}(z^7 + z^6 + z^3 + 1)) + z^{155}.
\end{aligned}
$$

If $c_{155} = 1$, then $z^{154} + z^{153} + z^{150} + z^{147}$ is added to c, and z^{155} is added to s. In this fashion, storage for $H(z^i)$ is eliminated for $i \in \{83, 85, \dots, 155\}$, the odd integers in $((m-1)/2, m - \deg r)$.

Algorithm 3.86 uses 44 field elements of precomputation. While this is roughly half that required by the basic algorithm, it is not minimal. For example, storage for $H(z^{51})$ may be eliminated, since

$$
\begin{aligned}
H(z^{51}) &= H(z^{102}) + z^{51} + \mathrm{Tr}(z^{51}) \\
&= H(z^{204}) + z^{102} + z^{51} + \mathrm{Tr}(z^{102}) + \mathrm{Tr}(z^{51}) \\
&= H(z^{163}z^{41}) + z^{102} + z^{51} \\
&= H(z^{48} + z^{47} + z^{44} + z^{41}) + z^{102} + z^{51}
\end{aligned}
$$

which corresponds to equation (3.43) with $j = 2$. The same technique eliminates storage for $H(z^i)$, $i \in \{51, 49, \dots, 41\}$. Similarly, if (3.43) is applied with $i = 21$ and $j = 3$, then

$$
H(z^{21}) = H(z^{12} + z^{11} + z^8 + z^5) + z^{84} + z^{42} + z^{21}.
$$

Note that the odd exponents 11 and 5 are less than 21, and hence storage for $H(z^{21})$ may be eliminated.

In summary, the use of (3.43) with $j \in \{1, 2, 3\}$ eliminates storage for odd values of $i \in \{21, 41, \dots, 51, 83, \dots, 155\}$, and a corresponding algorithm for solving the quadratic equation requires 37 elements of precomputation. Further reductions are possible, but there are some complications since the formula for $H(z^i)$ involves $H(z^j)$ for $j > i$. As an example,

$$
H(z^{23}) = H(z^{28} + z^{27} + z^{24} + z^{21}) + z^{92} + z^{46} + z^{23}
$$

and storage for $H(z^{23})$ may be exchanged for storage on $H(z^{27})$. These strategies reduce the precomputation to 30 field elements, significantly less than the 44 used in Algorithm 3.86. In fact, use of

$$
z^n = z^{157+n} + z^{n+1} + z^{n-3} + z^{n-6}
$$

together with the previous techniques reduces the storage to 21 field elements $H(z^i)$ for $i \in \{157, 73, 69, 65, 61, 57, 53, 39, 37, 33, 29, 27, 17, 15, 13, 11, 9, 7, 5, 3, 1\}$. However, this final reduction comes at a somewhat higher cost in required code compared with the 30-element version.

Experimentally, the algorithm for solving the quadratic equation (with 21 or 30 elements of precomputation) requires approximately 2/3 the time of a field multiplication. Special care should be given to branch misprediction factors (§5.1.4) as this algorithm performs many bit tests.

Computing square roots in $\mathbb{F}_{2^m}$

The basic method for computing $\sqrt{c}$, where $c \in \mathbb{F}_{2^m}$, is based on the little theorem of Fermat: $c^{2^m} = c$. Then $\sqrt{c}$ can be computed as $\sqrt{c} = c^{2^{m-1}}$, requiring $m-1$ squarings. A more efficient method is obtained from the observation that $\sqrt{c}$ can be expressed in terms of the square root of the element z. Let $c = \sum_{i=0}^{m-1} c_i z^i \in \mathbb{F}_{2^m}$, $c_i \in \{0, 1\}$. Since squaring is a linear operation in $\mathbb{F}_{2^m}$, the square root of c can be written as

$$\sqrt{c} = \left(\sum_{i=0}^{m-1} c_i z^i \right)^{2^{m-1}} = \sum_{i=0}^{m-1} c_i (z^{2^{m-1}})^i.$$

Splitting c into even and odd powers, we have

$$\sqrt{c} = \sum_{i=0}^{(m-1)/2} c_{2i} (z^{2^{m-1}})^{2i} + \sum_{i=0}^{(m-3)/2} c_{2i+1} (z^{2^{m-1}})^{2i+1}$$

$$= \sum_{i=0}^{(m-1)/2} c_{2i} z^i + \sum_{i=0}^{(m-3)/2} c_{2i+1} z^{2^{m-1}} z^i$$

$$= \sum_{i \text{ even}} c_i z^{\frac{i}{2}} + \sqrt{z} \sum_{i \text{ odd}} c_i z^{\frac{i-1}{2}}.$$

This reveals an efficient method for computing $\sqrt{c}$: extract the two half-length vectors $c_{\text{even}} = (c_{m-1}, \ldots, c_4, c_2, c_0)$ and $c_{\text{odd}} = (c_{m-2}, \ldots, c_5, c_3, c_1)$ from c (assuming m is odd), perform a field multiplication of c_{odd} of length $\lfloor m/2 \rfloor$ with the precomputed value $\sqrt{z}$, and finally add this result with c_{even}. The computation is expected to require approximately half the time of a field multiplication.

In the case that the reduction polynomial f is a trinomial, the computation of $\sqrt{c}$ can be further accelerated by the observation that an efficient formula for $\sqrt{z}$ can be derived directly from f. Let $f(z) = z^m + z^k + 1$ be an irreducible trinomial of degree m, where $m > 2$ is prime.

Consider the case that k is odd. Note that $1 \equiv z^m + z^k \pmod{f(z)}$. Then multiplying by z and taking the square root, we get

$$\sqrt{z} \equiv z^{\frac{m+1}{2}} + z^{\frac{k+1}{2}} \pmod{f(z)}.$$

Thus, the product $\sqrt{z} \cdot c_{\text{odd}}$ requires two shift-left operations and one modular reduction.

Now suppose k is even. Observe that $z^m \equiv z^k + 1 \pmod{f(z)}$. Then dividing by z^{m-1} and taking the square root, we get

$$\sqrt{z} \equiv z^{-\frac{m-1}{2}}(z^{\frac{k}{2}} + 1) \pmod{f(z)}.$$

In order to compute z^{-s} modulo $f(z)$, where $s = \frac{m-1}{2}$, one can use the congruences $z^{-t} \equiv z^{k-t} + z^{m-t} \pmod{f(z)}$ for $1 \leq t \leq k$ for writing z^{-s} as a sum of few positive powers of z. Hence, the product $\sqrt{z} \cdot c_{\text{odd}}$ can be performed with few shift-left operations and one modular reduction.

Example 3.88 (*square roots in* $\mathbb{F}_{2^{409}}$) The reduction polynomial for the NIST recommended finite field $\mathbb{F}_{2^{409}}$ is the trinomial $f(z) = z^{409} + z^{87} + 1$. Then, the new formula for computing the square root of $c \in \mathbb{F}_{2^{409}}$ is

$$\sqrt{c} = c_{\text{even}} + z^{205} \cdot c_{\text{odd}} + z^{44} \cdot c_{\text{odd}} \mod f(z).$$

Example 3.89 (*square roots in* $\mathbb{F}_{2^{233}}$) The reduction polynomial for the NIST recommended finite field $\mathbb{F}_{2^{233}}$ is the trinomial $f(z) = z^{233} + z^{74} + 1$. Since $k = 74$ is even, we have $\sqrt{z} = z^{-116} \cdot (z^{37} + 1) \mod f(z)$. Note that $z^{-74} \equiv 1 + z^{159} \pmod{f(z)}$ and $z^{-42} \equiv z^{32} + z^{191} \pmod{f(z)}$. Then one gets that $z^{-116} \equiv z^{32} + z^{117} + z^{191} \pmod{f(z)}$. Hence, the new method for computing the square root of $c \in \mathbb{F}_{2^{233}}$ is

$$\sqrt{c} = c_{\text{even}} + (z^{32} + z^{117} + z^{191})(z^{37} + 1) \cdot c_{\text{odd}} \mod f(z).$$

Compared to the standard method of computing square roots, the proposed technique eliminates the need of storage and replaces the required field multiplication by a faster operation. Experimentally, finding a root in Example 3.89 requires roughly $1/8$ the time of a field multiplication.

3.6.3 *Point multiplication*

Halve-and-add variants of the point multiplication methods discussed in §3.3 replace most point doublings with halvings. Depending on the application, it may be necessary to convert a given integer $k = (k_{t-1}, \ldots, k_0)_2$ for use with halving-based methods. If k' is defined by

$$k \equiv k'_{t-1}/2^{t-1} + \cdots + k'_2/2^2 + k'_1/2 + k'_0 \pmod{n}$$

then $kP = \sum_{i=0}^{t-1} k'_i/2^i P$; i.e., $(k'_{t-1}, \ldots, k'_0)$ is used by halving-based methods. This can be generalized to width-w NAF.

Lemma 3.90 Let $\sum_{i=0}^{t} k_i' 2^i$ be the w-NAF representation of $2^{t-1}k \bmod n$. Then

$$k \equiv \sum_{i=0}^{t-1} \frac{k_{t-1-i}'}{2^i} + 2k_t' \quad (\bmod \ n).$$

Proof: We have $2^{t-1}k \equiv \sum_{i=0}^{t} k_i' 2^i \pmod{n}$. Since n is prime, the congruence can be divided by 2^{t-1} to obtain

$$k \equiv \sum_{i=0}^{t} \frac{k_i'}{2^{t-1-i}} \equiv \sum_{i=0}^{t-1} \frac{k_{t-1-i}'}{2^i} + 2k_t' \quad (\bmod \ n). \qquad \square$$

Algorithm 3.91 presents a right-to-left version of the halve-and-add method with the input $2^{t-1}k \bmod n$ represented in w-NAF. Point halving occurs on the input P rather than on accumulators. Note that the coefficient k_t' is handled separately in step 2 as it corresponds to the special term $2k_t'$ in k. The expected running time is approximately

$$(\text{step 4 cost}) + (t/(w+1) - 2^{w-2})A' + tH \tag{3.44}$$

where H denotes a point halving and A' is the cost of a point addition when one of the inputs is in λ-representation. If projective coordinates are used for Q_i, then the additions in steps 3.1 and 3.2 are mixed-coordinate. Step 4 may be performed by conversion of Q_i to affine (with cost $I + (5 \cdot 2^{w-2} - 3)M$ if inverses are obtained by a simultaneous method), and then the sum is obtained by interleaving with appropriate signed-digit representations of the odd multipliers i. The cost of step 4 for $2 \le w \le 5$ is approximately $w - 2$ point doublings and 0, 2, 6, or 16 point additions, respectively.[3]

Algorithm 3.91 Halve-and-add w-NAF (right-to-left) point multiplication

---

INPUT: Window width w, $\text{NAF}_w(2^{t-1}k \bmod n) = \sum_{i=0}^{t} k_i' 2^i$, $P \in \mathcal{G}$.
OUTPUT: kP. (Note: $k = k_0'/2^{t-1} + \cdots + k_{t-2}'/2 + k_{t-1}' + 2k_t' \bmod n$.)

1. Set $Q_i \leftarrow \infty$ for $i \in I = \{1, 3, \ldots, 2^{w-1} - 1\}$.
2. If $k_t' = 1$ then $Q_1 = 2P$.
3. For i from $t - 1$ downto 0 do:
    3.1 If $k_i' > 0$ then $Q_{k_i'} \leftarrow Q_{k_i'} + P$.
    3.2 If $k_i' < 0$ then $Q_{-k_i'} \leftarrow Q_{-k_i'} - P$.
    3.3 $P \leftarrow P/2$.
4. $Q \leftarrow \sum_{i \in I} iQ_i$.
5. Return(Q).

---

[3] Knuth suggests calculating $Q_i \leftarrow Q_i + Q_{i+2}$ for i from $2^{w-1} - 3$ to 1, and then the result is given by $Q_1 + 2\sum_{i \in I \setminus \{1\}} Q_i$. The cost is comparable in the projective point case.

Consider the case $w = 2$. The expected running time of Algorithm 3.91 is then approximately $(1/3)tA' + tH$. If affine coordinates are used, then a point halving costs approximately $2M$, while a point addition costs $2M + V$ since the λ-representation of P must be converted to affine with one field multiplication. It follows that the field operation count with affine coordinates is approximately $(8/3)tM + (1/3)tV$. However, if Q is stored in projective coordinates, then a point addition requires $9M$. The field operation count of a mixed-coordinate Algorithm 3.91 with $w = 2$ is then approximately $5tM + (2M + I)$.

Algorithm 3.92 is a left-to-right method. Point halving occurs on the accumulator Q, whence projective coordinates cannot be used. The expected running time is approximately

$$(D + (2^{w-2} - 1)A) + (t/(w+1)A' + tH). \tag{3.45}$$

Algorithm 3.92 Halve-and-add w-NAF (left-to-right) point multiplication

---

INPUT: Window width w, $\mathrm{NAF}_w(2^{t-1}k \bmod n) = \sum_{i=0}^{t} k_i' 2^i$, $P \in \mathcal{G}$.
OUTPUT: kP. (Note: $k = k_0'/2^{t-1} + \cdots + k_{t-2}'/2 + k_{t-1}' + 2k_t' \bmod n$.)
    1. Compute $P_i = iP$, for $i \in \{1, 3, 5, \ldots, 2^{w-1} - 1\}$.
    2. $Q \leftarrow \infty$.
    3. For i from 0 to $t - 1$ do
        3.1 $Q \leftarrow Q/2$.
        3.2 If $k_i' > 0$ then $Q \leftarrow Q + P_{k_i'}$.
        3.3 If $k_i' < 0$ then $Q \leftarrow Q - P_{-k_i'}$.
    4. If $k_t' = 1$ then $Q \leftarrow Q + 2P$.
    5. Return(Q).

Analysis

In comparison to methods based on doubling, point halving looks best when I/M is small and kP is to be computed for P not known in advance. In applications, the operations kP and $kP + lQ$ with P known in advance are also of interest, and this section provides comparative results. The concrete example used is the NIST random curve over $\mathbb{F}_{2^{163}}$ (§A.2.2), although the general conclusions apply more widely.

Example 3.93 (*double-and-add vs. halve-and-add*) Table 3.11 provides an operation count comparison between double-and-add and halve-and-add methods for the NIST random curve over $\mathbb{F}_{2^{163}}$. For the field operations, the assumption is that $I/M = 8$ and that a field division has cost $I + M$.

The basic NAF halving method is expected to outperform the w-NAF doubling methods. However, the halving method has 46 field elements of precomputation. In contrast, Algorithm 3.36 with $w = 4$ (which runs in approximately the same time as with $w = 5$) requires only six field elements of extra storage.

Method	Storage (field elts)	Point operations	Field operations ($H = 2M, I/M = 8$)	
			affine	projective
NAF, doubling (Algorithm 3.36)	0	$163D + 54A$	$217(M+V) = 2173$	$1089M + I = 1097$
NAF, halving (Algorithm 3.91)	46	$163H + 54A'$	$435M + 54V = 924$	$817M + I = 825$
5-NAF, doubling (Algorithm 3.36)	14	$[D+7A] + 163D + 27A$	$198(M+V) = 1982$	$879M + 8V + I = 959$
4-NAF, halving (Algorithm 3.91)	55	$[3D+6A] + 163H + 30A'$	—	$671M + 2I = 687$
5-NAF, halving (Algorithm 3.92)	60	$[D+7A] + 163H + 27A'$	$388M + 35V = 705$	—

Table 3.11. *Point and field operation counts for point multiplication for the NIST random curve over $\mathbb{F}_{2^{163}}$. Halving uses 30 field elements of precomputation in the solve routine, and 16 elements for square root. $A' = A + M$, the cost of a point addition when one of the inputs is in λ-representation. Field operation counts assume that a division V costs $I + M$.*

The left-to-right w-NAF halving method requires that the accumulator be in affine coordinates, and point additions have cost $2M + V$ (since a conversion from λ-representation is required). For sufficiently large I/M, the right-to-left algorithm will be preferred; in the example, Algorithm 3.91 with $w = 2$ will outperform Algorithm 3.92 at roughly $I/M = 11$.

For point multiplication kP where P is not known in advance, the example case in Table 3.11 predicts that use of halving gives roughly 25% improvement over a similar method based on doubling, when $I/M = 8$.

The comparison is unbalanced in terms of storage required, since halving was permitted 46 field elements of precomputation in the solve and square root routines. The amount of storage in square root can be reduced at tolerable cost to halving; significant storage (e.g., 21–30 elements) for the solve routine appears to be essential. It should be noted, however, that the storage for the solve and square root routines is per field. In addition to the routines specific to halving, most of the support for methods based on doubling will be required, giving some code expansion.

Random curves vs. Koblitz curves The τ-adic methods on Koblitz curves (§3.4) share strategy with halving in the sense that point doubling is replaced by a less-expensive operation. In the Koblitz curve case, the replacement is the Frobenius map $\tau : (x, y) \mapsto (x^2, y^2)$, an inexpensive operation compared to field multiplication. Point multiplication on Koblitz curves using τ-adic methods will be faster than those based on halving, with approximate cost for kP given by

$$\left(2^{w-2} - 1 + \frac{t}{w+1}\right)A + t \cdot (\text{cost of } \tau)$$

when using a width-w τ-adic NAF in Algorithm 3.70. To compare with Table 3.11, assume that mixed coordinates are used, $w = 5$, and that field squaring has approximate cost $M/6$. In this case, the operation count is approximately $379M$, significantly less than the $687M$ required by the halving method.

Known point vs. unknown point In the case that P is known in advance (e.g., signature generation in ECDSA) and storage is available for precomputation, halving loses some of its performance advantages. For our case, and for relatively modest amounts of storage, the single-table comb method (Algorithm 3.44) is among the fastest and can be used to obtain meaningful operation count comparisons. The operation counts for kP using methods based on doubling and halving are approximately

$$\frac{t}{w}\Big(D + \frac{2^w - 1}{2^w}A\Big) \quad \text{and} \quad \frac{t}{w}\Big(H + \frac{2^w - 1}{2^w}A'\Big),$$

respectively. In contrast to the random point case, roughly half the operations are point additions. Note that the method based on doubling may use mixed-coordinate arithmetic (in which case $D = 4M$, $A = 8M$, and there is a final conversion to affine), while the method based on halving must work in affine coordinates (with $H = 2M$ and $A' = V + 2M$). If $V = I + M$, then values of t and w of practical interest give a threshold I/M between 7 and 8, above which the method based on doubling is expected to be superior (e.g., for $w = 4$ and $t = 163$, the threshold is roughly 7.4).

Simultaneous multiple point multiplication In ECDSA signature verification, the computationally expensive step is a calculation $kP + lQ$ where only P is known in advance. If interleaving (Algorithm 3.51) is used with widths w_1 and w_2, respectively, then the expected operation count for the method based on doubling is approximately

$$[D + (2^{w_2 - 2} - 1)A] + t\Big[D + \Big(\frac{1}{w_1 + 1} + \frac{1}{w_2 + 1}\Big)A\Big]$$

where the precomputation involving P is not included. (The expected count for the method using halving can be estimated by a similar formula; however, a more precise estimate must distinguish the case where consecutive additions occur, since the cost is $A' + V + M$ rather than $2A'$.)

For sufficiently large I/M, the method based on doubling will be superior; in Example 3.93, this occurs at roughly $I/M = 11.7$. When I/M is such that halving is preferred, the difference is less pronounced than in the case of a random point multiplication kP, due to the larger number of point additions relative to halvings. Note that the interleaving method cannot be efficiently converted to a right-to-left algorithm (where $w_1 = w_2 = 2$), since the halving or doubling operation would be required on two points at each step.

3.7 Point multiplication costs

Selection of point multiplication algorithms is complicated by platform characteristics, coordinate selection, memory and other constraints, security considerations (§5.3), and interoperability requirements. This section presents basic comparisons among algorithms for the NIST-recommended curves P-192 (over the prime field $\mathbb{F}_{p_{192}}$ for $p_{192} = 2^{192} - 2^{64} - 1$) and B-163 and K-163 (random and Koblitz curves over the binary field $\mathbb{F}_{2^{163}} = \mathbb{F}_2[z]/(z^{163} + z^7 + z^6 + z^3 + 1)$). The general assumptions are that inversion in prime fields is expensive relative to multiplication, a modest amount of storage is available for precomputation, and costs for point arithmetic can be estimated by considering only field multiplications, squarings, and inversions.

The execution times of elliptic curve cryptographic schemes are typically dominated by point multiplications. Estimates for point multiplication costs are presented for three cases: (i) kP where precomputation must be on-line; (ii) kP for P known in advance and precomputation may be off-line; and (iii) $kP + lQ$ where only the precomputation for P may be done off-line. The latter two cases are motivated by protocols such as ECDSA, where signature generation requires a calculation kP where P is fixed, and signature verification requires a calculation $kP + lQ$ where P is fixed and Q is not known a priori.

Estimates are given in terms of curve operations (point additions A and point doubles D), and the corresponding field operations (multiplications M and inversions I). The operation counts are roughly what are obtained using the basic approximations presented with the algorithms; however, the method here considers the coordinate representations used in precomputation and evaluation stages, and various minor optimizations. On the other hand, the various representations for the scalars are generally assumed to be of full length, overestimating some counts. Nevertheless, the estimation method is sufficiently accurate to permit meaningful comparisons.

Estimates for P-192

Table 3.12 presents rough estimates of costs in terms of elliptic curve operations and field operations for point multiplication methods for P-192, under the assumption that field inversion has the cost of roughly 80 field multiplications. The high cost of inversion encourages the use of projective coordinates and techniques such as simultaneous inversion. Most of the entries involving projective coordinates are not very sensitive to the precise value of I/M, provided that it is not dramatically smaller.

For point multiplication kP where precomputation must be done on-line, the cost of point doubles limits the improvements of windowing methods over the basic NAF method. The large inverse to multiplication ratio gives a slight edge to the use of Chudnovsky over affine in precomputation for window NAF. Fixed-base methods are significantly faster (even with only a few points of storage), where the precomputation costs are excluded and the number of point doubles at the evaluation stage is greatly reduced. The cost of processing Q in the multiple point methods for $kP + lQ$ diminishes the usefulness of techniques that reduce the number of point doubles for known-point multiplication. On the other hand, the cost of $kP + lQ$ is only a little higher than the cost for unknown-point multiplication.

Method	Coordinates	w	Points stored	EC operations A	D	Field operations M	I	Total[a]
Unknown point (kP, on-line precomputation)								
Binary	affine	–	0	95	191	977	286	23857
(Algorithm 3.27)	Jacobian-affine	–	0	95	191	2420	1	2500
Binary NAF	affine	–	0	63	191	886	254	21206
(Algorithm 3.31)	Jacobian-affine	–	0	63	191	2082	1	2162
Window NAF	Jacobian-affine	4	3	41	193	1840	4[b]	2160
(Algorithm 3.36)	Jacobian-Chudnovsky	5	7	38	192	1936	1	2016
Fixed base (kP, off-line precomputation)								
Interleave (Algorithm 3.51)	Jacobian-affine	3,3	3	47	95	1203	1	1283
Windowing (Algorithm 3.41)	Chudnovsky-affine & Jacobian-Chudnovsky	5	38	37^c+30^d	0	801	1	881
Windowing NAF (Algorithm 3.42)	Chudnovsky-affine & Jacobian-Chudnovsky	5	38	38^c+20^d	0	676	1	756
Comb (Algorithm 3.44)	Jacobian-affine	5	30	37	38	675	1	755
Comb 2-table (Algorithm 3.45)	Jacobian-affine	4	29	44	23	638	1	718
Multiple point multiplication ($kP+lQ$)								
Simultaneous (Algorithm 3.48[f])	Jacobian-affine & Jacobian-Chudnovsky	2	10	91	192	2592	1	2672
Simultaneous JSF (Alg. 3.48 & 3.50)	Jacobian-affine	–	2	97	191	2428	2[b]	2588
Interleave (Algorithm 3.51)	Jacobian-affine & Jacobian-Chudnovsky	6,5	22	32^e+34^d	192	2226	1	2306

[a]Total cost in field multiplications assuming field inversions have cost $I = 80M$.
[b]Simultaneous inversion used in precomputation. [c]$C + A \to C$. [d]$J + C \to J$. [e]$J + A \to J$.
[f]Sliding window variant.

Table 3.12. *Rough estimates of point multiplication costs for the NIST curve over $\mathbb{F}_{p_{192}}$ for prime $p_{192} = 2^{192} - 2^{64} - 1$. The unknown point methods for kP include the cost of precomputation, while fixed base methods do not. Multiple point methods find $kP + lQ$ where precomputation costs involving only P are excluded. Field squarings are assumed to have cost $S = .85M$.*

The entry for kP by interleaving when P is fixed is understood to mean that Algorithm 3.51 is used with inputs $v = 2$, $P_1 = P$, $P_2 = 2^d P$, and half-length scalars k^1 and k^2 defined by $k = 2^d k^2 + k^1$ where $d = \lceil t/2 \rceil$. Width-3 NAFs are found for each of k^1 and k^2. An alternative with essentially the same cost uses a simultaneous method (Algorithm 3.48) modified to process a single column of the joint sparse form (Algorithm 3.50) of k^1 and k^2 at each step. This modified "simultaneous JSF" algorithm is referenced in Table 3.12 for multiple point multiplication.

Estimates for B-163 and K-163

Table 3.13 presents rough estimates of costs in terms of elliptic curve operations and field operations for point multiplication methods for NIST random and Koblitz curves (B-163 and K-163) over the binary field $\mathbb{F}_{2^{163}} = \mathbb{F}_2[z]/(z^{163} + z^7 + z^6 + z^3 + 1)$. The estimates for TNAF algorithms are for K-163, while the other estimates are for B-163. The choice of algorithm and coordinate representations are sensitive to the ratio of field inversion to multiplication times, since the ratio is typically much smaller than for prime fields. Further, a small ratio encourages the development of a fast division algorithm for affine point arithmetic.

Estimates are presented for the cases $I/M = 5$ and $I/M = 8$ under the assumptions that field division V has approximate cost $I + M$ (i.e., division is roughly the same cost as inversion followed by multiplication), and that field squarings are inexpensive relative to multiplication. The assumptions and cases considered are motivated by reported results on common hardware and experimental evidence in §5.1.5. Note that if $V/M \leq 7$, then affine coordinates will be preferred over projective coordinates in point addition, although projective coordinates are still preferred in point doubling unless $V/M \leq 3$.

As discussed for P-192, the cost of the point doubling limits the improvements of windowing methods over the basic NAF method for B-163. However, the case is different for Koblitz curves, where doublings have been replaced by inexpensive field squarings. The squarings are not completely free, however, and the estimations for the TNAF algorithms include field squarings that result from applications of the Frobenius map τ under the assumption that a squaring has approximate cost $S \approx M/7$.

Methods based on point halving (§3.6) have been included in the unknown-point case, with the assumption that a halving has cost approximately $2M$. The predicted times are significantly better than those for B-163, but significantly slower than times for τ-adic methods on the special Koblitz curves. Note, however, that the storage listed for halving-based methods ignores the (fixed) field elements used in the solve and square root rotines. Similarly, it should be noted that the TNAF routines require support for the calculation of τ-adic NAFs.

Fixed-base methods are significantly faster (even with only a few points of storage), where the precomputation costs are excluded and the number of point doubles (for B-163) at the evaluation stage is greatly reduced. As with P-192, the cost of processing Q in the multiple point methods for $kP + lQ$ in B-163 diminishes the usefulness of techniques that reduce the number of point doubles for known-point multiplication. The case differs for the Koblitz curve, since field squarings replace most point doublings.

The discussion for P-192 clarifies the meaning of the entry for kP by interleaving when P is fixed. The JSF method noted in the entries for $kP + lQ$ has essentially the same cost and could have been used. The entry for interleaving with TNAFs is obtained by adapting the interleaving algorithm to process TNAFs.

Method	Coordinates	w	Points stored	EC operations		Field operations[a]			
				A	D	M	I	$I/M=5$	$I/M=8$
Unknown point (kP, on-line precomputation)									
Binary	affine	0	0	81	162	486	243	1701	2430
(Algorithm 3.27)	projective	0	0	81	162	1298	1	1303	1306
Binary NAF	affine	0	0	54	162	432	216	1512	2160
(Algorithm 3.31)	projective	0	0	54	162	1082	1	1087	1090
Window NAF	affine	4	3	35	163	396	198	1386	1980
(Algorithm 3.36)	projective	4	3	3^b+32	163	914	5	939	954
Montgomery	affine	–	0	162^c	162^d	328	325	1953	2928
(Algorithm 3.40)	projective	–	0	162^c	162^d	982	1	987	990
Halving w-NAF	affine	5	7	$7+27^e$	$1+163^f$	423	35	598	705
(Alg. 3.91 & 3.92)	projective	4	3	$6+30^e$	$3+163^f$	671	2	681	687
TNAF	affine	–	0	54	0^g	154	54	424	586
(Algorithm 3.66)	projective	–	0	54	0^g	503	1	508	511
Window TNAF	affine	5	7	34	0^g	114	34	284	386
(Algorithm 3.70)	projective	5	7	7^b+27	0^g	301	8	341	365
Fixed base (kP, off-line precomputation)									
Interleave	affine	3,3	3	41	81	244	122	854	1220
(Algorithm 3.51)	projective	3,3	3	41	81	654	1	659	662
Windowing	affine	5	32	61	0	122	61	427	610
(Algorithm 3.41)	projective	5	32	$31+30^h$	0	670	1	–	678
Windowing NAF	affine	5	32	52	0	104	52	364	520
(Algorithm 3.42)	projective	5	32	$32+20^h$	0	538	1	–	546
Comb	affine	5	30	31	32	126	63	441	630
(Algorithm 3.44)	projective	5	30	31	32	378	1	383	386
Window TNAF	affine	6	15	23	0^g	92	23	207	276
(Algorithm 3.70)	projective	6	15	23	0^g	255	1	260	263
Multiple point multiplication ($kP+lQ$)									
Simultaneous JSF	affine	–	2	83	162	490	245	1715	2450
(Alg. 3.48 & 3.50)	projective	–	2	83	162	1302	3	1317	1326
Simultaneous	affine	2	10	78	163	482	241	1687	2410
(Algorithm 3.48^i)	projective	2	10	78	163	1222	11	1277	1310
Interleave	affine	6,4	18	60	163	448	224	1568	2240
(Algorithm 3.51)	projective	6,4	18	60	163	1114	5	1139	1154
Interleave TNAF	affine	6,5	22	59	0^g	164	59	459	636
(Alg. 3.51 & 3.69)	projective	6,5	22	59	0^g	501	8	541	565

[a]Right columns give costs in terms of field multiplications for $I/M=5$ and $I/M=8$, resp.
[b]Affine. [c]Addition via (3.23). [d]x-coordinate only. [e]Cost $A+M$. [f]Halvings; estimated cost $2M$.
[g]Field ops include applications of τ with $S=M/7$. [h]$P+P\to P$. [i]Sliding window variant.

Table 3.13. *Rough estimates of point multiplication costs for the NIST curves over* $\mathbb{F}_{2^{163}} = \mathbb{F}_2[z]/(z^{163}+z^7+z^6+z^3+1)$. *The unknown point methods for kP include the cost of precomputation, while fixed base methods do not. Multiple point methods find $kP+lQ$ where precomputation costs involving only P are excluded. Precomputation is in affine coordinates.*

NIST curve	Method	Field mult M	Pentium III (800 MHz) normalized M	μs
Unknown point (kP, on-line precomputation)				
P-192	5-NAF (Algorithm 3.36, $w = 5$)	2016	2016	975
B-163	4-NAF (Algorithm 3.36, $w = 4$)	954	2953	1475
B-163	Halving (Algorithm 3.91, $w = 4$)	687	2126	1050
K-163	5-TNAF (Algorithm 3.70, $w = 5$)	365	1130	625
Fixed base (kP, off-line precomputation)				
P-192	Comb 2-table (Algorithm 3.45, $w = 4$)	718	718	325
B-163	Comb (Algorithm 3.44, $w = 5$)	386	1195	575
K-163	6-TNAF (Algorithm 3.70, $w = 6$)	263	814	475
Multiple point multiplication ($kP + lQ$)				
P-192	Interleave (Algorithm 3.51, $w = 6, 5$)	2306	2306	1150
B-163	Interleave (Algorithm 3.51, $w = 6, 4$)	1154	3572	1800
K-163	Interleave TNAF (Alg. 3.51 & 3.69, $w = 6, 5$)	565	1749	1000

Table 3.14. *Point multiplication timings on an 800 MHz Intel Pentium III using general-purpose registers. M is the estimated number of field multiplications under the assumption that $I/M = 80$ and $I/M = 8$ in the prime and binary fields, resp. The normalization gives equivalent P-192 field multiplications for this implementation.*

Summary

The summary multiplication counts in Tables 3.12 and 3.13 are not directly comparable, since the cost of field multiplication can differ dramatically between prime and binary fields on a given platform and between implementations. Table 3.14 gives field multiplication counts and actual execution times for a specific implementation on an 800 MHz Intel Pentium III. The ratio of binary to prime field multiplication times in this particular case is approximately 3.1 (see §5.1.5), and multiplication counts are normalized in terms of P-192 field multiplications.

As a rough comparison, the times show that unknown-point multiplications were significantly faster in the Koblitz (binary) case than for the random binary or prime curves, due to the inexpensive field squarings that have replaced most point doubles. In the known point case, precomputation can reduce the number of point doubles, and the faster prime field multiplication gives P-192 the edge. For $kP + lQ$ where only the precomputation for kP may be off-line, the times for K-163 and P-192 are comparable, and significantly faster than the corresponding time given for B-163.

The execution times for methods on the Koblitz curve are longer than predicted, in part because the cost of finding τ-adic NAFs is not represented in the estimates (but is included in the execution times). Algorithms 3.63 and 3.65 used in finding τ-adic NAFs were implemented with the "big number" routines from OpenSSL (see Appendix C). Note also that limited improvements in the known-point case for the Koblitz curve may be obtained via interleaving (using no more precomputation storage than granted to the method for P-192).

There are several limitations of the comparisons presented here. Only general-purpose registers were used in the implementation. Workstations commonly have special-purpose registers that can be employed to speed field arithmetic. In particular, the Pentium III has floating-point registers which can accelerate prime field arithmetic (see §5.1.2), and single-instruction multiple-data (SIMD) registers that are easily harnessed for binary field arithmetic (see §5.1.3). Although all Pentium family processors have a 32×32 integer multiplier giving a 64-bit result, multiplication with general-purpose registers on P6 family processors such as the Pentium III is faster than on earlier Pentium or newer Pentium 4 processors. The times for P-192 may be less competitive compared with Koblitz curve times on platforms where hardware integer multiplication is weaker or operates on fewer bits. For the most part, we have not distinguished between storage for data-dependent items and storage for items that are fixed for a given field or curve. The case where a large amount of storage is available for precomputation in known-point methods is not addressed.

3.8 Notes and further references

§3.1
A brief introduction to elliptic curves can be found in Chapter 6 of Koblitz's book [254]. Intermediate-level textbooks that provide proofs of many of the basic results used in elliptic curve cryptography include Charlap and Robbins [92, 93], Enge [132], Silverman and Tate [433], and Washington [474]. The standard advanced-level reference on the theory of elliptic curves are the two books by Silverman [429, 430].

Theorem 3.8 is due to Waterhouse [475]. Example 3.17 is from Wittmann [484].

§3.2
Chudnovsky and Chudnovsky [96] studied four basic models of elliptic curves including: (i) the *Weierstrass model* $y^2 + a_1 xy + a_3 y = x^3 + a_2 x^2 + a_4 x + a_6$ used throughout this book; (ii) the *Jacobi model* $y^2 = x^4 + ax^2 + b$; (iii) the *Jacobi form* which represents the elliptic curve as the intersection of two quadrics $x^2 + y^2 = 1$ and $k^2 x^2 + z^2 = 1$; and (iv) the *Hessian form* $x^3 + y^3 + z^3 = Dxyz$. Liardet and Smart [291] observed that the rules for adding and doubling points in the Jacobi form are the same, thereby potentially increasing resistance to power analysis attacks. Joye and Quisquater [231] showed that this property also holds for the Hessian form, and concluded that the addition formulas for the Hessian form require fewer field operations than the addition formulas for the Jacobi form (12 multiplications versus 16 multiplications). Smart [442] observed that the symmetry in the group law on elliptic curves in Hessian form can be exploited to parallelize (to three processors) the addition and doubling of points.

Note that since the group of $\mathbb{F}_q$-rational points on an elliptic curve in Hessian form defined over $\mathbb{F}_q$ must contain a point of order 3, the Hessian form cannot be used for the elliptic curves standardized by NIST. Elliptic curves in Hessian form were studied extensively by Frium [151].

Chudnovsky coordinates were proposed by Chudnovsky and Chudnovsky [96]. The different combinations for mixed coordinate systems were compared by Cohen, Miyaji and Ono [100]. Note that their modified Jacobian coordinates do not yield any speedups over (ordinary) Jacobian coordinates in point addition and doubling for elliptic curves $y^2 = x^3 + ax + b$ with $a = -3$; however, the strategy is useful in accelerating repeated doublings in Algorithm 3.23. Lim and Hwang [293] choose projective coordinates corresponding to $(X/Z^2, Y/2Z^3)$; the division by 2 is eliminated, but point addition then requires two more field additions.

LD coordinates were proposed by López and Dahab [300]. The formulas reflect an improvement due to Lim and Hwang [294] and Al-Daoud, Mahmod, Rushdan, and Kilicman [10] resulting in one fewer multiplication (and one more squaring) in mixed-coordinate point addition.

If field multiplication is via a method similar to Algorithm 2.36 with a data-dependent precomputation phase, then King [246] suggests organizing the point arithmetic to reduce the number of such precomputations (i.e., a table of precomputation may be used more than once). Depending on memory constraints, a single preserved table of precomputation is used, or multiple and possibly larger tables may be considered.

Algorithm 3.23 for repeated doubling is an example of an improvement possible when combinations of point operations are performed. An improvement of this type is suggested by King [246] for the point addition and doubling formulas given by López and Dahab [300]. A field multiplication can be traded for two squarings in the calculation of $2(P + Q)$, since the value $X_3 Z_3$ required in the addition may be used in the subsequent doubling. The proposal by Eisenträger, Lauter, and Montgomery [129] is similar in the sense that a field multiplication is eliminated in the calculation of $2P + Q$ in affine coordinates (by omitting the calculation of the y-coordinate of the intermediate value $P + Q$ in $2P + Q = (P + Q) + P$).

§3.3
The right-to-left binary method is described in Knuth [249], along with the generalization to an m-ary method. Cohen [99] discusses right-to-left and left-to-right algorithms with base 2^k. Gordon [179] provides a useful survey of exponentiation methods. Menezes, van Oorschot, and Vanstone [319] cover exponentiation algorithms of practical interest in more generality than presented here.

The density result in Theorem 3.29 is due to Morain and Olivos [333]. The window NAF method (Algorithms 3.36 and 3.35) is from Solinas [446], who remarks that "More elaborate window methods exist (see [179]), but they can require a great deal of initial calculation and seldom do much better than the technique presented here."

Möller [329] presents a *fractional window* technique that generalizes the sliding window and window NAF approaches. The method has more flexibility in the amount of precomputation, of particular interest when memory is constrained (see Note 3.39). For window width $w > 2$ and given odd parameter $v \leq 2^{w-1} - 3$, the fractional window representation has average density $1/(w + 1 + \frac{v+1}{2^{w-1}})$; the method is fractional in the sense that the effective window size has increased by $\frac{v+1}{2^{w-1}}$ compared with the width-w NAF.

Algorithm 3.40 is due to López and Dahab [299], and is based on an idea of Montgomery [331]. Okeya and Sakurai [359] extended this work to elliptic curves over finite fields of characteristic greater than three.

The fixed-base windowing method (Algorithm 3.41) is due to Brickell, Gordon, Mc-Curley, and Wilson [72]. Gordon [179] cites the papers of de Rooij [109] and Lim and Lee [295] for vector addition chain methods that address the "observation that the BGMW method tends to use too much memory." Special cases of the Lim-Lee method [295] appear in Algorithms 3.44 and 3.45; the general method is described in Note 3.47.

The use of simultaneous addition in Note 3.46 for Lim-Lee methods is described by Lim and Hwang [294]. An enhancement for combing parameter $v > 2$ (see Note 3.47) is given which reduces the number of inversions from $v - 1$ in a straightforward generalization to $\lceil \log_2 v \rceil$ (with $\lfloor v/2 \rfloor e$ elements of temporary storage).

"Shamir's trick" (Algorithm 3.48) for simultaneous point multiplication is attributed by ElGamal [131] to Shamir. The improvement with use of a sliding window is due to Yen, Laih, and Lenstra [487]. The joint sparse form is from Solinas [447]. Proos [383] generalizes the joint sparse form to any number of integers. A related "zero column combing" method is also presented, generalizing the Lim-Lee method with signed binary representations to increase the number of zero columns in the exponent array. The improvement (for similar amounts of storage) depends on the relative costs of point addition and doubling and the amount of storage for precomputation; if additions have the same cost as doubles, then the example with 160-bit k and 32 points or less of precomputation shows approximately 10% decrease in point operations (excluding precomputation) in calculating kP.

Interleaving (Algorithm 3.51) is due to Gallant, Lambert, and Vanstone [160] and Möller [326]. Möller [329] notes that the interleaving approach for kP where k is split and then w-NAFs are found for the fragments can "waste" part of each w-NAF. A *window NAF splitting* method is proposed, of particular interest when w is large. The basic idea is to calculate the w-NAF of k first, and then split.

§3.4

Koblitz curves are so named because they were first proposed for cryptographic use by Koblitz [253]. Koblitz explained how a τ-adic representation of an integer k can be used to eliminate the point doubling operations when computing kP for a point P on a

Koblitz curve. Meier and Staffelbach [312] showed how a short τ-adic representation of k can be obtained by first reducing k modulo $\tau^m - 1$ in $\mathbb{Z}[\tau]$. TNAFs and width-w TNAFs were introduced by Solinas [444]. The algorithms were further developed and analyzed in the extensive article by Solinas [446]. Park, Oh, Lee, Lim and Sung [370] presented an alternate method for obtaining short τ-adic representations. Their method reduces the length of the τ-adic representation by about $\log_2 h$, and thus offers a significant improvement only if the cofactor h is large.

Some of the techniques for fast point multiplication on Koblitz curves were extended to elliptic curves defined over small binary fields (e.g., $\mathbb{F}_{2^2}$, $\mathbb{F}_{2^3}$, $\mathbb{F}_{2^4}$ and $\mathbb{F}_{2^5}$) by Müller [334], and to elliptic curves defined over small extension fields of odd characteristic by Koblitz [256] and Smart [439]. Günther, Lange and Stein [185] proposed generalizations for point multiplication in the Jacobian of hyperelliptic curves of genus 2, focusing on the curves $y^2 + xy = x^5 + 1$ and $y^2 + xy = x^5 + x^2 + 1$ defined over $\mathbb{F}_2$. Their methods were extended by Choie and Lee [94] to hyperelliptic curves of genus 2, 3 and 4 defined over finite fields of any characteristic.

§3.5

The method for exploiting efficiently computable endomorphisms to accelerate point multiplication on elliptic curves is due to Gallant, Lambert and Vanstone [160], who also presented Algorithm 3.74 for computing a balanced length-two representation of a multiplier. The P-160 curve in Example 3.73 is from the wireless TLS specification [360]. Example 3.76 is due to Solinas [447].

Sica, Ciet and Quisquater [428] proved that the vector $v_2 = (a_2, b_2)$ in Algorithm 3.74 has small norm. Park, Jeong, Kim and Lim [368] presented an alternate method for computing balanced length-two representations and proved that their method always works. Their experiments showed that the performances of this alternate decomposition method and of Algorithm 3.74 are the same in practice. Another method was proposed by Kim and Lim [242]. The Gallant-Lambert-Vanstone method was generalized to balanced length-m multipliers by Müller [335] and shown to be effective for speeding up point multiplication on certain elliptic curves defined over optimal extensions fields. Generalizations to hyperelliptic curves having efficiently computable endomorphisms were proposed by Park, Jeong and Lim [369].

Ciet, Lange, Sica, and Quisquater [98] extend the technique of τ-adic expansions on Koblitz curves to curves over prime fields having an endomorphism ϕ with norm exceeding 1. In comparison with the Gallant-Lambert-Vanstone method, approximately $(\log_2 n)/2$ point doubles in the calculation of kP are replaced by twice as many applications of ϕ. A generalization of the joint sparse form (§3.3.3) to a ϕ-JSF is given for endomorphism ϕ having characteristic polynomial $x^2 \pm x + 2$.

§3.6

Point halving was proposed independently by Knudsen [247] and Schroeppel [413]. Additional comparisons with methods based on doubling were performed by Fong, Hankerson, López and Menezes [144].

The performance advantage of halving methods is clearest in the case of point multiplication kP where P is not known in advance, and smaller inversion to multiplication ratios generally favour halving. Knudsen's analysis [247] gives halving methods a 39% advantage for the unknown point case, under the assumption that $I/M \approx 3$. Fong, Hankerson, López and Menezes [144] suggest that this ratio is too optimistic on common SPARC and Pentium platforms, where the fastest times give $I/M > 8$. The larger ratio reduces the advantage to approximately 25% in the unknown-point case under a similar analysis; if P is known in advance and storage for a modest amount of precomputation is available, then methods based on halving are inferior. For $kP + lQ$ where only P is known in advance, the differences between methods based on halving and methods based on doubling are smaller, with halving methods faster for ratios I/M commonly reported.

Algorithm 3.91 partially addresses the challenge presented in Knudsen [247] to derive "an efficient halving algorithm for projective coordinates." While the algorithm does not provide halving on a projective point, it does illustrate an efficient windowing method with halving and projective coordinates, especially applicable in the case of larger I/M. Footnote 3 concerning the calculation of Q is from Knuth [249, Exercise 4.6.3-9]; see also Möller [326, 329].

§3.7

Details of the implementation used for Table 3.14 appear in §5.1.5. In short, only general-purpose registers were used, prime field arithmetic is largely in assembly, and binary field arithmetic is entirely in C except for a one-line fragment used in polynomial degree calculations. The Intel compiler version 6 along with the Netwide Assembler (NASM) were used on an Intel Pentium III running the Linux 2.2 operating system.

The 32-bit Intel Pentium III is roughly categorized as workstation-class, along with other popular processors such as the DEC Alpha (64-bit) and Sun SPARC (32-bit and 64-bit) family. Lim and Hwang [293, 294] give extensive field and curve timings for the Intel Pentium II and DEC Alpha, especially for OEFs. Smart [440] provides comparative timings on a Sun UltraSPARC IIi and an Intel Pentium Pro for curves over prime, binary, and optimal extension fields. The NIST curves are the focus in Hankerson, López, and Menezes [189] and Brown, Hankerson, López, and Menezes [77], with field and curve timings on an Intel Pentium II. De Win, Mister, Preneel, and Wiener [111] compare ECDSA to DSA and RSA signature algorithms, with timings on an Intel Pentium Pro. Weimerskirch, Stebila, and Chang Shantz [478] discuss implementations for binary fields that handle arbitrary field sizes and reduction polynomials; timings are given on a Pentium III and for 32- and 64-bit code on a Sun UltraSPARC III.

Special-purpose hardware commonly available on workstations can dramatically speed operations. Bernstein [43] gives timings for point multiplication on the NIST curve over $\mathbb{F}_p$ for $p = 2^{224} - 2^{96} + 1$ using floating-point hardware on AMD, DEC, Intel, and Sun processors at http://cr.yp.to/nistp224/timings.html. §5.1 provides an overview of the use of floating-point and SIMD hardware.

CHAPTER 4

Cryptographic Protocols

This chapter describes some elliptic curve-based signature, public-key encryption, and key establishment schemes. §4.1 surveys the state-of-the-art in algorithms for solving the elliptic curve discrete logarithm problem, whose intractability is necessary for the security of all elliptic curve cryptographic schemes. Also discussed briefly in §4.1 are the elliptic curve analogues of the Diffie-Hellman and decision Diffie-Hellman problems whose hardness is assumed in security proofs for some protocols. §4.2 and §4.3 consider the generation and validation of domain parameters and key pairs for use in elliptic curve protocols. The ECDSA and EC-KCDSA signature schemes, the ECIES and PSEC public-key encryption schemes, and the STS and ECMQV key establishment schemes are presented in §4.4, §4.5, and §4.6, respectively. Extensive chapter notes and references are provided in §4.7.

4.1 The elliptic curve discrete logarithm problem

The hardness of the elliptic curve discrete logarithm problem is essential for the security of all elliptic curve cryptographic schemes.

Definition 4.1 The *elliptic curve discrete logarithm problem (ECDLP)* is: given an elliptic curve E defined over a finite field $\mathbb{F}_q$, a point $P \in E(\mathbb{F}_q)$ of order n, and a point $Q \in \langle P \rangle$, find the integer $l \in [0, n-1]$ such that $Q = lP$. The integer l is called the *discrete logarithm of Q to the base P, denoted $l = \log_P Q$.

The elliptic curve parameters for cryptographic schemes should be carefully chosen in order to resist all known attacks on the ECDLP. The most naïve algorithm for solving the ECDLP is *exhaustive search* whereby one computes the sequence of points

$P, 2P, 3P, 4P, \ldots$ until Q is encountered. The running time is approximately n steps in the worst case and $n/2$ steps on average. Therefore, exhaustive search can be circumvented by selecting elliptic curve parameters with n sufficiently large to represent an infeasible amount of computation (e.g., $n \geq 2^{80}$). The best general-purpose attack known on the ECDLP is the combination of the Pohlig-Hellman algorithm and Pollard's rho algorithm, which has a fully-exponential running time of $O(\sqrt{p})$ where p is the largest prime divisor of n. To resist this attack, the elliptic curve parameters should be chosen so that n is divisible by a prime number p sufficiently large so that $\sqrt{p}$ steps is an infeasible amount of computation (e.g., $p > 2^{160}$). If, in addition, the elliptic curve parameters are carefully chosen to defeat all other known attacks (see §4.1.4), then the ECDLP is believed to be infeasible given the state of today's computer technology.

It should be noted that there is no mathematical proof that the ECDLP is intractable. That is, no one has proven that there does not exist an efficient algorithm for solving the ECDLP. Indeed, such a proof would be extremely surprising. For example, the non-existence of a polynomial-time algorithm for the ECDLP would imply that $P \neq NP$ thus settling one of the fundamental outstanding open questions in computer science.[1] Furthermore, there is no theoretical evidence that the ECDLP is intractable. For example, the ECDLP is not known to be NP-hard,[2] and it is not likely to be proven to be NP-hard since the decision version of the ECDLP is known to be in both NP and co-NP.[3]

Nonetheless, some evidence for the intractability of the ECDLP has been gathered over the years. First, the problem has been extensively studied by researchers since elliptic curve cryptography was first proposed in 1985 and no general-purpose subexponential-time algorithm has been discovered. Second, Shoup has proven a lower bound of $\sqrt{n}$ for the discrete logarithm problem in *generic groups* of prime order n, where the group elements are random bit strings and one only has access to the group operation through a hypothetical oracle. While Shoup's result does not imply that the ECDLP is indeed hard (since the elements of an elliptic curve group have a meaningful and non-random representation), it arguably offers some hope that the discrete logarithm problem is hard in *some* groups.

The Pohlig-Hellman and Pollard's rho algorithms for the ECDLP are presented in §4.1.1 and §4.1.2, respectively. In §4.1.3, we survey the attempts at devising general-purpose subexponential-time attacks for the ECDLP. *Isomorphism attacks* attempt to reduce the ECDLP to the DLP in an isomorphic group for which subexponential-time

---

[1] P is the complexity class of decision (YES/NO) problems with polynomial-time algorithms. *NP* is the complexity class of decision problems whose YES answers can be verified in polynomial-time if one is presented with an appropriate proof. While it can readily be seen that $P \subseteq NP$, it is not known whether $P = NP$.

[2] A problem is *NP-hard* if all NP problems polynomial-time reduce to it. NP-hardness of a problem is considered evidence for its intractability since the existence of a polynomial-time algorithm for the problem would imply that $P = NP$.

[3] *co-NP* is the complexity class of decision problems whose NO answers can be verified in polynomial-time if one is presented with an appropriate proof. It is not known whether $NP = co\text{-}NP$. However, the existence of an NP-hard decision problem that is in both NP and co-NP would imply that $NP = co\text{-}NP$.

(or faster) algorithms are known. These attacks include the Weil and Tate pairing attacks, attacks on prime-field-anomalous curves, and the Weil descent methodology. While the mathematics behind these isomorphism attacks is quite sophisticated, the cryptographic implications of the attacks can be easily explained and there are simple countermeasures known for verifying that a given elliptic curve is immune to them. For these reasons, we have chosen to restrict the presentation of the isomorphism attacks in §4.1.4 to the cryptographic implications and countermeasures, and have excluded the detailed mathematical descriptions of the attacks. Finally, §4.1.5 considers two problems of cryptographic interest that are related to the ECDLP, namely the elliptic curve Diffie-Hellman problem (ECDHP) and the elliptic curve decision Diffie-Hellman problem (ECDDHP).

4.1.1 Pohlig-Hellman attack

The Pohlig-Hellman algorithm efficiently reduces the computation of $l = \log_P Q$ to the computation of discrete logarithms in the prime order subgroups of $\langle P \rangle$. It follows that the ECDLP in $\langle P \rangle$ is no harder than the ECDLP in its prime order subgroups. Hence, in order to maximize resistance to the Pohlig-Hellman attack, the elliptic curve parameters should be selected so that the order n of P is divisible by a large prime. We now outline the Pohlig-Hellman algorithm.

Suppose that the prime factorization of n is $n = p_1^{e_1} p_2^{e_2} \cdots p_r^{e_r}$. The Pohlig-Hellman strategy is to compute $l_i = l \bmod p_i^{e_i}$ for each $1 \leq i \leq r$, and then solve the system of congruences

$$\begin{aligned}
l &\equiv l_1 \pmod{p_1^{e_1}} \\
l &\equiv l_2 \pmod{p_2^{e_2}} \\
&\;\;\vdots \\
l &\equiv l_r \pmod{p_r^{e_r}}
\end{aligned}$$

for $l \in [0, n-1]$. (The Chinese Remainder Theorem guarantees a unique solution.) We show how the computation of each l_i can be reduced to the computation of e_i discrete logarithms in the subgroup of order p_i of $\langle P \rangle$. To simplify the notation, we write p for p_i and e for e_i. Let the base-p representation of l_i be

$$l_i = z_0 + z_1 p + z_2 p^2 + \cdots + z_{e-1} p^{e-1}$$

where each $z_i \in [0, p-1]$. The digits $z_0, z_1, \ldots, z_{e-1}$ are computed one at a time as follows. We first compute $P_0 = (n/p)P$ and $Q_0 = (n/p)Q$. Since the order of P_0 is p, we have

$$Q_0 = \frac{n}{p} Q = l\left(\frac{n}{p}P\right) = l P_0 = z_0 P_0.$$

Hence $z_0 = \log_{P_0} Q_0$ can be obtained by solving an ECDLP instance in $\langle P_0 \rangle$. Next, we compute $Q_1 = (n/p^2)(Q - z_0 P)$. We have

$$Q_1 = \frac{n}{p^2}(Q - z_0 P) = \frac{n}{p^2}(l - z_0)P = (l - z_0)\left(\frac{n}{p^2}P\right)$$

$$= (z_0 + z_1 p - z_0)\left(\frac{n}{p^2}P\right) = z_1\left(\frac{n}{p}P\right) = z_1 P_0.$$

Hence $z_1 = \log_{P_0} Q_1$ can be obtained by solving an ECDLP instance in $\langle P_0 \rangle$. In general, if the digits $z_0, z_1, \ldots, z_{t-1}$ have been computed, then $z_t = \log_{P_0} Q_t$, where

$$Q_t = \frac{n}{p^{t+1}}\left(Q - z_0 P - z_1 p P - z_2 p^2 P - \cdots - z_{t-1} p^{t-1} P\right).$$

Example 4.2 (*Pohlig-Hellman algorithm for solving the ECDLP*) Consider the elliptic curve E defined over $\mathbb{F}_{7919}$ by the equation:

$$E : y^2 = x^3 + 1001x + 75.$$

Let $P = (4023, 6036) \in E(\mathbb{F}_{7919})$. The order of P is

$$n = 7889 = 7^3 \cdot 23.$$

Let $Q = (4135, 3169) \in \langle P \rangle$. We wish to determine $l = \log_P Q$.

(i) We first determine $l_1 = l \bmod 7^3$. We write $l_1 = z_0 + z_1 7 + z_2 7^2$ and compute

$$P_0 = 7^2 23 P = (7801, 2071)$$
$$Q_0 = 7^2 23 Q = (7801, 2071)$$

and find that $Q_0 = P_0$; hence $z_0 = 1$. We next compute

$$Q_1 = 7 \cdot 23(Q - P) = (7285, 14)$$

and find that $Q_1 = 3P_0$; hence $z_1 = 3$. Finally, we compute

$$Q_2 = 23(Q - P - 3 \cdot 7P) = (7285, 7905)$$

and find that $Q_2 = 4P_0$; hence $z_2 = 4$. Thus $l_1 = 1 + 3 \cdot 7 + 4 \cdot 7^2 = 218$.

(ii) We next determine $l_2 = l \bmod 23$. We compute

$$P_0 = 7^3 P = (7190, 7003)$$
$$Q_0 = 7^3 Q = (2599, 759)$$

and find that $Q_0 = 10 P_0$; hence $l_2 = 10$.

(iii) Finally, we solve the pair of congruences

$$l \equiv 218 \pmod{7^3}$$
$$l \equiv 10 \pmod{23}$$

and obtain $l = 4334$.

For the remainder of §4.1, we will assume that the order n of P is prime.

4.1.2 Pollard's rho attack

The main idea behind Pollard's rho algorithm is to find distinct pairs (c', d') and (c'', d'') of integers modulo n such that

$$c'P + d'Q = c''P + d''Q.$$

Then

$$(c' - c'')P = (d'' - d')Q = (d'' - d')lP$$

and so

$$(c' - c'') \equiv (d'' - d')l \pmod{n}.$$

Hence $l = \log_P Q$ can be obtained by computing

$$l = (c' - c'')(d'' - d')^{-1} \bmod n. \qquad (4.1)$$

A naïve method for finding such pairs (c', d') and (c'', d'') is to select random integers $c, d \in [0, n-1]$ and store the triples $(c, d, cP + dQ)$ in a table sorted by third component until a point $cP + dQ$ is obtained for a second time—such an occurrence is called a *collision*. By the birthday paradox,[4] the expected number of iterations before a collision is obtained is approximately $\sqrt{\pi n/2} \approx 1.2533\sqrt{n}$. The drawback of this algorithm is the storage required for the $\sqrt{\pi n/2}$ triples.

Pollard's rho algorithm finds (c', d') and (c'', d'') in roughly the same expected time as the naïve method, but has negligible storage requirements. The idea is to define an *iterating function* $f : \langle P \rangle \to \langle P \rangle$ so that given $X \in \langle P \rangle$ and $c, d \in [0, n-1]$ with $X = cP + dQ$, it is easy to compute $\overline{X} = f(X)$ and $\overline{c}, \overline{d} \in [0, n-1]$ with $\overline{X} = \overline{c}P + \overline{d}Q$. Furthermore, f should have the characteristics of a random function.

The following is an example of a suitable iterating function. Let $\{S_1, S_2, \ldots, S_L\}$ be a "random" partition of $\langle P \rangle$ into L sets of roughly the same size. Typical values for the

---

[4]Suppose that an urn has n balls numbered 1 to n. The balls are randomly drawn, one at a time with replacement, from the urn. Then the expected number of draws before some ball is drawn for the second time is approximately $\sqrt{\pi n/2}$. If $n = 365$ and the balls represent different days of the year, then the statement can be interpreted as saying that the expected number of people that have to be gathered in a room before one expects at least two of them to have the same birthday is approximately $\sqrt{\pi 365/2} \approx 24$. This number is surprisingly small and hence the nomenclature "birthday paradox."

number of *branches* L are 16 and 32. For example, if $L = 32$ then a point $X \in \langle P \rangle$ can be assigned to S_j if the five least significant bits of the x-coordinate of X represent the integer $j - 1$. We write $H(X) = j$ if $X \in S_j$ and call H the *partition function*. Finally, let $a_j, b_j \in_R [0, n-1]$ for $1 \le j \le L$. Then $f : \langle P \rangle \to \langle P \rangle$ is defined by

$$f(X) = X + a_j P + b_j Q \text{ where } j = H(X).$$

Observe that if $X = cP + dQ$, then $f(X) = \overline{X} = \overline{c}P + \overline{d}Q$ where $\overline{c} = c + a_j \bmod n$ and $\overline{d} = d + b_j \bmod n$.

Now, any point $X_0 \in \langle P \rangle$ determines a sequence $\{X_i\}_{i \ge 0}$ of points where $X_i = f(X_{i-1})$ for $i \ge 1$. Since the set $\langle P \rangle$ is finite, the sequence will eventually *collide* and then cycle forever; that is, there is a smallest index t for which $X_t = X_{t+s}$ for some $s \ge 1$, and then $X_i = X_{i-s}$ for all $i \ge t + s$ (see Figure 4.1). Here, t is called

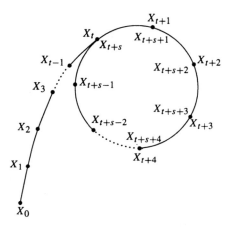

Figure 4.1. ρ-like shape of the sequence $\{X_i\}$ in Pollard's rho algorithm, where $t =$ tail length and $s =$ cycle length.

the *tail length* and s is called the *cycle length* of the sequence. If f is assumed to be a random function, then the sequence is expected to first collide after approximately $\sqrt{\pi n / 2}$ terms. Moreover, the expected tail length is $t \approx \sqrt{\pi n / 8}$ and the expected cycle length is $s \approx \sqrt{\pi n / 8}$.

A collision, that is, points X_i, X_j with $X_i = X_j$ and $i \ne j$, can be found using *Floyd's cycle-finding algorithm* wherein one computes pairs (X_i, X_{2i}) of points for $i = 1, 2, 3 \ldots$ until $X_i = X_{2i}$. After computing a new pair, the previous pair can be discarded; thus the storage requirements are negligible. The expected number k of such pairs that have to be computed before $X_i = X_{2i}$ is easily seen to satisfy $t \le k \le t + s$. In fact, assuming that f is a random function, the expected value of k is about $1.0308\sqrt{n}$, and hence the expected number of elliptic curve group operations is about

$3\sqrt{n}$. The complete algorithm is presented as Algorithm 4.3. Note that the probability of the algorithm terminating with failure (i.e., $d' = d''$ in step 7) is negligible.

Algorithm 4.3 Pollard's rho algorithm for the ECDLP (single processor)

INPUT: $P \in E(\mathbb{F}_q)$ of prime order n, $Q \in \langle P \rangle$.
OUTPUT: The discrete logarithm $l = \log_P Q$.
   1. Select the number L of branches (e.g., $L = 16$ or $L = 32$).
   2. Select a partition function $H : \langle P \rangle \to \{1, 2, \ldots, L\}$.
   3. For j from 1 to L do
        3.1 Select $a_j, b_j \in_R [0, n-1]$.
        3.2 Compute $R_j = a_j P + b_j Q$.
   4. Select $c', d' \in_R [0, n-1]$ and compute $X' = c'P + d'Q$.
   5. Set $X'' \leftarrow X', c'' \leftarrow c', d'' \leftarrow d'$.
   6. Repeat the following:
        6.1 Compute $j = H(X')$.
             Set $X' \leftarrow X' + R_j, c' \leftarrow c' + a_j \bmod n, d' \leftarrow d' + b_j \bmod n$.
        6.2 For i from 1 to 2 do
                Compute $j = H(X'')$.
                Set $X'' \leftarrow X'' + R_j, c'' \leftarrow c'' + a_j \bmod n, d'' \leftarrow d'' + b_j \bmod n$.
        Until $X' = X''$.
   7. If $d' = d''$ then return("failure");
        Else compute $l = (c' - c'')(d'' - d')^{-1} \bmod n$ and return(l).

Example 4.4 (*Pollard's rho algorithm for solving the ECDLP*) Consider the elliptic curve defined over $\mathbb{F}_{229}$ by the equation:

$$E : y^2 = x^3 + x + 44.$$

The point $P = (5, 116) \in E(\mathbb{F}_{229})$ has prime order $n = 239$. Let $Q = (155, 166) \in \langle P \rangle$. We wish to determine $l = \log_P Q$.
   We select the partition function $H : \langle P \rangle \to \{1, 2, 3, 4\}$ with $L = 4$ branches:

$$H(x, y) = (x \bmod 4) + 1,$$

and the four triples

$$[a_1, b_1, R_1] = [79, 163, (135, 117)]$$
$$[a_2, b_2, R_2] = [206, 19, (96, 97)]$$
$$[a_3, b_3, R_3] = [87, 109, (84, 62)]$$
$$[a_4, b_4, R_4] = [219, 68, (72, 134)].$$

The following table lists the triples (c', d', X') and (c'', d'', X'') computed in Algorithm 4.3 for the case $(c', d') = (54, 175)$ in step 4.

Iteration	c'	d'	X'	c''	d''	X''
–	54	175	(39,159)	54	175	(39,159)
1	34	4	(160, 9)	113	167	(130,182)
2	113	167	(130,182)	180	105	(36, 97)
3	200	37	(27, 17)	0	97	(108, 89)
4	180	105	(36, 97)	46	40	(223,153)
5	20	29	(119,180)	232	127	(167, 57)
6	0	97	(108, 89)	192	24	(57,105)
7	79	21	(81,168)	139	111	(185,227)
8	46	40	(223,153)	193	0	(197, 92)
9	26	108	(9, 18)	140	87	(194,145)
10	232	127	(167, 57)	67	120	(223,153)
11	212	195	(75,136)	14	207	(167, 57)
12	192	24	(57,105)	213	104	(57,105)

The algorithm finds

$$192P + 24Q = 213P + 104Q,$$

and hence

$$l = (192 - 213) \cdot (104 - 24)^{-1} \bmod 239 = 176.$$

Parallelized Pollard's rho attack

Suppose now that M processors are available for solving an ECDLP instance. A naïve approach would be to run Pollard's rho algorithm independently on each processor (with different randomly chosen starting points X_0) until any one processor terminates. A careful analysis shows that the expected number of elliptic curve operations performed by each processor before one terminates is about $3\sqrt{n/M}$. Thus the expected speedup is only by a factor of $\sqrt{M}$.

Van Oorschot and Wiener proposed a variant of Pollard's rho algorithm that yields a factor M speedup when M processors are employed. The idea is to allow the sequences $\{X_i\}_{i \geq 0}$ generated by the processors to collide with one another. More precisely, each processor randomly selects its own starting point X_0, but all processors use the same iterating function f to compute subsequent points X_i. Thus, if the sequences from two different processors ever collide, then, as illustrated in Figure 4.2, the two sequences will be identical from that point on.

Floyd's cycle-finding algorithm finds a collision in the sequence generated by a single processor. The following strategy enables efficient finding of a collision in the sequences generated by different processors. An easily testable *distinguishing property* of points is selected. For example, a point may be *distinguished* if the leading t bits of its x-coordinate are zero. Let θ be the proportion of points in $\langle P \rangle$ having this distinguishing property. Whenever a processor encounters a distinguished point, it transmits the point to a central server which stores it in a sorted list. When the server receives the same distinguished point for the second time, it computes the desired discrete logarithm via (4.1) and terminates all processors. The expected number of steps per processor before a collision occurs is $(\sqrt{\pi n/2})/M$. A subsequent distinguished point is expected after $1/\theta$ steps. Hence the expected number of elliptic curve operations performed by each processor before a collision of distinguished points is observed is

$$\frac{1}{M}\sqrt{\frac{\pi n}{2}} + \frac{1}{\theta}, \tag{4.2}$$

and this parallelized version of Pollard's rho algorithm achieves a speedup that is linear in the number of processors employed. Observe that the processors do not have to communicate with each other, and furthermore have limited communications with the central server. Moreover, the total space requirements at the central server can be controlled by careful selection of the distinguishing property. The complete algorithm is presented as Algorithm 4.5. Note that the probability of the algorithm terminating with failure (i.e., $d' = d''$ in step 7) is negligible.

Algorithm 4.5 Parallelized Pollard's rho algorithm for the ECDLP

INPUT: $P \in E(\mathbb{F}_q)$ of prime order n, $Q \in \langle P \rangle$.
OUTPUT: The discrete logarithm $l = \log_P Q$.
1. Select the number L of branches (e.g., $L = 16$ or $L = 32$).
2. Select a partition function $H : \langle P \rangle \to \{1, 2, \ldots, L\}$.
3. Select a distinguishing property for points in $\langle P \rangle$.
4. For j from 1 to L do
   4.1 Select $a_j, b_j \in_R [0, n-1]$.
   4.2 Compute $R_j = a_j P + b_j Q$.
5. Each of the M processors does the following:
   5.1 Select $c, d \in_R [0, n-1]$ and compute $X = cP + dQ$.
   5.2 Repeat the following:
       If X is distinguished then send (c, d, X) to the central server.
       Compute $j = H(X)$.
       Set $X \leftarrow X + R_j$, $c \leftarrow c + a_j \bmod n$, and $d \leftarrow d + b_j \bmod n$.
       Until the server receives some distinguished point Y for the second time.
6. Let the two triples associated with Y be (c', d', Y) and (c'', d'', Y).
7. If $d' = d''$ then return("failure");
   Else compute $l = (c' - c'')(d'' - d')^{-1} \bmod n$ and return(l).

Speeding Pollard's rho algorithm using automorphisms

Let $\psi : \langle P \rangle \to \langle P \rangle$ be a group automorphism, where $P \in E(\mathbb{F}_q)$ has order n. We assume that ψ can be computed very efficiently—significantly faster than a point addition. Suppose that ψ has order t, that is, t is the smallest positive integer such that

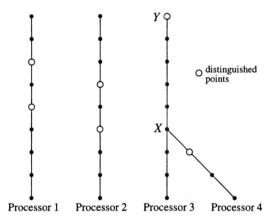

Figure 4.2. *Sequences generated by the parallelized Pollard's rho algorithm. The sequences generated by processors 3 and 4 first collide at X. The algorithm reports the collision at Y, the first subsequent distinguished point.*

$\psi^t(R) = R$ for all $R \in \langle P \rangle$. The relation $\sim$ on $\langle P \rangle$ defined by

$$R_1 \sim R_2 \text{ if and only if } R_1 = \psi^j(R_2) \text{ for some } j \in [0, t-1]$$

is an equivalence relation. The equivalence class $[R]$ containing a point $R \in \langle P \rangle$ is

$$[R] = \{R, \psi(R), \psi^2(R), \ldots, \psi^{l-1}(R)\},$$

where l is the smallest positive divisor of t such that $\psi^l(R) = R$.

The idea behind the speedup is to modify the iterating function f so that it is defined on the equivalence classes (rather than just on the points in $\langle P \rangle$). To achieve this, we define a canonical representative $\overline{R}$ for each equivalence class $[R]$. For example, $\overline{R}$ may be defined to be the point in $[R]$ whose x-coordinate is the smallest when considered as an integer (with ties broken by selecting the point with a smaller y-coordinate). Then, we can define an iterating function g on the canonical representatives by

$$g(R) = \overline{f(R)}.$$

Suppose now that we know the integer $\lambda \in [0, n-1]$ such that

$$\psi(P) = \lambda P.$$

Then, since ψ is a group automorphism, we have that $\psi(R) = \lambda R$ for all $R \in \langle P \rangle$. Thus, if we know integers a and b such that $X = aP + bQ$, then we can efficiently compute integers a' and b' such that $\overline{X} = a'P + b'Q$. Namely, if $\overline{X} = \psi^j(X)$, then $a' = \lambda^j a \bmod n$ and $b' = \lambda^j b \bmod n$.

The function g can now be used as the iterating function in the parallelized Pollard's rho algorithm. The initial point in a sequence is $X_0' = \overline{X_0}$ where $X_0 = a_0 P + b_0 Q$ and $a_0, b_0 \in_R [0, n-1]$. Subsequent terms of the sequence are computed iteratively: $X_i' = g(X_{i-1}')$ for $i \geq 1$. If most equivalence classes have size t, then the search space has size approximately n/t (versus n if equivalence classes are not employed) and thus the expected running time of the modified parallelized Pollard's rho algorithm is

$$\frac{1}{M}\sqrt{\frac{\pi n}{2t}} + \frac{1}{\theta},\tag{4.3}$$

a speedup by a factor of $\sqrt{t}$ over (4.2).

Example 4.6 (*using the negation map*) The negation map $\psi(P) = -P$ has order 2 and possesses the requisite properties described above. Thus, the parallelized Pollard's rho algorithm that uses equivalence classes under the negation map has an expected running time of

$$\frac{\sqrt{\pi n}}{2M} + \frac{1}{\theta}.\tag{4.4}$$

This is a speedup by a factor of $\sqrt{2}$ over (4.2) and is applicable to all elliptic curves.

Example 4.7 (*speeding Pollard's rho algorithm for Koblitz curves*) Recall from §3.4 that a Koblitz curve E_a (where $a \in \{0, 1\}$) is an elliptic curve defined over $\mathbb{F}_2$. The Frobenius map $\tau : E_a(\mathbb{F}_{2^m}) \to E_a(\mathbb{F}_{2^m})$, defined by $\tau(\infty) = \infty$ and $\tau(x, y) = (x^2, y^2)$, is also a group automorphism of order m and can be computed efficiently since squaring is a cheap operation in $\mathbb{F}_{2^m}$. If $P \in E_a(\mathbb{F}_{2^m})$ has prime order n such that n^2 does not divide $\#E_a(\mathbb{F}_{2^m})$, then $\tau(P) \in \langle P \rangle$ and hence τ is also a group automorphism of $\langle P \rangle$. Let $\mu = (-1)^{1-a}$. It follows from Note 3.72 that one of the two solutions λ to the modular equation

$$\lambda^2 - \mu\lambda + 2 \equiv 0 \pmod{n}$$

satisfies $\tau(P) = \lambda P$. Thus, τ has the requisite properties, and parallelized Pollard's rho algorithm that uses equivalence classes under the Frobenius map has an expected running time of

$$\frac{1}{M}\sqrt{\frac{\pi n}{2m}} + \frac{1}{\theta}.$$

Furthermore, the parallelized Pollard's rho algorithm can exploit both the Frobenius map and the negation map to achieve an expected running time of

$$\frac{1}{2M}\sqrt{\frac{\pi n}{m}} + \frac{1}{\theta}.\tag{4.5}$$

for Koblitz curves, a speedup by a factor of $\sqrt{2m}$ over (4.2).

Example 4.8 (*solving a 113-bit ECDLP instance on the Internet*) Let E be an elliptic curve defined over a prime field $\mathbb{F}_p$, and let $P \in E(\mathbb{F}_p)$ have prime order n. Suppose also that both p and n are 113-bit primes. Elliptic curves with these parameters would offer roughly the same security as provided by 56-bit DES. Assume that we have $M = 10,000$ computers available on the Internet to solve an instance of the ECDLP in $\langle P \rangle$, and that each computer can perform one iteration (of step 5.2 of Algorithm 4.5) in 10 microseconds. If we select the distinguishing property so that $\theta = 2^{-30}$, then the expected number of iterations performed by each computer before the logarithm is found is approximately

$$\frac{\sqrt{\pi 2^{113}}}{2 \cdot 10000} + 2^{30} \approx 9.03 \times 10^{13}.$$

Hence, the expected running time before the logarithm is found is about 1045 days, or three years. Since the x-coordinate and associated (c, d) pair of a distinguished point can be stored in 12 32-bit words, the total space required for storing the distinguished points at the central server is about

$$12\theta \frac{\sqrt{\pi n}}{2} \text{ words } \approx 3.8 \text{ Gigabytes.}$$

One concludes from these calculations that while solving a 113-bit ECDLP requires significant resources, 113-bit ECC provides adequate security only for low-security short-term applications.

Multiple logarithms

We show how the distinguished points stored during the solution of one ECDLP instance in $\langle P \rangle$ using (parallelized) Pollard's rho algorithm can be used to accelerate the solution of other ECDLP instances in $\langle P \rangle$. This property is relevant to the security of elliptic curve cryptographic systems because users typically share elliptic curve parameters $E, \mathbb{F}_q, P$, and select their own public keys $Q \in \langle P \rangle$. Thus, if one or more private keys can be found using Pollard's rho algorithm, then finding other private keys becomes progressively easier.

Suppose that $l = \log_P Q$ has been computed. For each stored triple (c, d, X) associated to distinguished points X encountered during the computation, the integer $s = c + dl \bmod n$ satisfies $X = sP$. Similarly, the integers $r_j = a_j + b_j l \bmod n$ satisfy $R_j = r_j P$ for $1 \leq j \leq L$. Now, to compute $l' = \log_P Q'$ where $Q' \in \langle P \rangle$, each processor computes the terms Y_i of a random sequence with starting point $Y_0 = c'_0 P + d'_0 Q'$ where $c'_0, d'_0 \in_R [0, n-1]$, and the *same* iterating function f as before. For each distinguished point Y encountered in the new sequences, a triple (c', d', Y) such that $Y = c'P + d'Q'$ is sent to the central server. A collision can occur between two new sequences or between a new sequence and an old one. In the former case, we have

$$c'P + d'Q' = c''P + d''Q',$$

whence $l' = (c' - c'')(d'' - d')^{-1} \bmod n$. In the latter case, we have

$$c'P + d'Q' = sP,$$

whence $l' = (s - c')(d')^{-1} \bmod n$.

The distinguished points collected during the first two ECDLP computations can similarly be used for the computation of the third ECDLP computation, and so on. The expected number W_k of random walk steps before k ECDLP instances are iteratively solved in the manner described has been shown to be

$$W_k \approx T \sum_{i=0}^{k-1} \frac{\binom{2i}{i}}{4^i},$$

where T is the expected number of random walk steps to solve a single ECDLP instance. Thus, solving the second, third, and fourth ECDLP instances take only 50%, 37%, 31%, respectively, of the time to solve the first instance.

Concerns that successive ECDLP computations become easier can be addressed by ensuring that the elliptic curve parameters are chosen so that the first ECDLP instance is infeasible to solve.

4.1.3 Index-calculus attacks

Index-calculus algorithms are the most powerful methods known for computing discrete logarithms in some groups including the multiplicative group $\mathbb{F}_q^*$ of a finite field, the jacobian $J_C(\mathbb{F}_q)$ of a hyperelliptic curve C of high genus g defined over a finite field $\mathbb{F}_q$, and the class group of an imaginary quadratic number field. It is natural then to ask whether index-calculus methods can lead to subexponential-time algorithms for the ECDLP.

We begin by outlining the index-calculus method in the general setting of an arbitrary cyclic group and illustrate how the method can be adapted to the multiplicative group of a prime field or binary field. We then explain why the natural ways to extend the index-calculus methods to elliptic curve groups are highly unlikely to yield subexponential-time algorithms for the ECDLP.

The main idea behind index-calculus methods

Let G be a cyclic group of order n generated by α. Suppose that we wish to find $\log_\alpha \beta$ for $\beta \in G$. The index-calculus method is the following.

1. *Factor base selection.* Choose a subset $S = \{p_1, p_2, \ldots, p_t\}$ of G, called the *factor base*, such that a "significant" proportion of elements in G can be efficiently expressed as a product of elements from S. The choice of S will depend on the characteristics of the particular group G.

2. *Compute logarithms of elements in S.* Select random integers $k \in [0, n-1]$ until α^k can be written as a product of elements in S:

$$\alpha^k = \prod_{i=1}^{t} p_i^{c_i}, \text{ where } c_i \geq 0. \tag{4.6}$$

Taking logarithms to the base α of both sides of (4.6) yields a linear equation where the unknowns are the logarithms of factor base elements:

$$k \equiv \sum_{i=1}^{t} c_i \log_\alpha p_i \pmod{n}. \tag{4.7}$$

This procedure is repeated until slightly more than t such equations have been obtained. The resulting linear system of equations can then be solved to obtain $\log_\alpha p_i$ for $1 \leq i \leq t$.

3. *Compute* $\log_\alpha \beta$. Select random integers k until $\alpha^k \beta$ can be written as a product of elements in S:

$$\alpha^k \beta = \prod_{i=1}^{t} p_i^{d_i}, \text{ where } d_i \geq 0. \tag{4.8}$$

Taking logarithms to the base α of both sides of (4.8) yields the desired logarithm of β:

$$\log_\alpha \beta = -k + \sum_{i=1}^{t} d_i \log_\alpha p_i \bmod n. \tag{4.9}$$

The running time of the index-calculus algorithm depends critically on the choice of the factor base S. There is also a trade-off in the size t of S. Larger t are preferred because then the probability of a random group element factoring over S is expected to be larger. On the other hand, smaller t are preferred because then the number of linear equations that need to be collected is smaller. The optimum choice of t depends on the proportion of elements in G that factor over S.

Consider now the case $G = \mathbb{F}_p^*$, the multiplicative group of a prime field. The elements of $\mathbb{F}_p^*$ can be regarded as the integers in $[1, p-1]$. There is a natural choice for S, namely the prime numbers $\leq B$ for some bound B. An element of $\mathbb{F}_p^*$ factors over S if it is B-smooth, that is, all its prime factors are $\leq B$. The optimal factor base size depends on the distribution of B-smooth integers in $[1, p-1]$, and yields a subexponential-time algorithm for the DLP in $\mathbb{F}_p^*$. The fastest variant of this algorithm is the number field sieve (NFS) and has an expected running time of $L_p[\frac{1}{3}, 1.923]$.

Consider next the case $G = \mathbb{F}_{2^m}^*$, the multiplicative group of a binary field. The elements of $\mathbb{F}_{2^m}^*$ can be regarded as the nonzero binary polynomials of degree less than m. Hence there is a natural choice for S, namely the irreducible binary polynomials of degree $\leq B$ for some bound B. An element of $\mathbb{F}_{2^m}^*$ factors over S if it is B-smooth, that is, all its irreducible factors have degree $\leq B$. The optimal factor base size depends on the distribution of B-smooth polynomials among the binary polynomials of degree $\leq B$, and yields a subexponential-time algorithm for the DLP in $\mathbb{F}_{2^m}^*$. The fastest variant of this algorithm is Coppersmith's algorithm and has an expected running time of $L_{2^m}[\frac{1}{3}, c]$ for some constant $c < 1.587$.

Failure of index-calculus attacks on the ECLDP

Suppose that we wish to solve instances of the ECDLP in $E(\mathbb{F}_p)$ where $E : y^2 = x^3 + ax + b$ is an elliptic curve defined over the prime field $\mathbb{F}_p$. For simplicity, suppose that $E(\mathbb{F}_p)$ has prime order so that $E(\mathbb{F}_p) = \langle P \rangle$ for some $P \in E(\mathbb{F}_p)$. The most natural index-calculus approach would first *lift* E to a curve $\widetilde{E}$ defined over the field $\mathbb{Q}$ of rational numbers, that is, to a curve $\widetilde{E} : y^2 = x^3 + \widetilde{a}x + \widetilde{b}$ where $\widetilde{a}, \widetilde{b} \in \mathbb{Q}$ and $a = \widetilde{a} \bmod p$ and $b = \widetilde{b} \bmod p$. Then, the *lift of a point* $R \in E(\mathbb{F}_p)$ is a point $\widetilde{R} \in \widetilde{E}(\mathbb{Q})$ whose coordinates reduce modulo p to those of R. This lifting process is analogous to the ones used in the index-calculus method described above for computing discrete logarithms in $\mathbb{F}_p^*$ and $\mathbb{F}_{2^m}^*$, where elements of $\mathbb{F}_p^*$ are "lifted" to integers in $\mathbb{Z}$, and elements of $\mathbb{F}_{2^m}^*$ are "lifted" to polynomials in $\mathbb{F}_2[z]$.

The celebrated Mordell-Weil Theorem states that the group structure of $\widetilde{E}(\mathbb{Q})$ is $E_{\text{tors}} \times \mathbb{Z}^r$, where E_{tors} is the set of points in $\widetilde{E}(\mathbb{Q})$ of finite order, and r is a nonnegative integer called the *rank* of $\widetilde{E}$. Furthermore, a theorem of Mazur states that E_{tors} has small size—in fact $\#E_{\text{tors}} \leq 16$. Thus a natural choice for the factor base is a set of points $P_1, P_2, \ldots, P_r$ such that $\widetilde{P}_1, \widetilde{P}_2, \ldots, \widetilde{P}_r$ are linearly independent in $\widetilde{E}(\mathbb{Q})$. Relations of the form (4.6) can then be found by selecting multiples kP of P in $E(\mathbb{F}_p)$ until the lift $\widetilde{kP}$ can be written as an integer linear combination of the basis points in $\widetilde{E}(\mathbb{Q})$:

$$\widetilde{kP} = c_1 \widetilde{P}_1 + c_2 \widetilde{P}_2 + \cdots + c_r \widetilde{P}_r.$$

Then, reducing the coordinates of the points modulo p yields a desired relation

$$kP = c_1 P_1 + c_2 P_2 + \cdots + c_r P_r$$

in $E(\mathbb{F}_p)$.

There are two main reasons why this index-calculus approach is doomed to fail. The first is that no one knows how to efficiently lift points in $E(\mathbb{F}_p)$ to $\widetilde{E}(\mathbb{Q})$. Certainly, for a lifting procedure to be feasible, the lifted points should have small *height*. (Roughly speaking, the height of a point $\widetilde{P} \in \widetilde{E}(\mathbb{Q})$ is the number of bits needed to write down the coordinates of $\widetilde{P}$.) However, it has been proven (under some reasonable assumptions) that the number of points of small height in any elliptic curve $\widetilde{E}(\mathbb{Q})$ is extremely small, so that only an insignificant proportion of points in $E(\mathbb{F}_p)$ can possibly be lifted to points of small height in $\widetilde{E}(\mathbb{Q})$—this is the second reason for unavoidable failure of this index-calculus approach.

For the ECDLP in elliptic curves E over non-prime fields $\mathbb{F}_q$, one could consider lifting E to an elliptic curve over a number field, or to an elliptic curve over a function field. These approaches are also destined to fail for the same reasons as for the prime field case.

Of course there may be other ways of applying the index-calculus methodology for solving the ECDLP. Thus far, no one has found an approach that yields a general subexponential-time (or better) algorithm for the ECDLP.

4.1.4 Isomorphism attacks

Let E be an elliptic curve defined over a finite field $\mathbb{F}_q$, and let $P \in E(\mathbb{F}_q)$ have prime order n. Let G be a group of order n. Since n is prime, $\langle P \rangle$ and G are both cyclic and hence isomorphic. If one could efficiently compute an isomorphism

$$\psi : \langle P \rangle \to G, \tag{4.10}$$

then ECDLP instances in $\langle P \rangle$ could be efficiently reduced to instances of the DLP in G. Namely, given P and $Q \in \langle P \rangle$, we have

$$\log_P Q = \log_{\psi(P)} \psi(Q). \tag{4.11}$$

Isomorphism attacks reduce the ECDLP to the DLP in groups G for which subexponential-time (or faster) algorithms are known. These attacks are *special-purpose* in that they result in ECDLP solvers that are faster than Pollard's rho algorithm only for special classes of elliptic curves. The isomorphism attacks that have been devised are the following:

(i) The *attack on prime-field-anomalous curves* reduces the ECDLP in an elliptic curve of order p defined over the prime field $\mathbb{F}_p$ to the DLP in the additive group $\mathbb{F}_p^+$ of integers modulo p.

(ii) In the case $\gcd(n, q) = 1$, the *Weil and Tate pairing attacks* establish an isomorphism between $\langle P \rangle$ and a subgroup of order n of the multiplicative group $\mathbb{F}_{q^k}^*$ of some extension field $\mathbb{F}_{q^k}$.

(iii) The *GHS Weil descent attack* attempts to reduce the ECDLP in an elliptic curve defined over a binary field $\mathbb{F}_{2^m}$ to the DLP in the jacobian of a hyperelliptic curve defined over a proper subfield of $\mathbb{F}_{2^m}$.

Since a polynomial-time algorithm is known for solving the DLP in $\mathbb{F}_p^+$, and since subexponential-time algorithms are known for the DLP in the multiplicative group of a finite field and for the jacobian of high-genus hyperelliptic curves, these isomorphism attacks can have important implications to the security of elliptic curve cryptographic schemes. We next discuss the cryptographic implications of and countermeasures to these attacks.

Attack on prime-field-anomalous curves

An elliptic curve E defined over a prime field $\mathbb{F}_p$ is said to be *prime-field-anomalous* if $\#E(\mathbb{F}_p) = p$. The group $E(\mathbb{F}_p)$ is cyclic since it has prime order, and hence $E(\mathbb{F}_p)$

is isomorphic to the *additive* group $\mathbb{F}_p^+$ of integers modulo p. Now, the DLP in $\mathbb{F}_p^+$ is the following: given p, $a \in \mathbb{F}_p^+$, $a \neq 0$, and $b \in \mathbb{F}_p^+$, find $l \in [0, p-1]$ such that $la \equiv b$ (mod p). Since $l = ba^{-1} \bmod p$, the DLP in $\mathbb{F}_p^+$ can be efficiently solved by using the extended Euclidean algorithm (Algorithm 2.20) to compute $a^{-1} \bmod p$.

In 1997, Araki, Satoh, Semaev and Smart showed than an isomorphism

$$\psi : E(\mathbb{F}_p) \rightarrow \mathbb{F}_p^+$$

can be efficiently computed for prime-field-anomalous elliptic curves. Consequently, the ECDLP in such curves can be efficiently solved and hence these elliptic curves must not be used in cryptographic protocols. Since it is easy to determine whether an elliptic curve E over a prime field $\mathbb{F}_p$ is prime-field-anomalous (by checking whether $\#E(\mathbb{F}_p) = p$), the Araki-Satoh-Semaev-Smart attack can easily be circumvented in practice.

Weil and Tate pairing attacks

Suppose now that the prime order n of $P \in E(\mathbb{F}_q)$ satisfies $\gcd(n, q) = 1$. Let k be the smallest positive integer such that $q^k \equiv 1$ (mod n); the integer k is the multiplicative order of q modulo n and therefore is a divisor of $n - 1$. Since n divides $q^k - 1$, the multiplicative group $\mathbb{F}_{q^k}^*$ of the extension field $\mathbb{F}_{q^k}$ has a unique subgroup G of order n. The Weil pairing attack constructs an isomorphism from $\langle P \rangle$ to G when the additional constraint $n \nmid (q - 1)$ is satisfied, while the Tate pairing attack constructs an isomorphism between $\langle P \rangle$ and G without requiring this additional constraint. The integer k is called the *embedding degree*.

For most elliptic curves one expects that $k \approx n$. In this case the Weil and Tate pairing attacks do not yield an efficient ECDLP solver since the finite field $\mathbb{F}_{q^k}$ has exponential size relative to the size of the ECDLP parameters. (The ECDLP parameters have size $O(\log q)$ bits, while elements of $\mathbb{F}_{q^k}$ have size $O(k \log q)$ bits.) However, some special elliptic curves do have small embedding degrees k. For these curves, the Weil and Tate pairing reductions take polynomial time. Since subexponential-time algorithms are known for the DLP in $\mathbb{F}_{q^k}^*$, this results in a subexponential-time algorithm for the ECDLP in these special elliptic curves.

The special classes of elliptic curves with small embedding degree include supersingular curves (Definition 3.10) and elliptic curves of trace 2 (with $\#E(\mathbb{F}_q) = q - 1$). These curves have $k \leq 6$ and consequently should not be used in the elliptic curve protocols discussed in this book unless the underlying finite field is large enough so that the DLP in $\mathbb{F}_{q^k}^*$ is considered intractable. We note that constructive applications have recently been discovered for supersingular elliptic curves, including the design of identity-based public-key encryption schemes (see page 199 for references).

To ensure that an elliptic curve E defined over $\mathbb{F}_q$ is immune to the Weil and Tate pairing attacks, it is sufficient to check that n, the order of the base point $P \in E(\mathbb{F}_q)$, does not divide $q^k - 1$ for all small k for which the DLP in $\mathbb{F}_{q^k}^*$ is considered tractable. If $n > 2^{160}$, then it suffices to check this condition for all $k \in [1, 20]$.

Weil descent

Suppose that E is a non-supersingular elliptic curve defined over a binary field $K = \mathbb{F}_{2^m}$, and suppose that $\#E(\mathbb{F}_{2^m}) = nh$ where n is prime and h is small (e.g., $h = 2$ or $h = 4$). In 1998, Frey proposed using Weil descent to reduce the ECDLP in $E(\mathbb{F}_{2^m})$ to the DLP in the jacobian variety of a curve of larger genus defined over a proper subfield $k = \mathbb{F}_{2^l}$ of K. Let $d = m/l$. In Frey's method, referred to as the *Weil descent attack methodology*, one first constructs the so-called Weil restriction $W_{K/k}$ of scalars of E, which is a d-dimensional abelian variety over k. One then attempts to find a curve C defined over k in $W_{K/k}$ such that (i) there are algorithms for solving the DLP in the jacobian $J_C(k)$ of C over k that are faster than Pollard's rho method; and (ii) ECDLP instances in $E(K)$ can be efficiently mapped to DLP instances in $J_C(k)$.

Gaudry, Hess and Smart (GHS) showed how the Weil restriction $W_{K/k}$ can be intersected with $n - 1$ hyperplanes to eventually obtain a hyperelliptic curve C of genus g defined over k from an irreducible component in the intersection. Furthermore, they gave an efficient algorithm that (in most cases) reduces ECDLP instances in $E(K)$ to instances of the hyperelliptic curve discrete logarithm problem (HCDLP) in $J_C(k)$. Now, the Enge-Gaudry index-calculus algorithm for the HCDLP in a genus-g hyperelliptic curve over $\mathbb{F}_q$ has a subexponential expected running time of $L_{q^g}[\sqrt{2}]$ bit operations for $g/\log q \to \infty$. Thus, provided that g is not too large, the GHS attack yields a subexponential-time algorithm for the original ECDLP.

It was subsequently shown that the GHS attack fails for *all* cryptographically interesting elliptic curves over $\mathbb{F}_{2^m}$ for *all* prime $m \in [160, 600]$. Note that such fields have only one proper subfield, namely $\mathbb{F}_2$. In particular, it was shown that the hyperelliptic curves C produced by the GHS attack either have genus too small (whence $J_C(\mathbb{F}_2)$ is too small to yield any non-trivial information about the ECDLP in $E(\mathbb{F}_{2^m})$), or have genus too large ($g \geq 2^{16} - 1$, whence the HCDLP in $J_C(\mathbb{F}_2)$ is infeasible using known methods for solving the HCDLP). The GHS attack has also been shown to fail for all elliptic curves over certain fields $\mathbb{F}_{2^m}$ where $m \in [160, 600]$ is composite; such fields include $\mathbb{F}_{2^{169}}$, $\mathbb{F}_{2^{209}}$ and $\mathbb{F}_{2^{247}}$.

However, the GHS attack *is* effective for solving the ECDLP in *some* elliptic curves over $\mathbb{F}_{2^m}$ where $m \in [160, 600]$ is composite. For example, the ECDLP in approximately 2^{94} of the 2^{162} isomorphism classes of elliptic curves over $\mathbb{F}_{2^{161}}$ can be solved in about 2^{48} steps by using the GHS attack to reduce the problem to an instance of the HCDLP in a genus-8 hyperelliptic curve over the subfield $\mathbb{F}_{2^{23}}$. Since Pollard's rho method takes roughly 2^{80} steps for solving the ECDLP in cryptographically interesting elliptic curves over $\mathbb{F}_{2^{161}}$, the GHS attack is deemed to be successful for the 2^{94} elliptic curves.

Let $\mathbb{F}_{2^m}$, where $m \in [160, 600]$ is composite, be a binary field for which the GHS attack exhibits some success. Then the proportion of elliptic curves over $\mathbb{F}_{2^m}$ that succumb to the GHS attack is relatively small. Thus, if one selects an elliptic curve over $\mathbb{F}_{2^m}$ at random, then there is a very high probability that the elliptic curve will resist the GHS attack. However, failure of the GHS attack does not imply failure of the Weil descent attack methodology—there may be other useful curves which lie on the Weil restriction that were not constructed by the GHS method. Thus, to account for potential future developments in the Weil descent attack methodology, it seems prudent to altogether avoid using elliptic curves over $\mathbb{F}_{2^m}$ where m is composite.

4.1.5 Related problems

While hardness of the ECDLP is necessary for the security of any elliptic curve cryptographic scheme, it is generally not sufficient. We present some problems related to the ECDLP whose hardness is assumed in the security proofs for some elliptic curve protocols. All these problems can be presented in the setting of a general cyclic group, however we restrict the discussion to elliptic curve groups.

Elliptic curve Diffie-Hellman problem

Definition 4.9 The *(computational) elliptic curve Diffie-Hellman problem (ECDHP)* is: given an elliptic curve E defined over a finite field $\mathbb{F}_q$, a point $P \in E(\mathbb{F}_q)$ of order n, and points $A = aP$, $B = bP \in \langle P \rangle$, find the point $C = abP$.

If the ECDLP in $\langle P \rangle$ can be efficiently solved, then the ECDHP in $\langle P \rangle$ can also be efficiently solved by first finding a from (P, A) and then computing $C = aB$. Thus the ECDHP is no harder than the ECDLP. It is not known whether the ECDHP is equally as hard as the ECDLP; that is, no one knows how to efficiently solve the ECDLP given a (hypothetical) oracle that efficiently solves the ECDHP. However, the equivalence of the ECDLP and ECDHP has been proven in some special cases where the ECDLP is believed to be hard, for example when n is prime and all the prime factors of $n - 1$ are small. The strongest evidence for the hardness of the ECDHP comes from a result of Boneh and Lipton who proved (under some reasonable assumptions about the distribution of smooth integers in a certain interval) that if n is prime and the ECDLP cannot be solved in $L_n[\frac{1}{2}, c]$ subexponential time (for some constant c), then the ECDHP cannot be solved in $L_n[\frac{1}{2}, c - 2]$ subexponential time. Further evidence for the hardness of the ECDHP comes from Shoup's lower bound of $\sqrt{n}$ for the Diffie-Hellman problem in generic groups of prime order n.

Elliptic curve decision Diffie-Hellman problem

The ECDHP is concerned with computing the Diffie-Hellman secret point abP given (P, aP, bP). For the security of some elliptic curve protocols, it may be necessary that an adversary does not learn *any* information about abP. This requirement can be formalized by insisting that the adversary cannot distinguish abP from a random element in $\langle P \rangle$.

Definition 4.10 The *elliptic curve decision Diffie-Hellman problem (ECDDHP)* is: given an elliptic curve E defined over a finite field $\mathbb{F}_q$, a point $P \in E(\mathbb{F}_q)$ of order n, and points $A = aP$, $B = bP$, and $C = cP \in \langle P \rangle$, determine whether $C = abP$ or, equivalently, whether $c \equiv ab \pmod{n}$.

If the ECDHP in $\langle P \rangle$ can be efficiently solved, then the ECDDHP in $\langle P \rangle$ can also be efficiently solved by first finding $C' = abP$ from (P, A, B) and then comparing C' with C. Thus the ECDDHP is no harder than the ECDHP (and also the ECDLP). The only hardness result that has been proved for ECDDHP is Shoup's lower bound of $\sqrt{n}$ for the decision Diffie-Hellman problem in generic groups of prime order n.

4.2 Domain parameters

Domain parameters for an elliptic curve scheme describe an elliptic curve E defined over a finite field $\mathbb{F}_q$, a base point $P \in E(\mathbb{F}_q)$, and its order n. The parameters should be chosen so that the ECDLP is resistant to all known attacks. There may also be other constraints for security or implementation reasons. Typically, domain parameters are shared by a group of entities; however, in some applications they may be specific to each user. For the remainder of this section we shall assume that the underlying field is either a prime field (§2.2), a binary field (§2.3), or an optimal extension field (§2.4).

Definition 4.11 *Domain parameters* $D = (q, \text{FR}, S, a, b, P, n, h)$ are comprised of:

1. The *field order* q.

2. An indication FR (*field representation*) of the representation used for the elements of $\mathbb{F}_q$.

3. A *seed* S if the elliptic curve was randomly generated in accordance with Algorithm 4.17, Algorithm 4.19, or Algorithm 4.22.

4. Two *coefficients* $a, b \in \mathbb{F}_q$ that define the equation of the elliptic curve E over $\mathbb{F}_q$ (i.e., $y^2 = x^3 + ax + b$ in the case of a prime field or an OEF, and $y^2 + xy = x^3 + ax^2 + b$ in the case of a binary field).

5. Two field elements x_P and y_P in $\mathbb{F}_q$ that define a finite point $P = (x_P, y_P) \in E(\mathbb{F}_q)$ in affine coordinates. P has prime order and is called the *base point*.

6. The *order* n of P.

7. The *cofactor* $h = \#E(\mathbb{F}_q)/n$.

Security constraints In order to avoid the Pohlig-Hellman attack (§4.1.1) and Pollard's rho attack (§4.1.2) on the ECDLP, it is necessary that $\#E(\mathbb{F}_q)$ be divisible by a sufficiently large prime n. At a minimum, one should have $n > 2^{160}$. Having fixed an underlying field $\mathbb{F}_q$, maximum resistance to the Pohlig-Hellman and Pollard's rho attacks is attained by selecting E so that $\#E(\mathbb{F}_q)$ is prime or *almost prime*, that is, $\#E(\mathbb{F}_q) = hn$ where n is prime and h is small (e.g., $h = 1, 2, 3$ or 4).

Some further precautions should be exercised to assure resistance to isomorphism attacks (§4.1.4). To avoid the attack on prime-field-anomalous curves, one should verify that $\#E(\mathbb{F}_q) \neq q$. To avoid the Weil and Tate pairing attacks, one should ensure that n does not divide $q^k - 1$ for all $1 \leq k \leq C$, where C is large enough so that the DLP in $\mathbb{F}_{q^c}^*$ is considered intractable (if $n > 2^{160}$ then $C = 20$ suffices). Finally, to ensure resistance to the Weil descent attack, one may consider using a binary field $\mathbb{F}_{2^m}$ only if m is prime.

Selecting elliptic curves verifiably at random A prudent way to guard against attacks on special classes of curves that may be discovered in the future is to select the elliptic curve E *at random* subject to the condition that $\#E(\mathbb{F}_q)$ is divisible by a large prime. Since the probability that a random curve succumbs to one of the known special-purpose isomorphism attacks is negligible, the known attacks are also prevented. A curve can be selected *verifiably at random* by choosing the coefficients of the defining elliptic curve as the outputs of a one-way function such as SHA-1 according to some pre-specified procedure. The input seed S to the function then serves as proof (under the assumption that SHA-1 cannot be inverted) that the elliptic curve was indeed generated at random. This provides some assurance to the user of the elliptic curve that it was not intentionally constructed with hidden weaknesses which could thereafter be exploited to recover the user's private keys.

4.2.1 Domain parameter generation and validation

Algorithm 4.14 is one way to generate cryptographically secure domain parameters—all the security constraints discussed above are satisfied. A set of domain parameters can be explicitly validated using Algorithm 4.15. The validation process proves that the elliptic curve in question has the claimed order and resists all known attacks on the ECDLP, and that the base point has the claimed order. An entity who uses elliptic curves generated by untrusted software or parties can use validation to be assured that the curves are cryptographically secure.

Sample sets of domain parameters are provided in §A.2.

Note 4.12 (*restrictions on n and L in Algorithms 4.14 and 4.15*)

(i) Since n is chosen to satisfy $n > 2^L$, the condition $L \geq 160$ in the input of Algorithm 4.14 ensures that $n > 2^{160}$.

(ii) The condition $L \leq \lfloor \log_2 q \rfloor$ ensures that $2^L \leq q$ whence an elliptic curve E over $\mathbb{F}_q$ with order $\#E(\mathbb{F}_q)$ divisible by an L-bit prime should exist (recall that $\#E(\mathbb{F}_q) \approx q$). In addition, if $q = 2^m$ then L should satisfy $L \leq \lfloor \log_2 q \rfloor - 1$ because $\#E(\mathbb{F}_{2^m})$ is even (cf. Theorem 3.18(iii)).

(iii) The condition $n > 4\sqrt{q}$ guarantees that $E(\mathbb{F}_q)$ has a unique subgroup of order n because $\#E(\mathbb{F}_q) \leq (\sqrt{q}+1)^2$ by Hasse's Theorem (Theorem 3.7) and so n^2 does not divide $\#E(\mathbb{F}_q)$. Furthermore, since $hn = \#E(\mathbb{F}_q)$ must lie in the Hasse interval, it follows that there is only one possible integer h such that $\#E(\mathbb{F}_q) = hn$, namely $h = \lfloor (\sqrt{q}+1)^2/n \rfloor$.

Note 4.13 (*selecting candidate elliptic curves*) In Algorithm 4.14, candidate elliptic curves E are generated verifiably at random using the procedures specified in §4.2.2. The orders $\#E(\mathbb{F}_q)$ can be determined using the SEA point counting algorithm for the prime field or OEF case, or a variant of Satoh's point counting algorithm for the binary field case (see §4.2.3). The orders $\#E(\mathbb{F}_q)$ of elliptic curves E over $\mathbb{F}_q$ are roughly uniformly distributed in the Hasse interval $[q+1-2\sqrt{q}, q+1+2\sqrt{q}]$ if $\mathbb{F}_q$ is a prime field or an OEF, and roughly uniformly distributed among the even integers in the Hasse interval if $\mathbb{F}_q$ is a binary field. Thus, one can use estimates of the expected number of primes in the Hasse interval to obtain fairly accurate estimates of the expected number of elliptic curves tried until one having prime or almost-prime order is found. The testing of candidate curves can be accelerated by deploying an *early-abort strategy* which first uses the SEA algorithm to quickly determine $\#E(\mathbb{F}_q)$ modulo small primes l, rejecting those curves where $\#E(\mathbb{F}_q)$ is divisible by l. Only those elliptic curves which pass these tests are subjected to a full point counting algorithm.

An alternative to using random curves is to select a subfield curve or a curve using the CM method (see §4.2.3). Algorithm 4.14 can be easily modified to accommodate these selection methods.

Algorithm 4.14 Domain parameter generation

INPUT: A field order q, a field representation FR for $\mathbb{F}_q$, security level L satisfying $160 \leq L \leq \lfloor \log_2 q \rfloor$ and $2^L \geq 4\sqrt{q}$.

OUTPUT: Domain parameters $D = (q, \text{FR}, S, a, b, P, n, h)$.

1. Select $a, b \in \mathbb{F}_q$ verifiably at random using Algorithm 4.17, 4.19 or 4.22 if $\mathbb{F}_q$ is a prime field, binary field, or OEF, respectively. Let S be the seed returned. Let E be $y^2 = x^3 + ax + b$ in the case $\mathbb{F}_q$ is a prime field or an OEF, and $y^2 + xy = x^3 + ax^2 + b$ in the case $\mathbb{F}_q$ is a binary field.
2. Compute $N = \#E(\mathbb{F}_q)$ (see §4.2.3).
3. Verify that N is divisible by a large prime n satisfying $n > 2^L$. If not, then go to step 1.
4. Verify that n does not divide $q^k - 1$ for $1 \leq k \leq 20$. If not, then go to step 1.
5. Verify that $n \neq q$. If not, then go to step 1.
6. Set $h \leftarrow N/n$.
7. Select an arbitrary point $P' \in E(\mathbb{F}_q)$ and set $P = hP'$. Repeat until $P \neq \infty$.
8. Return($q, \text{FR}, S, a, b, P, n, h$).

Algorithm 4.15 Explicit domain parameter validation

INPUT: Domain parameters $D = (q, \text{FR}, S, a, b, P, n, h)$.

OUTPUT: Acceptance or rejection of the validity of D.

1. Verify that q is a prime power ($q = p^m$ where p is prime and $m \geq 1$).
2. If $p = 2$ then verify that m is prime.
3. Verify that FR is a valid field representation.
4. Verify that a, b, x_P, y_P (where $P = (x, y)$) are elements of $\mathbb{F}_q$ (i.e., verify that they are of the proper format for elements of $\mathbb{F}_q$).
5. Verify that a and b define an elliptic curve over $\mathbb{F}_q$ (i.e., $4a^3 + 27b^2 \neq 0$ for fields with $p > 3$, and $b \neq 0$ for binary fields).
6. If the elliptic curve was randomly generated then
   6.1 Verify that S is a bit string of length at least l bits, where l is the bitlength of the hash function H.
   6.2 Use Algorithm 4.18 (for prime fields), Algorithm 4.21 (for binary fields) or Algorithm 4.23 (for OEFs) to verify that a and b were properly derived from S.
7. Verify that $P \neq \infty$.
8. Verify that P satisfies the elliptic curve equation defined by a, b.
9. Verify that n is prime, that $n > 2^{160}$, and that $n > 4\sqrt{q}$.
10. Verify that $nP = \infty$.
11. Compute $h' = \lfloor (\sqrt{q} + 1)^2 / n \rfloor$ and verify that $h = h'$.
12. Verify that n does not divide $q^k - 1$ for $1 \leq k \leq 20$.
13. Verify that $n \neq q$.
14. If any verification fails then return("Invalid"); else return("Valid").

4.2.2 Generating elliptic curves verifiably at random

Algorithms 4.17, 4.19 and 4.22 are specifications for generating elliptic curves verifiably at random over prime fields, binary fields, and OEFs, respectively. The corresponding verification procedures are presented as Algorithms 4.18, 4.21 and 4.23. The algorithms for prime fields and binary fields are from the ANSI X9.62 standard.

Note 4.16 (*explanation of the parameter r in Algorithms 4.17 and 4.22*) Suppose that $\mathbb{F}_q$ is a finite field of characteristic > 3. If elliptic curves $E_1 : y^2 = x^3 + a_1 x + b_1$ and $E_2 : y^2 = x^3 + a_2 x + b_2$ defined over $\mathbb{F}_q$ are isomorphic over $\mathbb{F}_q$ and satisfy $b_1 \neq 0$ (so $b_2 \neq 0$), then $a_1^3/b_1^2 = a_2^3/b_2^2$. The singular elliptic curves, that is, the curves $E : y^2 = x^3 + ax + b$ for which $4a^3 + 27b^2 = 0$ in $\mathbb{F}_q$, are precisely those which either have $a = 0$ and $b = 0$, or $a^3/b^2 = -27/4$. If $r \in \mathbb{F}_q$ with $r \neq 0$ and $r \neq -27/4$, then there are precisely two isomorphism classes of curves $E : y^2 = x^3 + ax + b$ with $a^3/b^2 = r$ in $\mathbb{F}_q$. Hence, there are essentially only two choices for (a, b) in step 10 of Algorithms 4.17 and 4.22. The conditions $r \neq 0$ and $r \neq -27/4$ imposed in step 9 of both algorithms ensure the exclusion of singular elliptic curves. Finally, we mention that this method of generating curves will never produce the elliptic curves with $a = 0$, $b \neq 0$, nor the elliptic curves with $a \neq 0$, $b = 0$. This is not a concern because such curves constitute a negligible fraction of all elliptic curves, and therefore are unlikely to ever be generated by any method which selects an elliptic curve uniformly at random.

Generating random elliptic curves over prime fields

Algorithm 4.17 Generating a random elliptic curve over a prime field $\mathbb{F}_p$

INPUT: A prime $p > 3$, and an l-bit hash function H.
OUTPUT: A seed S, and $a, b \in \mathbb{F}_p$ defining an elliptic curve $E : y^2 = x^3 + ax + b$.
1. Set $t \leftarrow \lceil \log_2 p \rceil$, $s \leftarrow \lfloor (t-1)/l \rfloor$, $v \leftarrow t - sl$.
2. Select an arbitrary bit string S of length $g \geq l$ bits.
3. Compute $h = H(S)$, and let r_0 be the bit string of length v bits obtained by taking the v rightmost bits of h.
4. Let R_0 be the bit string obtained by setting the leftmost bit of r_0 to 0.
5. Let z be the integer whose binary representation is S.
6. For i from 1 to s do:
   6.1 Let s_i be the g-bit binary representation of the integer $(z + i) \bmod 2^g$.
   6.2 Compute $R_i = H(s_i)$.
7. Let $R = R_0 \| R_1 \| \cdots \| R_s$.
8. Let r be the integer whose binary representation is R.
9. If $r = 0$ or if $4r + 27 \equiv 0 \pmod{p}$ then go to step 2.
10. Select arbitrary $a, b \in \mathbb{F}_p$, not both 0, such that $r \cdot b^2 \equiv a^3 \pmod{p}$.
11. Return(S, a, b).

Algorithm 4.18 Verifying that an elliptic curve over $\mathbb{F}_p$ was randomly generated

---

INPUT: Prime $p > 3$, l-bit hash function H, seed S of bitlength $g \geq l$, and $a, b \in \mathbb{F}_p$ defining an elliptic curve $E : y^2 = x^3 + ax + b$.
OUTPUT: Acceptance or rejection that E was generated using Algorithm 4.17.
1. Set $t \leftarrow \lceil \log_2 p \rceil$, $s \leftarrow \lfloor (t-1)/l \rfloor$, $v \leftarrow t - sl$.
2. Compute $h = H(S)$, and let r_0 be the bit string of length v bits obtained by taking the v rightmost bits of h.
3. Let R_0 be the bit string obtained by setting the leftmost bit of r_0 to 0.
4. Let z be the integer whose binary representation is S.
5. For i from 1 to s do:
   5.1 Let s_i be the g-bit binary representation of the integer $(z + i) \bmod 2^g$.
   5.2 Compute $R_i = H(s_i)$.
6. Let $R = R_0 \| R_1 \| \cdots \| R_s$.
7. Let r be the integer whose binary representation is R.
8. If $r \cdot b^2 \equiv a^3 \pmod{p}$ then return("Accept"); else return("Reject").

Generating random elliptic curves over binary fields

Algorithm 4.19 Generating a random elliptic curve over a binary field $\mathbb{F}_{2^m}$

INPUT: A positive integer m, and an l-bit hash function H.
OUTPUT: Seed S, and $a, b \in \mathbb{F}_{2^m}$ defining an elliptic curve $E : y^2 + xy = x^3 + ax^2 + b$.

1. Set $s \leftarrow \lfloor (m-1)/l \rfloor$, $v \leftarrow m - sl$.
2. Select an arbitrary bit string S of length $g \geq l$ bits.
3. Compute $h = H(S)$, and let b_0 be the bit string of length v bits obtained by taking the v rightmost bits of h.
4. Let z be the integer whose binary representation is S.
5. For i from 1 to s do:
   5.1 Let s_i be the g-bit binary representation of the integer $(z+i) \bmod 2^g$.
   5.2 Compute $b_i = H(s_i)$.
6. Let $b = b_0 \| b_1 \| \cdots \| b_s$.
7. If $b = 0$ then go to step 2.
8. Select arbitrary $a \in \mathbb{F}_{2^m}$.
9. Return(S, a, b).

Note 4.20 (*selection of a in Algorithm 4.19*) By Theorem 3.18(ii) on the isomorphism classes of elliptic curves over $\mathbb{F}_{2^m}$, it suffices to select a from $\{0, \gamma\}$ where $\gamma \in \mathbb{F}_{2^m}$ satisfies $\text{Tr}(\gamma) = 1$. Recall also from Theorem 3.18(iii) that $\#E(\mathbb{F}_{2^m})$ is always even, while if $a = 0$ then $\#E(\mathbb{F}_{2^m})$ is divisible by 4.

Algorithm 4.21 Verifying that an elliptic curve over $\mathbb{F}_{2^m}$ was randomly generated

---

INPUT: Positive integer m, l-bit hash function H, seed S of bitlength $g \geq l$, and $a, b \in \mathbb{F}_{2^m}$ defining an elliptic curve $E : y^2 + xy = x^3 + ax^2 + b$.
OUTPUT: Acceptance or rejection that E was generated using Algorithm 4.19.

1. Set $s \leftarrow \lfloor (m-1)/l \rfloor$, $v \leftarrow m - sl$.
2. Compute $h = H(S)$, and let b_0 be the bit string of length v bits obtained by taking the v rightmost bits of h.
3. Let z be the integer whose binary representation is S.
4. For i from 1 to s do:
   4.1 Let s_i be the g-bit binary representation of the integer $(z+i) \bmod 2^g$.
   4.2 Compute $b_i = H(s_i)$.
5. Let $b' = b_0 \| b_1 \| \cdots \| b_s$.
6. If $b' = b$ then return("Accept"); else return("Reject").

Generating random elliptic curves over OEFs

Algorithm 4.22 Generating a random elliptic curve over an OEF $\mathbb{F}_{p^m}$

INPUT: A prime $p > 3$, reduction polynomial $f(x) \in \mathbb{F}_p[x]$ of degree m, and an l-bit hash function H.

OUTPUT: A seed S, and $a, b \in \mathbb{F}_{p^m}$ defining an elliptic curve $E : y^2 = x^3 + ax + b$.

1. Set $W \leftarrow \lceil \log_2 p \rceil$, $t \leftarrow W \cdot m$, $s \leftarrow \lfloor (t-1)/l \rfloor$, $v \leftarrow t - sl$.
2. Select an arbitrary bit string S of length $g \geq l$ bits.
3. Compute $h = H(S)$, and let T_0 be the bit string of length v bits obtained by taking the v rightmost bits of h.
4. Let z be the integer whose binary representation is S.
5. For i from 1 to s do:
    5.1 Let s_i be the g-bit binary representation of the integer $(z + i) \bmod 2^g$.
    5.2 Compute $T_i = H(s_i)$.
6. Write $T_0 \| T_1 \| \cdots \| T_s = R_{m-1} \| \cdots \| R_1 \| R_0$ where each R_i is a W-bit string.
7. For each i, $0 \leq i \leq m-1$, let $r_i = \overline{R}_i \bmod p$, where $\overline{R}_i$ denotes the integer whose binary representation is R_i.
8. Let r be the element $(r_{m-1}, \ldots, r_1, r_0)$ in the OEF defined by p and $f(x)$.
9. If $r = 0$ or if $4r + 27 = 0$ in $\mathbb{F}_{p^m}$ then go to step 2.
10. Select arbitrary $a, b \in \mathbb{F}_{p^m}$, not both 0, such that $r \cdot b^2 = a^3$ in $\mathbb{F}_{p^m}$.
11. Return(S, a, b).

Algorithm 4.23 Verifying that an elliptic curve over $\mathbb{F}_{p^m}$ was randomly generated

---

INPUT: Prime $p > 3$, reduction polynomial $f(x) \in \mathbb{F}_p[x]$ of degree m, l-bit hash function H, seed S of bitlength $g \geq l$, and $a, b \in \mathbb{F}_{p^m}$ defining an elliptic curve $E : y^2 = x^3 + ax + b$.

OUTPUT: Acceptance or rejection that E was generated using Algorithm 4.22.

1. Set $W \leftarrow \lceil \log_2 p \rceil$, $t \leftarrow W \cdot m$, $s \leftarrow \lfloor (t-1)/l \rfloor$, $v \leftarrow t - sl$.
2. Compute $h = H(S)$, and let T_0 be the bit string of length v bits obtained by taking the v rightmost bits of h.
3. Let z be the integer whose binary representation is S.
4. For i from 1 to s do:
    4.1 Let s_i be the g-bit binary representation of the integer $(z + i) \bmod 2^g$.
    4.2 Compute $T_i = H(s_i)$.
5. Write $T_0 \| T_1 \| \cdots \| T_s = R_{m-1} \| \cdots \| R_1 \| R_0$ where each R_i is a W-bit string.
6. For each i, $0 \leq i \leq m-1$, let $r_i = \overline{R}_i \bmod p$, where $\overline{R}_i$ denotes the integer whose binary representation is R_i.
7. Let r be the element $(r_{m-1}, \ldots, r_1, r_0)$ in the OEF defined by p and $f(x)$.
8. If $r \cdot b^2 = a^3$ in $\mathbb{F}_{p^m}$ then return("Accept"); else return("Reject").

4.2.3   *Determining the number of points on an elliptic curve*

As discussed in the introduction to §4.2, the order $\#E(\mathbb{F}_q)$ of an elliptic curve E used in a cryptographic protocol should satisfy some constraints imposed by security considerations. Thus, determining the number of points on an elliptic curve is an important ingredient of domain parameter generation. A naïve algorithm for point counting is to find, for each $x \in \mathbb{F}_q$, the number of solutions $y \in \mathbb{F}_q$ to the Weierstrass equation for E. This method is clearly infeasible for field sizes of cryptographic interest. In practice, one of the following three techniques is employed for selecting an elliptic curve of known order.

Subfield curves   Let $q = p^{ld}$, where $d > 1$. One selects an elliptic curve E defined over $\mathbb{F}_{p^l}$, counts the number of points in $E(\mathbb{F}_{p^l})$ using a naïve method, and then easily determines $\#E(\mathbb{F}_q)$ using Theorem 3.11. The group used for the cryptographic application is $E(\mathbb{F}_q)$. Since the elliptic curve E is defined over a proper subfield $\mathbb{F}_{p^l}$ of $\mathbb{F}_q$, it is called a *subfield curve*. For example, Koblitz curves studied in §3.4 are subfield curves with $p = 2$ and $l = 1$. Since $\#E(\mathbb{F}_{p^{lc}})$ divides $\#E(\mathbb{F}_q)$ for all divisors c of d and an elliptic curve of prime or almost-prime order is desirable, l should be small (preferably $l = 1$) and d should be prime.

The complex-multiplication (CM) method   In this method, one first selects an order N that meets the required security constraints, and then constructs an elliptic curve with that order. For elliptic curves over prime fields, the CM method is also called the *Atkin-Morain method*; for binary fields it is called the *Lay-Zimmer* method. The CM method is very efficient provided that the finite field order q and the elliptic curve order $N = q + 1 - t$ are selected so that the complex multiplication field $\mathbb{Q}(\sqrt{t^2 - 4q})$ has small class number. Cryptographically suitable curves over 160-bit fields can be generated in one minute on a workstation. In particular, the CM method is much faster than the best algorithms known for counting the points on randomly selected elliptic curves over prime fields and OEFs. For elliptic curves over binary fields, the CM method has been superseded by faster point counting algorithms (see below).

Since the ECDLP is not known to be any easier for elliptic curves having small class number, elliptic curves generated using the CM method appear to offer the same level of security as those generated randomly.

Point counting   In 1985, Schoof presented the first polynomial-time algorithm for computing $\#E(\mathbb{F}_q)$ for an arbitrary elliptic curve E. The algorithm computes $\#E(\mathbb{F}_q) \bmod l$ for small prime numbers l, and then determines $\#E(\mathbb{F}_q)$ using the Chinese Remainder Theorem. It is inefficient in practice for values of q of practical interest, but was subsequently improved by several people including Atkin and Elkies resulting in the so-called *Schoof-Elkies-Atkin (SEA) algorithm*. The SEA algorithm, which is the best algorithm known for counting the points on arbitrary elliptic curves over prime fields or OEFs, takes a few minutes for values of q of practical interest. Since it can very quickly determine the number of points modulo small primes l, it can be used in an early-abort strategy to quickly eliminate candidate curves whose orders are divisible by a small prime number.

In 1999, Satoh proposed a fundamentally new method for counting the number of points over finite fields of small characteristic. Variants of Satoh's method, including the *Satoh-Skjernaa-Taguchi (SST)* and the *Arithmetic Geometric Mean (AGM) algorithms*, are extremely fast for the binary field case and can find cryptographically suitable elliptic curves over $\mathbb{F}_{2^{163}}$ in just a few seconds on a workstation.

4.3   *Key pairs*

An elliptic curve key pair is associated with a particular set of domain parameters $D = (q, \mathrm{FR}, S, a, b, P, n, h)$. The public key is a randomly selected point Q in the group $\langle P \rangle$ generated by P. The corresponding private key is $d = \log_P Q$. The entity A generating the key pair must have the assurance that the domain parameters are valid (see §4.2). The association between domain parameters and a public key must be verifiable by all entities who may subsequently use A's public key. In practice, this association can be achieved by cryptographic means (e.g., a certification authority generates a certificate attesting to this association) or by context (e.g., all entities use the same domain parameters).

Algorithm 4.24 Key pair generation

INPUT: Domain parameters $D = (q, \mathrm{FR}, S, a, b, P, n, h)$.
OUTPUT: Public key Q, private key d.
   1. Select $d \in_R [1, n-1]$.
   2. Compute $Q = dP$.
   3. Return(Q, d).

Observe that the problem of computing a private key d from the public key Q is precisely the elliptic curve discrete logarithm problem. Hence it is crucial that the domain parameters D be selected so that the ECDLP is intractable. Furthermore, it is important that the numbers d generated be "random" in the sense that the probability of any particular value being selected must be sufficiently small to preclude an adversary from gaining advantage through optimizing a search strategy based on such probability.

Public key validation

The purpose of public key validation is to verify that a public key possesses certain arithmetic properties. Successful execution demonstrates that an associated private key logically exists, although it does not demonstrate that someone has actually computed the private key nor that the claimed owner actually possesses it. Public key validation is especially important in Diffie-Hellman-based key establishment protocols where an entity A derives a shared secret k by combining her private key with a public key received from another entity B, and subsequently uses k in some symmetric-key protocol (e.g., encryption or message authentication). A dishonest B might select an invalid public key in such a way that the use of k reveals information about A's private key.

Algorithm 4.25 Public key validation

INPUT: Domain parameters $D = (q, \mathrm{FR}, S, a, b, P, n, h)$, public key Q.
OUTPUT: Acceptance or rejection of the validity of Q.
  1. Verify that $Q \neq \infty$.
  2. Verify that x_Q and y_Q are properly represented elements of $\mathbb{F}_q$ (e.g., integers in the interval $[0, q-1]$ if $\mathbb{F}_q$ is a prime field, and bit strings of length m bits if $\mathbb{F}_q$ is a binary field of order 2^m).
  3. Verify that Q satisfies the elliptic curve equation defined by a and b.
  4. Verify that $nQ = \infty$.
  5. If any verification fails then return("Invalid"); else return("Valid").

There may be much faster methods for verifying that $nQ = \infty$ than performing an expensive point multiplication nQ. For example, if $h = 1$ (which is usually the case for elliptic curves over prime fields that are used in practice), then the checks in steps 1, 2 and 3 of Algorithm 4.25 imply that $nQ = \infty$. In some protocols the check that $nQ = \infty$ may be omitted and either embedded in the protocol computations or replaced by the check that $hQ \neq \infty$. The latter check guarantees that Q is not in a small subgroup of $E(\mathbb{F}_q)$ of order dividing h.

Algorithm 4.26 Embedded public key validation

INPUT: Domain parameters $D = (q, \mathrm{FR}, S, a, b, P, n, h)$, public key Q.
OUTPUT: Acceptance or rejection of the (partial) validity of Q.
  1. Verify that $Q \neq \infty$.
  2. Verify that x_Q and y_Q are properly represented elements of $\mathbb{F}_q$ (e.g., integers in the interval $[0, q-1]$ if $\mathbb{F}_q$ is a prime field, and bit strings of length m bits if $\mathbb{F}_q$ is a binary field of order 2^m).
  3. Verify that Q lies on the elliptic curve defined by a and b.
  4. If any verification fails then return("Invalid"); else return("Valid").

Small subgroup attacks

We illustrate the importance of the checks in public key validation by describing a *small subgroup attack* on a cryptographic protocol that is effective if some checks are not performed. Suppose that an entity A's key pair (Q, d) is associated with domain parameters $D = (q, \mathrm{FR}, S, a, b, P, n, h)$. In the one-pass elliptic curve Diffie-Hellman

(ECDH) protocol, a second entity B who has authentic copies of D and Q selects $r \in_R [1, n-1]$ and sends $R = rP$ to A. A then computes the point $K = dR$, while B computes the same point $K = rQ$. Both A and B derive a shared secret key $k = \text{KDF}(K)$, where KDF is some key derivation function. Note that this key establishment protocol only provides unilateral authentication (of A to B), which may be desirable in some applications such as the widely deployed SSL protocol where the server is authenticated to the client but not conversely. We suppose that A and B subsequently use the key k to authenticate messages for each other using a message authentication code algorithm MAC.

Suppose now that A omits the check that $nQ = \infty$ in public key validation (step 4 in Algorithm 4.25). Let l be a prime divisor of the cofactor h. In the small subgroup attack, B sends to A a point R of order l (instead of a point in the group $\langle P \rangle$ of order n). A computes $K = dR$ and $k = \text{KDF}(K)$. Since R has order l, K also has order l (unless $d \equiv 0 \pmod{l}$ in which case $K = \infty$). Thus $K = d_l R$ where $d_l = d \bmod l$. Now, when A sends to B a message m and its authentication tag $t = \text{MAC}_k(m)$, B can repeatedly select $l' \in [0, l-1]$ until $t = \text{MAC}_{k'}(m)$ where $k' = \text{KDF}(K')$ and $K' = l'R$—then $d_l = l'$ with high probability. The expected number of trials before B succeeds is $l/2$. B can repeat the attack with different points R of pairwise relatively prime orders $l_1, l_2, \ldots, l_s$, and combine the results using the Chinese Remainder Theorem to obtain $d \bmod l_1 l_2 \cdots l_s$. If h is relatively large, then B can obtain significant information about A's private key d, and can perhaps then deduce all of d by exhaustive search.

In practice, h is usually small (e.g., $h = 1, 2$ or 4) in which case the small subgroup attack described above can only determine a very small number of bits of d. We next describe an attack that extends the small subgroup attack to elliptic curves different from the one specified in the domain parameters.

Invalid-curve attacks

The main observation in invalid-curve attacks is that the usual formulae for adding points on an elliptic curve E defined over $\mathbb{F}_q$ do not involve the coefficient b (see §3.1.2). Thus, if E' is any elliptic curve defined over $\mathbb{F}_q$ whose reduced Weierstrass equation differs from E's only in the coefficient b, then the addition laws for E' and E are the same. Such an elliptic curve E' is called an *invalid curve* relative to E.

Suppose now that A does not perform public key validation on points it receives in the one-pass ECDH protocol. The attacker B selects an invalid curve E' such that $E'(\mathbb{F}_q)$ contains a point R of small order l, and sends R to A. A computes $K = dR$ and $k = \text{KDF}(R)$. As with the small subgroup attack, when A sends B a message m and its tag $t = \text{MAC}_k(m)$, B can determine $d_l = d \bmod l$. By repeating the attack with points R (on perhaps different invalid curves) of relatively prime orders, B can eventually recover d.

The simplest way to prevent the invalid-curve attacks is to check that a received point does indeed lie on the legitimate elliptic curve.

4.4 Signature schemes

Signatures schemes are the digital counterparts to handwritten signatures. They can be used to provide data origin authentication, data integrity, and non-repudiation. Signature schemes are commonly used by trusted certification authorities to sign certificates that bind together an entity and its public key.

Definition 4.27 A *signature scheme* consists of four algorithms:

1. A *domain parameter generation algorithm* that generates a set D of domain parameters.

2. A *key generation algorithm* that takes as input a set D of domain parameters and generates key pairs (Q, d).

3. A *signature generation algorithm* that takes as input a set of domain parameters D, a private key d, and a message m, and produces a signature Σ.

4. A *signature verification algorithm* that takes as input the domain parameters D, a public key Q, a message m, and a purported signature Σ, and accepts or rejects the signature.

We assume that the domain parameters D are valid (see §4.2) and that the public key Q is valid and associated with D (see §4.3). The signature verification algorithm always accepts input (D, Q, m, Σ) if Σ was indeed generated by the signature generation algorithm with input (D, d, m).

The following notion of security of a signature scheme is due to Goldwasser, Micali and Rivest (GMR).

Definition 4.28 A signature scheme is said to be *secure* (or *GMR-secure*) if it is existentially unforgeable by a computationally bounded adversary who can mount an adaptive chosen-message attack. In other words, an adversary who can obtain signatures of any messages of its choosing from the legitimate signer is unable to produce a valid signature of any new message (for which it has not already requested and obtained a signature).

This security definition is a very strong one—the adversary is afforded tremendous powers (access to a signing oracle) while its goals are very weak (obtain the signature of *any* message not previously presented to the signing oracle). It can be argued that this notion is too strong for some applications—perhaps adversaries are unable to obtain signatures of messages of their choice, or perhaps the messages whose signatures they are able to forge are meaningless (and therefore harmless) within the context of the application. However, it is impossible for the designer of a signature scheme intended for widespread use to predict the precise abilities of adversaries in all environments in which the signature scheme will be deployed. Furthermore, it is impossible for the designer to formulate general criteria to determine which messages will be considered "meaningful." Therefore, it is prudent to design signature schemes that are secure under the strongest possible notion of security—GMR-security has gained acceptance as the "right" one.

Two standardized signature schemes are presented, ECDSA in §4.4.1, and EC-KCDSA in §4.4.2.

4.4.1 ECDSA

The Elliptic Curve Digital Signature Algorithm (ECDSA) is the elliptic curve analogue of the Digital Signature Algorithm (DSA). It is the most widely standardized elliptic curve-based signature scheme, appearing in the ANSI X9.62, FIPS 186-2, IEEE 1363-2000 and ISO/IEC 15946-2 standards as well as several draft standards.

In the following, H denotes a cryptographic hash function whose outputs have bitlength no more than that of n (if this condition is not satisfied, then the outputs of H can be truncated).

Algorithm 4.29 ECDSA signature generation

INPUT: Domain parameters $D = (q, \mathrm{FR}, S, a, b, P, n, h)$, private key d, message m.
OUTPUT: Signature (r, s).
1. Select $k \in_R [1, n-1]$.
2. Compute $kP = (x_1, y_1)$ and convert x_1 to an integer $\overline{x}_1$.
3. Compute $r = \overline{x}_1 \bmod n$. If $r = 0$ then go to step 1.
4. Compute $e = H(m)$.
5. Compute $s = k^{-1}(e + dr) \bmod n$. If $s = 0$ then go to step 1.
6. Return(r, s).

Algorithm 4.30 ECDSA signature verification

INPUT: Domain parameters $D = (q, \mathrm{FR}, S, a, b, P, n, h)$, public key Q, message m, signature (r, s).
OUTPUT: Acceptance or rejection of the signature.
1. Verify that r and s are integers in the interval $[1, n-1]$. If any verification fails then return("Reject the signature").
2. Compute $e = H(m)$.
3. Compute $w = s^{-1} \bmod n$.
4. Compute $u_1 = ew \bmod n$ and $u_2 = rw \bmod n$.
5. Compute $X = u_1 P + u_2 Q$.
6. If $X = \infty$ then return("Reject the signature");
7. Convert the x-coordinate x_1 of X to an integer $\overline{x}_1$; compute $v = \overline{x}_1 \bmod n$.
8. If $v = r$ then return("Accept the signature");
   Else return("Reject the signature").

Proof that signature verification works   If a signature (r, s) on a message m was indeed generated by the legitimate signer, then $s \equiv k^{-1}(e + dr) \pmod{n}$. Rearranging gives

$$k \equiv s^{-1}(e + dr) \equiv s^{-1}e + s^{-1}rd \equiv we + wrd \equiv u_1 + u_2 d \pmod{n}.$$

Thus $X = u_1 P + u_2 Q = (u_1 + u_2 d)P = kP$, and so $v = r$ as required. $\square$

Security notes

Note 4.31 (*security proofs for ECDSA*)   In order for ECDSA to be GMR-secure, it is necessary that the ECDLP in $\langle P \rangle$ be intractable, and that the hash function H be cryptographically secure (preimage resistant and collision resistant). It has not been proven that these conditions are also sufficient for GMR-security. ECDSA has, however, been proven GMR-secure in the generic group model (where the group $\langle P \rangle$ is replaced by a generic group) and under reasonable and concrete assumptions about H. While a security proof in the generic group model does not imply security in the real world where a specific group such as an elliptic curve group is used, it arguably inspires *some* confidence in the security of ECDSA.

Note 4.32 (*rationale for security requirements on the hash function*)   If H is not preimage resistant, then an adversary E may be able to forge signatures as follows. E selects an arbitrary integer l and computes r as the x-coordinate of $Q + lP$ reduced modulo n. E sets $s = r$ and computes $e = rl \bmod n$. If E can find a message m such that $e = H(m)$, then (r, s) is a valid signature for m.

  If H is not collision resistant, then E can forge signatures as follows. She first finds two different messages m and m' such that $H(m) = H(m')$. She then asks A to sign m; the resulting signature is also valid for m'.

Note 4.33 (*rationale for the checks on r and s in signature verification*)   Step 1 of the ECDSA signature verification procedure checks that r and s are integers in the interval $[1, n-1]$. These checks can be performed very efficiently, and are prudent measures in light of known attacks on related ElGamal signature schemes which do not perform these checks. The following is a plausible attack on ECDSA if the check $r \neq 0$ (and, more generally, $r \not\equiv 0 \pmod{n}$) is not performed. Suppose that A is using the elliptic curve $y^2 = x^3 + ax + b$ over a prime field $\mathbb{F}_p$, where b is a quadratic residue modulo p, and suppose that A uses a base point $P = (0, \sqrt{b})$ of prime order n. (It is plausible that all entities may select a base point with zero x-coordinate in order to minimize the size of domain parameters.) An adversary can now forge A's signature on any message m of its choice by computing $e = H(m)$. It can readily be checked that $(r = 0, s = e)$ is a valid signature for m.

Note 4.34 (*security requirements for per-message secrets*) The per-message secrets k in ECDSA signature generation have the same security requirements as the private key d. If an adversary E learns a single per-message secret k that A used to generate a signature (r, s) on some message m, then E can recover A's private key since

$$d = r^{-1}(ks - e) \bmod n \tag{4.12}$$

where $e = H(m)$ (see step 5 of ECDSA signature generation). Furthermore, Howgrave-Graham and Smart have shown that if an adversary somehow learns a few (e.g., five) consecutive bits of per-message secrets corresponding to several (e.g., 100) signed messages, then the adversary can easily compute the private key. These observations demonstrate that per-message secrets must be securely generated, securely stored, and securely destroyed after they have been used.

Note 4.35 (*repeated use of per-message secrets*) The per-message secrets k should be generated randomly. In particular, this ensures that per-message secrets never repeat, which is important because otherwise the private key d can be recovered. To see this, suppose that the same per-message secret k was used to generate ECDSA signatures (r, s_1) and (r, s_2) on two messages m_1 and m_2. Then $s_1 \equiv k^{-1}(e_1 + dr) \pmod{n}$ and $s_2 \equiv k^{-1}(e_2 + dr) \pmod{n}$, where $e_1 = H(m_1)$ and $e_2 = H(m_2)$. Then $ks_1 \equiv e_1 + dr \pmod{n}$ and $ks_2 \equiv e_2 + dr \pmod{n}$. Subtraction gives $k(s_1 - s_2) \equiv e_1 - e_2 \pmod{n}$. If $s_1 \not\equiv s_2 \pmod{n}$, which occurs with overwhelming probability, then

$$k \equiv (s_1 - s_2)^{-1}(e_1 - e_2) \pmod{n}.$$

Thus an adversary can determine k, and then use (4.12) to recover d.

4.4.2   EC-KCDSA

EC-KCDSA is the elliptic curve analogue of the Korean Certificate-based Digital Signature Algorithm (KCDSA). The description presented here is from the ISO/IEC 15946-2 standard.

In the following, H denotes a cryptographic hash function whose outputs are bit strings of length l_H. The bitlength of the domain parameter n should be at least l_H. *hcert* is the hash value of the signer's certification data that should include the signer's identifier, domain parameters, and public key. The signer's private key is an integer $d \in_R [1, n]$, while her public key is $Q = d^{-1}P$ (instead of dP which is the case with all other protocols presented in this book). This allows for the design of signature generation and verification procedures that do not require performing a modular inversion. In contrast, ECDSA signature generation and verification respectively require the computation of $k^{-1} \bmod n$ and $s^{-1} \bmod n$.

Algorithm 4.36 EC-KCDSA signature generation

INPUT: Domain parameters $D = (q, \text{FR}, S, a, b, P, n, h)$, private key d, hashed certification data *hcert*, message m.

OUTPUT: Signature (r, s).

1. Select $k \in_R [1, n-1]$.
2. Compute $kP = (x_1, y_1)$.
3. Compute $r = H(x_1)$.
4. Compute $e = H(hcert, m)$.
5. Compute $w = r \oplus e$ and convert w to an integer $\overline{w}$.
6. If $\overline{w} \geq n$ then $\overline{w} \leftarrow \overline{w} - n$.
7. Compute $s = d(k - \overline{w}) \bmod n$. If $s = 0$ then go to step 1.
8. Return(r, s).

Algorithm 4.37 EC-KCDSA signature verification

INPUT: Domain parameters $D = (q, \text{FR}, S, a, b, P, n, h)$, public key Q, hashed certification data *hcert*, message m, signature (r, s).

OUTPUT: Acceptance or rejection of the signature.

1. Verify that the bitlength of r is at most l_H and that s is an integer in the interval $[1, n-1]$. If any verification fails then return("Reject the signature").
2. Compute $e = H(hcert, m)$.
3. Compute $w = r \oplus e$ and convert w to an integer $\overline{w}$.
4. If $\overline{w} \geq n$ then $\overline{w} \leftarrow \overline{w} - n$.
5. Compute $X = sQ + \overline{w}P$.
6. Compute $v = H(x_1)$ where x_1 is the x-coordinate of X.
7. If $v = r$ then return("Accept the signature");
   Else return("Reject the signature").

Proof that signature verification works If a signature (r, s) on a message m was indeed generated by the legitimate signer, then $s \equiv d(k - \overline{w}) \pmod{n}$. Rearranging gives $k \equiv sd^{-1} + \overline{w} \pmod{n}$. Thus $X = sQ + \overline{w}P = (sd^{-1} + \overline{w})P = kP$, and so $v = r$ as required. $\square$

Note 4.38 (*use of* hcert) In practice, *hcert* can be defined to be the hash of the signer's public-key certificate that should include the signer's identity, domain parameters, and public key. Prepending *hcert* to the message m prior to hashing (i.e., when computing $e = H(hcert, m)$) can provide resistance to attacks based on manipulation of domain parameters.

Note 4.39 (*security proofs for EC-KCDSA*) KCDSA, which operates in a prime-order subgroup S of the multiplicative group of a finite field, has been proven GMR-secure under the assumptions that the discrete logarithm problem in S is intractable and that the hash function H is a random function. Actually, if different hash functions H_1

and H_2 are used in steps 3 and 4, respectively, of the signature generation procedure, then the security proof assumes that H_1 is a random function and makes the weaker assumption that H_2 is collision resistant.

A security proof for a protocol that makes the assumption that hash functions employed are random functions is said to hold in the *random oracle model*. Such proofs do not imply that the protocol is secure in the real world where the hash function is not a random function. Nonetheless, such security proofs do offer the assurance that the protocol is secure unless an adversary can exploit properties of the hash functions that distinguish them from random functions.

The security proof for KCDSA extends to the case of EC-KCDSA if the operation in step 3 of signature generation is replaced by $r = H(x_1, y_1)$.

4.5   *Public-key encryption*

Public-key encryption schemes can be used to provide confidentiality. Since they are considerably slower than their symmetric-key counterparts, they are typically used only to encrypt small data items such as credit card numbers and PINs, and to transport session keys which are subsequently used with faster symmetric-key algorithms for bulk encryption or message authentication.

Definition 4.40 A *public-key encryption scheme* consists of four algorithms:

1. A *domain parameter generation algorithm* that generates a set D of domain parameters.
2. A *key generation algorithm* that takes as input a set D of domain parameters and generates key pairs (Q, d).
3. An *encryption algorithm* that takes as input a set of domain parameters D, a public key Q, a plaintext message m, and produces a ciphertext c.
4. A *decryption algorithm* that takes as input the domain parameters D, a private key d, a ciphertext c, and either rejects c as invalid or produces a plaintext m.

We assume D is valid (see §4.2) and that Q is valid and associated with D (see §4.3). The decryption algorithm always accepts (D, d, c) and outputs m if c was indeed generated by the encryption algorithm on input (D, Q, m).

The following notion of security of a public-key encryption scheme is due to Goldwasser, Micali, Rackoff and Simon.

Definition 4.41 A public-key encryption scheme is said to be *secure* if it is indistinguishable by a computationally bounded adversary who can mount an adaptive chosen-ciphertext attack. In other words, an adversary who selects two plaintext messages m_1 and m_2 (of the same length) and is then given the ciphertext c of one of them is unable to decide with non-negligible advantage whether c is the encryption of m_1

or m_2. This is true even though the adversary is able to obtain the decryptions of any ciphertexts (different from the target ciphertext c) of its choosing.

This security definition is a very strong one—the adversary is unable to do better than guess whether c is the encryption of one of two plaintext messages m_1 and m_2 that the adversary itself chose even when it has access to a decryption oracle. Indistinguishability against adaptive chosen-ciphertext attacks has gained acceptance as the "right" notion of security for public-key encryption schemes.

Another desirable security property is that it should be infeasible for an adversary who is given a valid ciphertext c to produce a different valid ciphertext c' such that the (unknown) plaintext messages m and m' are related in some known way; this security property is called *non-malleability*. It has been proven that a public-key encryption scheme is indistinguishable against adaptive chosen-ciphertext attacks if and only if it is non-malleable against adaptive chosen-ciphertext attacks.

4.5.1 ECIES

The Elliptic Curve Integrated Encryption Scheme (ECIES) was proposed by Bellare and Rogaway, and is a variant of the ElGamal public-key encryption scheme. It has been standardized in ANSI X9.63 and ISO/IEC 15946-3, and is in the IEEE P1363a draft standard.

In ECIES, a Diffie-Hellman shared secret is used to derive two symmetric keys k_1 and k_2. Key k_1 is used to encrypt the plaintext using a symmetric-key cipher, while key k_2 is used to authenticate the resulting ciphertext. Intuitively, the authentication guards against chosen-ciphertext attacks since the adversary cannot generate valid ciphertexts on her own. The following cryptographic primitives are used:

1. KDF is a key derivation function that is constructed from a hash function H. If a key of l bits is required then KDF(S) is defined to be the concatenation of the hash values $H(S, i)$, where i is a counter that is incremented for each hash function evaluation until l bits of hash values have been generated.

2. ENC is the encryption function for a symmetric-key encryption scheme such as the AES, and DEC is the decryption function.

3. MAC is a message authentication code algorithm such as HMAC.

Algorithm 4.42 ECIES encryption

INPUT: Domain parameters $D = (q, \mathrm{FR}, S, a, b, P, n, h)$, public key Q, plaintext m.
OUTPUT: Ciphertext (R, C, t).
1. Select $k \in_R [1, n-1]$.
2. Compute $R = kP$ and $Z = hkQ$. If $Z = \infty$ then go to step 1.
3. $(k_1, k_2) \leftarrow \mathrm{KDF}(x_Z, R)$, where x_Z is the x-coordinate of Z.
4. Compute $C = \mathrm{ENC}_{k_1}(m)$ and $t = \mathrm{MAC}_{k_2}(C)$.
5. Return(R, C, t).

Algorithm 4.43 ECIES decryption

INPUT: Domain parameters $D = (q, \mathrm{FR}, S, a, b, P, n, h)$, private key d, ciphertext (R, C, t).

OUTPUT: Plaintext m or rejection of the ciphertext.

1. Perform an embedded public key validation of R (Algorithm 4.26). If the validation fails then return("Reject the ciphertext").
2. Compute $Z = hdR$. If $Z = \infty$ then return("Reject the ciphertext").
3. $(k_1, k_2) \leftarrow \mathrm{KDF}(x_Z, R)$, where x_Z is the x-coordinate of Z.
4. Compute $t' = \mathrm{MAC}_{k_2}(C)$. If $t' \neq t$ then return("Reject the ciphertext").
5. Compute $m = \mathrm{DEC}_{k_1}(C)$.
6. Return(m).

Proof that decryption works If ciphertext (R, C, t) was indeed generated by the legitimate entity when encrypting m, then

$$hdR = hd(kP) = hk(dP) = hkQ.$$

Thus the decryptor computes the same keys (k_1, k_2) as the encryptor, accepts the ciphertext, and recovers m. $\qquad\square$

Security notes

Note 4.44 (*security proofs for ECIES*) ECIES has been proven secure (in the sense of Definition 4.41) under the assumptions that the symmetric-key encryption scheme and MAC algorithm are secure, and that certain non-standard (but reasonable) variants of the computational and decision Diffie-Hellman problems are intractable. These Diffie-Hellman problems involve the key derivation function KDF.

Note 4.45 (*public key validation*) The shared secret point $Z = hdR$ is obtained by multiplying the Diffie-Hellman shared secret dkP by h. This ensures that Z is a point in the subgroup $\langle P \rangle$. Checking that $Z \neq \infty$ in step 2 of the decryption procedure confirms that Z has order exactly n. This, together with embedded key validation performed in step 1, provides resistance to the small subgroup and invalid-curve attacks described in §4.3 whereby an attacker learns information about the receiver's private key by sending invalid points R.

Note 4.46 (*inputs to the key derivation function*) The symmetric keys k_1 and k_2 are derived from the x-coordinate x_Z of the Diffie-Hellman shared secret Z as well as the one-time public key R of the sender. Inclusion of R as input to KDF is necessary because otherwise the scheme is malleable and hence also not indistinguishable. An adversary could simply replace R in the ciphertext (R, C, t) by $-R$ thus obtaining another valid ciphertext with the same plaintext as the original ciphertext.

4.5.2 PSEC

Provably Secure Encryption Curve scheme (PSEC) is due to Fujisaki and Okamoto. The version we present here is derived by combining PSEC-KEM, a *key encapsulation mechanism*, and *DEM1*, a *data encapsulation mechanism*, that are described in the ISO 18033-2 draft standard. PSEC-KEM has also been evaluated by NESSIE and CRYPTREC.

The following cryptographic primitives are used in PSEC:

1. KDF is a key derivation function that is constructed from a hash function.

2. ENC is the encryption function for a symmetric-key encryption scheme such as the AES, and DEC is the decryption function.

3. MAC is a message authentication code algorithm such as HMAC.

Algorithm 4.47 PSEC encryption

INPUT: Domain parameters $D = (q, \mathrm{FR}, S, a, b, P, n, h)$, public key Q, plaintext m.
OUTPUT: Ciphertext (R, C, s, t).

1. Select $r \in_R \{0, 1\}^l$, where l is the bitlength of n.
2. $(k', k_1, k_2) \leftarrow \mathrm{KDF}(r)$, where k' has bitlength $l + 128$.
3. Compute $k = k' \bmod n$.
4. Compute $R = kP$ and $Z = kQ$.
5. Compute $s = r \oplus \mathrm{KDF}(R, Z)$.
6. Compute $C = \mathrm{ENC}_{k_1}(m)$ and $t = \mathrm{MAC}_{k_2}(C)$.
7. Return(R, C, s, t).

Algorithm 4.48 PSEC decryption

INPUT: Domain parameters $D = (q, \mathrm{FR}, S, a, b, P, n, h)$, private key d, ciphertext (R, C, s, t).
OUTPUT: Plaintext m or rejection of the ciphertext.

1. Compute $Z = dR$.
2. Compute $r = s \oplus \mathrm{KDF}(R, Z)$.
3. $(k', k_1, k_2) \leftarrow \mathrm{KDF}(r)$, where k' has bitlength $l + 128$.
4. Compute $k = k' \bmod n$.
5. Compute $R' = kP$.
6. If $R' \neq R$ then return("Reject the ciphertext").
7. Compute $t' = \mathrm{MAC}_{k_2}(C)$. If $t' \neq t$ then return("Reject the ciphertext").
8. Compute $m = \mathrm{DEC}_{k_1}(C)$.
9. Return(m).

Proof that decryption works If ciphertext (R, C, s, t) was indeed generated by the legitimate entity when encrypting m, then $dR = d(kP) = k(dP) = kQ$. Thus the decryptor computes the same keys (k', k_1, k_2) as the encryptor, accepts the ciphertext, and recovers m.   □

Note 4.49 (*security proofs for PSEC*) PSEC has been proven secure (in the sense of Definition 4.41) under the assumptions that the symmetric-key encryption and MAC algorithms are secure, the computational Diffie-Helman problem is intractable, and the key derivation function is a random function.

4.6 *Key establishment*

The purpose of a key establishment protocol is to provide two or more entities communicating over an open network with a shared secret key. The key may then be used in a symmetric-key protocol to achieve some cryptographic goal such as confidentiality or data integrity.

A *key transport* protocol is a key establishment protocol where one entity creates the secret key and securely transfers it to the others. ECIES (see §4.5.1) can be considered to be a two-party key transport protocol when the plaintext message consists of the secret key. A *key agreement* protocol is a key establishment protocol where all participating entities contribute information which is used to derive the shared secret key. In this section, we will consider two-party key agreement protocols derived from the basic Diffie-Hellman protocol.

Security definition A key establishment protocol should ideally result in the sharing of secret keys that have the same attributes as keys that were established by people who know each other and meet in a secure location to select a key by repeatedly tossing a fair coin. In particular, subsequent use of the secret keys in a cryptographic protocol should not in any way reduce the security of that protocol. This notion of security has proved very difficult to formalize. Instead of a formal definition, we present an informal list of desirable security properties of a key establishment protocol.

Attack model A secure protocol should be able to withstand both *passive* attacks where an adversary attempts to prevent a protocol from achieving its goals by merely observing honest entities carrying out the protocol, and *active* attacks where an adversary additionally subverts the communications by injecting, deleting, altering or replaying messages. In order to limit the amount of data available for cryptanalytic attack (e.g., ciphertext generated using a fixed session key in an encryption application), each run of a key establishment protocol between two entities A and B should produce a unique secret key called a *session key*. The protocol should still achieve its goal in the face of an adversary who has learned some other session keys.

Fundamental security goal The fundamental security goals of a key establishment protocol are:

1. *Implicit key authentication.* A key establishment protocol is said to provide implicit key authentication (of B to A) if entity A is assured that no other entity aside from a specifically identified second entity B can possibly learn the value of a particular session key. The property does not imply that A is assured of B actually possessing the key.

2. *Explicit key authentication.* A key establishment protocol is said to provide *key confirmation* (of B to A) if entity A is assured that the second entity B can compute or has actually computed the session key. If both implicit key authentication and key confirmation (of B to A) are provided, then the key establishment protocol is said to provide *explicit key authentication* (of B to A).

Explicit key authentication of both entities normally requires three passes (messages exchanged). For a two-party three-pass key agreement protocol, the main security goal is explicit key authentication of each entity to the other.

Other desirable security attributes Other security attributes may also be desirable depending on the application in which a key establishment protocol is employed.

1. *Forward secrecy.* If long-term private keys of one or more entities are compromised, the secrecy of previous session keys established by honest entities should not be affected.

2. *Key-compromise impersonation resilience.* Suppose A's long-term private key is disclosed. Clearly an adversary who knows this value can now impersonate A, since it is precisely this value that identifies A. However, it may be desirable that this loss does not enable an adversary to impersonate other entities to A.

3. *Unknown key-share resilience.* Entity A cannot be coerced into sharing a key with entity B without A's knowledge, that is, when A believes the key is shared with some entity $C \neq B$, and B (correctly) believes the key is shared with A.

We present two elliptic curve-based key agreement schemes, the STS protocol in §4.6.1 and ECMQV in §4.6.2. Both these protocols are believed to provide explicit key authentication and possess the security attributes of forward secrecy, key-compromise impersonation resilience, and unknown key-share resilience.

4.6.1 Station-to-station

The station-to-station (STS) protocol is a discrete logarithm-based key agreement scheme due to Diffie, van Oorschot and Wiener. We present its elliptic curve analogue as described in the ANSI X9.63 standard.

In the following, $D = (q, \text{FR}, S, a, b, P, n, h)$ are elliptic curve domain parameters, KDF is a key derivation function (see §4.5.1), MAC is a message authentication code algorithm such as HMAC, and SIGN is the signature generation algorithm for a signature scheme with appendix such as ECDSA (see §4.4.1) or an RSA signature scheme. If any verification in Protocol 4.50 fails, then the protocol run is terminated with failure.

Protocol 4.50 Station-to-station key agreement

GOAL: A and B establish a shared secret key.

PROTOCOL MESSAGES:

$$A \to B: \quad A, R_A$$
$$A \leftarrow B: \quad B, R_B, s_B = \text{SIGN}_B(R_B, R_A, A), \ t_B = \text{MAC}_{k_1}(R_B, R_A, A)$$
$$A \to B: \quad s_A = \text{SIGN}_A(R_A, R_B, B), \ t_A = \text{MAC}_{k_1}(R_A, R_B, B)$$

1. A selects $k_A \in_R [1, n-1]$, computes $R_A = k_A P$, and sends A, R_A to B.
2. B does the following:
    2.1 Perform an embedded public key validation of R_A (see Algorithm 4.26).
    2.2 Select $k_B \in_R [1, n-1]$ and compute $R_B = k_B P$.
    2.3 Compute $Z = h k_B R_A$ and verify that $Z \neq \infty$.
    2.4 $(k_1, k_2) \leftarrow \text{KDF}(x_Z)$, where x_Z is the x-coordinate of Z.
    2.5 Compute $s_B = \text{SIGN}_B(R_B, R_A, A)$ and $t_B = \text{MAC}_{k_1}(R_B, R_A, A)$.
    2.6 Send B, R_B, s_B, t_B to A.
3. A does the following:
    3.1 Perform an embedded public key validation of R_B (see Algorithm 4.26).
    3.2 Compute $Z = h k_A R_B$ and verify that $Z \neq \infty$.
    3.3 $(k_1, k_2) \leftarrow \text{KDF}(x_Z)$, where x_Z is the x-coordinate of Z.
    3.4 Verify that s_B is B's signature on the message (R_B, R_A, A).
    3.5 Compute $t = \text{MAC}_{k_1}(R_B, R_A, A)$ and verify that $t = t_B$.
    3.6 Compute $s_A = \text{SIGN}_A(R_A, R_B, B)$ and $t_A = \text{MAC}_{k_1}(R_A, R_B, B)$.
    3.7 Send s_A, t_A to B.
4. B does the following:
    4.1 Verify that s_A is A's signature on the message (R_A, R_B, B).
    4.2 Compute $t = \text{MAC}_{k_1}(R_A, R_B, B)$ and verify that $t = t_A$.
5. The session key is k_2.

The shared secret is $Z = h k_A k_B P$, which is derived from the ephemeral (one-time) public keys R_A and R_B. Multiplication by h and the check $Z \neq \infty$ ensure that Z has order n and therefore is in $\langle P \rangle$. Successful verification of the signatures $s_A = \text{SIGN}_A(R_A, R_B, B)$ and $s_B = \text{SIGN}_B(R_B, R_A, A)$ convinces each entity of the identity of the other entity (since the signing entity can be identified by its public signing key), that the communications have not been tampered with (assuming that the signature scheme is secure), and that the other entity knows the identity of the entity with which it is communicating (since this identity is included in the signed message). Successful verification of the authentication tags t_A and t_B convinces each entity that the other entity has indeed computed the shared secret Z (since computing the tags requires knowledge of k_1 and therefore also of Z).

4.6.2 ECMQV

ECMQV is a three-pass key agreement protocol that has been been standardized in ANSI X9.63, IEEE 1363-2000, and ISO/IEC 15946-3.

In the following, $D = (q, \text{FR}, S, a, b, P, n, h)$ are elliptic curve domain parameters, (Q_A, d_A) is A's key pair, (Q_B, d_B) is B's key pair, KDF is a key derivation function (see §4.5.1), and MAC is a message authentication code algorithm such as HMAC. If R is an elliptic curve point then $\overline{R}$ is defined to be the integer $(\overline{x} \bmod 2^{\lceil f/2 \rceil}) + 2^{\lceil f/2 \rceil}$ where $\overline{x}$ is the integer representation of the x-coordinate of R, and $f = \lfloor \log_2 n \rfloor + 1$ is the bitlength of n. If any verification in Protocol 4.51 fails, then the protocol run is terminated with failure.

Protocol 4.51 ECMQV key agreement

GOAL: A and B establish a shared secret key.
PROTOCOL MESSAGES:

$\qquad A \rightarrow B$: $\quad A, R_A$
$\qquad A \leftarrow B$: $\quad B, R_B, t_B = \text{MAC}_{k_1}(2, B, A, R_B, R_A)$
$\qquad A \rightarrow B$: $\quad t_A = \text{MAC}_{k_1}(3, A, B, R_A, R_B)$

1. A selects $k_A \in_R [1, n-1]$, computes $R_A = k_A P$, and sends A, R_A to B.
2. B does the following:
   2.1 Perform an embedded public key validation of R_A (see Algorithm 4.26).
   2.2 Select $k_B \in_R [1, n-1]$ and compute $R_B = k_B P$.
   2.3 Compute $s_B = (k_B + \overline{R}_B d_B) \bmod n$ and $Z = h s_B (R_A + \overline{R}_A Q_A)$, and verify that $Z \neq \infty$.
   2.4 $(k_1, k_2) \leftarrow \text{KDF}(x_Z)$, where x_Z is the x-coordinate of Z.
   2.5 Compute $t_B = \text{MAC}_{k_1}(2, B, A, R_B, R_A)$.
   2.6 Send B, R_B, t_B to A.
3. A does the following:
   3.1 Perform an embedded public key validation of R_B (see Algorithm 4.26).
   3.2 Compute $s_A = (k_A + \overline{R}_A d_A) \bmod n$ and $Z = h s_A (R_B + \overline{R}_B Q_B)$, and verify that $Z \neq \infty$.
   3.3 $(k_1, k_2) \leftarrow \text{KDF}(x_Z)$, where x_Z is the x-coordinate of Z.
   3.4 Compute $t = \text{MAC}_{k_1}(2, B, A, R_B, R_A)$ and verify that $t = t_B$.
   3.5 Compute $t_A = \text{MAC}_{k_1}(3, A, B, R_A, R_B)$ and send t_A to B.
4. B computes $t = \text{MAC}_{k_1}(3, A, B, R_A, R_B)$ and verifies that $t = t_A$.
5. The session key is k_2.

Protocol 4.51 can be viewed as an extension of the ordinary Diffie-Hellman key agreement protocol. The quantity

$$s_A = (k_A + \overline{R}_A d_A) \bmod n$$

serves as an *implicit signature* for A's ephemeral public key R_A. It is a 'signature' in the sense that the only person who can compute s_A is A, and is 'implicit' in the sense that B indirectly verifies its validity by using

$$s_A P = R_A + \overline{R}_A Q_A$$

when deriving the shared secret Z. Similarly, s_B is an implicit signature for B's ephemeral public key R_B. The shared secret is $Z = h s_A s_B P$ rather than $k_A k_B P$ as would be the case with ordinary Diffie-Hellman; multiplication by h and the check $Z \neq \infty$ ensure that Z has order n and therefore is in $\langle P \rangle$. Note that Z is derived using the ephemeral public keys (R_A and R_B) as well as the long-term public keys (Q_A and Q_B) of the two entities. The strings "2" and "3" are included in the MAC inputs in order to distinguish authentication tags created by the initiator A and responder B. Successful verification of the authentication tags t_A and t_B convinces each entity that the other entity has indeed computed the shared secret Z (since computing the tags requires knowledge of k_1 and therefore also of Z), that the communications have not been tampered with (assuming that the MAC is secure), and that the other entity knows the identity of the entity with which it is communicating (since the identities are included in the messages that are MACed). No formal proof of security is known for Protocol 4.51.

4.7   Notes and further references

§4.1

The generic group model for proving lower bounds on the discrete logarithm problem was developed by Nechaev [344] and Shoup [425]. The Pohlig-Hellman algorithm is due to Pohlig and Hellman [376].

Although the ECDLP appears to be difficult to solve on classical computers, it is known to be easily solvable on *quantum computers* (computational devices that exploit quantum mechanical principles). In 1994, Shor [424] presented polynomial-time algorithms for computing discrete logarithms and factoring integers on a quantum computer. The ECDLP case was studied more extensively by Proos and Zalka [384] who devised quantum circuits for performing the elliptic curve group law. Proos and Zalka showed that a k-bit instance of the ECDLP can be efficiently solved on a K-qubit quantum computer where $K \approx 5k + 8\sqrt{k} + 5\log_2 k$ (a *qubit* is the quantum computer analogue of a classical bit). In contrast, Beauregard [31] showed that k-bit integers can be efficiently factored on a K-qubit quantum computer where $K \approx 2k$. For example, 256-bit instances of the ECDLP are roughly equally difficult to solve on classical computers as 3072-bit instances of the integer factorization problem. However, the former can be solved on a 1448-qubit quantum computer, while the latter seems to need a 6144-qubit quantum computer. Thus, it would appear that larger quantum machines (which presumably are more difficult to build) are needed to solve the integer factorization problem than the ECDLP for problem instances that are roughly equally difficult to solve on classical computers. The interesting question then is when or whether large-scale quantum computers can actually be built. This is an area of very active research and much speculation. The most significant experimental result achieved thus far is the 7-qubit machine built by Vandersypen et al. [464] in 2001 that was used to factor the integer 15 using Shor's algorithm. It remains to be seen whether experiments such as this can be scaled to factor integers and solve ECDLP instances that are of cryptographic interest. The book by Nielsen and Chuang [347] is an excellent and extensive overview of the field of quantum computing

Characteristics of random functions, including the expected tail length and the expected cyclic length of sequences obtained from random functions, were studied by Flajolet and Odlyzko [143]. The rho algorithm (Algorithm 4.3) for computing discrete logarithms was invented by Pollard [379]. Pollard's original algorithm used an iterating function with three branches. Teske [458] provided experimental evidence that Pollard's iterating function did not have optimal random characteristics, and proposed the iterating function used in Algorithm 4.3. Teske [458, 459] gave experimental and theoretical evidence that her iterating function very closely models a random function when the number of branches is $L = 20$.

Pollard's rho algorithm can be accelerated by using Brent's cycle finding algorithm [70] instead of Floyd's algorithm. This yields a reduction in the expected number of group operations from $3\sqrt{n}$ to approximately $2\sqrt{n}$. A method that is asymptotically faster but has significant storage requirements was proposed by Sedgewick, Szymanski and Yao [419].

The parallelized version of Pollard's rho algorithm (Algorithm 4.5) is due to van Oorschot and Wiener [463].

Gallant, Lambert and Vanstone [159] and Wiener and Zuccherato [482] independently discovered the methods for speeding (parallelized) Pollard's rho algorithm using automorphisms. They also described techniques for detecting when a processor has entered a short (and useless) cycle. These methods were generalized to hyperelliptic curves and other curves by Duursma, Gaudry and Morain [128].

Silverman and Stapleton [434] were the first to observe that the distinguished points encountered in Pollard's rho algorithm during the solution of an ECDLP instance can be used in the solution of subsequent ECDLP instances (with the same elliptic curve parameters). The use of Pollard's rho algorithm to iteratively solve multiple ECDLP instances was analyzed by Kuhn and Struik [271]. Kuhn and Struik also proved that the best strategy for solving any one of k given ECDLP instances is to arbitrarily select one of these instances and devote all efforts to solving that instance.

Pollard's *kangaroo algorithm* [379] (introduced under the name *lambda method*), was designed to find discrete logarithms that are known to lie in an interval of length b. Its expected running time is $3.28\sqrt{b}$ group operations and has negligible storage requirements. Van Oorschot and Wiener [463] presented a variant that has modest storage requirements and an expected running time of approximately $2\sqrt{b}$ group operations. They also showed how to parallelize the kangaroo method, achieving a speedup that is linear in the number of processors employed. The parallelized kangaroo method is slower than the parallelized rho algorithm when no information is known a priori about the discrete logarithm (i.e., $b = n$). It becomes faster when $b < 0.39n$. The parallelized kangaroo method was further analyzed by Pollard [381].

The arguments in §4.1.3 for failure of the index-calculus method for the ECDLP were presented by Miller [325] and further elaborated by Silverman and Suzuki [432]. For an excellent exposition of the failure of this and other attacks, see Koblitz [257].

Silverman [431] proposed an attack on the ECDLP that he termed *xedni calculus*. Given an ECDLP instance (P, Q) on an elliptic curve E over a prime field $\mathbb{F}_p$, one first takes $r \leq 9$ different integer linear combinations of P and Q and lifts these r points to points in the rational plane $\mathbb{Q} \times \mathbb{Q}$. One then attempts to find an elliptic curve $\widetilde{E}$ defined over $\mathbb{Q}$ that passes through these points. (This procedure is the reverse of the index-calculus method which first lifts the curve and then the points; hence the name "xedni".) If $\widetilde{E}(\mathbb{Q})$ has rank $< r$, then an integer linear dependence relation among the r points can be found thereby (almost certainly) yielding a solution to the original ECDLP. In order to increase the probability that $\widetilde{E}(\mathbb{Q})$ has rank $< r$, Silverman required that $\widetilde{E}$ be chosen so that $\#\widetilde{E}(\mathbb{F}_t)$ is as small as possible for all small primes t, that is, $\#E(\mathbb{F}_t) \approx t + 1 - 2\sqrt{t}$. (The opposite conditions, $\#E(\mathbb{F}_t) \approx t + 1 + 2\sqrt{t}$, called *Mestre conditions*, were proposed by Mestre [324] and have been successfully used to obtain elliptic curves over $\mathbb{Q}$ of higher than expected rank.) Shortly after Silverman proposed xedni calculus, Koblitz (see Appendix K of [431]) observed that xedni calculus could be adapted to solve both the ordinary discrete logarithm problem and the integer factorization problem. Thus, if the xedni-calculus attack were efficient, then it would adversely affect the security of all the important public-key schemes. Fortunately (for proponents of public-key cryptography), Jacobson, Koblitz, Silverman, Stein and Teske [222] were able to prove that xedni calculus is ineffective asymptotically (as $p \to \infty$), and also provided convincing experimental evidence that it is extremely inefficient for primes p of the sizes used in cryptography.

Isomorphism attacks on prime-field-anomalous elliptic curves were discovered independently by Satoh and Araki [401], Semaev [420] and Smart [438]. Semaev's attack was generalized by Rück [397] to the DLP in subgroups of order p of the jacobian of an arbitrary curve (including a hyperelliptic curve) defined over a finite field of characteristic p.

The Weil pairing and Tate pairing attacks are due to Menezes, Okamoto and Vanstone [314], and Frey and Rück [150], respectively. Balasubramanian and Koblitz [27] proved that the embedding degree k is large for most elliptic curves of prime order defined over prime fields. The Tate pairing attack applies to the jacobian of any non-singular irreducible curve over a finite field $\mathbb{F}_q$ (subject to the condition that the order n of the base element satisfies $\gcd(n, q) = 1$). Galbraith [155] derived upper bounds $k(g)$ on the embedding degree k for supersingular abelian varieties of dimension g over finite fields; these varieties include the jacobians of genus-g supersingular curves. The bounds were improved by Rubin and Silverberg [396]. Constructive applications of supersingular curves (and bilinear maps in general) include the three-party one-round Diffie-Hellman protocol of Joux [227], the identity-based public-key encryption scheme of Boneh and Franklin [58, 59], the hierarchical identity-based encryption and signature schemes of Horwitz and Lynn [199] and Gentry and Silverberg [170], the short signature scheme of Boneh, Lynn and Shacham [62], the aggregate signature scheme of Boneh, Gentry, Lynn and Shacham [60], the self-blindable certificate scheme of Verheul [472], and the efficient provably secure signature scheme of Boneh, Mironov and Shoup [63].

Frey first presented the Weil descent attack methodology in his lecture at the ECC '98 conference (see [149]). Frey's ideas were further elaborated by Galbraith and Smart [158]. The GHS attack was presented by Gaudry, Hess and Smart [167] (see also Hess [196]). It was shown to fail for all cryptographically interesting elliptic curves over $\mathbb{F}_{2^m}$ for all prime $m \in [160, 600]$ by Menezes and Qu [315]. Jacobson, Menezes and Stein [223] used the GHS attack to solve an actual ECDLP instance over $\mathbb{F}_{2^{124}}$ by first reducing it to an HCDLP instance in a genus-31 hyperelliptic curve over $\mathbb{F}_{2^4}$, and then solving the latter with the Enge-Gaudry subexponential-time algorithm [163, 133]. Maurer, Menezes and Teske [304] completed the analysis of the GHS attack by identifying and enumerating the isomorphism classes of elliptic curves over $\mathbb{F}_{2^m}$ for composite $m \in [160, 600]$ that are most vulnerable to the GHS attack. Menezes, Teske and Weng [318] showed that the fields $\mathbb{F}_{2^m}$, where $m \in [185, 600]$ is divisible by 5, are *weak* for elliptic curve cryptography in the sense that the GHS attack can be used to solve the ECDLP significantly faster than Pollard's rho algorithm for all cryptographically interesting elliptic curves over these fields.

Elliptic curves E_1 and E_2 defined over $\mathbb{F}_{q^n}$ are said to be *isogenous* over $\mathbb{F}_{q^n}$ if $\#E_1(\mathbb{F}_{q^n}) = \#E_2(\mathbb{F}_{q^n})$. Galbraith, Hess and Smart [156] presented a practical algorithm for explicitly computing an isogeny between two isogenous elliptic curves over $\mathbb{F}_{q^n}$. They observed that their algorithm could be used to extend the effectiveness of the GHS attack as follows. Given an ECDLP instance on some cryptographically interesting elliptic curve E_1 over $\mathbb{F}_{2^m}$, one can check if E_1 is isogenous to some elliptic curve E_2 over $\mathbb{F}_{2^m}$ for which the GHS reduction yields an easier HCDLP instance than E_1. One can then use an isogeny $\phi : E_1 \to E_2$ to map the ECDLP instance to an ECDLP instance in $E_2(\mathbb{F}_{2^m})$ and solve the latter using the GHS attack. For example, in the case $m = 155$, we can expect that roughly 2^{104} out of the 2^{156} isomorphism classes of elliptic curves over $\mathbb{F}_{2^{155}}$ are isogeous to one of the approximately 2^{32} elliptic curves over $\mathbb{F}_{2^{155}}$ originally believed to be susceptible to the GHS attack. Thus, the GHS attack may now be effective on 2^{104} out of the 2^{156} elliptic curves over $\mathbb{F}_{2^{155}}$.

Arita [18] showed that some elliptic curves over finite fields $\mathbb{F}_{3^m}$ of characteristic three may also be susceptible to the Weil descent attack. Diem [118, 119] has shown that the GHS attack can be extended to elliptic curves over $\mathbb{F}_{p^m}$ where $p \geq 5$ is prime. He concludes that his particular variant of the GHS attack will always fail when m is prime and $m \geq 11$—that is, the discrete logarithm problem in the resulting higher-genus curves is intractable. However, he provide some evidence that the attack might suceed for *some* elliptic curves when $m = 3, 5$ or 7. Further research and experimentation is necessary before the cryptographic implications of Diem's work are fully understood.

Den Boer [112] proved the equivalence of the discrete logarithm and Diffie-Hellman problems in arbitrary cyclic groups of order n where $\phi(n)$ has no large prime factors ($\phi(n)$ is the Euler phi function). These results were generalized by Maurer [305]; see also Maurer and Wolf [307]. Boneh and Lipton [61] formulated problems in generic fields (which they call *black-box fields*), and proved the result that hardness of the ECDLP implies hardness of the ECDHP. Boneh and Shparlinski [64] proved that if the ECDHP is hard in a prime-order subgroup $\langle P \rangle \subseteq E(\mathbb{F}_p)$ of an elliptic curve E defined over a prime field $\mathbb{F}_p$, then there does not exist an efficient algorithm that predicts the least significant bit of either the x-coordinate or the y-coordinate of the Diffie-Hellman secret point for most elliptic curves isomorphic to E. This does not exclude the existence of efficient prediction algorithms for each of the isomorphic elliptic curves. Boneh and Shparlinski's work provides some evidence that computing the least significant bit of either the x-coordinate or the y-coordinate of the Diffie-Hellman secret point abP from (P, aP, bP) is as hard as computing the entire point abP.

A comprehensive survey (circa 1998) of the decision Diffie-Hellman problem and its cryptographic applications is given by Boneh [54]. Joux and Nguyen [229] (see also Verheul [471]) give examples of supersingular elliptic curves for which the discrete logarithm and Diffie-Hellman problems are equivalent (and not known to be solvable in polynomial time), but for which the decision Diffie-Hellman problem can be efficiently solved.

§4.2

Algorithms 4.14 and 4.15 (domain parameter generation and validation), and Algorithms 4.17, 4.18, 4.19 and 4.21 (generation and verification of random elliptic curves over prime fields and binary fields) are extracted from ANSI X9.62 [14]. Vaudenay [467] studied the procedures for generating random elliptic curves and suggested some enhancements. In particular, he proposed including the field order and representation as input in the binary field case.

Lenstra [285] proved that the orders of elliptic curves over a prime field are roughly uniformly distributed in the Hasse interval. Howe [201] extended Lenstra's results to obtain, for any finite field $\mathbb{F}_q$ and prime power l^k, estimates for the probability that a randomly selected elliptic curve over $\mathbb{F}_q$ has order $\#E(\mathbb{F}_q)$ divisible by l^k. The early-abort strategy was first studied by Lercier [287].

The complex multiplication method for prime fields is described by Atkin and Morain [20] (see also Buchmann and Baier [79]), for binary fields by Lay and Zimmer [276], and for optimal extension fields by Baier and Buchmann [24]. Weng [479] introduced a CM method for generating hyperelliptic curves of genus 2 that are suitable for cryptographic applications.

Schoof's algorithm [411], originally described for elliptic curves over finite fields over odd characteristic, was adapted to the binary field case by Koblitz [252]. An extensive treatment of Schoof's algorithm [411] and its improvements by Atkin and Elkies (and others) is given by Blake, Seroussi and Smart [49, Chapter VII]. Lercier and Morain [289] and Izu, Kogure, Noro and Yokoyama [218] report on their implementations of the SEA algorithm for the prime field case. The latter implementation on a 300 MHz Pentium II counts the number of points on a 240-bit prime field in about 7.5 minutes, and can generate an elliptic curve of prime order over a 240-bit prime field in about 3 hours. Extensions of Schoof's algorithm to genus-2 hyperelliptic curves were studied by Gaudry and Harley [166].

Satoh [400] presented his point counting algorithm for elliptic curves over finite fields of small characteristic greater than five. It was extended to elliptic curves over binary fields by Fouquet, Gaudry and Harley [146] and Skjernaa [436]. Many variants for the binary field case have subsequently been proposed. A variant that has lower memory requirements was devised by Vercauteren, Preneel and Vandewalle [470]. Fouquet, Gaudry and Harley [147] explore combinations with an early abort strategy for the purpose of generating elliptic curves of almost-prime orders. The SST variant was proposed by Satoh, Skjernaa and Taguchi [402]. The AGM method, developed by Mestre, Harley and Gaudry is described by Gaudry [164] who also presents refinements and comparisons of the AGM and SST algorithms. Gaudry reports that his modified-SST algorithm can determine the number of points on randomly chosen elliptic curves over $\mathbb{F}_{2^{163}}$ and $\mathbb{F}_{2^{239}}$ in 0.13 seconds and 0.40 seconds, respectively, on a 700 MHz Pentium III. Further enhancements for binary fields having a Gaussian normal basis of small type have been reported by Kim et al. [243], Lercier and Lubicz [288], and Harley [192].

Another noteworthy algorithm is that of Kedlaya [240] for counting the points on hyperelliptic curves (of any genus) over finite fields of small odd characteristic. Kedlaya's algorithm was extended by Vercauteren [469] to hyperelliptic curve over binary fields, by Gaudry and Gürel [165] to superelliptic curves $y^r = f(x)$ over finite fields of small characteristic different from r, and by Denef and Vercauteren [113] to Artin-Schreier curves $y^2 + x^m y = f(x)$ over binary fields.

§4.3
The need for public key validation was evangelized by Johnson [224, 225] at various standards meetings. Small subgroup attacks on discrete logarithm protocols are due to Vanstone (as presented by Menezes, Qu and Vanstone [316]), van Oorschot and Wiener [462], Anderson and Vaudenay [13], and Lim and Lee [296]. The invalid-curve attacks are extensions of the small subgroup attacks to invalid curves, using the ideas behind the differential fault attacks on elliptic curve schemes by Biehl, Meyer and Müller [46]. Invalid-curve attacks were first described by Antipa, Brown, Menezes, Struik and Vanstone [16] who also demonstrated their potential effectiveness on the ECIES encryption scheme and the one-pass ECMQV key agreement protocol.

§4.4

The concept of a signature scheme was introduced in 1976 by Diffie and Hellman [121]. The first signature scheme based on the discrete logarithm problem was proposed in 1984 by ElGamal [131]. There are many variants of ElGamal's scheme including DSA, KCDSA, and schemes proposed by Schnorr [410] and Okamoto [354]. The notion of GMR-security (Definition 4.28) is due to Goldwasser, Micali and Rivest [175].

ECDSA is described by Johnson, Menezes and Vanstone [226]. An extensive security analysis was undertaken by Brown [75] who proved the GMR-security of ECDSA in the generic group model. Dent [114] demonstrated that security proofs in the generic group model may not provide any assurances in practice by describing a signature scheme that is provably secure in the generic group model but is provably insecure when any specific group is used. Stern, Pointcheval, Malone-Lee and Smart [452] noticed that ECDSA has certain properties that no longer hold in the generic group model, further illustrating limitations of security proofs in the generic group model.

Howgrave-Graham and Smart [202] first showed that an adversary can efficiently recover a DSA or ECDSA private key if she knows a few bits of each per-message secret corresponding to some signed messages (see Note 4.34). Their attacks were formally proven to work for DSA and ECDSA by Nguyen and Shparlinski [345, 346], and for the Nyberg-Rueppel signature scheme by El Mahassni, Nguyen and Shparlinski [130]. Römer and Seifert [392] presented a variant of this attack on ECDSA.

EC-KCDSA was first described by Lim and Lee [297]. The description provided in §4.4.2 is based on the ISO/IEC 15946-2 standard [212]. The random oracle model was popularized by Bellare and Rogaway [37]. Canetti, Goldreich and Halevi [83] presented public-key encryption and signature schemes which they proved are secure in the random oracle model, but insecure for any concrete instantiation of the random function. Their work demonstrates that caution must be exercised when assessing the real-world security of protocols that have been proven secure in the random oracle model. Pointcheval and Stern [378] and Brickell, Pointcheval, Vaudenay and Yung [73] proved the security of several variants of DSA (and also ECDSA) in the random oracle model. The security proofs do not appear to extend to DSA and ECDSA. The security proof of KCDSA mentioned in Note 4.39 is due to Brickell, Pointcheval, Vaudenay and Yung [73].

Signature schemes such as ECDSA and EC-KCDSA are sometimes called signature schemes *with appendix* because the message *m* is a required input to the verification process. Signature schemes *with (partial) message recovery* are different in that they do not require the (entire) message as input to the verification algorithm. The message, or a portion of it, is recovered from the signature itself. Such schemes are desirable in environments where bandwidth is extremely constrained. The Pintsov-Vanstone (PV) signature scheme [375] is an example of a signature scheme with partial message recovery. It is based on a signature scheme of Nyberg and Rueppel [350] and was extensively analyzed by Brown and Johnson [76] who provided security proofs under various assumptions. Another elliptic curve signature scheme providing partial message recovery is that of Naccache and Stern [341].

§4.5

The notion of indistinguishability (also known as *polynomial security*) for public-key encryption schemes (Definition 4.41) was conceived by Goldwasser and Micali [174]. They also formalized the security notion of *semantic security*—where a computationally bounded adversary is unable to obtain any information about a plaintext corresponding to a given ciphertext—and proved that the two security notions are equivalent (under chosen-plaintext attacks). The concept of non-malleability was introduced by Dolev, Dwork and Naor [123, 124]. Rackoff and Simon [389] are usually credited for the requirement that these security properties hold under adaptive chosen-ciphertext attacks. Bellare, Desai, Pointcheval and Rogaway [36] studied the relationships between various security notions for public-key encryption schemes and proved the equivalence of indistinguishability and non-malleability against adaptive chosen-ciphertext attacks.

The security definitions are in the *single-user setting* where there is only one legitimate entity who can decrypt data and the adversary's goal is to compromise the security of this task. Bellare, Boldyreva and Micali [35] presented security definitions for public-key encryption in the *multi-user setting*. The motivation for their work was to account for attacks such as Håstad's attacks [195] whereby an adversary can easily recover a plaintext m if the same m (or linearly related m) is encrypted for three legitimate entities using the basic RSA encryption scheme with encryption exponent $e = 3$. Note that Håstad's attacks cannot be considered to defeat the security goals of public-key encryption in the single-user setting where there is only one legitimate entity. Bellare, Boldyreva and Micali proved that security in the single-user setting implies security in the multi-user setting.

ECIES, a variant of the ElGamal public-key encryption scheme [131], was proposed by Bellare and Rogaway [40]. Abdalla, Bellare and Rogaway [1] formulated three variants of the computational and decision Diffie-Hellman problems whose intractability was sufficient for the security of ECIES. Smart [441] adapted the proof to the generic group model where the Diffie-Hellman intractability assumptions are replaced by the assumption that the group is generic. Cramer and Shoup [106] proved the security of ECIES in the random oracle model under the assumption that the ECDHP problem is hard even if an efficient algorithm for the ECDDHP is known. Solving the Diffie-Hellman problem given an oracle for the decision Diffie-Hellman problem is an example of a *gap problem*, a notion introduced by Okamoto and Pointcheval [356].

PSEC is based on the work of Fujisaki and Okamoto [152]. Key encapsulation mechanisms were studied by Cramer and Shoup [106]. PSEC-KEM, DEM1, and the security proof of PSEC were presented by Shoup in ISO 18033-2 [215].

Cramer and Shoup [105] presented a discrete logarithm-based public-key encryption scheme that is especially notable because it was proven secure in a standard model (i.e., not in idealized models such as the generic group or random oracle model). The security proof assumes the intractability of the decision Diffie-Hellman problem and makes reasonable assumptions about the hash function employed. An extension of the scheme for encrypting messages of arbitrary lengths was proved secure by Shoup [426] under the computational Diffie-Hellman assumption in the random oracle model where the hash function is modeled as a random function. One drawback of the Cramer-Shoup scheme is that the encryption and decryption procedures require more group exponentiations (point multiplications in the elliptic curve case) than competing schemes.

Some other notable discrete logarithm-based public-key encryption schemes are those that can be derived from the general constructions of Pointcheval [377], and Okamoto and Pointcheval [357]. These constructions convert any public-key encryption scheme that is indistinguishable against passive attacks (such as the basic ElGamal scheme) to one that is provably indistinguishable against adaptive chosen-ciphertext attacks in the random oracle model.

§4.6

The Diffie-Hellman key agreement protocol was introduced in the landmark paper of Diffie and Hellman [121]. Boyd and Mathuria [68] provide a comprehensive and up-to-date treatment of key transport and key agreement protocols. See also Chapter 12 of Menezes, van Oorschot and Vanstone [319], and the survey of authenticated Diffie-Hellman protocols by Blake-Wilson and Menezes [50].

The most convincing formal definition of a secure key establishment protocol is that of Canetti and Krawczyk [84]; see also Canetti and Krawczyk [85].

The STS key agreement protocol (Protocol 4.50) is due to Diffie, van Oorschot and Wiener [122]. Blake-Wilson and Menezes [51] presented some plausible unknown key-share attacks on the STS protocol when the identity of the intended recipient is not included in the messages that are signed and MACed. Protocols that are similar (but not identical) to Protocol 4.50 were proven secure by Canetti and Krawczyk [84].

The ECMQV key agreement protocol (Protocol 4.51) was studied by Law, Menezes, Qu, Solinas and Vanstone [275], who provide some heuristic arguments for its security and also present a one-pass variant. Kaliski [237] described an unknown key-share attack on a two-pass variant of the ECMQV protocol that does not provide key confirmation. The three-pass Protocol 4.51 appears to resist this attack.

Many different authenticated Diffie-Hellman key agreement protocols have been proposed and analyzed. Some well-known examples are the OAKLEY protocol of Orman [363], the SKEME protocol of Krawczyk [269], and the Internet Key Exchange (IKE) protocol due to Harkins and Carrell [190] and analyzed by Canetti and Krawczyk [85].

CHAPTER **5**

Implementation Issues

This chapter introduces some engineering aspects of implementing cryptographic solutions based on elliptic curves efficiently and securely in specific environments. The presentation will often be by selected examples, since the material is necessarily platform-specific and complicated by competing requirements, physical constraints and rapidly changing hardware, inelegant designs, and different objectives. The coverage is admittedly narrow. Our goal is to provide a glimpse of engineering considerations faced by software developers and hardware designers. The topics and examples chosen illustrate general principles or involve hardware or software in wide use.

Selected topics on efficient software implementation are presented in §5.1. Although the coverage is platform-specific (and hence also about hardware), much of the material has wider applicability. The section includes notes on use of floating-point and single-instruction multiple-data (vector) operations found on common workstations to speed field arithmetic. §5.2 provides an introduction to the hardware implementation of finite field and elliptic curve arithmetic. §5.3 on secure implementation introduces the broad area of side-channel attacks. Rather than a direct mathematical assault on security mechanisms, such attacks attempt to glean secrets from information leaked as a consequence of physical processes or implementation decisions, including power consumption, electromagnetic radiation, timing of operations, fault analysis, and analysis of error messages. In particular, simple and differential power analysis have been shown to be effective against devices such as smart cards where power consumption can be accurately monitored. For such devices, tamper-proof packaging may be ineffective (or at least expensive) for protecting embedded secrets. The section discusses some algorithmic countermeasures which can minimize or mitigate the effectiveness of side-channel attacks, typically at the cost of some efficiency.

5.1 Software implementation

This section collects a few topics which involve platform-specific details to a greater extent than earlier chapters. At this level, software implementation decisions are driven by underlying hardware characteristics, and hence this section is also about hardware. No attempt has been made to be comprehensive; rather, the coverage is largely by example. For material which focuses on specific platforms, we have chosen the Intel IA-32 family (commonly known as $x86$ processors, in wide use since the 1980s) and the Sun SPARC family.

§5.1.1 discusses some shortcomings of traditional approaches for integer multiplication, in particular, on the Intel Pentium family processors. §5.1.2 and §5.1.3 present an overview of technologies and implementation issues for two types of hardware acceleration. Many common processors possess floating-point hardware that can be used to implement prime field arithmetic. A fast method presented by Bernstein using floating-point methods is outlined in §5.1.2. §5.1.3 considers the single-instruction multiple-data (SIMD) registers present on Intel and AMD processors, which can be used to speed field arithmetic. The common MMX subset is suitable for binary field arithmetic, and extensions on the Pentium 4 can be used to speed multiplication in prime fields using integer operations rather than floating point methods. §5.1.4 consists of miscellaneous optimization techniques and implementation notes, some of which concern requirements, characteristics, flaws, and quirks of the development tools the authors have used. Selected timings for field arithmetic are presented in §5.1.5.

5.1.1 Integer arithmetic

In "classical" implementations of field arithmetic for $\mathbb{F}_p$ where p is prime, the field element a is represented as a series of W-bit integers $0 \le a_i < 2^W$, where W is the wordsize on the target machine (e.g., $W = 32$) and $a = \sum_{i=0}^{t-1} a_i 2^{Wi}$. Schoolbook multiplication uses various scanning methods, of which product scanning (Algorithm 2.10) consecutively computes each output word of $c = ab$ (and reduction is done separately). A multiply-and-accumulate strategy with a three-register accumulator (r_2, r_1, r_0) consists primarily of t^2 repeated fragments of the form

$$
\begin{aligned}
(uv) &\leftarrow a_i b_j \\
(\varepsilon, r_0) &\leftarrow r_0 + v \\
(\varepsilon, r_1) &\leftarrow r_1 + u + \varepsilon \\
r_2 &\leftarrow r_2 + \varepsilon
\end{aligned}
\tag{5.1}
$$

where (uv) is the $2W$-bit product of a_i and b_j and ε is the carry bit. Karatsuba-Ofman techniques (see §2.2.2) reduce the number of multiplications and are faster asymptotically, but the overhead often makes such methods uncompetitive for field sizes of practical interest.

Processor	Year	MHz	Cache (KB)	Selected features
386	1985	16		First IA-32 family processor with 32-bit operations and parallel stages.
486	1989	25	L1: 8	Decode and execution units expanded in five pipelined stages in the 486; processor is capable of one instruction per clock cycle.
Pentium	1993	60	L1: 16	Dual-pipeline: optimal pairing in U-V pipes could give throughput of two instructions per clock cycle. MMX added eight special-purpose 64-bit "multimedia" registers, supporting operations on vectors of 1, 2, 4, or 8-byte integers.
Pentium MMX	1997	166	L1: 32	
Pentium Pro	1995	150	L1: 16 L2: 256,512	P6 architecture introduced more sophisticated pipelining and out-of-order execution. Instructions decoded to μ-ops, with up to three μ-ops executed per cycle. Improved branch prediction, but misprediction penalty much larger than on Pentium. Integer multiplication latency/throughput 4/1 vs 9/9 on Pentium. Pentium II and newer have MMX; the III introduced SSE extensions with 128-bit registers supporting operations on vectors of single-precision floating-point values.
Pentium II	1997	233	L1: 32 L2: 256,512	
Celeron	1998	266	L2: 0,128	
Pentium III	1999	500	L1: 32 L2: 512	
Pentium 4	2000	1400	L1: 8 L2: 256	NetBurst architecture runs at significantly higher clock speeds, but many instructions have worse cycle counts than P6 family processors. New 12K μ-op "execution trace cache" mechanism. SSE2 extensions have double-precision floating-point and 128-bit packed integer data types.

Table 5.1. Partial history and features of the Intel IA-32 family of processors. Many variants of a given processor exist, and new features appear over time (e.g., the original Celeron had no cache). Cache comparisons are complicated by the different access speeds and mechanisms (e.g., newer Pentium IIIs use an advanced transfer cache with smaller level 1 and level 2 cache sizes).

To illustrate the considerations involved in evaluating strategies for multiplication, we briefly examine the case for the Intel Pentium family of processors, some of which appear in Table 5.1. The Pentium is essentially a 32-bit architecture, and said to be "superscalar" as it can process instructions in parallel. The pipelining capability is easiest to describe for the original Pentium, where there were two general-purpose integer pipelines, and optimization focused on organizing code to keep both pipes filled subject to certain pipelining constraints. The case is more complicated in the newer processors of the Pentium family, which use more sophisticated pipelining and techniques such as out-of-order execution. For the discussion presented here, only fairly general properties of the processor are involved.

The Pentium possesses an integer multiplier that can perform a 32×32-bit multiplication (giving a 64-bit result). However, there are only eight (mostly) general-purpose registers, and the multiplication of interest is restrictive in the registers used. Of fundamental interest are instruction *latency* and *throughput*, some of which are given in Table 5.2. Roughly speaking, latency is the number of clock cycles required before the result of an operation may be used, and throughput is the number of cycles that must pass before the instruction may be executed again.[1] Note that small latency and small throughput are desirable under these definitions.

Instruction	Pentium II/III	Pentium 4
Integer add, xor,...	1 / 1	.5 / .5
Integer add, sub with carry	1 / 1	6–8 / 2–3
Integer multiplication	4 / 1	14–18 / 3–5
Floating-point multiply	5 / 2	7 / 2
MMX ALU	1 / 1	2 / 2
MMX multiply	3 / 1	8 / 2

Table 5.2. Instruction latency / throughput for the Intel Pentium II/III vs the Pentium 4.

Fragment (5.1) has two performance bottlenecks: the dependencies between instructions work against pipelining, and there is a significant latency period after the multiply (especially on the Pentium 4). Strategies for improving field multiplication (e.g., by reducing simultaneously) using general-purpose registers are constrained by the very few such registers available, carry handling, and the restriction to fixed output registers for the multiplication of interest. Some useful memory move instructions can be efficiently inserted into (5.1). On the Pentium II/III, it appears that no reorganization of the code can make better use of the latency period after the multiply, and multiplication of t-word integers requires an average of approximately seven cycles to process each 32×32 multiplication. Code similar to fragment (5.1) will do much worse on the Pentium 4.

Redundant representations   The cost of carry handling can be reduced in some cases by use of a different field representation. The basic idea is to choose $W' < W$ and represent elements as $a = \sum a_i 2^{W'i}$ where $|a_i|$ may be somewhat larger than $2^{W'-1}$ (and hence such representations are not unique, and more words may be required to represent a field element). Additions, for example, may be done without any processing of carry. For field multiplication, choosing W' so that several terms $a_i b_j$ in $c = ab$ may be accumulated without carrying into a third word may be desirable. Roughly

---

[1] Intel defines *latency* as the number of clock cycles that are required for the execution core to complete all of the μops that form an IA-32 instruction, and *throughput* as the number of clock cycles required to wait before the issue ports are free to accept the same instruction again. For many IA-32 instructions, the throughput of an instruction can be significantly less than its latency.

speaking, this is the strategy discussed in the next section, where W' is such that the approximately $2W'$-bit quantity $a_i b_j$ can be stored in a single (wide) floating-point register.

5.1.2   Floating-point arithmetic

The floating-point hardware present on many workstations can be used to perform integer arithmetic. The basic techniques are not new, although the performance benefits on common hardware has perhaps not been fully appreciated. As in the preceding section, the examples will be drawn primarily from the Intel Pentium family; however, much of the discussion applies to other platforms.

A rational number of the form $2^e m$ where e and m are integers with $|m| < 2^b$ is said to be a *b-bit floating-point number*. Given a real number z, $\mathrm{fp}_b(z)$ denotes a b-bit floating-point value close to z in the sense that $|z - \mathrm{fp}_b(z)| \le 2^{e-1}$ if $|z| \le 2^{e+b}$. A b-bit floating-point value $2^e m$ is the desired approximation for $|z| \in ((2^{b+e} - 2^{e-1})/2, 2^{b+e} - 2^{e-1})$; a simple example in the case $b = 3$ appears in the following table.

e	z-interval	3-bit approximation	max error
-1	$[2 - 1/8, 4 - 1/4]$	$2^{-1}m = 1a_1.a_0$	$1/4$
0	$[4 - 1/4, 8 - 1/2]$	$2^0 m = 1a_1 a_0$	$1/2$
1	$[8 - 1/2, 16 - 1]$	$2^1 m = 1a_1 a_0 0$	1

If z is a b-bit floating-point value, then $z = \mathrm{fp}_b(z)$. Subject to constraints on the exponents, floating-point hardware can find $\mathrm{fp}_b(x \pm y)$ and $\mathrm{fp}_b(xy)$ for b-bit floating-point values x and y, where b depends on the hardware.

IEEE single- and double-precision floating-point formats consist of a sign bit s, biased exponent e, and fraction f. A double-precision floating-point format

s	e (11-bit exponent)	f (52-bit fraction)
63	62 52	51 0

represents numbers $z = (-1)^s \times 2^{e-1023} \times 1.f$; the normalization of the significand $1.f$ increases the effective precision to 53 bits.[2] Floating-point operations are sometimes described using the length of the significand, such as 53-bit for double precision. The Pentium has eight floating-point registers, where the length of the significand is selected in a control register. In terms of fp_b, the Pentium has versions for $b \in \{24, 53, 64\}$ (corresponding to formats of size 32, 64, and 80 bits).

Coding with floating-point operations requires strategies that are not merely direct translations of what is done in the classical case. The numbers are stored in different formats, and it is not economical to repeatedly move between the formats. Bit operations that are convenient in integer format (e.g., extraction of specific bits) are generally

---

[2] A similar normalization occurs for 32-bit single-precision and the 80-bit double extended-precision formats; however, the entire 64-bit significand is retained in extended-precision format.

clumsy (and slow) if attempted on values in floating point registers. On the other hand, floating-point addition operates on more bits than addition with integer instructions if $W = 32$, and the extra registers are welcomed on register-poor machines such as the Pentium. Multiplication latency is still a factor (in fact, it's worse on the Pentium II/III than for integer multiplication—see Table 5.2); however, there are more registers and the requirement for specific register use is no longer present, making it possible to do useful operations during the latency period.

A multiprecision integer multiplication can be performed by a combination of floating-point and integer operations. If the input and output are in canonical (multi-word integer) format, the method is not effective on Intel P6-family processors; however, the longer latencies of the Pentium 4 encourage a somewhat similar strategy using SIMD capabilities (§5.1.3), and the combination has been used on SPARC processors.

Example 5.1 (*SPARC multiplication*) The SPARC (Scalable Processor ARChitecture) specification is the basis for RISC (Reduced Instruction Set Computer) designs from Sun Microsystems. Unlike the Pentium where an integer multiply instruction is available, the 32-bit SPARC-V7 processors had only a "multiply step" instruction MULScc, and multiplication is essentially shift-and-add with up to 32 repeated steps.

The SPARC-V9 architecture extends V8 to include 64-bit address and data types, additional registers and instructions, improved processing of conditionals and branching, and advanced support for superscalar designs. In particular, the V7 and V8 multiply operations are deprecated in favour of a new MULX instruction that produces the lower 64 bits of the product of 64-bit integers. In the Sun UltraSPARC, MULX is relatively slow for generic 32×32 multiplication; worse, the instruction does not cooperate with the superscalar design which can issue four instructions per cycle (subject to moderately restrictive constraints).

Due to the limitations of MULX, the multiprecision library GNU MP (see Appendix C) implements integer multiplication using floating-point registers on V9-compatible processors. Multiplication of a with 64-bit b splits a into 32-bit half-words and b into four 16-bit pieces, and eight floating-point multiplications are performed for each 64-bit word of a. Pairs (four per word of a) of 48-bit partial products are summed using floating-point addition; the remaining operations are performed after transfer to integer form. On an UltraSPARC I or II, the 56 instructions in the main loop of the calculation for ab (where 64-bits of a are processed per iteration and b is 64-bit) are said to execute in 14 cycles (4 instructions per cycle).

The conversions between integer and floating-point formats on each field multiplication allow floating-point variations to be inserted relatively painlessly into existing code. However, more efficient curve arithmetic may be constructed if the number of conversions can be minimized across curve operations.

Scalar multiplication for P-224

We outline a fast method due to Bernstein for performing elliptic curve point multiplication kP using floating-point hardware for the NIST-recommended curve over $\mathbb{F}_p$ with $p = 2^{224} - 2^{96} + 1$. All of the performance improvements are in field arithmetic (and in the organization of field operations in point doubling and addition). On the Pentium, which can use a 64-bit significand, field elements were represented as

$$a = \sum_i a_i 2^{W'i} = \sum_{i=0}^{7} a_i 2^{28i}$$

where $|a_i|$ is permitted to be somewhat larger than 2^{27} (as outlined at the end of §5.1.1). In comparison with the representation as a vector of 32-bit positive integers, this representation is not unique, and an additional word is required. Field multiplication will require more than 64 (floating-point) multiplications, compared with 49 in the classical method. On the positive side, more registers are available, multiplication can occur on any register, and terms $a_i b_j$ may be directly accumulated in a register without any carry handling.

Field arithmetic Field multiplication and (partial) reduction is performed simultaneously, calculating $c = ab$ from most-significant to least-significant output word. Portions of the code for computing the term c_k are of the form

$$r_2 \leftarrow \sum_{i+j=k} a_i b_j$$
$$r_1 \leftarrow \text{fp}_{64}(r_2 + \alpha_k) - \alpha_k$$
$$r_0 \leftarrow r_2 - r_1$$

where r_i are floating-point registers and $\alpha_k = 3 \cdot 2^{90+28k}$. Roughly speaking, the addition and subtraction of α_k is an efficient way to extract bits from a floating-point number. Consider the case $k = 0$ and that rounding is via round-to-nearest. If r_2 is a 64-bit floating-point value with $|r_2| < 2^{90}$, then $r_1 \in 2^{28}\mathbb{Z}$, $|r_0| \leq 2^{27}$, and $r_2 = r_0 + r_1$. Figure 5.1 shows the values for r_1 and r_0 when $0 \leq r_2 = v \cdot 2^{28} + u < 2^{90}$ and the case $u = 2^{27}$ is handled by a "round-to-even" convention.

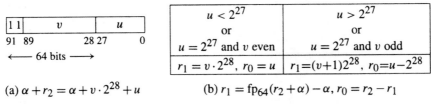

	$u < 2^{27}$ or $u = 2^{27}$ and v even	$u > 2^{27}$ or $u = 2^{27}$ and v odd
	$r_1 = v \cdot 2^{28}$, $r_0 = u$	$r_1 = (v+1)2^{28}$, $r_0 = u - 2^{28}$

(a) $\alpha + r_2 = \alpha + v \cdot 2^{28} + u$ (b) $r_1 = \text{fp}_{64}(r_2 + \alpha) - \alpha$, $r_0 = r_2 - r_1$

Figure 5.1. *Splitting of a 64-bit floating-point number r_2 for the case $0 \leq r_2 = v \cdot 2^{28} + u < 2^{90}$ and $\alpha = 3 \cdot 2^{90}$. The round-to-nearest convention is used, with round-to-even when $u = 2^{27}$.*

The r_0 and r_1 calculated for a given $k > 7$ are folded into lower-order terms. The first step finds $r_2 = a_7 b_7$, and then $c_{14} = r_0$ and $c_{15} = r_1$. Let $c_k' = c_k \cdot 2^{-28k}$ and consider

$$
\begin{aligned}
c_k = c_k' \cdot 2^{28k} &= c_k' \cdot 2^{28(k-8)} 2^{224} \\
&= c_k' \cdot 2^{28(k-8)} (p + 2^{96} - 1) \\
&\equiv c_k' \cdot 2^{28(k-5)} 2^{12} - c_k' \cdot 2^{28(k-8)} \pmod{p}.
\end{aligned}
$$

This says that $c_k \cdot 2^{-128}$ is added to c_{k-5}, and $c_k \cdot 2^{-224}$ is subtracted from c_{k-8}; for example, c_{15} is folded into c_{10} and c_7. The process eventually produces a partially reduced product $c = ab$ as a vector of eight floating-point values.

Curve arithmetic Bernstein's point multiplication method for computing kP uses a width-4 window method (without sliding), with an expected $3 + (15/16)(224/4)$ point additions.[3] On the Pentium II/III, point multiplication required roughly 730,000 cycles, significantly faster than other implementations reported in the literature. Most of the improvement may be obtained by scheduling only field multiplication and squaring. However, the point arithmetic was organized so that some operations could be efficiently folded into field multiplication; for example, the field arithmetic for point doubling $(x_2, y_2, z_2) = 2(x_1, y_1, z_1)$ is organized as

$$
\delta \leftarrow z_1^2, \quad \gamma \leftarrow y_1^2 \quad \beta \leftarrow x_1 \gamma, \quad \alpha \leftarrow 3(x_1 - \delta)(x_1 + \delta)
$$
$$
x_2 \leftarrow \alpha^2 - 8\beta, \quad z_2 \leftarrow (y_1 + z_1)^2 - \gamma - \delta, \quad y_2 \leftarrow \alpha(4\beta - x_2) - 8\gamma^2
$$

requiring three multiplications, five squarings, and seven reductions. Conversion of the output to canonical form is expensive, but is done only at the end of the point multiplication.

Programming considerations Except for a fragment to set the floating-point control register, all of the code is in C. However, the scheduling and management of registers is processor-specific, and involves some of the same work necessary for assembly language versions. There are also a number of requirements on the development tools. It is essential that 80-bit extended-double registers not be unexpectedly spilled to 64-bit doubles by the compiler. Typically, data must be aligned properly (e.g., on 8-byte boundaries), and some environments do not manage this properly. Alignment for automatic variables may require extra steps. An alternate strategy using SIMD integer capabilities is discussed in §5.1.3.

---

[3] The reference implementation processes k as $k = \sum_{i=0}^{55} k_i 2^{4i}$ where $-8 \le k_i < 8$. The precomputation phase stores iP in Chudnovsky coordinates $(X:Y:Z:Z^2:Z^3)$ for nonzero $i \in [-8, 8)$, requiring three point squarings and three point doublings. The excessive storage is not essential for performance.

5.1.3 SIMD and field arithmetic

Single-instruction multiple-data (SIMD) capabilities perform operations in parallel on vectors. In the Intel Pentium family (see Table 5.1), such hardware is present on all but the original Pentium and the Pentium Pro. The features were initially known as "MMX Technology" for the multimedia applications, and consisted of eight 64-bit registers, operating on vectors with components of 1, 2, 4, or 8 bytes. The capabilities were extended in subsequent processors: streaming SIMD (SSE) in the Pentium III has 128-bit registers and single-precision floating-point arithmetic, and SSE2 extends SSE to include double-precision floating-point and integer operations in the Pentium 4. Advanced Micro Devices (AMD) introduced MMX support on their K6 processor, and added various extensions in newer chips.

In this section, we consider the use of SIMD capabilities on AMD and Intel processors to speed field arithmetic. The general idea is to use these special-purpose registers to implement fast 64-bit operations on what is primarily a 32-bit machine. For binary fields, the common MMX subset can be used to speed multiplication and inversion. For prime fields, the SSE2 extensions (specific to the Pentium 4) provide an alternative approach to the floating-point methods of §5.1.2.

Binary field arithmetic with MMX

The eight 64-bit MMX registers found on Pentium and AMD processors are relatively easy to employ to speed operations in binary fields $\mathbb{F}_{2^m}$. Although restrictive in the functions supported, the essential shift and xor operations required for binary field arithmetic are available. The strengths and shortcomings of the MMX subset for field multiplication and inversion are examined in this section.

Naïvely, the 64-bit registers should improve performance by a factor of 2 compared with code using only general-purpose 32-bit registers. In practice, the results depend on the algorithm and the coding method. Implementations may be a mix of conventional and MMX code, and only a portion of the algorithm benefits from the wide registers. Comparison operations produce a mask vector rather than setting status flags, and data-dependent branching is not directly supported. The MMX registers cannot be used to address memory. On the other hand, the Pentium has only eight general-purpose registers, so effective use of the extra registers may contribute collateral benefits to general register management. As noted in Table 5.2, there is no latency or throughput penalty for use of MMX on the Pentium II/III; on the Pentium 4, scheduling will be of more concern.

Field multiplication Comb multiplication (Algorithm 2.36) with reduction is efficiently implemented with MMX. Consider the field $\mathbb{F}_{2^{163}}$, with reduction polynomial $f(z) = z^{163} + z^7 + z^6 + z^3 + 1$. The precomputation step 1 uses MMX, and the accumulator C is maintained in six MMX registers; processing of the input a is accomplished with general-purpose registers. The algorithm adapts well to use of the wide registers, since the operations required are simple xor and shifts, there are no comparisons on MMX registers, and (for this case) the accumulator C can be maintained entirely in registers. Field multiplication is roughly twice the speed of a traditional approach.

Field inversion For inversion, Algorithm 2.48 (a Euclidean Algorithm variant) was implemented. In contrast to multiplication, the inversion algorithm requires some operations which are less-efficiently implemented with MMX. A degree calculation is required in step 3.1, and step 3.3 requires an extra register load since the shift is by a non-constant value. Two strategies were tested. The first used MMX only on g_1 and g_2, applying conventional code to track the lengths of u and v and find degrees. The second strategy obtained somewhat better performance by using MMX for all four variables. Lengths of u and v were tracked in 32-bit increments, in order to more efficiently perform degree calculations (by extracting appropriate 32-bit halves and passing to conventional code for degree). A factor 1.5 improvement was observed in comparison with a non-MMX version.

Programming considerations Unlike the commitment required for use of floating-point registers as described in §5.1.2, the use of MMX capabilities may be efficiently isolated to specific routines such as field multiplication—other code in an elliptic curve scheme could remain unchanged if desired. Implementation in C may be done with assembly-language fragments or with intrinsics. Assembly-language coding allows the most control over register allocation and scheduling, and was the method used to implement Algorithm 2.36. Programming with intrinsics is somewhat similar to assembly-language coding, but the compiler manages register allocation and can perform optimizations. The inversion routines were coded with intrinsics.

Intel provides intrinsics with its compiler, and the features were added to gcc-3.1. As in §5.1.2, data alignment on 8-byte boundaries is required for performance. The MMX and floating point registers share the same address space, and there is a penalty for switching from MMX operations to floating-point operations. Code targeted for the Pentium 4 could use the SSE2 enhancements, which do not have the interaction problem with the floating-point stack, and which have wider 128-bit vector operations.

SIMD and prime field arithmetic

The Pentium III has eight 128-bit SIMD registers, and SSE2 extensions on the Pentium 4 support operations on vectors of double-precision floating-point values and 64-bit integers. In contrast to the floating-point implementation described in §5.1.2, use of the integer SSE2 capabilities can be efficiently isolated to specific routines such as field multiplication.

Multiplication in SSE2 hardware does not increase the maximum size of operands over conventional instructions (32 bits in both cases, giving a 64-bit result); however, there are more registers which can participate in multiplication, the multiplication latency is lower, and products may be accumulated with 64-bit operations. With conventional code, handling carry is a bottleneck but is directly supported since arithmetic operations set condition codes that can be conveniently used. The SSE2 registers are not designed for this type of coding, and explicit tests for carry are expensive. Implementing the operand-scanning multiplication of Algorithm 2.9 is straightforward with scalar SSE2 operations, since the additions may be done without concern for carry. The approach has two additions and a subsequent shift associated with each multiplication in the inner product operation $(UV) \leftarrow C[i+j] + A[i] \cdot B[j] + U$. The total number of additions and shifts can be reduced by adapting the product-scanning approach in Algorithm 2.10 at the cost of more multiplications. To avoid tests for carry, one or both of the input values are represented in the form $a = \sum a_i 2^{W'i}$ where $W' < 32$ so that products may be accumulated in 64-bit registers.

Example 5.2 (*multiplication with SSE2 integer operations*) Suppose inputs consist of integers represented as seven 32-bit words (e.g., in P-224 discussed in §5.1.2). A scalar implementation of Algorithm 2.9 performs 49 multiplications, 84 additions, and 49 shifts in the SSE2 registers. If the input is split into 28-bit fragments, then Algorithm 2.10 performs 64 multiplications, 63 additions, and 15 shifts to obtain the product as 16 28-bit fragments.

The multiprecision library GNU MP (see Appendix C) uses an operand-scanning approach, with an 11-instruction inner loop. The code is impressively compact, and generic in that it handles inputs of varying lengths. If the supplied testing harness is used with parameters favourable to multiplication times, then timings are comparable to those obtained using more complicated code. However, under more realistic tests, a product-scanning method using code specialized to the 7-word case is 20% faster, even though the input must be split into 28-bit fragments and the output reassembled into 32-bit words. A straightforward SSE2 integer implementation of multiplication on 7-word inputs and producing 14-word output (32-bit words) requires approximately 325 cycles, less than half the time of a traditional approach (which is especially slow on the Pentium 4 due to the instruction latencies in Table 5.2).

5.1.4 Platform miscellany

This section presents selected notes on optimization techniques and platform characteristics, some of which are specific to development environments the authors have used. Compiler-specific notes are restricted to those for the C programming language, a common choice when a higher-level language is used. Even if implementation in hand-crafted assembly (for performance) is planned, prototyping in a higher-level language may speed development and comparisons of algorithms. In this case, it will be desirable that the prototype provide meaningful benchmark and other information for performance estimates of assembly-language versions.

Common optimization considerations

We present basic performance considerations and techniques with wide applicability.

Loop unrolling Among common strategies for improving performance, loop unrolling is one of the most basic and most profitable. Loops are expanded so that more operations are done per iteration, reducing the number of instructions executed but increasing code size. The longer sequences are generally better-optimized, especially in the case of fully-unrolled loops. As an example, the comb multiplication in Algorithm 2.36 can be done efficiently with an outer loop over the w-bit windows, and a completely unrolled inner loop to perform addition and shifting.

Typically, user-specified options influence the amount of loop unrolling performed by the compiler. At the current state of compiler technology, this automatic method cannot replace programmer-directed efforts, especially when unrolling is combined with coding changes that reduce data-dependencies.

Local data On register-poor machines such as the Intel Pentium, the consumption of registers to address data can frustrate optimization efforts. Copying data to the stack allows addressing to be done with the same register used for other local variables. Note that the use of a common base register can result in longer instructions (on processors such as the Pentium with variable-length instructions) as displacements increase.

Duplicated code For some algorithms, duplicating code or writing case-specific fragments is effective. As an example, the Euclidean algorithm variants for inversion call for repeated interchange of the contents of arrays holding field elements. This can be managed by copying contents or interchanging pointers to the arrays; however, faster performance may be obtained with separate code fragments which are essentially identical except that the names of variables are interchanged.

Similarly, case-specific code fragments can be effective at reducing the number of conditionals and other operations. The Euclidean algorithm variants, for example, have arrays which are known a priori to grow or shrink during execution. If the lengths can be tracked efficiently, then distinct code fragments can be written, and a transfer to the appropriate fragment is performed whenever a length crosses a boundary. A somewhat extreme case of this occurs with the Almost Inverse Algorithm 2.50, where two of the variables grow and two shrink. If t words are used to represent a field element, then t^2 length-specific fragments can be employed. In tests on the Intel Pentium and Sun SPARC, this was in fact required for the algorithm to be competitive with Algorithm 2.48.

Use of "bail-out" strategies can be especially effective with code duplication. The basic idea is to remove code which handles unlikely or contrived data, and transfer execution to a different routine if such data is encountered. Such methods can have dismal worst-case performance, but may optimize significantly better (in part, because less code is required). The technique is effective in the Euclidean Algorithm 2.48, where the "unlikely data" is that giving large shifts at step 3.3.

Duplicated and case-specific coding can involve significant code expansion. Platform characteristics and application constraints may limit the use of such strategies.

Branch misprediction Conditional expressions can significantly degrade optimizations and performance, especially if the outcome is poorly-predicted. Branch prediction in the Intel Pentium family, for example, was improved in the P6 processors, but the cost of misprediction is in fact much higher. Care must be exercised when timing routines containing a significant number of conditional expressions. Timing by repeated calls with the same data can give wildly misleading results if typical usage differs. This is easily seen in OEF arithmetic if implemented in the natural way suggested by the mathematics, and in the routine described in §3.6.2 for solving $x^2 + x = c$ in binary fields, since branch prediction will be very poor with realistic data.

Techniques to reduce the number of frequently-executed poorly-predicted conditionals include algorithm changes, table-lookup, and specialized instructions. In the case of OEF multiplication in §2.4.2, the natural method which performs many subfield operations is replaced by an algorithm with fewer conditional expressions. Table-lookup is a widely used method, which is effective if the size of the table is manageable. (Table-lookup can eliminate code, so the combined code and table may require less storage than the non-table version.) The method is effective in Algorithm 3.86 for solving $x^2 + x = c$, eliminating conditionals at step 3 and processing multiple bits concurrently. Finally, the specialized instructions are illustrated by the Pentium II or later, which contain conditional move and other instructions eliminating branching at the cost of some dependency between instructions.

Assembly coding Performance considerations, shortcuts, register allocation, and access to platform features are often sufficiently compelling to justify coding critical sections in assembler. If many platforms must be supported, coding entire routines may involve significant effort—even within the same family of processors, different scheduling may be required for best performance.

Consider the multiply-and-accumulate fragment (5.1). This is commonly coded in assembler for two reasons: some compilers do not process the $2W$-bit product from W-bit input efficiently, and instructions that access the carry flag rather than explicit tests for carry should be used. In longer fragments, it may also be possible to outperform the compiler in register allocation.

Inline assembly, supported by some compilers, is especially desirable for inserting short fragments. As an example, the Euclidean Algorithm 2.48 requires polynomial degree calculations. A relatively fast method uses a binary search and table lookup, once the nonzero word of interest is located. Some processors have instruction sets from which a fast "bit scan" may be built: the Pentium has single instructions (*bsr* and *bsf*) for finding the position of the most or least significant bit in a word.[4] Similarly, Sun suggests using a Hamming weight (population) instruction to build a fast bit scan from the right for the SPARC. The GNU C and Intel compilers work well for inlining such code, since it is possible to direct cooperation with surrounding code. In contrast,

---

[4]The number of cycles required by the bit scan instructions varies across the Pentium family. The floating point hardware can be used to provide an alternative to bit scan.

the Microsoft compiler has only limited support for such cooperation, and can suffer from poor register management.

Compiler characteristics and flaws

The remaining notes in this section are decidedly platform-specific. The compilers referenced are GNU C (gcc-2.95), Intel (6.0), Microsoft (6.0), and Sun Workshop (6U2), producing 32-bit code for the Intel Pentium family and 32- or 64-bit code for the Sun UltraSPARC.

Scalars vs arrays Some compilers will produce slower code when arrays are used rather than scalars (even though the array indices are known at compile-time). Among the compilers tested, GNU C exhibits this optimization weakness.

Instruction scheduling Compared with the Intel and Sun compilers, GNU C is weaker at instruction scheduling on the Pentium and SPARC platforms, but can be coerced into producing somewhat better sequences by relatively small changes to the source. In particular, significantly different times were observed in tests with Algorithm 2.36 on SPARC with minor reorganizations of code. The Sun Workshop compiler is less-sensitive to such changes, and generally produces faster code.

On the Intel processors, scheduling and other optimizations using general-purpose registers are frustrated by the few such registers available. A common strategy is to allow the frame pointer (ebp) to be used as a general-purpose register; in GNU C, this is '-fomit-frame-pointer'.

Alignment Processors typically have alignment requirements on data (e.g., 32-bit integers appear on 4-byte boundaries), and unaligned accesses may fault or be slow. This is of particular concern with double-precision floating-point values and data for SIMD operations, since some environments do not manage the desired alignment properly. It is likely that these shortcomings will be corrected in subsequent releases of the development tools. Regardless, alignment for automatic (stack) variables may require additional steps.

Flaws Despite the maturity of the compilers tested, it was relatively easy to uncover weaknesses. For example, an apparent optimization flaw in the Sun Workshop compiler was triggered by a small code change in the 64-bit implementation of Algorithm 2.36, causing shifts by 4 to be processed as multiplication by 16, a much slower operation on that platform. Workarounds include post-processing the assembler output or using a weaker optimization setting.

Significant optimization problems were observed in the Microsoft compiler concerning inlining of C code; in particular, multiplication in a short OEF routine would sometimes be replaced by a function call. This bug results in larger and much slower code. The widely-used Microsoft compiler produces code which is competitive with that of the Intel compiler (provided no bugs are triggered). However, the limited ability for inline assembler to cooperate with surrounding code is a design weakness compared with that of GNU C or the Intel compilers, which have the additional advantage that they can be used on Unix-like systems.

5.1.5 Timings

Selected field operation timings are presented for Intel Pentium family processors and the Sun UltraSPARC, commonly used in workstations. The NIST recommended binary and prime fields (§A.2) are the focus, although some data for an OEF (§2.4) is presented for comparison.

It is acknowledged that timings can be misleading, and are heavily influenced by the programmer's talent and effort (or lack thereof), compiler selection, and the precise method of obtaining the data. The timings presented here should be viewed with the same healthy dose of skepticism prescribed for all such data. Nonetheless, timings are essential for algorithm analysis, since rough operation counts are often insufficient to capture platform characteristics. For the particular timings presented here, there has generally been independent "sanity check" data available from other implementations.

Tables 5.3–5.5 give basic comparisons for the NIST recommended binary and prime fields, along with a selected OEF. Inversion and multiplication times for binary fields on two platforms appear in Table 5.6, comparing compilers, inversion algorithms, and 32-bit vs 64-bit code. The 64-bit code on the Intel Pentium III is via special-purpose registers. These capabilities were extended in the Pentium 4, and Table 5.7 includes timings for prime field multiplication via these registers along with an approach using floating-point registers.

Field arithmetic comparisons

Timings for the smallest of the NIST recommended binary and prime fields, along with an OEF, are presented in Table 5.3. Specifically, these are the binary field $\mathbb{F}_{2^{163}}$ with reduction polynomial $f(z) = z^{163} + z^7 + z^6 + z^3 + 1$, the prime field $\mathbb{F}_{p_{192}}$ with $p_{192} = 2^{192} - 2^{64} - 1$, and the OEF $\mathbb{F}_{p^6}$ with prime $p = 2^{31} - 1$ and reduction polynomial $f(z) = z^6 - 7$. Realistic branch misprediction penalties are obtained using a sequence of pseudo randomly generated field elements, and the timings include framework overhead such as function calls. The Intel compiler version 6 along with the Netwide Assembler (NASM) were used on an Intel Pentium III running the Linux 2.2 operating system.

Algorithms for binary fields were coded entirely in C except for a one-line assembler fragment used in polynomial degree calculations in inversion. Assembly coding may be required in prime fields and OEFs in order to use hardware multipliers producing a 64-bit product from 32-bit input, and to directly access the carry bit, both of which are essential to performance in conventional methods. The first of the $\mathbb{F}_{p_{192}}$ columns in Table 5.3 gives timings for code written primarily in C. For most entries, a signifi-

	$\mathbb{F}_{2^{163}}$	$\mathbb{F}_{p_{192}}$ [a]	$\mathbb{F}_{p_{192}}$	$\mathbb{F}_{(2^{31}-1)^6}$
Addition	0.04	0.18	0.07	0.06
Reduction				
Fast reduction	0.11[b]	0.25[c]	0.11[c]	N/A
Barrett reduction (Algorithm 2.14)	N/A	1.55[d]	0.49	N/A
Multiplication (including fast reduction)	1.30[e]	0.57[d,f]	0.42[f]	0.40[g]
Squaring (including fast reduction)	0.20[h]	—	0.36[i]	0.32[g]
Inversion	10.5[j]	58.3[k]	25.2[k]	2.9[l]
I/M	8.1	102.3	60.0	7.3

[a]Coded primarily in C. [b]Algorithm 2.41. [c]Algorithm 2.27. [d]Uses a 32×32 multiply-and-add.
[e]Algorithm 2.36. [f]Algorithm 2.10. [g]Example 2.56. [h]Algorithm 2.39.
[i]Algorithm 2.13. [j]Algorithm 2.48. [k]Algorithm 2.22. [l]Algorithm 2.59.

Table 5.3. Timings (in μs) for field arithmetic on an 800 MHz Intel Pentium III. The binary field $\mathbb{F}_{2^{163}} = \mathbb{F}_2[z]/(z^{163}+z^7+z^6+z^3+1)$ and the prime field $\mathbb{F}_{p_{192}}$ for $p_{192} = 2^{192} - 2^{64} - 1$ are from the NIST recommendations (§A.2). The rightmost column is the optimal extension field $\mathbb{F}_{p^6} = \mathbb{F}_p[z]/(z^6 - 7)$ for prime $p = 2^{31} - 1$.

cant penalty is seen relative to the timings with assembly. However, the multiplication routine uses an in-line assembly fragment for a 32×32 multiply with a three-word accumulation. If reduction is excluded, the time is very close to that obtained with the assembly language version, an indication that the Intel compiler handles insertion of short in-line assembly fragments well.

Reduction Barrett reduction does not exploit the special form of the NIST prime, and the entries can be interpreted as rough cost estimates of reduction with a random 192-bit prime. In contrast to special primes, this estimate shows that reduction is now a very significant part of field multiplication timings, encouraging the use of Montgomery (§2.2.4) and other multiplication methods. Significant performance degradation in the C version of the fast reduction algorithm is largely explained by the many conditionals in the clumsy handling of carry.

OEF The OEF $\mathbb{F}_{(2^{31}-1)^6}$ in the rightmost column of Table 5.3 is roughly the same size as $\mathbb{F}_{p_{192}}$. The multiplication is accomplished with an accumulation method (Example 2.56) resembling the method used in $\mathbb{F}_{p_{192}}$, and the resulting times are comparable. As expected, inversion is significantly faster for the OEF.

NIST fields Tables 5.4 and 5.5 provide timings for the NIST recommended binary and prime fields. Note that optimizations in the larger fields were limited to techniques employed for $\mathbb{F}_{2^{163}}$ and $\mathbb{F}_{p_{192}}$. In particular, Karatsuba-Ofman methods were not competitive in our tests on this platform for the smaller fields, but were not examined carefully in the larger fields.

	$\mathbb{F}_{2^{163}}$	$\mathbb{F}_{2^{233}}$	$\mathbb{F}_{2^{283}}$	$\mathbb{F}_{2^{409}}$	$\mathbb{F}_{2^{571}}$
Addition	0.04	0.04	0.04	0.06	0.07
Reduction (Algorithms 2.41–2.45)	0.11	0.13	0.19	0.14	0.33
Multiplication (Algorithm 2.36)	1.30	2.27	2.92	5.53	10.23
Squaring (Algorithm 2.39)	0.20	0.23	0.32	0.31	0.56
Inversion (Algorithm 2.48)	10.5	18.6	28.2	53.9	96.4
I/M	8.1	8.2	9.7	9.8	9.4

Table 5.4. Timings (in μs) for binary field arithmetic on an 800 MHz Intel Pentium III, including reduction to canonical form. The fields are from the NIST recommendations (§A.2) with reduction polynomials $z^{163} + z^7 + z^6 + z^3 + 1$, $z^{233} + z^{74} + 1$, $z^{283} + z^{12} + z^7 + z^5 + 1$, $z^{409} + z^{87} + 1$, and $z^{571} + z^{10} + z^5 + z^2 + 1$, respectively.

	$\mathbb{F}_{p_{192}}$	$\mathbb{F}_{p_{224}}$	$\mathbb{F}_{p_{256}}$	$\mathbb{F}_{p_{384}}$	$\mathbb{F}_{p_{521}}$
Addition	0.07	0.07	0.08	0.10	0.10
Reduction (Algorithms 2.27–2.31)	0.11	0.12	0.30	0.38	0.20
Multiplication (Algorithm 2.10)	0.42	0.52	0.81	1.47	2.32
Squaring (Algorithm 2.13)	0.36	0.44	0.71	1.23	1.87
Inversion (Algorithm 2.22)	25.2	34.3	44.3	96.3	163.8
I/M	60.0	70.0	54.7	65.5	70.6

Table 5.5. Timings (in μs) for prime field arithmetic on an 800 MHz Intel Pentium III, including reduction to canonical form. The fields are from the NIST recommendations (§A.2) with $p_{192} = 2^{192} - 2^{64} - 1$, $p_{224} = 2^{224} - 2^{96} + 1$, $p_{256} = 2^{256} - 2^{224} + 2^{192} + 2^{96} - 1$, $p_{384} = 2^{384} - 2^{128} - 2^{96} + 2^{32} - 1$, and $p_{521} = 2^{521} - 1$.

Multiplication and inversion in binary fields

In point multiplication on elliptic curves (§3.3), the cost of field inversion relative to field multiplication is of particular interest. This section presents estimates of the ratio for the NIST binary fields (where the ratio is expected to be relatively small) for two platforms. The three inversion methods discussed in §2.3.6 are compared, along with timings for 32-bit and 64-bit code. The results also show significant differences among the compilers used.

Table 5.6 gives comparative timings on two popular platforms, the Intel Pentium III and Sun UltraSPARC IIe. Both processors are capable of 32- and 64-bit operations, although only the UltraSPARC is 64-bit. The 64-bit operations on the Pentium III are via the single-instruction multiple-data (SIMD) registers, introduced on the Pentium MMX (see Table 5.1). The inversion methods are the extended Euclidean algorithm (EEA) in Algorithm 2.48, the binary Euclidean algorithm (BEA) in Algorithm 2.49, and the almost inverse algorithm (AIA) in Algorithm 2.50. The example fields are taken from the NIST recommendations, with reduction polynomials $f(z) = z^{163} + z^7 + z^6 + z^3 + 1$ and $f(z) = z^{233} + z^{74} + 1$. Both allow fast reduction, but only the latter is favourable to the almost inverse algorithm. Field multiplication based on the comb

Algorithm	Pentium III (800 MHz)			SPARC (500 MHz)		
	32-bit		64-bit	32-bit		64-bit
	gcc	icc	mmx	gcc	cc	cc
Arithmetic in $\mathbb{F}_2^{163}$						
multiplication	1.8	1.3	.7	1.9	1.8	.9
Euclidean algorithm	10.9	10.5	7.1	21.4	14.8	—
binary Euclidean algorithm	20.7	16.0	—	16.8	14.9	10.6
almost inverse	16.4	15.2	—	22.6	15.2	—
I/M	6.1	8.1	9.8	8.8	8.2	12.1
Arithmetic in $\mathbb{F}_2^{233}$						
multiplication	3.0	2.3	—	4.0	2.9	1.7
Euclidean algorithm	18.3	18.8	—	45.5	25.7	—
binary Euclidean algorithm	36.2	28.9	—	42.0	34.0	16.9
almost inverse	22.7	20.1	—	36.8	24.7	—
I/M	6.1	8.2	—	9.2	8.5	9.9

Table 5.6. Multiplication and inversion times for the Intel Pentium III and Sun UltraSPARC IIe. The compilers are GNU C 2.95 (gcc), Intel 6 (icc), and Sun Workshop 6U2 (cc). The 64-bit "multimedia" registers were employed for the entries under "mmx." Inversion to multiplication (I/M) uses the best inversion time.

method (Algorithm 2.36) appears to be fastest on these platforms. A width-4 comb was used, and the times include reduction. Other than the MMX code and a one-line assembler fragment for EEA, algorithms were coded entirely in C.

Some table entries are as expected, for example, the relatively good times for almost inverse in $\mathbb{F}_2^{233}$. Other entries illustrate the significant differences between platforms or compilers on a single platform. Apparent inconsistencies remain in Table 5.6, but we believe that the fastest times provide meaningful estimates of inversion and multiplication costs on these platforms.

Division The timings do not make a very strong case for division using a modification of the BEA (§2.3.6). For the 32-bit code, unless EEA or AIA can be converted to efficiently perform division, then only the entry for $\mathbb{F}_2^{163}$ on the SPARC supports use of BEA-like division. Furthermore, the ratio I/M is at least 8 in most cases, and hence the savings from use of a division algorithm would be less than 10%. With such a ratio, elliptic curve methods will be chosen to reduce the number of inversions, so the savings on a point multiplication kP would be significantly less than 10%.

On the other hand, if affine-only arithmetic is in use in a point multiplication method based on double-and-add, then a fast division would be especially welcomed even if I/M is significantly larger than 5. If BEA is the algorithm of choice, then division has essentially the same cost as inversion.

Implementation notes General programming considerations for the implementations used here are covered in §5.1.4. In particular, to obtain acceptable multiplication times with gcc on the Sun SPARC, code was tuned to be more "gcc-friendly." Limited tuning for gcc was also performed on the inversion code. Optimizing the inversion code is tedious, in part because rough operation counts at this level often fail to capture processor or compiler characteristics adequately.

Multimedia registers The Intel Pentium family (all but the original and the Pentium Pro) and AMD processors possess eight 64-bit "multimedia" registers that were employed for the timings in the column marked "mmx." Use of these capabilities for field arithmetic is discussed in §5.1.3.

EEA Algorithm 2.48 requires polynomial degree calculations. On the SPARC, degree was found by binary search and table lookup, once the nonzero word of interest is located. On the Pentium, a bit scan instruction (bsr) that finds the position of the most significant bit in a word was employed via in-line assembly, resulting in an improvement of approximately 15% in inversion times.

   The code tracks the lengths of u and v using t fragments of similar code, each fragment corresponding to the current "top" of u and v. Here, t was chosen to be the number of words required to represent field elements.

BEA Algorithm 2.49 was implemented with a t-fragment split to track the lengths of u and v efficiently. Rather than the degree calculation indicated in step 3.3, a simpler comparison on the appropriate words was used.

AIA Algorithm 2.50 allows efficient tracking of the lengths of g_1 and g_2 (in addition to the lengths of u and v). A total of t^2 similar fragments of code were used, a significant amount of code expansion unless t is small. As with BEA, a simple comparison replaces the degree calculations. Note that only the reduction polynomial for $\mathbb{F}_{2^{233}}$ is favourable to the almost inverse algorithm.

Prime field multiplication methods

For prime fields, traditional approaches for field multiplication are often throttled by limitations of hardware integer multipliers and carry propagation. Both the Ultra-SPARC and the Pentium family processors suffer from such limitations. The Intel Pentium 4 is in fact much slower (in terms of processor cycles) in some operations than the preceding generation of Pentium processors. As an example, field multiplication in $\mathbb{F}_{p_{224}}$ using Algorithm 2.10 with code targeted at the Pentium II/III appears in Table 5.5 (from a Pentium III) and Table 5.7 (from a Pentium 4). Despite a factor 2 clock speed advantage for the Pentium 4, the timing is in fact slower than obtained on the Pentium III.

Karatsuba-Ofman Methods based on Karatsuba-Ofman do not appear to be competitive with classical methods on the Pentium II/III for fields of this size. Table 5.7 includes times on the Pentium 4 using a depth-2 approach outlined in Example 2.12.

Multiplication in $\mathbb{F}_{p_{224}}$	Time (μs)
Classical integer (Algorithm 2.10)	0.62
Karatsuba-Ofman (Example 2.12)	0.82
SIMD (Example 5.2)	0.27
Floating-point (P-224 in §5.1.2)	0.20[a]

[a]Excludes conversion to/from canonical form.

Table 5.7. Multiplication in $\mathbb{F}_{p_{224}}$ for the 224-bit NIST prime $p_{224} = 2^{224} - 2^{96} + 1$ on a 1.7 GHz Intel Pentium 4. The time for the floating-point version includes (partial) reduction to eight floating-point values, but not to or from canonical form; other times include reduction.

The classical and the Karatsuba-Ofman implementations would benefit from additional tuning specifically for the Pentium 4; regardless, both approaches will be inferior to the methods using special-purpose registers discussed next.

Floating-point arithmetic A strategy with wide applicability involves floating-point hardware commonly found on workstations. The basic idea, discussed in more detail in §5.1.2, is to exploit fast floating-point capabilities to perform integer arithmetic using a suitable field element representation. In applications such as elliptic curve point multiplication, the expensive conversions between integer and floating-point formats can be limited to an insignificant portion of the overall computation, provided that the curve operations are written to cooperate with the new field representation. This strategy is outlined for the NIST recommended prime field $\mathbb{F}_{p_{224}}$ for $p_{224} = 2^{224} - 2^{96} + 1$ in §5.1.2. Timings for multiplication using a floating-point approach on the Pentium 4 are presented in Table 5.7. Note that the time includes partial reduction to eight floating-point values (each of size roughly 28 bits), but excludes the expensive conversion to canonical reduced form.

SIMD Fast multiplication can also be built using the single-instruction multiple-data (SIMD) registers on the Pentium 4. The common MMX subset was noted in the previous section for binary field arithmetic, and SSE2 extensions on the Pentium 4 are suitable for integer operations on vectors of 64-bit integers. §5.1.3 discusses the special registers in more detail. Compared with the floating-point approach, conversion between the field representation used with the SIMD registers and canonical form is relatively inexpensive, and insertion of SIMD code into a larger framework is relatively painless. The time for the SIMD approach in Table 5.7 includes the conversions and reduction to canonical form.

5.2   Hardware implementation

In some applications, a software implementation of an elliptic curve cryptographic scheme at required security levels may not provide the desired performance levels. In these cases it may be advantageous to design and fabricate hardware accelerators to meet the performance requirements. This section gives an introduction to hardware implementation of elliptic curve systems. The main design issues are discussed in §5.2.1. Architectures for finite field processors are introduced in §5.2.2. We begin with an overview of some basic concepts of hardware design.

Gate A *gate* is a small electronic circuit that modifies its inputs and produces a single output. The most common gate has two inputs (but may have more). Gates comprise the basic building blocks of modern computing devices. The most common gates are NOT (inverting its input), NAND (logical AND of two inputs followed by inversion), NOR (logical OR of two inputs followed by inversion), and their more costly cousins AND and OR. Gate count typically refers to the equivalent numbers of 2-input NAND gates.

VLSI *Very large scale integration* (VLSI) refers to the building of circuits with gate counts exceeding 10,000. A VLSI circuit starts with a description in VHDL, Verilog, or other hardware-description languages that is compiled either into information needed to produce the circuit (known as *synthesis*) or into source code to be run on general-purpose machines (known as a *simulation*). The design of VLSI circuits involves a trade-off between circuit-delay caused by the speed of signal propagation and power dissipation. Judicious layouts of the physical circuit affect both. Other tools available include layout editors to assist with block placement and timing-analysis tools to tune the design. These custom designs can be costly in terms of time, money and other resources.

FPGA A *field-programmable gate array* (FPGA) consists of a number of logic blocks each of which typically contains more than a single gate and interconnections between them. These can be converted into circuits by judicious application of power to close or open specific electrical paths. In essence, the FPGA is programmed. The change is reversible, allowing circuits to be created and modified after manufacture (hence "field-programmable"). An FPGA can be large with a sea of gates numbering 20,000 or more. FPGAs were originally introduced as a means of prototyping but are increasingly being used to create application-specific circuits that will often outperform binary code running on generic processors. Programming is typically done with vendor-specific tools similar to those used in creating VLSI circuits.

Gate Array A *gate array* consists of a regular array of logic blocks where each logic block typically contains more than a single gate and also interconnections between these blocks. Circuits are formed by judiciously fusing connections between blocks. This process is irreversible. With the advent of FPGAs that provide considerably more flexibility, gate array technology seems to be used far less.

ASIC *Application-specific integrated circuit* (ASIC) is the terminology used in regard to VLSI or gate array.

Multiplexor A *multiplexor* is a multiple-input single-output device with a controller that selects which input becomes the output. These devices provide the conditional control of a circuit.

Pipelining *Pipelining* is a design feature that allows a second computation to begin before the current computation is completed.

Parallel Processing *Parallel processing* is a technique that permits two or more computations to happen simultaneously.

5.2.1 *Design criteria*

The operation that dominates the execution time of an elliptic curve cryptographic protocol is point multiplication. Efficient implementation of point multiplication can be separated into three distinct layers:

1. finite field arithmetic (Chapter 2);
2. elliptic curve point addition and doubling (§3.2); and
3. point multiplication technique (§3.3).

Accordingly, there is a hierarchy of operations involved in point multiplication with point multiplication techniques near the top and the fundamental finite field arithmetic at the base. The hierarchy, depicted in Figure 5.2, has been extended to the protocol level. For example, one could decide to implement ECDSA signature generation (§4.4.1) entirely in hardware so that the only input to the device is the message to be signed, and the only output is the signature for that message.

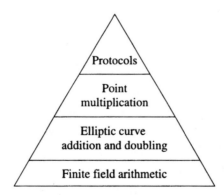

Figure 5.2. Hierarchy of operations in elliptic curve cryptographic schemes.

An important element of hardware design is to determine those layers of the hierarchy that should be implemented in silicon. Clearly, finite field arithmetic must be designed into any hardware implementation. One possibility is to design a hardware accelerator for finite field arithmetic only, and then use an off-the-shelf microprocessor to perform the higher-level functions of elliptic curve point arithmetic. It is important to note that an efficient finite field multiplier does not necessarily yield an efficient point multiplier—all layers of the hierarchy need to be optimized.

Moving point addition and doubling and then point multiplication to hardware provides a more efficient ECC processor at the expense of more complexity. In all cases a combination of both efficient algorithms and hardware architectures is required.

One approach to higher functionality is the processor depicted in Figure 5.3. Along with program and data memory, the three main components are an arithmetic logic unit (AU), an arithmetic unit controller (AUC), and a main controller (MC). The AU performs the basic field operations of addition, squaring, multiplication, and inversion, and is controlled by the AUC. The AUC executes the elliptic curve operations of point addition and doubling. The MC coordinates and executes the method chosen for point multiplication, and interacts with the host system.

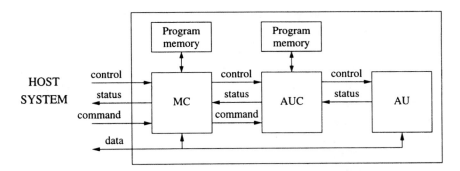

Figure 5.3. Elliptic curve processor architecture.

Let's consider how a higher functionality processor might handle the computation of kP for a randomly chosen integer k. The host commands the processor to generate kP where the integer k and the (affine) coordinates of P are provided by the host. The integer k is loaded into the MC, and the coordinates of P are loaded into the AU. The MC instructs the AUC to do its initialization which may include converting the affine coordinates of P to projective coordinates needed by the point addition and doubling formulae. The MC scans the bits of k and instructs the AUC to perform the appropriate elliptic curve operations, which in turn instructs the AU to perform the appropriate finite field operations. After all bits of k are processed, the MC instructs the AUC to convert the result back to affine coordinates. The host reads the coordinates of kP from the registers in the AU. Two important consequences of having two controllers are the ability to permit parallel processing and pipelining of operations. The MC can also use the data storage capability to implement algorithms that use precomputation to compute kP more efficiently (see §3.3).

Criteria for selecting hardware designs

The following are some of the issues that have to considered in hardware design. It should be emphasized that a good design demands a thorough understanding of the target platform, operating environment, and performance and security requirements.

1. *Cost* is always a significant issue with hardware designers, and is driven by all of the criteria that follow.

2. *Hardware vs. software.* Is there a compelling argument to choose a hardware accelerator over a software implementation?

3. *Throughput.* A device that will be installed into a server will likely need to do hundreds or thousands of elliptic curve operations per second whereas devices designed for handheld computers will require only a small fraction of this.

4. *Complexity.* The more levels of the hierarchy that the device implements, the more complex the circuitry becomes. This translates into more silicon area on a custom VLSI device or a much larger FPGA. It will also result in higher cost.

5. *Flexibility.* Issues pertinent here include the ability of the device to perform computations on curves over binary fields and prime fields.

6. *Algorithm agility.* Many cryptographic protocols require cryptographic algorithms to be negotiated on a per-session basis (e.g., SSL). Reconfigurable hardware might be an attractive feature provided that performance is not significantly impacted.

7. *Power consumption.* Depending on the environment where the device will operate, power consumption may or may not be a major issue. For example, contactless smart cards are very constrained by the amount of power available for cryptographic operations whereas a server can afford much higher power consumption.

8. *Security* should always be paramount in any design consideration. If the device is designed to perform only point additions and doublings, then it is activated during a point multiplication kP by the bits associated with the random value k. Without careful design of the overall architecture, bits of k could be leaked by side-channel attacks. Countermeasures to attacks based on timing, power analysis, and electromagnetic radiation (see §5.3) should be considered based on the environment in which the device will operate.

9. *Overall system architecture.* If the overall system has a microprocessor with enough free cycles to handle protocol functionality above finite field arithmetic (see Figure 5.2), then, depending on other criteria, this may be good reason to design the device for finite field arithmetic only.

10. *Implementation platform.* A custom VLSI or gate array design or an FPGA may be used. FPGAs typically have a high per unit cost versus VLSI and gate array devices. Design costs are however significantly higher for VLSI implementations.

11. *Scalability*. If it is desirable that the device can provide various levels of security (for example by implementing all the NIST curves in §A.2), then one must design the underlying finite field processor to accommodate variable field sizes.

The relative importance of these design criteria depends heavily on the application. For example, cost is less of a concern if the hardware is intended for a high-end server than if the hardware is intended for a low-end device such as a light switch. Table 5.8 lists design criteria priorities for these two extreme situations.

High-end device		Low-end device	
High priority	Low priority	High Priority	Low priority
Throughput	Cost	Cost	Throughput
Security	Power consumption	Hardware vs. software	Flexibility
Scalability	Complexity	Complexity	Algorithm agility
System architecture		Power consumption	Scalability
Implementation platform		Security	
Algorithm agility		System architecture	
Flexibility		Implementation platform	
Hardware vs. software			

Table 5.8. Priorities for hardware design criteria.

5.2.2 Field arithmetic processors

This section describes hardware circuits for performing addition, multiplication, squaring, and inversion operations in a binary field $\mathbb{F}_{2^m}$. The operations in $\mathbb{F}_{2^m}$ are typically easier to implement in hardware than their counterparts in prime fields $\mathbb{F}_p$ because bitwise addition in $\mathbb{F}_{2^m}$ does not have any carry propagation. Moreover, unlike the case of $\mathbb{F}_{2^m}$, squaring in $\mathbb{F}_p$ is roughly as costly as a general multiplication. As a consequence of squaring being more expensive in $\mathbb{F}_p$ than $\mathbb{F}_{2^m}$, inversion using multiplication (as described below for $\mathbb{F}_{2^m}$) is slower in $\mathbb{F}_p$.

Addition

Recall from §2.3.1 that addition of elements in a binary field $\mathbb{F}_{2^m}$ is performed bitwise. There is no carry propagation, and hence addition in $\mathbb{F}_{2^m}$ is considerably simpler to implement in hardware than addition in prime fields $\mathbb{F}_p$.

Multiplication

We discuss the design of a hardware circuit to multiply elements in a binary field $\mathbb{F}_{2^m}$. We shall only consider the case where the elements of $\mathbb{F}_{2^m}$ are represented with respect to a polynomial basis. If $f(z)$ is the reduction polynomial, then we write

$$f(z) = z^m + r(z), \quad \text{where } \deg r \le m - 1.$$

Moreover, if $r(z) = r_{m-1}z^{m-1} + \cdots + r_2 z^2 + r_1 z + r_0$, then we represent $r(z)$ by the binary vector

$$r = (r_{m-1}, \ldots, r_2, r_1, r_0).$$

A multiplier is said to be *bit-serial* if it generates one bit of the product at each clock cycle. It is *digit-serial* if it generates more than one bit of the product at each clock cycle. We present bit-serial multipliers for the three cases:

(i)   fixed field size with arbitrary reduction polynomial;

(ii) fixed field size with fixed reduction polynomial; and

(iii) variable field size (with arbitrary or fixed reduction polynomials).

We also describe a digit-serial multiplier for the fourth case:

(iv) fixed field size with fixed reduction polynomial.

In Figures 5.4–5.11, the following symbols are used to denote operations on bits A, B, C:

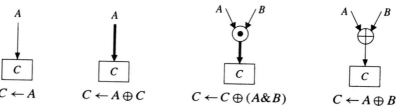

$$C \leftarrow A \qquad\qquad C \leftarrow A \oplus C \qquad\qquad C \leftarrow C \oplus (A \& B) \qquad\qquad C \leftarrow A \oplus B$$

(i) Fixed field size with arbitrary reduction polynomial Algorithm 5.3, which multiplies a multiplicand $a \in \mathbb{F}_{2^m}$ and a multiplier $b \in \mathbb{F}_{2^m}$, processes the bits of b from left (most significant) to right (least significant). The multiplier, called a *most significant bit first (MSB) multiplier*, is depicted in Figure 5.4 for the case $m = 5$. In Figure 5.4 b is a shift register and c is a shift register whose low-end bit is tied to 0. An MSB multiplier can perform a multiplication in $\mathbb{F}_{2^m}$ in m clock cycles.

Algorithm 5.3 Most significant bit first (MSB) multiplier for $\mathbb{F}_{2^m}$

INPUT: $a = (a_{m-1}, \ldots, a_1, a_0)$, $b = (b_{m-1}, \ldots, b_1, b_0) \in \mathbb{F}_{2^m}$, and reduction polynomial
$\qquad f(z) = z^m + r(z)$.
OUTPUT: $c = a \cdot b$.
   1. Set $c \leftarrow 0$.
   2. For i from $m - 1$ downto 0 do
     2.1 $c \leftarrow \text{leftshift}(c) + c_{m-1} r$.
     2.2 $c \leftarrow c + b_i a$.
   3. Return(c).

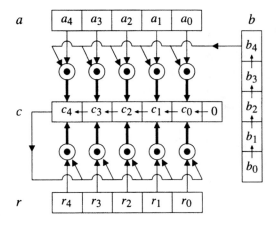

Figure 5.4. *Most significant bit first (MSB) multiplier for* $\mathbb{F}_{2^5}$.

Algorithm 5.4, which multiplies a multiplicand $a \in \mathbb{F}_{2^m}$ and a multiplier $b \in \mathbb{F}_{2^m}$, processes the bits of b from right (least significant) to left (most significant). The multiplier, called a *least significant bit first (LSB) multiplier*, is depicted in Figure 5.5.

Algorithm 5.4 Least significant bit first (LSB) multiplier for $\mathbb{F}_{2^m}$

INPUT: $a = (a_{m-1}, \ldots, a_1, a_0), b = (b_{m-1}, \ldots, b_1, b_0) \in \mathbb{F}_{2^m}$, and reduction polynomial
  $f(z) = z^m + r(z)$.
OUTPUT: $c = a \cdot b$.
  1. Set $c \leftarrow 0$.
  2. For i from 0 to $m-1$ do
    2.1 $c \leftarrow c + b_i a$.
    2.2 $a \leftarrow \text{leftshift}(a) + a_{m-1} r$.
  3. Return(c).

One difference between the MSB and LSB multipliers is that the contents of two of the four registers in Figure 5.4 are not altered during a multiplication, while three of the four registers in Figure 5.5 are altered. In other words, the MSB multiplier only has to clock two registers per clock cycle, as compared to three for the LSB multiplier.

(ii) Fixed field size with fixed reduction polynomial If the reduction polynomial $f(z)$ is fixed and is selected to be a trinomial or pentanomial, then the design of the multiplier is significantly less complex since a register to hold the reduction polynomial is no longer needed. Figure 5.6 illustrates an MSB multiplier for $\mathbb{F}_{2^5}$ with fixed reduction polynomial $f(z) = z^5 + z^2 + 1$.

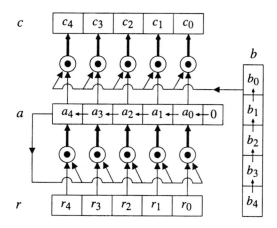

Figure 5.5. *Least significant bit first (LSB) multiplier for* $\mathbb{F}_{2^5}$.

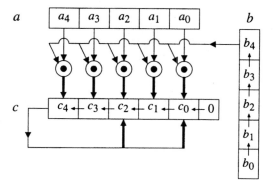

Figure 5.6. *MSB multiplier with fixed reduction polynomial* $f(z) = z^5 + z^2 + 1$.

(iii) Variable field size The MSB multiplier in Figure 5.4 can be extended to multiply elements in the fields $\mathbb{F}_{2^m}$ for $m \in \{m_1, m_2, \ldots, m_t\}$, where $m_1 < m_2 < \cdots < m_t$. Each register has length m_t. Figure 5.7 illustrates an MSB multiplier that can implement multiplication in any field $\mathbb{F}_{2^m}$ for $m \in \{1, 2, \ldots, 10\}$, and for any reduction polynomial. Note that only the contents of registers b and c change at each clock cycle. The controller loads the bits of a, b and r from high-order to low-order and sets the unused bits to 0. Although the unused cells are clocked, they consume little power since their contents do not change.

The circuit can be simplified if each field has a fixed reduction polynomial, preferably a trinomial or a pentanomial. Figure 5.8 illustrates a variable field size MSB multiplier for $\mathbb{F}_{2^5}$, $\mathbb{F}_{2^7}$, and $\mathbb{F}_{2^{10}}$ with the fixed reduction polynomials $z^5 + z^2 + 1$,

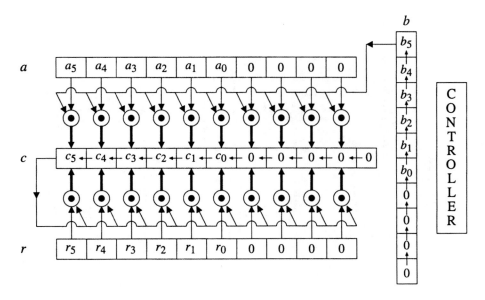

Figure 5.7. MSB multiplier for fields $\mathbb{F}_{2^m}$ with $1 \leq m \leq 10$. A multiplier for $\mathbb{F}_{2^6}$ is shown.

$z^7 + z + 1$, and $z^{10} + z^3 + 1$, respectively. A multiplexor is used to select the desired field. Loading registers and controlling the multiplexor is the function of the controller.

(iv) Digit-serial multiplier for fixed field size with fixed reduction polynomial We consider multiplication of two elements a and b in $\mathbb{F}_{2^m}$ where the multiplier b is expressed as a polynomial having $l = \lceil m/k \rceil$ digits

$$b = \sum_{i=0}^{l-1} B_i z^{ki},$$

where each digit B_i is a binary polynomial of degree at most $k - 1$. One way to express the product $a \cdot b$ is the following:

$$a \cdot b = a \left(\sum_{i=0}^{l-1} B_i z^{ki} \right) \bmod f(z)$$

$$= \left(\sum_{i=0}^{l-1} B_i (az^{ki} \bmod f(z)) \right) \bmod f(z)$$

where $f(z)$ is the reduction polynomial for $\mathbb{F}_{2^m}$. Algorithm 5.5 is a digit-serial multiplier derived from this observation.

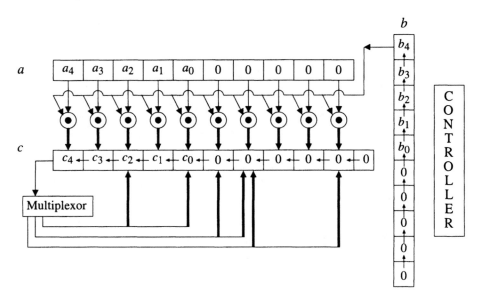

Figure 5.8. MSB multiplier for fields $\mathbb{F}_{2^5}$, $\mathbb{F}_{2^7}$, and $\mathbb{F}_{2^{10}}$ with reduction polynomials $z^5 + z^2 + 1$, $z^7 + z + 1$, and $z^{10} + z^3 + 1$. The multiplier for $\mathbb{F}_{2^5}$ is shown.

Algorithm 5.5 Digit-serial multiplier for $\mathbb{F}_{2^m}$

INPUT: $a = \sum_{i=0}^{m-1} a_i z^i \in \mathbb{F}_{2^m}$, $b = \sum_{i=0}^{l-1} B_i z^{ki} \in \mathbb{F}_{2^m}$, reduction polynomial $f(z)$.
OUTPUT: $c = a \cdot b$.
  1. Set $c \leftarrow 0$.
  2. For i from 0 to $l-1$ do
       2.1 $c \leftarrow c + B_i a$.
       2.2 $a \leftarrow a \cdot z^k \bmod f(z)$.
  3. Return($c \bmod f(z)$).

A hardware circuit for executing Algorithm 5.5 consists of a shift register to hold the multiplicand a, another shift register to hold the multiplier b, and an accumulating register (not a shift register) to hold c. The registers holding a and b are each m bits in length, whereas c is $(m + k - 1)$ bits long. At the ith iteration, the content of a is $az^{ki} \bmod f(z)$. The product $B_i \cdot (az^{ki} \bmod f(z))$ is called a *digit multiplication*. The result of this digit multiplication is at most $m + k - 1$ bits in length and is XORed into the accumulator c. If the circuit can compute $az^{ki} \bmod f(z)$ and $B_i \cdot (az^{ki} \bmod f(z))$ in a single clock, then the entire multiplication can be completed in l clock cycles. While the complexity of the circuit increases with k, a k-fold speedup for multiplication can be achieved.

Figure 5.9 shows the a register for a 2-digit multiplier for $\mathbb{F}_{2^5}$ where the field is defined by the reduction polynomial $f(z) = z^5 + z^2 + 1$. In this example, we have

$k = 2$ and $l = 3$. Figure 5.10 shows the circuit for digit multiplication excluding the interconnect of Figure 5.9 and the interconnect on the c register for the final reduction modulo $f(z)$. The final reduction interconnect will require multiplexors.

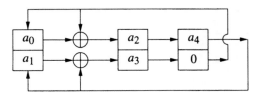

Figure 5.9. *Circuit to compute* az^{ki} *mod* $f(z)$, *where* $f(z) = z^5 + z^2 + 1$ *and* $k = 2$.

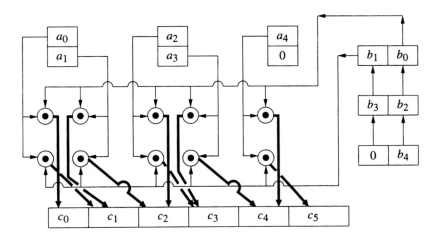

Figure 5.10. *A 2-digit multiplier for* $\mathbb{F}_{2^5}$ *defined by* $f(z) = z^5 + z^2 + 1$.

Squaring

Squaring can of course be performed using any of the multipliers described above. If the reduction polynomial $f(z)$ is fixed and is a trinomial or a pentanomial, then it is possible to design a circuit that will perform a squaring operation in a single clock cycle (vs. m clock cycles for the bit-serial multipliers). Moreover, the squaring circuit will add very little complexity to the multiplication circuit. A squaring circuit that takes only one clock cycle is important when inversion is done by multiplication (see below).

For example, consider the field $\mathbb{F}_{2^7}$ with reduction polynomial $f(z) = z^7 + z + 1$. If $a = a_6 z^6 + a_5 z^5 + a_4 z^4 + a_3 z^3 + a_2 z^2 + a_1 z + a_0$, then

$$c = a^2$$
$$= a_6 z^{12} + a_5 z^{10} + a_4 z^8 + a_3 z^6 + a_2 z^4 + a_1 z^2 + a_0$$
$$= (a_6 + a_3)z^6 + a_6 z^5 + (a_5 + a_2)z^4 + a_5 z^3 + (a_4 + a_1)z^2 + a_4 z + a_0.$$

A squaring circuit is illustrated in Figure 5.11.

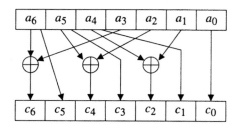

Figure 5.11. *Squaring circuit for* $\mathbb{F}_{2^7}$ *with fixed reduction polynomial* $f(z) = z^7 + z + 1$.

Inversion

The most difficult finite field operation to implement in hardware is inversion. There are two basic types of inversion algorithms: those based on the extended Euclidean algorithm and its variants (cf. §2.3.6), and those that use field multiplication. Inversion by multiplication does not add significantly to the complexity of a hardware design, but can severely impact performance if it is needed frequently. This is the reason why most hardware (and for that matter software) designers prefer projective coordinates over affine. Additional functionality must be incorporated into the controller but extensive modifications to the core circuit are not required. If affine coordinates are preferred, then inversion will undoubtedly be the bottleneck in performance thereby necessitating an inversion circuit based on the extended Euclidean algorithm. Such a circuit will add more complexity to both the core circuit and the controller. It seems that the added complexity does not justify implementing inversion by the extended Euclidean algorithm, and therefore we restrict our attention to inversion methods that use multiplication.

Let a be a nonzero element in $\mathbb{F}_{2^m}$. Inversion by multiplication uses the fact that

$$a^{-1} = a^{2^m - 2}. \tag{5.2}$$

Since $2^m - 2 = \sum_{i=1}^{m-1} 2^i$, we have

$$a^{-1} = a^{\sum_{i=1}^{m-1} 2^i} = \prod_{i=1}^{m-1} a^{2^i}. \tag{5.3}$$

Thus, a^{-1} can be computed by $m-1$ squarings and $m-2$ multiplications. We next show how the number of multiplications can be reduced. First observe that

$$a^{-1} = a^{2^m-2} = (a^{2^{m-1}-1})^2.$$

Hence a^{-1} can be computed in one squaring once $a^{2^{m-1}-1}$ has been evaluated. Now if m is odd then

$$2^{m-1} - 1 = (2^{(m-1)/2} - 1)(2^{(m-1)/2} + 1). \tag{5.4}$$

If we let

$$b = a^{2^{(m-1)/2}-1},$$

then by (5.4) we have

$$a^{2^{m-1}-1} = b \cdot b^{2^{(m-1)/2}}.$$

Hence $a^{2^{m-1}-1}$ can be computed with one multiplication and $(m-1)/2$ squarings once b has been evaluated. Similarly, if m is even then

$$2^{m-1} - 1 = 2(2^{m-2} - 1) + 1 = 2(2^{(m-2)/2} - 1)(2^{(m-2)/2} + 1) + 1. \tag{5.5}$$

If we let

$$c = a^{2^{(m-2)/2}-1},$$

then by (5.5) we have

$$a^{2^{m-1}-1} = a \cdot \left(c \cdot c^{2^{(m-2)/2}}\right)^2.$$

Hence $a^{2^{m-1}-1}$ can be computed with two multiplications and $m/2$ squarings once c has been evaluated. This procedure can be repeated recursively to eventually compute a^{-1}. The total number of multiplications in this procedure can be shown to be

$$\lfloor \log_2(m-1) \rfloor + w(m-1) - 1, \tag{5.6}$$

where $w(m-1)$ denotes the number of 1s in the binary representation of $m-1$, while the total number of squarings is $m-1$. This inversion procedure is shown in Algorithm 5.6 when m is odd.

Algorithm 5.6 Inversion in $\mathbb{F}_{2^m}$ (m odd)

INPUT: Nonzero element $a \in \mathbb{F}_{2^m}$.
OUTPUT: a^{-1}.
   1. Set $A \leftarrow a^2$, $B \leftarrow 1$, $x \leftarrow (m-1)/2$.
   2. While $x \neq 0$ do
      2.1 $A \leftarrow A \cdot A^{2^x}$.
      2.2 If x is even then $x \leftarrow x/2$;
           Else $B \leftarrow B \cdot A$, $A \leftarrow A^2$, $x \leftarrow (x-1)/2$.
   3. Return(B).

Table 5.9 shows the number of squarings and multiplications needed to compute inverses in the NIST binary fields $\mathbb{F}_{2^{163}}$, $\mathbb{F}_{2^{233}}$, $\mathbb{F}_{2^{283}}$, $\mathbb{F}_{2^{409}}$ and $\mathbb{F}_{2^{571}}$ using Algorithm 5.6. The last squaring of A in step 2.2 is not required, and therefore is not included in the operation counts.

m	$\lfloor \log_2(m-1) \rfloor$	$w(m-1)$	multiplications	squarings
163	7	3	9	162
233	7	4	10	232
283	8	4	11	282
409	8	4	11	408
571	9	5	13	570

Table 5.9. Operation counts for inversion in the binary fields $\mathbb{F}_{2^{163}}$, $\mathbb{F}_{2^{233}}$, $\mathbb{F}_{2^{283}}$, $\mathbb{F}_{2^{409}}$ and $\mathbb{F}_{2^{571}}$ using Algorithm 5.6.

5.3 Secure implementation

When assessing the security of a cryptographic protocol, one usually assumes that the adversary has a complete description of the protocol, is in possession of all public keys, and is only lacking knowledge of the secret keys. In addition, the adversary may have intercepted some data exchanged between the legitimate participants, and may even have some control over the nature of this data (e.g., by selecting the messages in a chosen-message attack on a signature scheme, or by selecting the ciphertext in a chosen-ciphertext attack on a public-key encryption scheme). The adversary then attempts to compromise the protocol goals by either solving an underlying problem assumed to be intractable, or by exploiting some design flaw in the protocol.

The attacks considered in this traditional security model exploit the mathematical specification of the protocol. In recent years, researchers have become increasingly aware of the possibility of attacks that exploit specific properties of the implementation and operating environment. Such *side-channel attacks* utilize information leaked during the protocol's execution and are not considered in traditional security models. For example, the adversary may be able to monitor the power consumed or the electromagnetic radiation emitted by a smart card while it performs private-key operations such as decryption and signature generation. The adversary may also be able to measure the time it takes to perform a cryptographic operation, or analyze how a cryptographic device behaves when certain errors are encountered. Side-channel information may be easy to gather in practice, and therefore it is essential that the threat of side-channel attacks be quantified when assessing the overall security of a system.

It should be emphasized that a particular side-channel attack may not be a realistic threat in some environments. For example, attacks that measure power consumption of a cryptographic device can be considered very plausible if the device is a smart card that draws power from an external, untrusted source. On the other hand, if the device is a workstation located in a secure office, then power consumption attacks are not a significant threat.

The objective of this section is to provide an introduction to side-channel attacks and their countermeasures. We consider power analysis attacks, electromagnetic analysis attacks, error message analysis, fault analysis, and timing attacks in §5.3.1, §5.3.2, §5.3.3, §5.3.4, and §5.3.5, respectively. The countermeasures that have been proposed are algorithmic, software-based, hardware-based, or combinations thereof. None of these countermeasures are guaranteed to defeat all side-channel attacks. Furthermore, they may slow cryptographic computations and have expensive memory or hardware requirements. The efficient and secure implementation of cryptographic protocols on devices such as smart cards is an ongoing and challenging research problem that demands the attention of both cryptographers and engineers.

5.3.1 Power analysis attacks

CMOS (Complementary Metal-Oxide Semiconductor) logic is the dominant semiconductor technology for microprocessors, memories, and application specific integrated circuits (ASICs). The basic building unit in CMOS logic is the inverter, or NOT gate, depicted in Figure 5.12. It consists of two transistors, one P-type and one N-type, that

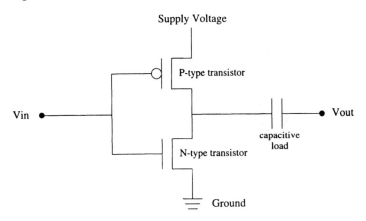

Figure 5.12. CMOS logic inverter.

serve as voltage-controlled switches. A high voltage signal is interpreted as a logical '1', while a low voltage signal is interpreted as a logical '0'. If the input voltage Vin is low, then the P-type transistor is conducting (i.e., the switch is closed) while the N-type transistor is non-conducting; in this case, there is a path from the supply voltage to the output and therefore Vout is high. Conversely, if Vin is high, then the P-type transistor is non-conducting while the N-type transistor is conducting; in this case, there is a path from the output to the ground and therefore Vout is low. When the inverter switches state, there is a short period of time during which both transistors conduct current. This causes a short circuit from the power supply to the ground. There is also current flow when internal capacitive loads attached to the inverter's output are charged or discharged.

During a clock cycle, current flows through only a small proportion of the gates in a CMOS device—those gates that are active during the execution of a particular instruction. Thus, the power consumed by the device can be expected to change continuously as the device executes a complicated series of instructions.

If the power to the device is supplied at a constant voltage, then the power consumed by the device is proportional to the flow of current. The current flow, and thus also the power consumption, can be measured by placing a resistor in series with the power supply and using an oscilloscope to measure the voltage difference across the resistor. One can then plot a *power trace*, which shows the power consumed by the device during each clock cycle.

The hypothesis behind power analysis attacks is that the power traces are correlated to the instructions the device is executing as well as the values of the operands it is manipulating. Therefore, examination of the power traces can reveal information about the instructions being executed and contents of data registers. In the case that the device is executing a secret-key cryptographic operation, it may then be possible to deduce the secret key.

Simple power analysis

In *simple power analysis* (SPA) attacks, information about secret keying material is deduced directly by examining the power trace from a single secret key operation. Implementations of elliptic curve point multiplication algorithms are particularly vulnerable because the usual formulas for adding and doubling points are quite different and therefore may have power traces which can readily be distinguished. Figure 5.13 shows the power trace for a sequence of addition (S) and double (D) operations on an elliptic curve over a prime field. Points were represented using Jacobian coordinates (see §3.2.1) whereby an addition operation takes significantly longer than a double operation.

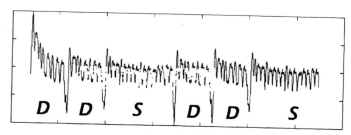

Figure 5.13. *Power trace for a sequence of addition (S) and double (D) operations on an elliptic curve over a prime field. Points were represented using Jacobian coordinates. The traces were obtained from an SC140 DSP processor core.*

Consider, for example, a device that performs a point multiplication kP during ECDSA signature generation (Algorithm 4.29). Here, P is a publicly-known elliptic curve point and k is a secret integer. Recall that knowledge of a single per-message secret k and the corresponding message and signature allows one to easily recover the long-term private key (cf. Note 4.34). Suppose first that one of the binary methods for point multiplication (Algorithms 3.26 and 3.27) is used. If examination of a power trace of a point multiplication reveals the sequence of double and addition operations, then one immediately learns the individual bits of k. Suppose now that a more sophisticated point multiplication method is employed; for concreteness consider the binary NAF method (Algorithm 3.31). If the power trace reveals the sequence of double and addition operations, then an adversary learns the digits of NAF(k) that are 0, which yields substantial information about k.

Knowledge of how the algorithm is used and implementated facilitate SPA attacks. Any implementation where the execution path is determined by the key bits has a potential vulnerability.

Countermeasures Numerous techniques for resisting SPA attacks have been proposed. These countermeasures involve modifications to the algorithms, software implementations, hardware implementations, or combinations thereof. The effectiveness of the countermeasures is heavily dependent on the characteristics of the hardware platform, the operating environment, and the capabilities of the adversary, and must be evaluated on a case-by-case basis. As an example, Figure 5.14 shows for the power trace for a sequence of addition (S) and double (D) operations on an elliptic curve over a prime field. Dummy operations were inserted in the algorithms for addition and doubling in such a way that the sequence of elementary operations involved in a doubling operation is repeated exactly twice in an addition operation. Compared to Figure 5.13, it seems impossible to distinguish the addition and double operations by casual inspection of the power trace in Figure 5.14.

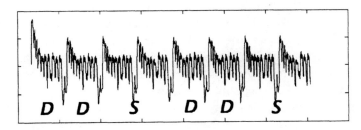

Figure 5.14. Power trace for a sequence of addition (S) and double (D) operations on an elliptic curve over a prime field. Points were represented using Jacobian coordinates. SPA resistance was achieved by insertion of dummy operations in the addition and double algorithms (compare with Figure 5.13). The traces were obtained from an SC140 DSP processor core.

None of the countermeasures that have been proposed are guaranteed to provide adequate protection. It is also important to note that resistance to SPA attacks does not guarantee resistance to other side-channel attacks such as differential power analysis and electromagnetic analysis attacks. It is therefore impossible at present to provide general recommendations for the best countermeasures to SPA attacks. Instead we just give one example and list other methods in the Notes section starting on page 254.

Algorithm 5.7 is a modification of the left-to-right binary point multiplication method to provide enhanced resistance to SPA attacks. Dummy operations are included in the main loop so that the same basic elliptic curve operations (one double and one addition) are performed in each iteration. Thus the sequence of double and additions deduced from the power trace does not reveal any information about the bits of k. As with most algorithmic countermeasures, the increased security comes at the expense of slower performance.

Algorithm 5.7 SPA-resistant left-to-right binary point multiplication

---

INPUT: $k = (k_{t-1}, \ldots, k_1, k_0)_2$, $P \in E(\mathbb{F}_q)$.
OUTPUT: kP.

    1. $Q_0 \leftarrow \infty$.
    2. For i from $t-1$ downto 0 do
        2.1 $Q_0 \leftarrow 2Q_0$.
        2.2 $Q_1 \leftarrow Q_0 + P$.
        2.3 $Q_0 \leftarrow Q_{k_i}$.
    3. Return(Q_0).

Differential power analysis

Differential power analysis (DPA) attacks exploit variations in power consumption that are correlated to the data values being manipulated. These variations are typically much smaller than those associated with different instruction sequences, and may be obfuscated by noise and measurement errors. Statistical methods are used on a collection of power traces in order reduce the noice and strengthen the differential signals.

To launch a DPA attack, an adversary first selects an internal variable V that is encountered during the execution of the cryptographic operation and has the property that knowledge of the input message m and a portion k' of the unknown secret key determines the value of V. The determining function $V = f(k', m)$ is called the *selection function*. Let us assume for simplicity that V is a single bit. The adversary collects a number of power traces (e.g., a few thousand) from the device that performs the cryptographic operation. She then makes a guess for k', and partitions the power traces into two groups according to the predicted value of the bit V. The power traces in each group are averaged, and the difference of the averages, called the *differential trace*, is plotted. The idea is that the value of V will have some (possibly very small) influence on the power trace. Thus, if the guess for k' is incorrect, then the partition of power traces was essentially done randomly, and so one would expect the differential trace to be flat. On the other hand, if the guess for k' is correct then the two averaged power traces will have some noticeable differences; one would expect the plot of the differential trace to be flat with spikes in regions influenced by V. This process is repeated (using the same collection of power traces) until k' is determined.

These ideas are illustrated in the following DPA attack on the SPA-resistant point multiplication method of Algorithm 5.7. The attack demonstrates that SPA countermeasures do not necessarily resist DPA attacks.

DPA attacks are generally not applicable to point multiplication in the signature generation procedure for elliptic curve signature schemes such as ECDSA (Algorithm 4.29) since the secret key k is different for each signature while the base point P is fixed. However, the attacks can be mounted on point multiplication in elliptic curve encryption and key agreement schemes. For example, for the point multiplication in the ECIES decryption procedure (Algorithm 4.43), the multiplier is $k = hd$ where d is the long-term private key and h is the cofactor, and the base point is $P = R$ where R is the point included in the ciphertext.

Suppose now that an adversary has collected the power traces as a cryptographic device computed kP_1, $kP_2, \ldots, kP_r$ using Algorithm 5.7. The adversary knows $P_1, P_2, \ldots, P_r$ and wishes to determine k. If $Q_0 = \infty$ then the doubling operation in step 2.1 is trivial and therefore can likely be distinguished from a non-trivial doubling operation by examination of a single power trace. Thus, the attacker can easily determine the leftmost bit of k that is 1. Let us suppose that $k_{t-1} = 1$. The following assignments are made in the first iteration of step 2 (with $i = t - 1$): $Q_0 \leftarrow \infty$, $Q_1 \leftarrow P$, $Q_0 \leftarrow P$. In the second iteration of step 2 (with $i = t - 2$) the assignments are $Q_0 \leftarrow 2P$, $Q_1 \leftarrow 3P$, and either $Q_0 \leftarrow 2P$ (if $k_{t-2} = 0$) or $Q_0 \leftarrow 3P$ (if $k_{t-2} = 1$). It follows that the point $4P$ is computed in a subsequent iteration if and only if $k_{t-2} = 0$. A position in the binary representation of a point is selected, and the power traces are divided into two groups depending on whether the selected bit of $4P_i$ is 0 or 1. In the notation of the generic description of DPA attacks, the key portion is $k' = k_{t-2}$, $m = P_i$, and the selection function f computes the selected bit of $4P_i$. If the differential trace has some noticeable spikes, then the adversary concludes that $k_{t-2} = 0$; otherwise $k_{t-2} = 1$. Once k_{t-2} has been determined, the adversary can similarly infer k_{t-3} and so on.

Countermeasures As is the case with SPA attacks, numerous techniques for resisting DPA attacks have been proposed. Again, none of them are guaranteed to be sufficient and their effectiveness must be evaluated on a case-by-case basis. These countermeasures are surveyed in the Notes section starting on page 254. Here we only present one countermeasure that provides resistance to the particular DPA attack described above for point multiplication.

Suppose that the field $\mathbb{F}_q$ had characteristic > 3, and suppose that mixed Jacobian-affine coordinates (see §3.2.2) are used in Algorithm 5.7. Thus, the point P is stored in affine coordinates, while the points Q_0 and Q_1 are stored in Jacobian coordinates.

The first assignment of Q_1 is $Q_1 \leftarrow P$; if $P = (x, y)$ in affine coordinates, then $Q_1 = (x : y : 1)$ in Jacobian coordinates. After this first assignment, the coordinates of Q_1 are randomized to $(\lambda^2 x, \lambda^3 y, \lambda)$, where λ is a randomly selected nonzero element in $\mathbb{F}_q$, and the algorithm proceeds as before. The DPA attack described above is thwarted because the adversary is unable to predict any specific bit of $4P_i$ (or other multiples of P_i) in randomized Jacobian coordinates.

5.3.2 *Electromagnetic analysis attacks*

The flow of current through a CMOS device also induces electromagnetic (EM) emanations. The EM signals can be collected by placing a sensor close to the device. As with power analysis attacks, one can now analyze the EM signals in the hope that they reveal information about the instructions being executed and contents of data registers. Simple ElectroMagnetic Analysis (SEMA) attacks and Differential ElectroMagnetic Analysis (DEMA) attacks, analogues of SPA and DPA attacks, can be launched. As with power analysis attacks, these electromagnetic analysis (EMA) attacks are non-intrusive and can be performed with relatively inexpensive equipment.

Since EM emanations may depend on the physical characteristics of the active gates, a single EM sensor captures multiple EM signals of different types. These signals can be separated and analyzed individually. This is unlike the case of power analysis attacks where the power consumption measured is the single aggregation of power consumed by all active units. Consequently, EMA attacks can potentially reveal more information than power analysis attacks, and therefore constitute a more significant threat.

The most comprehensive study on EMA attacks was undertaken in 2002 by IBM researchers Agrawal, Archambeault, Rao and Rohatgi, who conducted experiments on several smart cards and a server containing an SSL accelerator. Their experiments provide convincing evidence that the output of a single wideband EM sensor consists of multiple EM signals, each of which can encode somewhat different information about the device's state. Moreover, they succeeded in using EMA attacks to compromise the security of some commercially available cryptographic devices that had built-in countermeasures for resisting power analysis attacks, thus demonstrating that EMA attacks can indeed be more powerful than power analysis attacks.

As with power analysis, EMA countermeasures could be hardware based (e.g., metal layers to contain the EM emanations or circuit redesign to reduce the EM emanations) or software based (e.g., use of randomization). The study of EMA attacks is relatively new, and it remains to be seen which countermeasures prove to be the most effective.

5.3.3 *Error message analysis*

Another side channel that may be available to an adversary is the list of error messages generated by the victim's cryptographic device. Consider, for example, the decryption process of a public-key encryption scheme such as ECIES (see §4.5.1). A ciphertext might be rejected as invalid because some data item encountered during decryption is not of requisite form. In the case of ECIES decryption (Algorithm 4.43), a ciphertext (R, C, t) will be rejected if embedded public key validation of R fails, or if $Z = hdR = \infty$, or if the authentication tag t is invalid. There are several ways in which the adversary may learn the reason for rejection. For example, the error message may be released by the protocol that used the encryption scheme, the adversary may be able to access the error log file, or the adversary may be able to accurately time the decryption process thereby learning the precise point of failure. An adversary who learns the reason for rejection may be able to use this information to its advantage.

To illustrate this kind of side-channel attack, we consider Manger's attack on the RSA-OAEP encryption scheme. Manger's attack is very effective, despite the fact that RSA-OAEP has been proven secure (in the random oracle model). This supports the contention that a cryptographic scheme that is secure in a traditional security model is not necessarily secure when deployed in a real-world setting.

RSA-OAEP encryption scheme

RSA-OAEP is intended for the secure transport of short messages such as symmetric session keys. It first formats the plaintext message using Optimal Asymmetric Encryption Padding (OAEP), and then encrypts the formatted message using the basic RSA function. RSA-OAEP has been proven secure (in the sense of Definition 4.41) under the assumption that the problem of finding eth roots modulo n is intractable, and that the hash functions employed are random functions. The following notation is used in the descriptions of the encryption and decryption procedures.

1. A's RSA public key is (n, e), and d is A's corresponding private key. The integer n is k bytes in length. For example, if n is a 1024-bit modulus, then $k = 128$.

2. H is a hash function with l-byte outputs. For example, H may be SHA-1 in which case $l = 20$.

3. P consists of some encoding parameters.

4. *padding* consists of a string of 00 bytes (possibly empty) followed by a 01 byte.

5. G is a *mask generating function*. It takes as input a byte string s and an output length t, and generates a (pseudorandom) byte string of length t bytes. In practice, $G(s, t)$ may be defined by concatenating successive hash values $H(s \| i)$, for $0 \le i \le \lceil t/l \rceil - 1$, and deleting any rightmost bytes if necessary.

The concatenation $\overline{m}$ of *maskedS* and *maskedPM* is a byte string of length $k - 1$. This ensures that the integer representation m of $\overline{m}$ is less than the modulus n which is k bytes in length, and hence m can be recovered from c.

Algorithm 5.8 RSA-OAEP encryption

INPUT: RSA public key (n, e), message M of length at most $k - 2 - 2l$ bytes.
OUTPUT: Ciphertext c.

1. Select a random seed S of length l bytes.
2. Apply the OAEP encoding operation, depicted in Figure 5.15, with inputs S, P and M to obtain an integer m:
    2.1 Form the padded message PM of length $k - l - 1$ bytes by concatenating $H(P)$, a padding string of the appropriate length, and M.
    2.2 Compute $maskedPM = PM \oplus G(S, k - l - 1)$.
    2.3 Compute $maskedS = S \oplus G(maskedPM, l)$.
    2.4 Concatenate the strings $maskedS$ and $maskedPM$ and convert the result $\overline{m}$ to an integer m.
3. Compute $c = m^e \bmod n$.
4. Return(c).

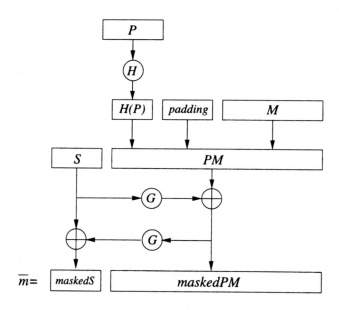

Figure 5.15. OAEP encoding function.

Algorithm 5.9 RSA-OAEP decryption

INPUT: RSA public key (n, e), private key d, ciphertext c.

OUTPUT: Plaintext M or rejection of the ciphertext.

1. Check that $c \in [0, n - 1]$; if not then return("Reject the ciphertext").
2. Compute $m = c^d \bmod n$.
3. Convert m to a byte string $\overline{m}$ of length k. Let X denote the first byte of $\overline{m}$.
4. If $X \neq 00$ then return("Reject the ciphertext").
5. Apply the OAEP decoding operation, depicted in Figure 5.16 with inputs $P, \overline{m}$:
   5.1 Parse $\overline{m}$ to obtain X, a byte string $maskedS$ of length l, and a byte string $maskedPM$ of length $k - l - 1$.
   5.2 Compute $S = maskedS \oplus G(maskedPM, l)$.
   5.3 Compute $PM = maskedPM \oplus G(S, k - l - 1)$.
   5.4 Separate PM into a byte string Q consisting of the first l bytes of PM, a (possibly empty) byte string PS consisting of all consecutive zero bytes following Q, a byte T, and a byte string M.
   5.5 If $T \neq 01$ then return("Reject the ciphertext").
   5.6 If $Q \neq H(P)$ then return("Reject the ciphertext").
6. Return(M).

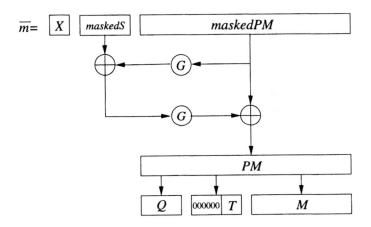

Figure 5.16. OAEP decoding function.

Manger's attack and countermeasures

A ciphertext $c' \in [0, n - 1]$ may be invalid for several reasons: either $X \neq 00$ in step 4 of Algorithm 5.9, or $T \neq 01$ in step 5.5, or $Q \neq H(P)$ in step 5.6. Manger's attack assumes that an adversary is able to ascertain whether $X \neq 00$ in the case that c' is found to be invalid by the decryptor. The attack does not require the full power of a chosen-ciphertext attack—the adversary does not need to learn the plaintexts corresponding to ciphertexts of her choosing.

Suppose now that the adversary wishes to decrypt a target ciphertext c that was encrypted using A's RSA key. Since c is valid, the adversary knows a priori that $m = c^d \bmod n$ lies in the interval $I = [0, 2^{8(k-1)} - 1]$. The adversary selects ciphertexts c' related to c in such a way that knowledge of whether the leftmost byte X' of $\overline{m'}$ satisfies $X' \neq 00$ allows her to decrease the length of interval I known to contain m by a factor (roughly) of 2. We will not present the technical details of how c' is chosen but only mention that this can be done very efficiently. After presenting about $8k$ such ciphertexts c' to A and learning where the corresponding X' satisfy $X' \neq 00$, the interval I will have only one integer in it, and adversary will thereby have recovered m and can easily compute the plaintext M. If n is a 1024-bit integer, then only about 1024 interactions are required with the victim and hence the attack should be viewed as being quite practical.

The attack can be prevented by ensuring that the decryption process returns identical error messages if any of the three checks fail. Moreover, to prevent the possibility of an adversary deducing the point of error by timing the decryption operation, the checks in steps 4 and 5.5 of Algorithm 5.9 should be deferred until $H(P)$ has been computed and is being compared with Q in step 5.6.

5.3.4   *Fault analysis attacks*

Boneh, DeMillo and Lipton observed that if an error occurs while a cryptographic device is performing a private-key operation, then the output of the cryptographic operation may be incorrect and thereby provide exploitable information to an adversary. Such errors may be introduced by non-malicious agents (e.g., hardware failures, software bugs, or external noise) or may be induced by a malicious adversary who has physical access to the device.

Fault analysis attacks generally do not pose a significant threat in practice. However, if the environment in which cryptographic operations are being performed is conducive to either non-malicious or induced errors, then suitable precautions should be taken. These include verifying the result of a computation before exposing it, and using error-control techniques to detect or correct data errors in internal memory.

We illustrate the basic ideas by presenting fault analysis attacks and countermeasures on the RSA signature scheme.

RSA signature generation

Consider the FDH (Full Domain Hash) variant of the RSA signature scheme with public key (n, e) and private key d. The signature of a message M is

$$s = m^d \bmod n, \tag{5.7}$$

where $m = H(M)$ and H is a hash function whose outputs are integers in the interval $[0, n-1]$. The signature s on M is verified by computing $m = H(M)$ and $m' = s^e \bmod n$, and then checking that $m = m'$.

In order to accelerate the signing operation (5.7), the signer computes

$$s_p = m^{d_p} \bmod p \quad \text{and} \quad s_q = m^{d_q} \bmod q, \tag{5.8}$$

where p and q are the prime factors of n, $d_p = d \bmod (p-1)$, and $d_q = d \bmod (q-1)$. Then the signature s can be computed as

$$s = a s_p + b s_q \bmod n,$$

where a and b are integers satisfying

$$a \equiv \begin{cases} 1 & (\bmod\ p) \\ 0 & (\bmod\ q) \end{cases} \quad \text{and} \quad b \equiv \begin{cases} 0 & (\bmod\ p) \\ 1 & (\bmod\ q). \end{cases}$$

The integers d_p, d_q, a and b can be precomputed by the signer. This signing procedure is faster because the two modular exponentiations in (5.8) have exponents and moduli that are half the bitlengths of the exponent and modulus in (5.7).

Suppose now that an error occurs during the computation of s_p and that no errors occur during the computation of s_q. In particular, suppose that $s_p \not\equiv m^{d_p} \pmod{p}$ and $s_q \equiv m^{d_q} \pmod{q}$. Thus

$$s \not\equiv m^{d_p} \pmod{p} \quad \text{and} \quad s \equiv m^{d_q} \pmod{q}$$

whence

$$s^e \not\equiv m \pmod{p} \quad \text{and} \quad s^e \equiv m \pmod{q}.$$

It follows that

$$\gcd(s^e - m, n) = q, \tag{5.9}$$

and so an adversary who obtains the message representative m and the (incorrect) signature s can easily factor n and thereafter compute the private key d.

One method for resisting this particular fault analysis attack on RSA signatures is to incorporate some randomness in the formation of the message representative m from the message M in such a way that an adversary cannot learn m from an erroneous signature (and thus cannot evaluate the gcd in (5.9)). This property holds in the PSS (Probabilistic Signature Scheme) variant of the RSA signature scheme. Note, however, that there may exist other kinds of fault analysis attacks that are effective on PSS.

The simplest and most effective countermeasure is to insist that the device verify the signature before transmission.

5.3.5   Timing attacks

The premise behind timing attacks is that the amount of time to execute an arithmetic operation can vary depending on the value of its operands. An adversary who is capable of accurately measuring the time a device takes to execute cryptographic operations (e.g., signature generation on a smart card) can analyze the measurements obtained to deduce information about the secret key. Timing attacks are generally not as serious a threat as power analysis attacks to devices such as smart cards because they typically require a very large number of measurements. However, recent work by Boneh and Brumley has shown that timing attacks can be a concern even when launched against a workstation running a protocol such as SSL with RSA over a local network (where power analysis attacks may not be applicable). Thus, it is prudent that security engineers consider resistance of their systems to timing attacks.

While experimental results on timing attacks on RSA and DES implementations have been reported in the literature, there have not been any published reports on timing attacks on implementations of elliptic curve systems. The attacks are expected to be especially difficult to mount on elliptic curve signature schemes such as ECDSA since a fresh per-message secret k is chosen each time the signature generation procedure is invoked.

5.4   Notes and further references

§5.1
The features of the Intel IA-32 family of processors are described in [210]. References for optimization techniques for the Pentium family of processors include the Intel manuals [208, 209] and Gerber [171]. SIMD capabilities of the AMD K6 processor are detailed in [4]. Footnote 1 on instruction latency and throughput is from Intel [209].

The SPARC specification is created by the Architecture Committee of SPARC International (http://www.sparc.org), and is documented in Weaver and Germond [476]; see also Paul [371]. The V9 design was preceded by the Texas Instruments and Sun Super-SPARC and the Ross Technology HyperSPARC, both superscalar. Examples 5.1 and 5.2 are based in part on GNU MP version 4.1.2.

The fast implementations for finite field and elliptic curve arithmetic in P-224 using floating-point operations described in §5.1.2 are due to Bernstein [42, 43]. Historical information and references are provided in [42]. Required numerical analyses of the proposed methods for P-224 were not complete as of 2002. Bernstein has announced that "Fast point multiplication on the NIST P-224 elliptic curve" is expected to be included in his forthcoming book on *High-speed Cryptography*.

Although SIMD is often associated with image and speech applications, Intel [209] also suggests the use of such capabilities in "encryption algorithms." Aoki and Lipmaa

[17] evaluated the effectiveness of MMX-techniques on the AES finalists, noting that MMX was particularly effective for Rijndael; see also Lipmaa's [298] implementation of the IDEA block cipher. In cross-platform code distributed for solving the Certicom ECC2K-108 Challenge [88] (an instance of the elliptic curve discrete logarithm problem for a Koblitz curve over a 109-bit binary field), Robert Harley [191] provided several versions of field multiplication routines. The MMX version was "about twice as fast" as the version using only general-purpose registers. The Karatsuba-style approach worked well for the intended target; however, the fastest versions of Algorithm 2.36 using only general-purpose registers were competitive in our tests.

Integer multiplication in Example 5.2 uses only scalar operations in the SSE2 instruction set. Moore [332] exploits vector capabilities of the 128-bit SSE2 registers to perform two products simultaneously from 32-bit values in each 64-bit half of the register. The method is roughly operand scanning, obtaining the matrix $(a_i b_j)$ of products of 29-bit values a_i and b_j in submatrices of size 4×4 (corresponding to values in a pair of 128-bit registers). A shuffle instruction (pshufd) is used extensively to load a register with four 32-bit components selected from a given register. Products are accumulated, but "carry processing" is handled in a second stage. The supplied code adapts easily to inputs of fairly general size; however, for the specific case discussed in Example 5.2, the method was not as fast as a (fixed size) product-scanning approach using scalar operations.

Of recent works that include implementation details and timings on common general-purpose processors, the pair of papers by Lim and Hwang [293, 294] are noted for the extensive benchmark data (on the Intel Pentium II and DEC Alpha), especially for OEFs. Smart [440] compares representative prime, binary, and optimal extension fields of approximately the same size, in the context of elliptic curve methods. Timings on a Sun UltraSPARC IIi and an Intel Pentium Pro are provided for field and elliptic curve operations. Coding is in C++ with limited in-line assembly; a Karatsuba-Ofman method with lookup tables for multiplication of polynomials of degree less than 8 is used for the binary field. Hankerson, López, and Menezes [189] and Brown, Hankerson, López, and Menezes [77] present an extensive study of software implementation for the NIST curves, with field and curve timings on an Intel Pentium II. De Win, Mister, Preneel, and Wiener [111] compare ECDSA to DSA and RSA signature algorithms. Limited assembly on an Intel Pentium Pro was used for the prime field; reduction is via Barrett. The binary field arithmetic follows Schroeppel, Orman, O'Malley, and Spatscheck [415]; in particular, the almost inverse algorithm (Algorithm 2.50) is timed for two reduction trinomials, one of which is favourable to the almost inverse method.

Implementors for constrained devices such as smartcards and handhelds face a different set of challenges and objectives. An introductory survey of smartcards with cryptographic capabilities circa 1995 is given by Naccache and M'Raïhi [339]. Durand [126] compares inversion algorithms for prime characteristic fields, and provides timings for RSA decryption and elliptic curve point multiplication on RISC processors from SGS-Thomson. Hasegawa, Nakajima, Matsui [194] implement ECDSA on a 16-bit CISC M16C processor from Mitsubishi. Low memory consumption was paramount, and elliptic curve point operations are written to use only two temporary variables. The ECDSA implementation including SHA-1 required 4000 bytes. A prime of the form $p = e2^a \pm 1$ is proposed for efficiency, where e fits within a word (16 bits in this case), and a is a multiple of the word size; in particular, $p = 65112 \cdot 2^{144} - 1$ of 160 bits is used for the implementation. Itoh, Takenaka, Torii, Temma, and Kurihara [216] implement RSA, DSA, and ECDSA on the Texas Instruments digital signal processor TMS320C620. Pipelining improvements are proposed for a Montgomery multiplication algorithm discussed in [260]. A consecutive doubling algorithm reduces the number of field multiplications (with a method related to the modified Jacobian coordinates in Cohen, Miyaji, and Ono [100]); field additions are also reduced under the assumption that division by 2 has cost comparable to field addition (see §3.2.2). Guajardo, Blümel, Krieger, and Paar [182] target low-power and low-cost devices based on the Texas Instruments MSP430x33x family of 16-bit RISC microcontrollers. Implementation is over $\mathbb{F}_p$ for prime $p = 2^{128} - 2^{97} - 1$, suitable for lower-security applications. Inversion is based on Fermat's theorem, and the special form of the modulus is used to reduce the amount of precomputation in a k-ary exponentiation method.

OEFs have been attractive for some constrained devices. Chung, Sim, and Lee [97] discuss performance and implementation considerations for a low-power Samsung CalmRISC 8-bit processor with a MAC2424 math coprocessor. The coprocessor operates in 24-bit or 16-bit mode; the 16-bit mode was selected due to performance restrictions. Timings are provided for field and curve operations over $\mathbb{F}_{p^{10}}$ with $p = 2^{16} - 165$ and reduction polynomial $f(z) = z^{10} - 2$. Woodbury, Bailey, and Paar [486] examine point multiplication on very low-cost Intel 8051 family processors. Only 256 bytes of RAM are available, along with slower external XRAM used for precomputation. Implementation is for a curve over the OEF $\mathbb{F}_{(2^8 - 17)^{17}}$ with reduction polynomial $f(z) = 2^{17} - 2$, suitable for lower-security applications.

Personal Digital Assistants such as the Palm and RIM offerings have substantial memory and processing capability compared with the constrained devices noted above, but are less powerful than common portable computers and have power and communication bandwidth constraints. Weimerskirch, Paar, and Chang Shantz [477] present implementation results for the Handspring Visor with 2 MB of memory and a 16 MHz Motorola Dragonball running the Palm OS. Timings are provided for the NIST recommended random and Koblitz curves over $\mathbb{F}_{2^{163}}$.

§5.2

The elliptic curve processor architecture depicted in Figure 5.3 is due to Orlando and Paar [361].

Beth and Gollmann [45] describe several circuits for $\mathbb{F}_{2^m}$ multipliers including the MSB and LSB versions, and ones that use normal and dual basis representations. The digit-serial multiplier (Algorithm 5.5) was proposed by Song and Parhi [449]. Algorithm 5.6 for inversion in $\mathbb{F}_{2^m}$ is due to Itoh and Tsujii [217] (see also Agnew, Beth, Mullin and Vanstone [5]). The algorithm is presented in the context of a normal basis representation for the elements of $\mathbb{F}_{2^m}$. Guajardo and Paar [183] adapted the algorithm for inversion in general extension fields (including optimal extension fields) that use a polynomial basis representation.

There are many papers that describe hardware implementations of elliptic curve operations. The majority of these papers consider elliptic curves over binary fields. Orlando and Paar [361] proposed a scalable processor architecture suitable for the FPGA implementation of elliptic curve operations over binary fields. Multiplication is performed with the digit-serial circuit proposed by Song and Parhi [449]. Timings are provided for the field $\mathbb{F}_{2^{167}}$. Okada, Torii, Itoh and Takenaka [353] describe an FPGA implementation for elliptic curves over $\mathbb{F}_{2^{163}}$. Bednara et al. [32] (see also Bednara et al. [33]) compared their FPGA implementations of elliptic curve operations over the field $\mathbb{F}_{2^{191}}$ with polynomial and normal basis representations. They concluded that a polynomial basis multiplier will require fewer logic gates to implement than a normal basis multiplier, and that Montgomery's method (Algorithm 3.40) is preferred for point multiplication.

The hardware design of Ernst, Jung, Madlener, Huss and Blümel [134] uses the Karatsuba-Ofman method for multiplying binary polynomials. Hardware designs intended to minimize power consumption were considered by Goodman and Chandrakasan [177], and by Schroeppel, Beaver, Gonzales, Miller and Draelos [414]. Gura et al. [186] designed hardware accelerators that permit any elliptic curve over any binary field $\mathbb{F}_{2^m}$ with $m \leq 255$. Architectures that exploit subfields of a binary field were studied by Paar and Soria-Rodriguez [365].

Hardware implementations of binary field arithmetic that use a normal basis representation are described by Agnew, Mullin, Onyszchuk and Vanstone [6] (for the field $\mathbb{F}_{2^{593}}$), Agnew, Mullin and Vanstone [7] (for the field $\mathbb{F}_{2^{155}}$), Gao, Shrivastava and Sobelman [162] (for arbitrary binary fields), and Leong and Leung [286] (for the fields $\mathbb{F}_{2^{113}}$, $\mathbb{F}_{2^{155}}$ and $\mathbb{F}_{2^{173}}$). The latter two papers include both the finite field operations and the elliptic curve operations.

Koren's book [266] is an excellent introduction to hardware architectures for performing the basic integer operations of addition, subtraction and multiplication. Orlando and Paar [362] detail a scalable hardware architecture for performing elliptic curve arithmetic over prime fields.

Savaş, Tenca and Koç [404] and Großschädl [181] introduced scalable multipliers for performing multiplication in both prime fields and binary fields. For both designs, the unified multipliers require only slightly more area than for a multiplier solely for prime fields. Multiplication in the Savaş, Tenca and Koç design is performed using Montgomery's technique (cf. §2.2.4), while Großschädl's design uses the more conventional approach of accumulating partial products. Unified designs for Montgomery inversion in both prime fields and binary fields were studied by Gutub, Tenca, Savaş and Koç [187]. An architecture with low power consumption for performing all operations in both binary fields and prime fields was presented by Wolkerstorfer [485].

Bertoni et al. [44] present hardware architectures for performing multiplication in $\mathbb{F}_{p^m}$ where p is odd, with an emphasis on the case $p = 3$; see also Page and Smart [366].

§5.3

Much of the research being conducted on side-channel attacks and their counter-measures is presented at the conference on "Cryptographic Hardware and Embedded Systems" that have been held annually since 1999. The proceedings of these conferences are published by Springer-Verlag [262, 263, 261, 238]. Side-channel attacks do not include exploitation of common programming and operational errors such as buffer overflows, predictable random number generators, race conditions, and poor password selection. For a discussion of the security implications of such errors, see the books by Anderson [11] and Viega and McGraw [473].

SPA and DPA attacks were introduced in 1998 by Kocher, Jaffe and Jun [265]. Coron [104] was the first to apply these attacks to elliptic curve cryptographic schemes, and proposed the SPA-resistant method for point multiplication (Algorithm 5.7), and the DPA-resistant method of randomizing projective coordinates. Oswald [364] showed how a multiplier k can be determined using the partial information gained about NAF(k) from a power trace of an execution of the binary NAF point multiplication method (Algorithm 3.31). Experimental results with power analysis attacks on smart cards were reported by Akkar, Bevan, Dischamp and Moyart [9] and Messerges, Dabbish and Sloan [323], while those on a DSP processor core are reported by Gebotys and Gebotys [168]. Figures 5.13 and 5.14 are taken from Gebotys and Gebotys [168].

Chari, Jutla, Rao and Rohatgi [91] presented some general SPA and DPA countermeasures, and a formal methodology for evaluating their effectiveness. Proposals for hardware-based defenses against power analysis attacks include using an internal power source, randomizing the order in which instructions are executed (May, Muller and Smart [308]), randomized register renaming (May, Muller and Smart [309]), and using two capacitors, one of which is charged by an external power supply and the other supplies power to the device (Shamir [422]).

One effective method for guarding against SPA attacks on point multiplication is to employ elliptic curve addition formulas that can also be used for doubling. This approach was studied by Liardet and Smart [291] for curves in Jacobi form, by Joye and Quisquater [231] for curves in Hessian form, and by Brier and Joye [74] for curves in general Weierstrass form. Izu and Takagi [221] devised an active attack (not using power analysis) on the Brier-Joye formula that can reveal a few bits of the private key in elliptic curve schemes that use point multiplication with a fixed multiplier. Another strategy for SPA resistance is to use point multiplication algorithms such as Coron's

(Algorithm 5.7) where the pattern of addition and double operations is independent of the multiplier. Other examples are Montgomery point multiplication (see page 102 and also Okeya and Sakurai [358]), and the methods presented by Möller [327, 328], Hitchcock and Montague [198], and Izu and Takagi [220]. The security and efficiency of (improved versions) of the Möller [327] and Izu-Takagi [220] methods were carefully analyzed by Izu, Möller and Takagi [219]. Another approach taken by Trichina and Bellezza [461] and Gebotys and Gebotys [168] is to devise formulas for the addition and double operations that have the same pattern of field operations (addition, subtraction, multiplication and squaring).

Hasan [193] studied power analysis attacks on point multiplication for Koblitz curves (see §3.4) and proposed some countermeasures which do not significantly degrade performance.

Joye and Tymen [232] proposed using a randomly chosen elliptic curve isomorphic to the given one, and a randomly chosen representation for the underlying fields, as countermeasures to DPA attacks. Goubin [180] showed that even if point multiplication is protected with an SPA-resistant method such as Algorithm 5.7 and a DPA-resistant method such as randomized projective coordinates, randomized elliptic curve, or randomized field representation, the point multiplication may still be vulnerable to a DPA attack in situations where an attacker can select the base point (as is the case, for example, with ECIES). Goubin's observations highlight the difficulty in securing point multiplication against power analysis attacks.

The potential of exploiting electromagnetic emanations has been known in military circles for a long time. For example, see the recently declassified TEMPEST document written by the National Security Agency [343] that investigates different compromising emanations including electromagnetic radiation, line conduction, and acoustic emissions. The unclassified literature on attack techniques and countermeasures is also extensive. For example, Kuhn and Anderson [272] discuss software-based techniques for launching and preventing attacks based on deducing the information on video screens from the electromagnetic radiations emitted. Loughry and Umphress [302] describe how optical radiation emitted from computer LED (light-emitting diodes) status indicators can be analyzed to infer the data being processed by a device. Chapter 15 of Anderson's book [11] provides an excellent introduction to emission security. Experimental results on electromagnetic analysis (EMA) attacks on cryptographic devices such as smart cards and comparisons to power analysis attacks were first presented by Quisquater and Samyde [386] and Gandolfi, Mourtel and Olivier [161]. The most comprehensive unclassified study on EMA attacks to date is the work of Agrawal, Archambeault, Rao and Rohatgi [8].

The first prominent example of side-channel attacks exploiting error messages was Bleichenbacher's 1998 attack [53] on the RSA encryption scheme as specified in the PKCS#1 v1.5 standard [394]. This version of RSA encryption, which specifies a method for formatting the plaintext message prior to application of the RSA function, is widely deployed in practice including in the SSL protocol for secure web communications. For 1024-bit RSA moduli, Bleichenbacher's attack enables an adversary to obtain the decryption of a target ciphertext c by submitting about one million carefully-chosen ciphertexts related to c to the victim and learning whether the ciphertexts were rejected or not. The attack necessitated a patch to numerous SSL implementations. The RSA-OAEP encryption scheme was proposed by Bellare and Rogaway [38] and proved secure in the random oracle model by Shoup [427] and Fujisaki, Okamoto, Pointcheval and Stern [153]. It has been included in many standards including the v2.2 update of PKCS#1 [395]. Manger [303] presented his attack on RSA-OAEP in 2001. Vaudenay [466] described error message analysis attacks on symmetric-key encryption when messages are first formatted by padding and then encrypted with a block cipher in CBC mode.

Fault analysis attacks were first considered in 1997 by Boneh, DeMillo and Lipton [56, 57], who described such attacks on the RSA signature scheme and the Fiat-Shamir and Schnorr identification protocols. Bao et al. [28] presented fault analysis attacks on the ElGamal, Schnorr and DSA signature schemes. The FDH and PSS variants of the RSA signature scheme are due to Bellare and Rogaway [39], who proved their security (in the sense of Definition 4.28) under the assumptions that finding eth roots modulo n is intractable and that the hash functions employed are random functions. Fault analysis attacks on elliptic curve public-key encryption schemes were presented by Biehl, Meyer and Müller [46]. Their attacks succeed if an error during the decryption process produces a point that is not on the valid elliptic curve. The attacks can be prevented by ensuring that points that are the result of a cryptographic calculation indeed lie on the correct elliptic curve. Biham and Shamir [48] presented fault analysis attacks on the DES symmetric-key encryption scheme. Anderson and Kuhn [12] discuss some realistic ways of inducing transient faults, which they call *glitches*. More recently, Skorobogatov and Anderson [437] demonstrated that inexpensive equipment can be used to induce faults in a smart card by illuminating specific transistors; they also propose countermeasures to these *optical fault induction attacks*.

Timing attacks were introduced in 1996 by Kocher [264], who described attacks on RSA modular exponentiation. Schindler [407] presented timing attacks on implementation of RSA exponentation that employ the Chinese Remainder Theorem. Experimental results for an RSA implementation on a smart card were reported by Dhem et al. [117]. Timing attacks on DES that recover the Hamming weight of the secret key were described by Hevia and Kiwi [197]. Brumley and Boneh [78] demonstrated that timing attacks can reveal RSA private keys from an OpenSSL-based web server over a local network. Canvel, Hiltgen, Vaudenay and Vuagnoux [86] devised timing attacks on the CBC-mode encryption schemes used in SSL and TLS; their attacks can decrypt commonly used ciphertext such as the encryption of a password.

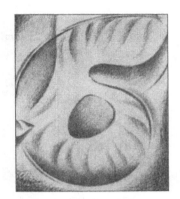

APPENDIX A

Sample Parameters

This appendix presents elliptic curve domain parameters $D = (q, \text{FR}, S, a, b, P, n, h)$ that are suitable for cryptographic use; see §4.2 for a review of the notation. In §A.1, an algorithm for testing irreducibility of a polynomial is presented. This algorithm can be used to generate a reduction polynomial for representing elements of the finite field $\mathbb{F}_{p^m}$. Also included in §A.1 are tables of irreducible binary polynomials that are recommended by several standards including ANSI X9.62 and ANSI X9.63 as reduction polynomials for representing the elements of binary fields $\mathbb{F}_{2^m}$. The 15 elliptic curves recommended by NIST in the FIPS 186-2 standard for U.S. federal government use are listed in §A.2.

A.1 Irreducible polynomials

A polynomial $f(z) = a_m z^m + \cdots + a_1 z + a_0 \in \mathbb{F}_p[z]$ of degree $m \geq 1$ is *irreducible* over $\mathbb{F}_p$ if $f(z)$ cannot be factored as a product of polynomials in $\mathbb{F}_p[z]$ each of degree less than m. Since $f(z)$ is irreducible if and only if $a_m^{-1} f(z)$ is irreducible, it suffices to only consider *monic* polynomials (i.e., polynomials with leading coefficient $a_m = 1$).

For any prime p and integer $m \geq 1$, there exists at least one monic irreducible polynomial of degree m in $\mathbb{F}_p[z]$. In fact, the exact number of such polynomials is

$$N_p(m) = \frac{1}{m} \sum_{d \mid m} \mu(d) p^{m/d},$$

where the summation index d ranges over all positive divisors of m, and the *Möbius function* μ is defined as follows:

$$\mu(d) = \begin{cases} 1, & \text{if } d = 1, \\ 0, & \text{if } d \text{ is divisible by the square of a prime,} \\ (-1)^l, & \text{if } d \text{ is the product of } l \text{ distinct primes.} \end{cases}$$

It has been shown that

$$\frac{1}{2m} \leq \frac{N_p(m)}{p^m} \approx \frac{1}{m}.$$

Thus, if polynomials in $\mathbb{F}_p[z]$ can be efficiently tested for irreducibility, then irreducible polynomials of degree m can be efficiently found by selecting random monic polynomials of degree m in $\mathbb{F}_p[z]$ until an irreducible one is found—the expected number of trials is approximately m.

Algorithm A.1 is an efficient test for deciding irreducibility. It is based on the fact that a polynomial $f(z)$ of degree m is irreducible over $\mathbb{F}_p$ if and only if $\gcd(f(z), z^{p^i} - z) = 1$ for each i, $1 \leq i \leq \lfloor \frac{m}{2} \rfloor$.

Algorithm A.1 Testing a polynomial for irreducibility

INPUT: A prime p and a polynomial $f(z) \in \mathbb{F}_p[z]$ of degree $m \geq 1$.
OUTPUT: Irreducibility of $f(z)$.
1. $u(z) \leftarrow z$.
2. For i from 1 to $\lfloor \frac{m}{2} \rfloor$ do:
   2.1 $u(z) \leftarrow u(z)^p \bmod f(z)$.
   2.2 $d(z) \leftarrow \gcd(f(z), u(z) - z)$.
   2.3 If $d(z) \neq 1$ then return("reducible").
3. Return("irreducible").

For each m, $2 \leq m \leq 600$, Tables A.1 and A.2 list an irreducible trinomial or pentanomial $f(z)$ of degree m over $\mathbb{F}_2$. The entries in the column labeled "T" are the degrees of the nonzero terms of the polynomial excluding the leading term z^m and the constant term 1. For example, $T = k$ represents the trinomial $z^m + z^k + 1$, and $T = (k_3, k_2, k_1)$ represents the pentanomial $z^m + z^{k_3} + z^{k_2} + z^{k_1} + 1$. The following criteria from the ANSI X9.62 and ANSI X9.63 standards were used to select the reduction polynomials:

(i) If there exists an irreducible trinomial of degree m over $\mathbb{F}_2$, then $f(z)$ is the irreducible trinomial $z^m + z^k + 1$ for the smallest possible k.

(ii) If there does not exist an irreducible trinomial of degree m over $\mathbb{F}_2$, then $f(z)$ is the irreducible pentanomial $z^m + z^{k_3} + z^{k_2} + z^{k_1} + 1$ for which (a) k_3 is the smallest possible; (b) for this particular value of k_3, k_2 is the smallest possible; and (c) for these particular values of k_3 and k_2, k_1 is the smallest possible.

m	T	m	T	m	T	m	T	m	T	m	T
1	−	51	6, 3, 1	101	7, 6, 1	151	3	201	14	251	7, 4, 2
2	1	52	3	102	29	152	6, 3, 2	202	55	252	15
3	1	53	6, 2, 1	103	9	153	1	203	8, 7, 1	253	46
4	1	54	9	104	4, 3, 1	154	15	204	27	254	7, 2, 1
5	2	55	7	105	4	155	62	205	9, 5, 2	255	52
6	1	56	7, 4, 2	106	15	156	9	206	10, 9, 5	256	10, 5, 2
7	1	57	4	107	9, 7, 4	157	6, 5, 2	207	43	257	12
8	4, 3, 1	58	19	108	17	158	8, 6, 5	208	9, 3, 1	258	71
9	1	59	7, 4, 2	109	5, 4, 2	159	31	209	6	259	10, 6, 2
10	3	60	1	110	33	160	5, 3, 2	210	7	260	15
11	2	61	5, 2, 1	111	10	161	18	211	11, 10, 8	261	7, 6, 4
12	3	62	29	112	5, 4, 3	162	27	212	105	262	9, 8, 4
13	4, 3, 1	63	1	113	9	163	7, 6, 3	213	6, 5, 2	263	93
14	5	64	4, 3, 1	114	5, 3, 2	164	10, 8, 7	214	73	264	9, 6, 2
15	1	65	18	115	8, 7, 5	165	9, 8, 3	215	23	265	42
16	5, 3, 1	66	3	116	4, 2, 1	166	37	216	7, 3, 1	266	47
17	3	67	5, 2, 1	117	5, 2, 1	167	6	217	45	267	8, 6, 3
18	3	68	9	118	33	168	15, 3, 2	218	11	268	25
19	5, 2, 1	69	6, 5, 2	119	8	169	34	219	8, 4, 1	269	7, 6, 1
20	3	70	5, 3, 1	120	4, 3, 1	170	11	220	7	270	53
21	2	71	6	121	18	171	6, 5, 2	221	8, 6, 2	271	58
22	1	72	10, 9, 3	122	6, 2, 1	172	1	222	5, 4, 2	272	9, 3, 2
23	5	73	25	123	2	173	8, 5, 2	223	33	273	23
24	4, 3, 1	74	35	124	19	174	13	224	9, 8, 3	274	67
25	3	75	6, 3, 1	125	7, 6, 5	175	6	225	32	275	11, 10, 9
26	4, 3, 1	76	21	126	21	176	11, 3, 2	226	10, 7, 3	276	63
27	5, 2, 1	77	6, 5, 2	127	1	177	8	227	10, 9, 4	277	12, 6, 3
28	1	78	6, 5, 3	128	7, 2, 1	178	31	228	113	278	5
29	2	79	9	129	5	179	4, 2, 1	229	10, 4, 1	279	5
30	1	80	9, 4, 2	130	3	180	3	230	8, 7, 6	280	9, 5, 2
31	3	81	4	131	8, 3, 2	181	7, 6, 1	231	26	281	93
32	7, 3, 2	82	8, 3, 1	132	17	182	81	232	9, 4, 2	282	35
33	10	83	7, 4, 2	133	9, 8, 2	183	56	233	74	283	12, 7, 5
34	7	84	5	134	57	184	9, 8, 7	234	31	284	53
35	2	85	8, 2, 1	135	11	185	24	235	9, 6, 1	285	10, 7, 5
36	9	86	21	136	5, 3, 2	186	11	236	5	286	69
37	6, 4, 1	87	13	137	21	187	7, 6, 5	237	7, 4, 1	287	71
38	6, 5, 1	88	7, 6, 2	138	8, 7, 1	188	6, 5, 2	238	73	288	11, 10, 1
39	4	89	38	139	8, 5, 3	189	6, 5, 2	239	36	289	21
40	5, 4, 3	90	27	140	15	190	8, 7, 6	240	8, 5, 3	290	5, 3, 2
41	3	91	8, 5, 1	141	10, 4, 1	191	9	241	70	291	12, 11, 5
42	7	92	21	142	21	192	7, 2, 1	242	95	292	37
43	6, 4, 3	93	2	143	5, 3, 2	193	15	243	8, 5, 1	293	11, 6, 1
44	5	94	21	144	7, 4, 2	194	87	244	111	294	33
45	4, 3, 1	95	11	145	52	195	8, 3, 2	245	6, 4, 1	295	48
46	1	96	10, 9, 6	146	71	196	3	246	11, 2, 1	296	7, 3, 2
47	5	97	6	147	14	197	9, 4, 2	247	82	297	5
48	5, 3, 2	98	11	148	27	198	9	248	15, 14, 10	298	11, 8, 4
49	9	99	6, 3, 1	149	10, 9, 7	199	34	249	35	299	11, 6, 4
50	4, 3, 2	100	15	150	53	200	5, 3, 2	250	103	300	5

Table A.1. Irreducible binary polynomials of degree m, $2 \leq m \leq 300$.

m	T	m	T	m	T	m	T	m	T	m	T
301	9, 5, 2	351	34	401	152	451	16, 10, 1	501	5, 4, 2	551	135
302	41	352	13, 11, 6	402	171	452	6, 5, 4	502	8, 5, 4	552	19, 16, 9
303	1	353	69	403	9, 8, 5	453	15, 6, 4	503	3	553	39
304	11, 2, 1	354	99	404	65	454	8, 6, 1	504	15, 14, 6	554	10, 8, 7
305	102	355	6, 5, 1	405	13, 8, 2	455	38	505	156	555	10, 9, 4
306	7, 3, 1	356	10, 9, 7	406	141	456	18, 9, 6	506	23	556	153
307	8, 4, 2	357	11, 10, 2	407	71	457	16	507	13, 6, 3	557	7, 6, 5
308	15	358	57	408	5, 3, 2	458	203	508	9	558	73
309	10, 6, 4	359	68	409	87	459	12, 5, 2	509	8, 7, 3	559	34
310	93	360	5, 3, 2	410	10, 4, 3	460	19	510	69	560	11, 9, 6
311	7, 5, 3	361	7, 4, 1	411	12, 10, 3	461	7, 6, 1	511	10	561	71
312	9, 7, 4	362	63	412	147	462	73	512	8, 5, 2	562	11, 4, 2
313	79	363	8, 5, 3	413	10, 7, 6	463	93	513	26	563	14, 7, 3
314	15	364	9	414	13	464	19, 18, 13	514	67	564	163
315	10, 9, 1	365	9, 6, 5	415	102	465	31	515	14, 7, 4	565	11, 6, 1
316	63	366	29	416	9, 5, 2	466	14, 11, 6	516	21	566	153
317	7, 4, 2	367	21	417	107	467	11, 6, 1	517	12, 10, 2	567	28
318	45	368	7, 3, 2	418	199	468	27	518	33	568	15, 7, 6
319	36	369	91	419	15, 5, 4	469	9, 5, 2	519	79	569	77
320	4, 3, 1	370	139	420	7	470	9	520	15, 11, 2	570	67
321	31	371	8, 3, 2	421	5, 4, 2	471	1	521	32	571	10, 5, 2
322	67	372	111	422	149	472	11, 3, 2	522	39	572	12, 8, 1
323	10, 3, 1	373	8, 7, 2	423	25	473	200	523	13, 6, 2	573	10, 6, 4
324	51	374	8, 6, 5	424	9, 7, 2	474	191	524	167	574	13
325	10, 5, 2	375	16	425	12	475	9, 8, 4	525	6, 4, 1	575	146
326	10, 3, 1	376	8, 7, 5	426	63	476	9	526	97	576	13, 4, 3
327	34	377	41	427	11, 6, 5	477	16, 15, 7	527	47	577	25
328	8, 3, 1	378	43	428	105	478	121	528	11, 6, 2	578	23, 22, 16
329	50	379	10, 8, 5	429	10, 8, 7	479	104	529	42	579	12, 9, 7
330	99	380	47	430	14, 6, 1	480	15, 9, 6	530	10, 7, 3	580	237
331	10, 6, 2	381	5, 2, 1	431	120	481	138	531	10, 5, 4	581	13, 7, 6
332	89	382	81	432	13, 4, 3	482	9, 6, 5	532	1	582	85
333	2	383	90	433	33	483	9, 6, 4	533	4, 3, 2	583	130
334	5, 2, 1	384	12, 3, 2	434	12, 11, 5	484	105	534	161	584	14, 13, 3
335	10, 7, 2	385	6	435	12, 9, 5	485	17, 16, 6	535	8, 6, 2	585	88
336	7, 4, 1	386	83	436	165	486	81	536	7, 5, 3	586	7, 5, 2
337	55	387	8, 7, 1	437	6, 2, 1	487	94	537	94	587	11, 6, 1
338	4, 3, 1	388	159	438	65	488	4, 3, 1	538	195	588	35
339	16, 10, 7	389	10, 9, 5	439	49	489	83	539	10, 5, 4	589	10, 4, 3
340	45	390	9	440	4, 3, 1	490	219	540	9	590	93
341	10, 8, 6	391	28	441	7	491	11, 6, 3	541	13, 10, 4	591	9, 6, 4
342	125	392	13, 10, 6	442	7, 5, 2	492	7	542	8, 6, 1	592	13, 6, 3
343	75	393	7	443	10, 6, 1	493	10, 5, 3	543	16	593	86
344	7, 2, 1	394	135	444	81	494	17	544	8, 3, 1	594	19
345	22	395	11, 6, 5	445	7, 6, 4	495	76	545	122	595	9, 2, 1
346	63	396	25	446	105	496	16, 5, 2	546	8, 2, 1	596	273
347	11, 10, 3	397	12, 7, 6	447	73	497	78	547	13, 7, 4	597	14, 12, 9
348	103	398	7, 6, 2	448	11, 6, 4	498	155	548	10, 5, 3	598	7, 6, 1
349	6, 5, 2	399	26	449	134	499	11, 6, 5	549	16, 4, 3	599	30
350	53	400	5, 3, 2	450	47	500	27	550	193	600	9, 5, 2

Table A.2. *Irreducible binary polynomials of degree* m, $301 \leq m \leq 600$.

A.2 Elliptic curves

In the FIPS 186-2 standard, NIST recommended 15 elliptic curves of varying security levels for U.S. federal government use. The curves are of three types:

(i) random elliptic curves over a prime field $\mathbb{F}_p$;

(ii) random elliptic curves over a binary field $\mathbb{F}_{2^m}$; and

(iii) Koblitz elliptic curves over a binary field $\mathbb{F}_{2^m}$.

Their parameters are listed in §A.2.1, §A.2.2 and §A.2.3, respectively.

In the tables that follow, integers and polynomials are sometimes represented as hexadecimal strings. For example, "0x1BB5" is the hexadecimal representation of the integer 7093. The coefficients of the binary polynomial $z^{13} + z^{11} + z^5 + z^2 + z + 1$ form a binary string "10100000100111" which has hexadecimal representation "0x2827".

A.2.1 Random elliptic curves over $\mathbb{F}_p$

Table A.3 lists domain parameters for the five NIST-recommended randomly chosen elliptic curves over prime fields $\mathbb{F}_p$. The primes p were specially chosen to allow for very fast reduction of integers modulo p (see §2.2.6). The selection $a = -3$ for the coefficient in the elliptic curve equation was made so that elliptic curve points represented in Jacobian projective coordinates could be added using one fewer field multiplication (see §3.2.2). The following parameters are given for each curve:

p	The order of the prime field $\mathbb{F}_p$.
S	The seed selected to randomly generate the coefficients of the elliptic curve using Algorithm 4.17.
r	The output of SHA-1 in Algorithm 4.17.
a, b	The coefficients of the elliptic curve $y^2 = x^3 + ax + b$ satisfying $rb^2 \equiv a^3 \pmod{p}$.
n	The (prime) order of the base point P.
h	The cofactor.
x, y	The x and y coordinates of P.

P-192: $p = 2^{192} - 2^{64} - 1$, $a = -3$, $h = 1$

$S =$ 0x 3045AE6F C8422F64 ED579528 D38120EA E12196D5

$r =$ 0x 3099D2BB BFCB2538 542DCD5F B078B6EF 5F3D6FE2 C745DE65

$b =$ 0x 64210519 E59C80E7 0FA7E9AB 72243049 FEB8DEEC C146B9B1

$n =$ 0x FFFFFFFF FFFFFFFF FFFFFFFF 99DEF836 146BC9B1 B4D22831

$x =$ 0x 188DA80E B03090F6 7CBF20EB 43A18800 F4FF0AFD 82FF1012

$y =$ 0x 07192B95 FFC8DA78 631011ED 6B24CDD5 73F977A1 1E794811

P-224: $p = 2^{224} - 2^{96} + 1$, $a = -3$, $h = 1$

$S =$ 0x BD713447 99D5C7FC DC45B59F A3B9AB8F 6A948BC5

$r =$ 0x 5B056C7E 11DD68F4 0469EE7F 3C7A7D74 F7D12111 6506D031 218291FB

$b =$ 0x B4050A85 0C04B3AB F5413256 5044B0B7 D7BFD8BA 270B3943 2355FFB4

$n =$ 0x FFFFFFFF FFFFFFFF FFFFFFFF FFFF16A2 E0B8F03E 13DD2945 5C5C2A3D

$x =$ 0x B70E0CBD 6BB4BF7F 321390B9 4A03C1D3 56C21122 343280D6 115C1D21

$y =$ 0x BD376388 B5F723FB 4C22DFE6 CD4375A0 5A074764 44D58199 85007E34

P-256: $p = 2^{256} - 2^{224} + 2^{192} + 2^{96} - 1$, $a = -3$, $h = 1$

$S =$ 0x C49D3608 86E70493 6A6678E1 139D26B7 819F7E90

$r =$ 0x 7EFBA166 2985BE94 03CB055C 75D4F7E0 CE8D84A9 C5114ABC AF317768 0104FA0D

$b =$ 0x 5AC635D8 AA3A93E7 B3EBBD55 769886BC 651D06B0 CC53B0F6 3BCE3C3E 27D2604B

$n =$ 0x FFFFFFFF 00000000 FFFFFFFF FFFFFFFF BCE6FAAD A7179E84 F3B9CAC2 FC632551

$x =$ 0x 6B17D1F2 E12C4247 F8BCE6E5 63A440F2 77037D81 2DEB33A0 F4A13945 D898C296

$y =$ 0x 4FE342E2 FE1A7F9B 8EE7EB4A 7C0F9E16 2BCE3357 6B315ECE CBB64068 37BF51F5

P-384: $p = 2^{384} - 2^{128} - 2^{96} + 2^{32} - 1$, $a = -3$, $h = 1$

$S =$ 0x A335926A A319A27A 1D00896A 6773A482 7ACDAC73

$r =$ 0x 79D1E655 F868F02F FF48DCDE E14151DD B80643C1 406D0CA1 0DFE6FC5 2009540A
       495E8042 EA5F744F 6E184667 CC722483

$b =$ 0x B3312FA7 E23EE7E4 988E056B E3F82D19 181D9C6E FE814112 0314088F 5013875A
       C656398D 8A2ED19D 2A85C8ED D3EC2AEF

$n =$ 0x FFFFFFFF FFFFFFFF FFFFFFFF FFFFFFFF FFFFFFFF FFFFFFFF C7634D81 F4372DDF
       581A0DB2 48B0A77A ECEC196A CCC52973

$x =$ 0x AA87CA22 BE8B0537 8EB1C71E F320AD74 6E1D3B62 8BA79B98 59F741E0 82542A38
       5502F25D BF55296C 3A545E38 72760AB7

$y =$ 0x 3617DE4A 96262C6F 5D9E98BF 9292DC29 F8F41DBD 289A147C E9DA3113 B5F0B8C0
       0A60B1CE 1D7E819D 7A431D7C 90EA0E5F

P-521: $p = 2^{521} - 1$, $a = -3$, $h = 1$

$S =$ 0x D09E8800 291CB853 96CC6717 393284AA A0DA64BA

$r =$ 0x 000000B4 8BFA5F42 0A349495 39D2BDFC 264EEEEB 077688E4 4FBF0AD8 F6D0EDB3
       7BD6B533 28100051 8E19F1B9 FFBE0FE9 ED8A3C22 00B8F875 E523868C 70C1E5BF
       55BAD637

$b =$ 0x 00000051 953EB961 8E1C9A1F 929A21A0 B68540EE A2DA725B 99B315F3 B8B48991
       8EF109E1 56193951 EC7E937B 1652C0BD 3BB1BF07 3573DF88 3D2C34F1 EF451FD4
       6B503F00

$n =$ 0x 000001FF FFFFFFFF FFFFFFFF FFFFFFFF FFFFFFFF FFFFFFFF FFFFFFFF FFFFFFFF
       FFFFFFFA 51868783 BF2F966B 7FCC0148 F709A5D0 3BB5C9B8 899C47AE BB6FB71E
       91386409

$x =$ 0x 000000C6 858E06B7 0404E9CD 9E3ECB66 2395B442 9C648139 053FB521 F828AF60
       6B4D3DBA A14B5E77 EFE75928 FE1DC127 A2FFA8DE 3348B3C1 856A429B F97E7E31
       C2E5BD66

$y =$ 0x 00000118 39296A78 9A3BC004 5C8A5FB4 2C7D1BD9 98F54449 579B4468 17AFBD17
       273E662C 97EE7299 5EF42640 C550B901 3FAD0761 353C7086 A272C240 88BE9476
       9FD16650

Table A.3. NIST-recommended random elliptic curves over prime fields.

A.2.2   Random elliptic curves over $\mathbb{F}_{2^m}$

Table A.4 lists domain parameters for the five NIST-recommended randomly chosen elliptic curves over binary fields $\mathbb{F}_{2^m}$. The extension degrees m are prime and were selected so that there exists a Koblitz curve over $\mathbb{F}_{2^m}$ having almost-prime group order (see §A.2.3). Algorithm 4.19 was used to generate the coefficient b of an elliptic curve over $\mathbb{F}_{2^m}$ from the seed S. The output b of the algorithm was interpreted as an element of $\mathbb{F}_{2^m}$ represented with respect to the Gaussian normal basis specified in FIPS 186-2. A change-of-basis matrix was then used to transform b to a polynomial basis representation—see FIPS 186-2 for more details. The following parameters are given for each curve:

m	The extension degree of the binary field $\mathbb{F}_{2^m}$.
$f(z)$	The reduction polynomial of degree m.
S	The seed selected to randomly generate the coefficients of the elliptic curve.
a, b	The coefficients of the elliptic curve $y^2 + xy = x^3 + ax^2 + b$.
n	The (prime) order of the base point P.
h	The cofactor.
x, y	The x and y coordinates of P.

A.2.3   Koblitz elliptic curves over $\mathbb{F}_{2^m}$

Table A.5 lists domain parameters for the five NIST-recommended Koblitz curves over binary fields. The binary fields $\mathbb{F}_{2^m}$ are the same as for the random curves in §A.2.2. Koblitz curves were selected because point multiplication can be performed faster than for the random curves (see §3.4). The following parameters are given for each curve:

m	The extension degree of the binary field $\mathbb{F}_{2^m}$.
$f(z)$	The reduction polynomial of degree m.
a, b	The coefficients of the elliptic curve $y^2 + xy = x^3 + ax^2 + b$.
n	The (prime) order of the base point P.
h	The cofactor.
x, y	The x and y coordinates of P.

B-163: $m = 163$, $f(z) = z^{163} + z^7 + z^6 + z^3 + 1$, $a = 1$, $h = 2$

S = 0x 85E25BFE 5C86226C DB12016F 7553F9D0 E693A268
b = 0x 00000002 0A601907 B8C953CA 1481EB10 512F7874 4A3205FD
n = 0x 00000004 00000000 00000000 000292FE 77E70C12 A4234C33
x = 0x 00000003 F0EBA162 86A2D57E A0991168 D4994637 E8343E36
y = 0x 00000000 D51FBC6C 71A0094F A2CDD545 B11C5C0C 797324F1

B-233: $m = 233$, $f(z) = z^{233} + z^{74} + 1$, $a = 1$, $h = 2$

S = 0x 74D59FF0 7F6B413D 0EA14B34 4B20A2DB 049B50C3
b = 0x 00000066 647EDE6C 332C7F8C 0923BB58 213B333B 20E9CE42 81FE115F 7D8F90AD
n = 0x 00000100 00000000 00000000 00000000 0013E974 E72F8A69 22031D26 03CFE0D7
x = 0x 000000FA C9DFCBAC 8313BB21 39F1BB75 5FEF65BC 391F8B36 F8F8EB73 71FD558B
y = 0x 00000100 6A08A419 03350678 E58528BE BF8A0BEF F867A7CA 36716F7E 01F81052

B-283: $m = 283$, $f(z) = z^{283} + z^{12} + z^7 + z^5 + 1$, $a = 1$, $h = 2$

S = 0x 77E2B073 70EB0F83 2A6DD5B6 2DFC88CD 06BB84BE
b = 0x 027B680A C8B8596D A5A4AF8A 19A0303F CA97FD76 45309FA2 A581485A F6263E31
        3B79A2F5
n = 0x 03FFFFFF FFFFFFFF FFFFFFFF FFFFFFFF FFFFEF90 399660FC 938A9016 5B042A7C
        EFADB307
x = 0x 05F93925 8DB7DD90 E1934F8C 70B0DFEC 2EED25B8 557EAC9C 80E2E198 F8CDBECD
        86B12053
y = 0x 03676854 FE24141C B98FE6D4 B20D02B4 516FF702 350EDDB0 826779C8 13F0DF45
        BE8112F4

B-409: $m = 409$, $f(z) = z^{409} + z^{87} + 1$, $a = 1$, $h = 2$

S = 0x 4099B5A4 57F9D69F 79213D09 4C4BCD4D 4262210B
b = 0x 0021A5C2 C8EE9FEB 5C4B9A75 3B7B476B 7FD6422E F1F3DD67 4761FA99 D6AC27C8
        A9A197B2 72822F6C D57A55AA 4F50AE31 7B13545F
n = 0x 01000000 00000000 00000000 00000000 00000000 00000000 000001E2 AAD6A612
        F33307BE 5FA47C3C 9E052F83 8164CD37 D9A21173
x = 0x 015D4860 D088DDB3 496B0C60 64756260 441CDE4A F1771D4D B01FFE5B 34E59703
        DC255A86 8A118051 5603AEAB 60794E54 BB7996A7
y = 0x 0061B1CF AB6BE5F3 2BBFA783 24ED106A 7636B9C5 A7BD198D 0158AA4F 5488D08F
        38514F1F DF4B4F40 D2181B36 81C364BA 0273C706

B-571: $m = 571$, $f(z) = z^{571} + z^{10} + z^5 + z^2 + 1$, $a = 1$, $h = 2$

S = 0x 2aa058f7 3a0e33ab 486b0f61 0410c53a 7f132310
b = 0x 02F40E7E 2221F295 DE297117 B7F3D62F 5C6A97FF CB8CEFF1 CD6BA8CE 4A9A18AD
        84FFABBD 8EFA5933 2BE7AD67 56A66E29 4AFD185A 78FF12AA 520E4DE7 39BACA0C
        7FFEFF7F 2955727A
n = 0x 03FFFFFF FFFFFFFF FFFFFFFF FFFFFFFF FFFFFFFF FFFFFFFF FFFFFFFF FFFFFFFF
        FFFFFFFF E661CE18 FF559873 08059B18 6823851E C7DD9CA1 161DE93D 5174D66E
        8382E9BB 2FE84E47
x = 0x 0303001D 34B85629 6C16C0D4 0D3CD775 0A93D1D2 955FA80A A5F40FC8 DB7B2ABD
        BDE53950 F4C0D293 CDD711A3 5B67FB14 99AE6003 8614F139 4ABFA3B4 C850D927
        E1E7769C 8EEC2D19
y = 0x 037BF273 42DA639B 6DCCFFFE B73D69D7 8C6C27A6 009CBBCA 1980F853 3921E8A6
        84423E43 BAB08A57 6291AF8F 461BB2A8 B3531D2F 0485C19B 16E2F151 6E23DD3C
        1A4827AF 1B8AC15B

Table A.4. NIST-recommended random elliptic curves over binary fields.

K-163: $m = 163$, $f(z) = z^{163} + z^7 + z^6 + z^3 + 1$, $a = 1$, $b = 1$, $h = 2$
n = 0x 00000004 00000000 00000000 00020108 A2E0CC0D 99F8A5EF
x = 0x 00000002 FE13C053 7BBC11AC AA07D793 DE4E6D5E 5C94EEE8
y = 0x 00000002 89070FB0 5D38FF58 321F2E80 0536D538 CCDAA3D9

K-233: $m = 233$, $f(z) = z^{233} + z^{74} + 1$, $a = 0$, $b = 1$, $h = 4$
n = 0x 00000080 00000000 00000000 00000000 00069D5B B915BCD4 6EFB1AD5 F173ABDF
x = 0x 00000172 32BA853A 7E731AF1 29F22FF4 149563A4 19C26BF5 0A4C9D6E EFAD6126
y = 0x 000001DB 537DECE8 19B7F70F 555A67C4 27A8CD9B F18AEB9B 56E0C110 56FAE6A3

K-283: $m = 283$, $f(z) = z^{283} + z^{12} + z^7 + z^5 + 1$, $a = 0$, $b = 1$, $h = 4$
n = 0x 01FFFFFF FFFFFFFF FFFFFFFF FFFFFFFF FFFFE9AE 2ED07577 265DFF7F 94451E06
         1E163C61
x = 0x 0503213F 78CA4488 3F1A3B81 62F188E5 53CD265F 23C1567A 16876913 B0C2AC24
         58492836
y = 0x 01CCDA38 0F1C9E31 8D90F95D 07E5426F E87E45C0 E8184698 E4596236 4E341161
         77DD2259

K-409: $m = 409$, $f(z) = z^{409} + z^{87} + 1$, $a = 0$, $b = 1$, $h = 4$
n = 0x 007FFFFF FFFFFFFF FFFFFFFF FFFFFFFF FFFFFFFF FFFFFFFF FFFFFE5F 83B2D4EA
         20400EC4 557D5ED3 E3E7CA5B 4B5C83B8 E01E5FCF
x = 0x 0060F05F 658F49C1 AD3AB189 0F718421 0EFD0987 E307C84C 27ACCFB8 F9F67CC2
         C460189E B5AAAA62 EE222EB1 B35540CF E9023746
y = 0x 01E36905 0B7C4E42 ACBA1DAC BF04299C 3460782F 918EA427 E6325165 E9EA10E3
         DA5F6C42 E9C55215 AA9CA27A 5863EC48 D8E0286B

K-571: $m = 571$, $f(z) = z^{571} + z^{10} + z^5 + z^2 + 1$, $a = 0$, $b = 1$, $h = 4$
n = 0x 02000000 00000000 00000000 00000000 00000000 00000000 00000000 00000000
         00000000 131850E1 F19A63E4 B391A8DB 917F4138 B630D84B E5D63938 1E91DEB4
         5CFE778F 637C1001
x = 0x 026EB7A8 59923FBC 82189631 F8103FE4 AC9CA297 0012D5D4 60248048 01841CA4
         43709584 93B205E6 47DA304D B4CEB08C BBD1BA39 494776FB 988B4717 4DCA88C7
         E2945283 A01C8972
y = 0x 0349DC80 7F4FBF37 4F4AEADE 3BCA9531 4DD58CEC 9F307A54 FFC61EFC 006D8A2C
         9D4979C0 AC44AEA7 4FBEBBB9 F772AEDC B620B01A 7BA7AF1B 320430C8 591984F6
         01CD4C14 3EF1C7A3

Table A.5. *NIST-recommended Koblitz curves over binary fields.*

APPENDIX B

ECC Standards

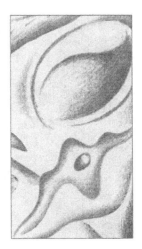

Cryptographic standards are important for two reasons: (i) to facilitate the widespread use of cryptographically sound and well-specified techniques; and (ii) to promote interoperability between different implementations. Interoperability is encouraged by completely specifying the steps of the cryptographic schemes and the formats for shared data such as domain parameters, keys and exchanged messages, and by limiting the number of options available to the implementor.

This section describes the salient features of selected standards and draft standards that describe elliptic curve mechanisms for signatures, encryption, and key establishment. A summary is provided in Table B.1. Electronic copies of the standards can be obtained online from the web sites listed in Table B.2. It should be noted that many of these standards are updated periodically. Readers should consult the web sites for the latest drafts.

American National Standards Institute (ANSI) The ANSI X9F subcommittee of the ANSI X9 committee develops information security standards for the financial services industry. Two elliptic curve standards have been completed: ANSI X9.62 which specifies the ECDSA (§4.4.1), and ANSI X9.63 which specifies numerous elliptic curve key agreement and key transport protocols including STS (§4.6.1), ECMQV (§4.6.2), and ECIES (§4.5.1). The objective of these standards is to achieve a high degree of security and interoperability. The underlying finite field is restricted to being a prime field $\mathbb{F}_p$ or a binary field $\mathbb{F}_{2^m}$. The elements of $\mathbb{F}_{2^m}$ may be represented using a polynomial basis or a normal basis over $\mathbb{F}_2$. If a polynomial basis is desired, then the reduction polynomial must be an irreducible trinomial, if one exists, and an irreducible pentanomial otherwise. To facilitate interoperability, a specific reduction polynomial is recommended for each field $\mathbb{F}_{2^m}$; these polynomials of degree m, where $2 \leq m \leq 600$, are listed in Tables A.1 and A.2. If a normal basis is desired, a specific Gaussian normal

Standard	Year	Abbreviated Title	Ref.
ANSI X9.62	1999	The elliptic curve digital signature algorithm	[14]
ANSI X9.63	2001	Key agreement and key transport	[15]
FIPS 186-2	2000	Digital signature standard (DSS)	[140]
IEEE 1363-2000	2000	Standard specifications for public-key cryptography	[204]
IEEE P1363a	(draft)	Amendment 1: Additional techniques	[203]
ISO/IEC 15946-1	2002	Techniques based on elliptic curves–Part 1: General	[211]
ISO/IEC 15946-2	2002	Part 2: Digital signatures	[212]
ISO/IEC 15946-3	2002	Part 3: Key establishment	[213]
ISO/IEC 15946-4	(draft)	Part 4: Digital signatures giving message recovery	[214]
ISO/IEC 18033-2	(draft)	Encryption algorithms–Part 2: Asymmetric ciphers	[215]
SEC 1	2000	Elliptic curve cryptography	[417]
SEC 2	2000	Recommended elliptic curve domain parameters	[418]

Table B.1. Selected standards and draft standards that specify cryptographic mechanisms based on elliptic curves.

ANSI	American National Standards Institute
	http://www.ansi.org
X9	Standards for the Financial Services Industry
	http://www.x9.org
IEEE	Institute of Electrical and Electronics Engineers
	http://www.ieee.org
P1363	Specifications for Public-Key Cryptography
	http://grouper.ieee.org/groups/1363
ISO	International Organization for Standardization
	http://www.iso.ch
IEC	International Electrotechnical Commission
	http://www.iec.ch
SC 27	Information Technology – Security Techniques
	http://www.din.de/ni/sc27
NIST	National Institute of Standards and Technology
	http://www.nist.gov
FIPS	Federal Information Processing Standards
	http://www.itl.nist.gov/fipspubs
SECG	Standards for Efficient Cryptography Group
	http://www.secg.org
SEC	Standards for Efficient Cryptography documents
	http://www.secg.org/secg_docs.htm
NESSIE	New European Schemes for Signatures, Integrity and Encryption
	http://www.cryptonessie.org
IPA	Information-technology Promotion Agency
	http://www.ipa.go.jp/ipa-e/index-e.html
CRYPTREC	Cryptographic Research and Evaluation Committee
	http://www.ipa.go.jp/security/enc/CRYPTREC/index-e.html

Table B.2. URLs for standards bodies and working groups.

basis is mandated. The primary security requirement is that the order n of the base point P should be greater than 2^{160}. The only hash function employed is SHA-1; however, it is anticipated that ANSI X9.62 and X9.63 will be updated in the coming years to allow for hash functions of varying output lengths.

National Institute of Standards and Technology (NIST) NIST is a non-regulatory federal agency within the U.S. Commerce Department's Technology Administration. Included in its mission is the development of security-related Federal Information Processing Standards (FIPS) intended for use by U.S. federal government departments. The FIPS standards widely adopted and depolyed around the world include the Data Encryption Standard (DES: FIPS 46), the Secure Hash Algorithms (SHA-1, SHA-256, SHA-384 and SHA-512: FIPS 180-2 [138]), the Advanced Encryption Standard (AES: FIPS 197 [141]), and Hash-based Message Authentication Code (HMAC: FIPS 198 [142]). FIPS 186-2, also known as the Digital Signature Standard (DSS), specifies the RSA, DSA and ECDSA signature schemes. ECDSA is specified simply by reference to ANSI X9.62 with a recommendation to use the 15 elliptic curves listed in §A.2.1, §A.2.2 and §A.2.3. NIST is in the process of developing a recommendation [342] for elliptic curve key establishment schemes that will include a selection of protocols from ANSI X9.63.

Institute of Electrical and Electronics Engineers (IEEE) The IEEE P1363 working group is developing a suite of standards for public-key cryptography. The scope of P1363 is very broad and includes schemes based on the intractability of integer factorization, discrete logarithm in finite fields, elliptic curve discrete logarithms, and lattice-based schemes. The 1363-2000 standard includes elliptic curve signature schemes (ECDSA and an elliptic curve analogue of a signature scheme due to Nyberg and Rueppel), and elliptic curve key agreement schemes (ECMQV and variants of elliptic curve Diffie-Hellman (ECDH)). It differs fundamentally from the ANSI standards and FIPS 186-2 in that there are no mandated minimum security requirements and there is an abundance of options. Its primary purpose, therefore, is to serve as a reference for specifications of a variety of cryptographic protocols from which other standards and applications can select. The 1363-2000 standard restricts the underlying finite field to be a prime field $\mathbb{F}_p$ or a binary field $\mathbb{F}_{2^m}$. The P1363a draft standard is an addendum to 1363-2000. It contains specifications of ECIES and the Pintsov-Vanstone signature scheme providing message recovery, and allows for extension fields $\mathbb{F}_{p^m}$ of odd characteristic including optimal extension fields (see §2.4).

International Organization for Standardization (ISO) ISO and the International Electrotechnical Commission (IEC) jointly develop cryptographic standards within the SC 27 subcommittee. ISO/IEC 15946 is a suite of elliptic curve cryptographic standards that specifies signature schemes (including ECDSA and EC-KCDSA), key establishment schemes (including ECMQV and STS), and digital signature schemes providing message recovery. ISO/IEC 18033-2 provides detailed descriptions and security analyses of various public-key encryption schemes including ECIES-KEM and PSEC-KEM.

Standards for Efficient Cryptography Group (SECG) SECG is a consortium of companies formed to address potential interoperability problems with cryptographic standards. SEC 1 specifies ECDSA, ECIES, ECDH and ECMQV, and attempts to be compatible with all ANSI, NIST, IEEE and ISO/IEC elliptic curve standards. Some specific elliptic curves, including the 15 NIST elliptic curves, are listed in SEC 2.

New European Schemes for Signatures, Integrity and Encryption (NESSIE) The NESSIE project was funded by the European Union's Fifth Framework Programme. Its main objective was to assess and select various symmetric-key primitives (block ciphers, stream ciphers, hash functions, message authentication codes) and public-key primitives (public-key encryption, signature and identification schemes). The elliptic curve schemes selected were ECDSA and the key transport protocols PSEC-KEM and ACE-KEM.

Cryptographic Research and Evaluation Committee (CRYPTREC) The Information-technology Promotion Agency (IPA) in Japan formed the CRYPTREC committee for the purpose of evaluating cryptographic protocols for securing the Japanese government's electronic business. Numerous symmetric-key and public-key primitives are being evaluated, including ECDSA, ECIES, PSEC-KEM and ECDH.

APPENDIX C

Software Tools

This appendix lists software tools of interest to practitioners and educators. The listing is separated into two sections. §C.1 includes research and other tools, most of which are fairly general-purpose and do not necessarily require programming. §C.2 entries are more specialized or contain libraries to be used with programming languages such as C. Generally speaking, §C.1 is of interest to those involved in education and with prototyping, while developers may be primarily interested in §C.2. Researchers have used packages from both sections. The descriptions provided are, for the most part, adapted directly from those given by the package authors.

C.1   General-purpose tools

The entries in this section vary in capability and interface, with bc and calc as fairly basic tools, and Maple, Mathematica, and MuPAD offering sophisticated graphics and advanced user interfaces. Magma is significantly more specialized than tools such as Mathematica, and has excellent support for elliptic curve operations such as point counting. GAP and KANT/KASH can be regarded as the most specialized of the packages in this section.

bc http://www.gnu.org

> bc is a language that supports arbitrary precision numbers with interactive execution. There are some similarities in the syntax to the C programming language. bc has the advantage of its wide availability and may be useful as a calculator and in prototyping. Keith Matthews has written several bc programs in number theory, http://www.numbertheory.org/gnubc/.

Calc http://www.gnu.org

Calc is an interactive calculator providing for easy large numeric calculations. It can also be programmed for difficult or long calculations. Functions are provided for basic modular arithmetic. Calc, developed by David I. Bell and Landon Curt Noll with contributions, is hosted on SourceForge, http://sourceforge.net/projects/calc/.

GAP http://www.gap-system.org

GAP (Groups, Algorithms and Programming) is a system for computational discrete algebra with particular emphasis on computational group theory. Capabilities include long integer and rational arithmetic, cyclotomic fields, finite fields, residue class rings, p-adic numbers, polynomials, vectors and matrices, various combinatorial functions, elementary number theory, and a wide variety of list operations. GAP was developed at Lehrstuhl D für Mathematik, RWTH Aachen, Germany beginning in 1986, and then transferred to the University of St. Andrews, Scotland in 1997.

KANT/KASH http://www.math.tu-berlin.de/~kant/kash.html

The Computational Algebraic Number Theory package is designed for sophisticated computations in number fields and in global function fields. KASH is the KAnt SHell, a front-end to KANT. Development is directed by Prof. Dr. M. Pohst at the Technische Universität Berlin.

Magma http://magma.maths.usyd.edu.au

The Magma Computational Algebra System "is a large, well-supported software package designed to solve computationally hard problems in algebra, number theory, geometry and combinatorics. It provides a mathematically rigorous environment for computing with algebraic, number-theoretic, combinatoric and geometric objects." In particular, there is extensive support for elliptic curve operations.

Magma is produced and distributed by the Computational Algebra Group within the School of Mathematics and Statistics of the University of Sydney. "While Magma is a non-commercial system, we are required to recover all costs arising from its distribution and support."

Maple http://www.maplesoft.com

Maple is an advanced mathematical problem-solving and programming environment. The University of Waterloo's Symbolic Computation Group (Waterloo, Canada) initially developed the Maple symbolic technology. Maple is commercial—historically, student and academic licensing has been relatively generous.

Mathematica http://www.wolfram.com

Mathematica is a general-purpose technical computing system, combining fast, high-precision numeric and symbolic computation with easy-to-use data visualization and programming capabilities. Wolfram Research, the developer of Mathematica, was founded by Stephen Wolfram in 1987.

MuPAD http://www.mupad.de

MuPAD is a general-purpose computer algebra system for symbolic and numerical computations. Users can view the library code, implement their own routines and data types easily, and can also dynamically link C/C++ compiled modules for raw speed and flexibility.

MuPAD was originally developed by the MuPAD Research Group under direction of Prof. B. Fuchssteiner at the University of Paderborn (Germany). Free licenses are available; commercial versions can be obtained from SciFace Software. Several books on MuPAD have been published, including the paperback *MuPAD Tutorial: A version and platform independent introduction*, by J. Gerhard, W. Oevel, F. Postel, and S. Wehmeier, Springer-Verlag, 2000.

C.2 Libraries

In contrast to most of the entries in §C.1, the packages in this section are more specialized. For example, some are libraries intended for programmers using languages such as C or C++.

The most basic is GNU MP, a library supporting arbitrary-precision arithmetic routines. It is recommended for its performance across many platforms. Crypto++ offers an extensive list of routines for cryptographic use, in an elegant C++ framework. OpenSSL, MIRACL, and cryptlib are similarly ambitious. Developed from SSLeay, OpenSSL is widely used in applications such as the Apache web server and OpenSSH, and has also been used strictly for its big number routines. MIRACL provides executables for elliptic curve point counting.

In addition to integer and polynomial arithmetic, LiDIA and NTL provide sophisticated number-theoretic algorithms. Along with PARI-GP, these tools may be of particular interest to researchers.

cryptlib http://www.cs.auckland.ac.nz/~pgut001/cryptlib/

Although elliptic curve methods are not included, the cryptlib security toolkit from Peter Gutmann is notable for its range of encryption, digital signature, key and certificate management, and message security services, with support for a wide variety of crypto hardware. In particular, cryptlib emphasizes ease of use of high-level services such as SSH, SSL, S/MIME, and PGP. The big number routines are from OpenSSL. The toolkit runs on a wide range of platforms, has a dual-license for open source and commercial use, and substantial documentation is available.

Crypto++ http://www.eskimo.com/~weidai/cryptlib.html

Crypto++ is a free C++ library from Wei Dai for cryptography, and includes ciphers, message authentication codes, one-way hash functions, public-key cryptosystems, and key agreement schemes. The project is hosted on SourceForge, http://sourceforge.net/projects/cryptopp/.

GNU MP http://www.swox.com/gmp/

GMP is a free library for arbitrary precision arithmetic, operating on signed integers, rational numbers, and floating point numbers. It focuses on speed rather than simplicity or elegance.

Libgcrypt http://www.gnu.org/directory/security/libgcrypt.html

Libgcrypt is a general-purpose cryptographic library based on the code from GnuPG (an OpenPGP compliant application). It provides functions for cryptographic building blocks including symmetric ciphers, hash algorithms, MACs, public key algorithms, large integers (using code derived from GNU MP), and random numbers.

LiDIA http://www.informatik.tu-darmstadt.de/TI/LiDIA/

LiDIA is a C++ library for computational number theory which provides a collection of highly optimized implementations of various multiprecision data types and time-intensive algorithms. In particular, the library contains algorithms for factoring and for point counting on elliptic curves. The developer is the LiDIA Group at the Darmstadt University of Technology (Germany).

MIRACL http://indigo.ie/~mscott/

The Multiprecision Integer and Rational Arithmetic C/C++ Library implements primitives supporting symmetric-key and public-key methods, including elliptic curve methods and point counting. Licensed through Shamus Software Ltd. (Ireland), it is "FREE for non-profit making, educational, or any non-commercial use."

NTL: A Library for doing Number Theory http://www.shoup.net/ntl/

NTL is a high-performance portable C++ library providing data structures and algorithms for arbitrary length integers; for vectors, matrices, and polynomials over the integers and over finite fields; and for arbitrary precision floating point arithmetic. In particular, the library contains state-of-the-art implementations for lattice basis reduction. NTL is maintained by Victor Shoup.

OpenSSL http://www.openssl.org

> The OpenSSL Project is a collaborative effort to develop a robust, full-featured, and Open Source toolkit implementing the Secure Sockets Layer (SSL v2/v3) and Transport Layer Security (TLS v1) protocols as well as a general-purpose cryptography library. OpenSSL is based on the SSLeay library developed by Eric A. Young and Tim J. Hudson.

PARI-GP http://www.parigp-home.de

> PARI-GP is a computer-aided number theory package, consisting of a C library and the programmable interactive gp calculator. Originally developed at Bordeaux by a team led by Henri Cohen, PARI-GP is now maintained by Karim Belabas at the Université Paris-Sud Orsay with many contributors.

Bibliography

[1] M. ABDALLA, M. BELLARE, AND P. ROGAWAY. The oracle Diffie-Hellman assumptions and an analysis of DHIES. *Topics in Cryptology—CT-RSA 2001* (LNCS 2020) [338], 143–158, 2001.

[2] C. ADAMS AND S. LLOYD. *Understanding PKI: Concepts, Standards, and Deployment Considerations.* Addison-Wesley, 2nd edition, 2002.

[3] L. M. ADLEMAN AND M.-D. A. HUANG, editors. *Algorithmic Number Theory—ANTS-I*, volume 877 of *Lecture Notes in Computer Science.* Springer-Verlag, 1994.

[4] ADVANCED MICRO DEVICES. *AMD-K6 Processor Multimedia Technology*, 2000. Publication 20726, available from http://www.amd.com.

[5] G. AGNEW, T. BETH, R. MULLIN, AND S. VANSTONE. Arithmetic operations in $GF(2^m)$. *Journal of Cryptology*, 6:3–13, 1993.

[6] G. AGNEW, R. MULLIN, I. ONYSZCHUK, AND S. VANSTONE. An implementation for a fast public-key cryptosystem. *Journal of Cryptology*, 3:63–79, 1991.

[7] G. AGNEW, R. MULLIN, AND S. VANSTONE. An implementation of elliptic curve cryptosystems over $\mathbb{F}_{2^{155}}$. *IEEE Journal on Selected Areas in Communications*, 11:804–813, 1993.

[8] D. AGRAWAL, B. ARCHAMBEAULT, J. RAO, AND P. ROHATGI. The EM side-channel(s). *Cryptographic Hardware and Embedded Systems—CHES 2002* (LNCS 2523) [238], 29–45, 2002.

[9] M. AKKAR, R. BEVAN, P. DISCHAMP, AND D. MOYART. Power analysis, what is now possible... *Advances in Cryptology—ASIACRYPT 2000* (LNCS 1976) [355], 489–502, 2000.

[10] E. AL-DAOUD, R. MAHMOD, M. RUSHDAN, AND A. KILICMAN. A new addition formula for elliptic curves over $GF(2^n)$. *IEEE Transactions on Computers*, 51:972–975, 2002.

[11] R. ANDERSON. *Security Engineering: A Guide to Building Dependable Distributed Systems.* Wiley, 2001.

[12] R. ANDERSON AND M. KUHN. Low cost attacks on tamper resistant devices. *Security Protocols 1997* (LNCS 1361) [95], 125–136, 1998.

[13] R. ANDERSON AND S. VAUDENAY. Minding your p's and q's. *Advances in Cryptology—ASIACRYPT '96* (LNCS 1163) [245], 26–35, 1996.

[14] ANSI X9.62. Public Key Cryptography for the Financial Services Industry: The Elliptic Curve Digital Signature Algorithm (ECDSA). American National Standards Institute, 1999.

[15] ANSI X9.63. Public Key Cryptography for the Financial Services Industry: Key Agreement and Key Transport Using Elliptic Curve Cryptography. American National Standards Institute, 2001.

[16] A. ANTIPA, D. BROWN, A. MENEZES, R. STRUIK, AND S. VANSTONE. Validation of elliptic curve public keys. *Public Key Cryptography—PKC 2003* (LNCS 2567) [116], 211–223, 2003.

[17] K. AOKI AND H. LIPMAA. Fast implementation of AES candidates. *Third AES Candidate Conference (AES3)*, 2000. Available from http://csrc.nist.gov/encryption/aes/round2/conf3/aes3conf.htm.

[18] S. ARITA. Weil descent of elliptic curves over finite fields of characteristic three. *Advances in Cryptology—ASIACRYPT 2000* (LNCS 1976) [355], 248–258, 2000.

[19] D. ASH, I. BLAKE, AND S. VANSTONE. Low complexity normal bases. *Discrete Applied Mathematics*, 25:191–210, 1989.

[20] A. ATKIN AND F. MORAIN. Elliptic curves and primality proving. *Mathematics of Computation*, 61:29–68, 1993.

[21] I. ATTALI AND T. JENSEN, editors. *Smart Card Programming and Security*, volume 2140 of *Lecture Notes in Computer Science*. International Conference on Research in Smart Cards, E-smart 2001, Cannes, France, September 19-21, 2001, Springer-Verlag, 2001.

[22] D. AUCSMITH, editor. *Information Hiding—IH '98*, volume 1525 of *Lecture Notes in Computer Science*. Second International Workshop, IH'98, Portland, Oregon, April 1998, Springer-Verlag, 1998.

[23] E. BACH AND J. SHALLIT. *Algorithmic Number Theory, Volume I: Efficient Algorithms*. MIT Press, 1996.

[24] H. BAIER AND J. BUCHMANN. Elliptic curves of prime order over optimal extension fields for use in cryptography. *Progress in Cryptology—INDOCRYPT 2001* (LNCS 2247) [367], 99–107, 2001.

[25] D. BAILEY AND C. PAAR. Optimal extension fields for fast arithmetic in public-key algorithms. *Advances in Cryptology—CRYPTO '98* (LNCS 1462) [270], 472–485, 1998.

[26] ———. Efficient arithmetic in finite field extensions with application in elliptic curve cryptography. *Journal of Cryptology*, 14:153–176, 2001.

[27] R. BALASUBRAMANIAN AND N. KOBLITZ. The improbability that an elliptic curve has subexponential discrete log problem under the Menezes-Okamoto-Vanstone algorithm. *Journal of Cryptology*, 11:141–145, 1998.

[28] F. BAO, H. DENG, Y. HAN, A. JENG, D. NARASIMHALU, AND T. NGAIR. Breaking public key cryptosystems on tamper resistant devices in the presence of transient faults. *Security Protocols 1997* (LNCS 1361) [95], 115–124, 1998.

[29] P. BARRETT. Implementing the Rivest Shamir and Adleman public key encryption algorithm on a standard digital signal processor. *Advances in Cryptology—CRYPTO '86* (LNCS 263) [351], 311–323, 1987.

[30] L. BATTEN AND J. SEBERRY, editors. *Information Security and Privacy 2002*, volume 2384 of *Lecture Notes in Computer Science*. 7th Australasian Conference, July 3-5, 2001, Melbourne, Australia, Springer-Verlag, 2002.

[31] S. BEAUREGARD. Circuit for Shor's algorithm using $2n + 3$ qubits. *Quantum Information and Computation*, 3:175–185, 2003.

[32] M. BEDNARA, M. DALDRUP, J. SHOKROLLAHI, J. TEICH, AND J. VON ZUR GATHEN. Reconfigurable implementation of elliptic curve crypto algorithms. *Proceedings of the International Parallel and Distributed Processing Symposium (IPDPS 2002)*, 2002. Available from http://computer.org/proceedings/ipdps/1573/workshops/1573toc.htm.

[33] ———. Tradeoff analysis of FPGA based elliptic curve cryptography. *Proceedings of the IEEE International Symposium on Circuits and Systems (ISCAS 2002)*, 2002.

[34] M. BELLARE, editor. *Advances in Cryptology—CRYPTO 2000*, volume 1880 of *Lecture Notes in Computer Science*. 20th Annual International Cryptology Conference, Santa Barbara, California, August 2000, Springer-Verlag, 2000.

[35] M. BELLARE, A. BOLDYREVA, AND S. MICALI. Public-key encryption in a multi-user setting: Security proofs and improvements. *Advances in Cryptology—EUROCRYPT 2000* (LNCS 1807) [382], 259–274, 2000.

[36] M. BELLARE, A. DESAI, D. POINTCHEVAL, AND P. ROGAWAY. Relations among notions of security for public-key encryption schemes. *Advances in Cryptology—CRYPTO '98* (LNCS 1462) [270], 26–45, 1998.

[37] M. BELLARE AND P. ROGAWAY. Random oracles are practical: A paradigm for designing efficient protocols. *First ACM Conference on Computer and Communications Security*, 62–73. ACM Press, 1993.

[38] ———. Optimal asymmetric encryption. *Advances in Cryptology—EUROCRYPT '94* (LNCS 950) [110], 92–111, 1995.

[39] ———. The exact security of digital signatures — how to sign with RSA and Rabin. *Advances in Cryptology—EUROCRYPT '96* (LNCS 1070) [306], 399–416, 1996.

[40] ———. Minimizing the use of random oracles in authenticated encryption schemes. *Information and Communications Security '97* (LNCS 1334) [188], 1–16, 1997.

[41] D. BERNSTEIN. Circuits for integer factorization: A proposal. Preprint, 2001. Available from http://cr.yp.to/papers.html.

[42] ———. Floating-point arithmetic and message authentication. Preprint, 2000. Available from http://cr.yp.to/papers.html.

[43] ———. A software implementation of NIST P-224. Presentation at the 5th Workshop on Elliptic Curve Cryptography (ECC 2001), University of Waterloo, October 29-31, 2001. Slides available from http://cr.yp.to/talks.html.

[44] G. BERTONI, J. GUAJARDO, S. KUMAR, G. ORLANDO, C. PAAR, AND T. WOLLINGER. Efficient $GF(p^m)$ arithmetic architectures for cryptographic applications. *Topics in Cryptology—CT-RSA 2003* (LNCS 2612) [230], 158–175, 2003.

[45] T. BETH AND D. GOLLMANN. Algorithm engineering for public key algorithms. *IEEE Journal on Selected Areas in Communications*, 7:458–465, 1989.

[46] I. BIEHL, B. MEYER, AND V. MÜLLER. Differential fault analysis on elliptic curve cryptosystems. *Advances in Cryptology—CRYPTO 2000* (LNCS 1880) [34], 131–146, 2000.

[47] E. BIHAM, editor. *Advances in Cryptology—EUROCRYPT 2003*, volume 2656 of *Lecture Notes in Computer Science*. International Conference on the Theory and Applications of Cryptographic Techniques, Warsaw, Poland, May 4-8, 2003, Springer-Verlag, 2003.

[48] E. BIHAM AND A. SHAMIR. Differential fault analysis of secret key cryptosystems. *Advances in Cryptology—CRYPTO '97* (LNCS 1294) [235], 513–525, 1997.

[49] I. BLAKE, G. SEROUSSI, AND N. SMART. *Elliptic Curves in Cryptography*. Cambridge University Press, 1999.

[50] S. BLAKE-WILSON AND A. MENEZES. Authenticated Diffie-Hellman key agreement protocols. *Selected Areas in Cryptography—SAC '98* (LNCS 1556) [457], 339–361, 1999.

[51] ———. Unknown key-share attacks on the station-to-station (STS) protocol. *Public Key Cryptography—PKC '99* (LNCS 1560) [206], 154–170, 1999.

[52] D. BLEICHENBACHER. On the security of the KMOV public key cryptosystem. *Advances in Cryptology—CRYPTO '97* (LNCS 1294) [235], 235–248, 1997.

[53] ———. Chosen ciphertext attacks against protocols based on the RSA encryption standard PKCS #1. *Advances in Cryptology—CRYPTO '98* (LNCS 1462) [270], 1–12, 1998.

[54] D. BONEH. The decision Diffie-Hellman problem. *Algorithmic Number Theory—ANTS-III* (LNCS 1423) [82], 48–63, 1998.

[55] ———, editor. *Advances in Cryptology—CRYPTO 2003*, volume 2729 of *Lecture Notes in Computer Science*. 23rd Annual International Cryptology Conference, Santa Barbara, California, August 17-21, 2003, Springer-Verlag, 2003.

[56] D. BONEH, R. DeMILLO, AND R. LIPTON. On the importance of checking cryptographic protocols for faults. *Advances in Cryptology—EUROCRYPT '97* (LNCS 1233) [154], 37–51, 1997.

[57] ———. On the importance of eliminating errors in cryptographic computations. *Journal of Cryptology*, 14:101–119, 2001.

[58] D. BONEH AND M. FRANKLIN. Identity-based encryption from the Weil pairing. *Advances in Cryptology—CRYPTO 2001* (LNCS 2139) [241], 213–229, 2001.

[59] ———. Identity-based encryption from the Weil pairing. *SIAM Journal on Computing*, 32:586–615, 2003.

[60] D. BONEH, C. GENTRY, B. LYNN, AND H. SHACHAM. Aggregate and verifiably encrypted signatures from bilinear maps. *Advances in Cryptology—EUROCRYPT 2003* (LNCS 2656) [47], 416–432, 2003.

[61] D. BONEH AND R. LIPTON. Algorithms for black-box fields and their application to cryptography. *Advances in Cryptology—CRYPTO '96* (LNCS 1109) [255], 283–297, 1996.

[62] D. BONEH, B. LYNN, AND H. SHACHAM. Short signatures from the Weil pairing. *Advances in Cryptology—ASIACRYPT 2001* (LNCS 2248) [67], 514–532, 2001.

[63] D. BONEH, I. MIRONOV, AND V. SHOUP. A secure signature scheme from bilinear maps. *Topics in Cryptology—CT-RSA 2003* (LNCS 2612) [230], 98–110, 2003.

[64] D. BONEH AND I. SHPARLINSKI. On the unpredictability of bits of the elliptic curve Diffie-Hellman scheme. *Advances in Cryptology—CRYPTO 2001* (LNCS 2139) [241], 201–212, 2001.

[65] W. BOSMA, editor. *Algorithmic Number Theory—ANTS-IV*, volume 1838 of *Lecture Notes in Computer Science*. 4th International Symposium, ANTS-IV, Leiden, The Netherlands, July 2000, Springer-Verlag, 2000.

[66] A. BOSSELAERS, R. GOVAERTS, AND J. VANDEWALLE. Comparison of three modular reduction functions. *Advances in Cryptology—CRYPTO '93* (LNCS 773) [453], 175–186, 1994.

[67] C. BOYD, editor. *Advances in Cryptology—ASIACRYPT 2001*, volume 2248 of *Lecture Notes in Computer Science*. 7th International Conference on the Theory and Application of Cryptology and Information Security, Gold Coast, Australia, December 9-13, 2001, Springer-Verlag, 2001.

[68] C. BOYD AND A. MATHURIA. *Protocols for Key Establishment and Authentication*. Springer-Verlag, 2003.

[69] G. BRASSARD, editor. *Advances in Cryptology–CRYPTO '89*, volume 435 of *Lecture Notes in Computer Science*. Springer-Verlag, 1990.

[70] R. BRENT. An improved Monte Carlo factorization algorithm. *BIT*, 20:176–184, 1980.

[71] E. BRICKELL, editor. *Advances in Cryptology—CRYPTO '92*, volume 740 of *Lecture Notes in Computer Science*. 12th Annual International Cryptology Conference, Santa Barbara, California, August 1992, Springer-Verlag, 1993.

[72] E. BRICKELL, D. GORDON, K. McCURLEY, AND D. WILSON. Fast exponentiation with precomputation. *Advances in Cryptology—EUROCRYPT '92* (LNCS 658) [398], 200–207, 1993.

[73] E. BRICKELL, D. POINTCHEVAL, S. VAUDENAY, AND M. YUNG. Design validations for discrete logarithm based signature schemes. *Public Key Cryptography—PKC 2000* (LNCS 1751) [207], 276–292, 2000.

[74] É. BRIER AND M. JOYE. Weierstraß elliptic curves and side-channel attacks. *Public Key Cryptography—PKC 2002* (LNCS 2274) [340], 335–345, 2002.

[75] D. BROWN. Generic groups, collision resistance, and ECDSA. Cryptology ePrint Archive: Report 2002/026. Available from http://eprint.iacr.org/2002/026/, February 2002.

[76] D. BROWN AND D. JOHNSON. Formal security proofs for a signature scheme with partial message recovery. *Topics in Cryptology—CT-RSA 2001* (LNCS 2020) [338], 126–142, 2001.

[77] M. BROWN, D. HANKERSON, J. LÓPEZ, AND A. MENEZES. Software implementation of the NIST elliptic curves over prime fields. *Topics in Cryptology—CT-RSA 2001* (LNCS 2020) [338], 250–265, 2001.

[78] D. BRUMLEY AND D. BONEH. Remote timing attacks are practical. *Proceedings of the Twelfth USENIX Security Symposium*. USENIX Association, 2003.

[79] J. BUCHMANN AND H. BAIER. Efficient construction of cryptographically strong elliptic curves. *Progress in Cryptology—INDOCRYPT 2000* (LNCS 1977) [393], 191–202, 2000.

[80] J. BUCHMANN AND H. WILLIAMS. A key-exchange system based on imaginary quadratic fields. *Journal of Cryptology*, 1:107–118, 1988.

[81] ——. A key exchange system based on real quadratic fields. *Advances in Cryptology–CRYPTO '89* (LNCS 435) [69], 335–343, 1990.

[82] J. BUHLER, editor. *Algorithmic Number Theory—ANTS-III*, volume 1423 of *Lecture Notes in Computer Science*. Third International Symposium, ANTS-III, Portland, Oregon, June 1998, Springer-Verlag, 1998.

[83] R. CANETTI, O. GOLDREICH, AND S. HALEVI. The random oracle methodology, revisited. *Proceedings of the 30th Annual ACM Symposium on Theory of Computing*, 209–218, 1998.

[84] R. CANETTI AND H. KRAWCZYK. Analysis of key-exchange protocols and their use for building secure channels. *Advances in Cryptology—EUROCRYPT 2001* (LNCS 2045) [372], 453–474, 2001.

[85] ———. Security analysis of IKE's signature-based key-exchange protocol. *Advances in Cryptology—CRYPTO 2002* (LNCS 2442) [488], 143–161, 2002.

[86] B. CANVEL, A. HILTGEN, S. VAUDENAY, AND M. VUAGNOUX. Password interception in a SSL/TLS channel. *Advances in Cryptology—CRYPTO 2003* (LNCS 2729) [55], 583–599, 2003.

[87] S. CAVALLAR, B. DODSON, A. LENSTRA, W. LIOEN, P. MONTGOMERY, B. MURPHY, H. TE RIELE, K. AARDAL, J. GILCHRIST, G. GUILLERM, P. LEYLAND, J. MARCHAND, F. MORAIN, A. MUFFETT, C. PUTNAM, C. PUTNAM, AND P. ZIMMERMANN. Factorization of a 512-bit RSA modulus. *Advances in Cryptology—EUROCRYPT 2000* (LNCS 1807) [382], 1–18, 2000.

[88] CERTICOM CORP. ECC Challenge. http://www.certicom.com/resources/ecc_chall/challenge.html, 1997.

[89] A. CHAN AND V. GLIGOR, editors. *Information Security 2002*, volume 2433 of *Lecture Notes in Computer Science*. 5th International Conference, September 30 – October 23, 2002, Sao Paulo, Brazil, Springer-Verlag, 2002.

[90] S. CHANG SHANTZ. From Euclid's GCD to Montgomery multiplication to the great divide. Technical Report SMLI TR-2001-95, Sun Microsystems Laboratories, 2001.

[91] S. CHARI, C. JUTLA, J. RAO, AND P. ROHATGI. Towards sound approaches to counteract power-analysis attacks. *Advances in Cryptology—CRYPTO '99* (LNCS 1666) [480], 398–412, 1999.

[92] L. CHARLAP AND D. ROBBINS. An elementary introduction to elliptic curves. CRD Expository Report 31, Center for Communications Research, Princeton, 1988.

[93] ———. An elementary introduction to elliptic curves II. CRD Expository Report 34, Center for Communications Research, Princeton, 1990.

[94] Y. CHOIE AND J. LEE. Speeding up the scalar multiplication in the jacobians of hyperelliptic curves using frobenius map. *Progress in Cryptology—INDOCRYPT 2002* (LNCS 2551) [317], 285–295, 2002.

[95] B. CHRISTIANSON, B. CRISPO, M. LOMAS, AND M. ROE, editors. *Security Protocols 1997*, volume 1361 of *Lecture Notes in Computer Science*. 5th International Workshop, April 1997, Paris, France, Springer-Verlag, 1998.

[96] D. CHUDNOVSKY AND G. CHUDNOVSKY. Sequences of numbers generated by addition in formal groups and new primality and factoring tests. *Advances in Applied Mathematics*, 7:385–434, 1987.

[97] J. CHUNG, S. SIM, AND P. LEE. Fast implementation of elliptic curve defined over $GF(p^m)$ on CalmRISC with MAC2424 coprocessor. *Cryptographic Hardware and Embedded Systems—CHES 2000* (LNCS 1965) [263], 57–70, 2000.

[98] M. CIET, T. LANGE, F. SICA, AND J. QUISQUATER. Improved algorithms for efficient arithmetic on elliptic curves using fast endomorphisms. *Advances in Cryptology—EUROCRYPT 2003* (LNCS 2656) [47], 388–400, 2003.

[99] H. COHEN. *A Course in Computational Algebraic Number Theory.* Springer-Verlag, 1993.

[100] H. COHEN, A. MIYAJI, AND T. ONO. Efficient elliptic curve exponentiation using mixed coordinates. *Advances in Cryptology—ASIACRYPT '98* (LNCS 1514) [352], 51–65, 1998.

[101] P. COMBA. Exponentiation cryptosystems on the IBM PC. *IBM Systems Journal*, 29:526–538, 1990.

[102] D. COPPERSMITH. Fast evaluation of logarithms in fields of characteristic two. *IEEE Transactions on Information Theory*, 30:587–594, 1984.

[103] ———, editor. *Advances in Cryptology—CRYPTO '95*, volume 963 of *Lecture Notes in Computer Science*. 15th Annual International Cryptology Conference, Santa Barbara, California, August 1995, Springer-Verlag, 1995.

[104] J. CORON. Resistance against differential power analysis for elliptic curve cryptosystems. *Cryptographic Hardware and Embedded Systems—CHES '99* (LNCS 1717) [262], 292–302, 1999.

[105] R. CRAMER AND V. SHOUP. A practical public key cryptosystem provably secure against adaptive chosen ciphertext attack. *Advances in Cryptology—CRYPTO '98* (LNCS 1462) [270], 13–25, 1998.

[106] ———. Design and analysis of practical public-key encryption schemes secure against adaptive chosen ciphertext attack. *SIAM Journal on Computing*, to appear.

[107] I. DAMGÅRD, editor. *Advances in Cryptology—EUROCRYPT '90*, volume 473 of *Lecture Notes in Computer Science*. Workshop on the Theory and Application of Cryptographic Techniques, Aarhus, Denmark, May 1990, Springer-Verlag, 1991.

[108] G. DAVID AND Y. FRANKEL, editors. *Information Security 2001*, volume 2200 of *Lecture Notes in Computer Science*. 4th International Conference, October 1-3, 2001, Malaga, Spain, Springer-Verlag, 2001.

[109] P. DE ROOIJ. Efficient exponentiation using precomputation and vector addition chains. *Advances in Cryptology—EUROCRYPT '94* (LNCS 950) [110], 389–399, 1995.

[110] A. DE SANTIS, editor. *Advances in Cryptology—EUROCRYPT '94*, volume 950 of *Lecture Notes in Computer Science*. Workshop on the Theory and Application of Cryptographic Techniques, Perugia, Italy, May 1994, Springer-Verlag, 1995.

[111] E. DE WIN, S. MISTER, B. PRENEEL, AND M. WIENER. On the performance of signature schemes based on elliptic curves. *Algorithmic Number Theory—ANTS-III* (LNCS 1423) [82], 252–266, 1998.

[112] B. DEN BOER. Diffie-Hellman is as strong as discrete log for certain primes. *Advances in Cryptology—CRYPTO '88* (LNCS 403) [172], 530–539, 1990.

[113] J. DENEF AND F. VERCAUTEREN. An extension of Kedlaya's algorithm to Artin-Schreier curves in characteristic 2. *Algorithmic Number Theory—ANTS-V* (LNCS 2369) [137], 308–323, 2002.

[114] A. DENT. Adapting the weaknesses of the random oracle model to the generic group model. *Advances in Cryptology—ASIACRYPT 2002* (LNCS 2501) [489], 100–109, 2002.

[115] Y. DESMEDT, editor. *Advances in Cryptology—CRYPTO '94*, volume 839 of *Lecture Notes in Computer Science*. 14th Annual International Cryptology Conference, Santa Barbara, California, August 1994, Springer-Verlag, 1994.

[116] ——, editor. *Public Key Cryptography—PKC 2003*, volume 2567 of *Lecture Notes in Computer Science*. 6th International Workshop on Practice and Theory in Public Key Cryptography Miami, Florida, January 6-8, 2003, Springer-Verlag, 2003.

[117] J. DHEM, F. KOEUNE, P. LEROUX, P. MESTRÉ, J. QUISQUATER, AND J. WILLEMS. A practical implementation of the timing attack. *Smart Card Research and Applications* (LNCS 1820) [387], 175–190, 2000.

[118] C. DIEM. *A Study on Theoretical and Practical Aspects of Weil-Restriction of Varieties*. Ph.D. thesis, University of Essen, Germany, 2001.

[119] ——. The GHS-Attack in odd characteristic. *Journal of the Ramanujan Mathematical Society*, 18:1–32, 2003.

[120] W. DIFFIE. The first ten years of public key cryptology. In Simmons [435], chapter 3, 135–175.

[121] W. DIFFIE AND M. HELLMAN. New directions in cryptography. *IEEE Transactions on Information Theory*, 22:644–654, 1976.

[122] W. DIFFIE, P. VAN OORSCHOT, AND M. WIENER. Authentication and authenticated key exchanges. *Designs, Codes and Cryptography*, 2:107–125, 1992.

[123] D. DOLEV, C. DWORK, AND M. NAOR. Non-malleable cryptography. *Proceedings of the 23rd Annual ACM Symposium on Theory of Computing*, 542–552, 1991.

[124] ——. Non-malleable cryptography. *SIAM Journal on Computing*, 30:391–437, 2000.

[125] J. DOMINGO-FERRER, D. CHAN, AND A. WATSON, editors. *Smart Card Research and Advanced Applications*, volume 180 of *IFIP International Federation for Information Processing*. Fourth Working Conference on Smart Card Research and Advanced Applications (CARDIS 2000), Bristol, UK, September 20-22, 2000, Kluwer, 2000.

[126] A. DURAND. Efficient ways to implement elliptic curve exponentiation on a smart card. *Smart Card Research and Applications* (LNCS 1820) [387], 357–365, 2000.

[127] S. DUSSÉ AND B. KALISKI. A cryptographic library for the Motorola DSP56000. *Advances in Cryptology—EUROCRYPT '90* (LNCS 473) [107], 230–244, 1991.

[128] I. DUURSMA, P. GAUDRY, AND F. MORAIN. Speeding up the discrete log computation on curves with automorphisms. *Advances in Cryptology—ASIACRYPT '99* (LNCS 1716) [274], 103–121, 1999.

[129] K. EISENTRÄGER, K. LAUTER, AND P. MONTGOMERY. Fast elliptic curve arithmetic and improved Weil pairing evaluation. *Topics in Cryptology—CT-RSA 2003* (LNCS 2612) [230], 343–354, 2003.

[130] E. EL MAHASSNI, P. NGUYEN, AND I. SHPARLINSKI. The insecurity of Nyberg-Rueppel and other DSA-like signature schemes with partially known nonces. *Cryptography and Lattices—CaLC 2001*, volume 2146 of *Lecture Notes in Computer Science*, 97–109. Springer-Verlag, 2001.

[131] T. ELGAMAL. A public key cryptosystem and a signature scheme based on discrete logarithms. *IEEE Transactions on Information Theory*, 31:469–472, 1985.

[132] A. ENGE. *Elliptic Curves and Their Applications to Cryptography: An Introduction*. Kluwer Academic Publishers, 1999.

[133] A. ENGE AND P. GAUDRY. A general framework for subexponential discrete logarithm algorithms. *Acta Arithmetica*, 102:83–103, 2002.

[134] M. ERNST, M. JUNG, F. MADLENER, S. HUSS, AND R. BLÜMEL. A reconfigurable system on chip implementation for elliptic curve cryptography over $GF(2^n)$. *Cryptographic Hardware and Embedded Systems—CHES 2002* (LNCS 2523) [238], 381–399, 2002.

[135] J. FEIGENBAUM, editor. *Advances in Cryptology—CRYPTO '91*, volume 576 of *Lecture Notes in Computer Science*. Springer-Verlag, 1992.

[136] N. FERGUSON AND B. SCHNEIER. *Practical Cryptography*. Wiley, 2003.

[137] C. FIEKER AND D. KOHEL, editors. *Algorithmic Number Theory—ANTS-V*, volume 2369 of *Lecture Notes in Computer Science*. 5th International Symposium, ANTS-V, Sydney, Australia, July 2002, Springer-Verlag, 2002.

[138] FIPS 180-2. Secure Hash Standard. Federal Information Processing Standards Publication 180-2, National Institute of Standards and Technology, 2002.

[139] FIPS 186. Digital Signature Standard (DSS). Federal Information Processing Standards Publication 186, National Institute of Standards and Technology, 1994.

[140] FIPS 186-2. Digital Signature Standard (DSS). Federal Information Processing Standards Publication 186-2, National Institute of Standards and Technology, 2000.

[141] FIPS 197. Advanced Encryption Standard (AES). Federal Information Processing Standards Publication 197, National Institute of Standards and Technology, 2001.

[142] FIPS 198. HMAC – Keyed-Hash Message Authentication. Federal Information Processing Standards Publication 198, National Institute of Standards and Technology, 2002.

[143] P. FLAJOLET AND A. ODLYZKO. Random mapping statistics. *Advances in Cryptology —EUROCRYPT '89* (LNCS 434) [388], 329–354, 1990.

[144] K. FONG, D. HANKERSON, J. LÓPEZ, AND A. MENEZES. Field inversion and point halving revisited. Technical Report CORR 2003-18, Department of Combinatorics and Optimization, University of Waterloo, Canada, 2003.

[145] W. FORD AND M. BAUM. *Secure Electronic Commerce: Building the Infrastructure for Digital Signatures and Encryption*. Prentice Hall, 2nd edition, 2000.

[146] M. FOUQUET, P. GAUDRY, AND R. HARLEY. An extension of Satoh's algorithm and its implementation. *Journal of the Ramanujan Mathematical Society*, 15:281–318, 2000.

[147] ———. Finding secure curves with the Satoh-FGH algorithm and an early-abort strategy. *Advances in Cryptology—EUROCRYPT 2001* (LNCS 2045) [372], 14–29, 2001.

[148] Y. FRANKEL, editor. *Financial Cryptography—FC 2000*, volume 1962 of *Lecture Notes in Computer Science*. 4th International Conference, FC 2000, Anguilla, British West Indies, February 2000, Springer-Verlag, 2001.

[149] G. FREY. Applications of arithmetical geometry to cryptographic constructions. *Proceedings of the Fifth International Conference on Finite Fields and Applications*, 128–161. Springer-Verlag, 2001.

[150] G. FREY AND H. RÜCK. A remark concerning m-divisibility and the discrete logarithm in the divisor class group of curves. *Mathematics of Computation*, 62:865–874, 1994.

[151] H. FRIUM. The group law on elliptic curves on Hesse form. *Finite Fields with Applications to Coding Theory, Cryptography and Related Areas*, 123–151. Springer-Verlag, 2002.

[152] E. FUJISAKI AND T. OKAMOTO. Secure integration of asymmetric and symmetric encryption schemes. *Advances in Cryptology—CRYPTO '99* (LNCS 1666) [480], 537–554, 1999.

[153] E. FUJISAKI, T. OKAMOTO, D. POINTCHEVAL, AND J. STERN. RSA-OAEP is secure under the RSA assumption. *Advances in Cryptology—CRYPTO 2001* (LNCS 2139) [241], 260–274, 2001.

[154] W. FUMY, editor. *Advances in Cryptology—EUROCRYPT '97*, volume 1233 of *Lecture Notes in Computer Science*. International Conference on the Theory and Application of Cryptographic Techniques, Konstanz, Germany, May 1997, Springer-Verlag, 1997.

[155] S. GALBRAITH. Supersingular curves in cryptography. *Advances in Cryptology—ASIACRYPT 2001* (LNCS 2248) [67], 495–513, 2001.

[156] S. GALBRAITH, F. HESS, AND N. SMART. Extending the GHS Weil descent attack. *Advances in Cryptology—EUROCRYPT 2002* (LNCS 2332) [248], 29–44, 2002.

[157] S. GALBRAITH, S. PAULUS, AND N. SMART. Arithmetic on superelliptic curves. *Mathematics of Computation*, 71:393–405, 2002.

[158] S. GALBRAITH AND N. SMART. A cryptographic application of Weil descent. *Cryptography and Coding*, volume 1746 of *Lecture Notes in Computer Science*, 191–200. Springer-Verlag, 1999.

[159] R. GALLANT, R. LAMBERT, AND S. VANSTONE. Improving the parallelized Pollard lambda search on anomalous binary curves. *Mathematics of Computation*, 69:1699–1705, 2000.

[160] ———. Faster point multiplication on elliptic curves with efficient endomorphisms. *Advances in Cryptology—CRYPTO 2001* (LNCS 2139) [241], 190–200, 2001.

[161] K. GANDOLFI, C. MOURTEL, AND F. OLIVIER. Electromagnetic analysis: concrete results. *Cryptographic Hardware and Embedded Systems—CHES 2001* (LNCS 2162) [261], 251–261, 2001.

[162] L. GAO, S. SHRIVASTAVA, AND G. SOBELMAN. Elliptic curve scalar multiplier design using FPGAs. *Cryptographic Hardware and Embedded Systems—CHES '99* (LNCS 1717) [262], 257–268, 1999.

[163] P. GAUDRY. An algorithm for solving the discrete log problem in hyperelliptic curves. *Advances in Cryptology—EUROCRYPT 2000* (LNCS 1807) [382], 19–34, 2000.

[164] ———. A comparison and a combination of SST and AGM algorithms for counting points of elliptic curves in characteristic 2. *Advances in Cryptology—ASIACRYPT 2002* (LNCS 2501) [489], 311–327, 2002.

[165] P. GAUDRY AND N. GÜREL. An extension of Kedlaya's point-counting algorithm to superelliptic curves. *Advances in Cryptology—ASIACRYPT 2001* (LNCS 2248) [67], 480–494, 2001.

[166] P. GAUDRY AND R. HARLEY. Counting points on hyperelliptic curves over finite fields. *Algorithmic Number Theory—ANTS-IV* (LNCS 1838) [65], 313–332, 2000.

[167] P. GAUDRY, F. HESS, AND N. SMART. Constructive and destructive facets of Weil descent on elliptic curves. *Journal of Cryptology*, 15:19–46, 2002.

[168] C. GEBOTYS AND R. GEBOTYS. Secure elliptic curve implementations: An analysis of resistance to power-attacks in a DSP. *Cryptographic Hardware and Embedded Systems—CHES 2002* (LNCS 2523) [238], 114–128, 2002.

[169] W. GEISELMANN AND R. STEINWANDT. A dedicated sieving hardware. *Public Key Cryptography—PKC 2003* (LNCS 2567) [116], 267–278, 2003.

[170] C. GENTRY AND A. SILVERBERG. Hierarchical ID-based cryptography. *Advances in Cryptology—ASIACRYPT 2002* (LNCS 2501) [489], 548–566, 2002.

[171] R. GERBER. *The Software Optimization Cookbook – High-Performance Recipes for the Intel Architecture.* Intel Press, 2002.

[172] S. GOLDWASSER, editor. *Advances in Cryptology—CRYPTO '88*, volume 403 of *Lecture Notes in Computer Science.* Springer-Verlag, 1990.

[173] S. GOLDWASSER AND J. KILIAN. Almost all primes can be quickly certified. *Proceedings of the 18th Annual ACM Symposium on Theory of Computing*, 316–329, 1986.

[174] S. GOLDWASSER AND S. MICALI. Probabilistic encryption. *Journal of Computer and System Sciences*, 29:270–299, 1984.

[175] S. GOLDWASSER, S. MICALI, AND R. RIVEST. A digital signature scheme secure against adaptive chosen-message attacks. *SIAM Journal on Computing*, 17:281–308, 1988.

[176] G. GONG AND L. HARN. Public-key cryptosystems based on cubic finite field extensions. *IEEE Transactions on Information Theory*, 45:2601–2605, 1999.

[177] J. GOODMAN AND A. CHANDRAKASAN. An energy efficient reconfigurable public-key cryptography processor architecture. *Cryptographic Hardware and Embedded Systems—CHES 2000* (LNCS 1965) [263], 175–190, 2000.

[178] D. GORDON. Discrete logarithms in $GF(p)$ using the number field sieve. *SIAM Journal on Discrete Mathematics*, 6:124–138, 1993.

[179] ——. A survey of fast exponentiation methods. *Journal of Algorithms*, 27:129–146, 1998.

[180] L. GOUBIN. A refined power-analysis attack on elliptic curve cryptosystems. *Public Key Cryptography—PKC 2003* (LNCS 2567) [116], 199–210, 2003.

[181] J. GROSSSCHÄDL. A bit-serial unified multiplier architecture for finite fields $GF(p)$ and $GF(2^m)$. *Cryptographic Hardware and Embedded Systems—CHES 2001* (LNCS 2162) [261], 202–219, 2001.

[182] J. GUAJARDO, R. BLÜMEL, U. KRIEGER, AND C. PAAR. Efficient implementation of elliptic curve cryptosystems on the TI MSP430x33x family of microcontrollers. *Public Key Cryptography—PKC 2001* (LNCS 1992) [244], 365–382, 2001.

[183] J. GUAJARDO AND C. PAAR. Itoh-Tsujii inversion in standard basis and its application in cryptography and codes. *Designs, Codes and Cryptography*, 25:207–216, 2002.

[184] L. GUILLOU AND J. QUISQUATER, editors. *Advances in Cryptology—EUROCRYPT '95*, volume 921 of *Lecture Notes in Computer Science.* International Conference on the Theory and Application of Cryptographic Techniques, Saint-Malo, France, May 1995, Springer-Verlag, 1995.

[185] C. GÜNTHER, T. LANGE, AND A. STEIN. Speeding up the arithmetic on Koblitz curves of genus two. *Selected Areas in Cryptography—SAC 2000* (LNCS 2012) [455], 106–117, 2001.

[186] N. GURA, S. CHANG SHANTZ, H. EBERLE, D. FINCHELSTEIN, S. GUPTA, V. GUPTA, AND D. STEBILA. An end-to-end systems approach to elliptic curve cryptography. *Cryptographic Hardware and Embedded Systems—CHES 2002* (LNCS 2523) [238], 349–365, 2002.

[187] A. GUTUB, A. TENCA, E. SAVAŞ, AND C. KOÇ. Scalable and unified hardware to compute Montgomery inverse in $GF(p)$ and $GF(2^n)$. *Cryptographic Hardware and Embedded Systems—CHES 2002* (LNCS 2523) [238], 484–499, 2002.

[188] Y. HAN, T. OKAMOTO, AND S. QING, editors. *Information and Communications Security '97*, volume 1334 of *Lecture Notes in Computer Science*. First Inernational Conference, November 11-14, 1997, Beijing, China, Springer-Verlag, 1997.

[189] D. HANKERSON, J. LÓPEZ, AND A. MENEZES. Software implementation of elliptic curve cryptography over binary fields. *Cryptographic Hardware and Embedded Systems—CHES 2000* (LNCS 1965) [263], 1–24, 2000.

[190] D. HARKINS AND D. CARREL. The Internet Key Exchange (IKE). Internet Request for Comments 2409, Available from http://www.ietf.org/rfc/rfc2409.txt, November 1998.

[191] R. HARLEY. The Elliptic Curve Discrete Logarithms Project. http://pauillac.inria.fr/~harley/ecdl/, 1997.

[192] ———. Asymptotically optimal p-adic point-counting. Contribution to the Number Theory List, 2002.

[193] M. HASAN. Power analysis attacks and algorithmic approaches to their countermeasures for Koblitz curve cryptosystems. *IEEE Transactions on Computers*, 50:1071–1083, 2001.

[194] T. HASEGAWA, J. NAKAJIMA, AND M. MATSUI. A practical implementation of elliptic curve cryptosystems over $GF(p)$ on a 16-bit microcomputer. *Public Key Cryptography—PKC '98* (LNCS 1431) [205], 182–194, 1998.

[195] J. HÅSTAD. Solving simultaneous modular equations of low degree. *SIAM Journal on Computing*, 17:336–341, 1988.

[196] F. HESS. The GHS attack revisited. *Advances in Cryptology—EUROCRYPT 2003* (LNCS 2656) [47], 374–387, 2003.

[197] A. HEVIA AND M. KIWI. Strength of two Data Encryption Standard implementations under timing attacks. *ACM Transactions on Information and System Security*, 2:416–437, 1999.

[198] Y. HITCHCOCK AND P. MONTAGUE. A new elliptic curve scalar multiplication algorithm to resist simple power analysis. *Information Security and Privacy 2002* (LNCS 2384) [30], 214–225, 2002.

[199] J. HORWITZ AND B. LYNN. Toward hierarchical identity-based encryption. *Advances in Cryptology—EUROCRYPT 2002* (LNCS 2332) [248], 466–481, 2002.

[200] R. HOUSLEY AND T. POLK. *Planning for PKI: Best Practices Guide for Deploying Public Key Infrastructure*. Wiley, 2001.

[201] E. HOWE. On the group orders of elliptic curves over finite fields. *Compositio Mathematica*, 85:229–247, 1993.

[202] N. Howgrave-Graham and N. Smart. Lattice attacks on digital signature schemes. *Designs, Codes and Cryptography*, 23:283–290, 2001.

[203] IEEE P1363A. Standard Specifications for Public-Key Cryptography—Amendment 1: Additional Techniques, working draft 12bis, May 12 2003.

[204] IEEE Std 1363-2000. IEEE Standard Specifications for Public-Key Cryptography, 2000.

[205] H. Imai and Y. Zheng, editors. *Public Key Cryptography—PKC '98*, volume 1431 of *Lecture Notes in Computer Science*. First International Workshop on Practice and Theory in Public Key Cryptography, Pacifico Yokohama, Japan, February 1998, Springer-Verlag, 1998.

[206] ——, editors. *Public Key Cryptography—PKC '99*, volume 1560 of *Lecture Notes in Computer Science*. Second International Workshop on Practice and Theory in Public Key Cryptography, Kamakura, Japan, March 1999, Springer-Verlag, 1999.

[207] ——, editors. *Public Key Cryptography—PKC 2000*, volume 1751 of *Lecture Notes in Computer Science*. Third International Workshop on Practice and Theory in Public Key Cryptosystems, Melbourne, Australia, January 2000, Springer-Verlag, 2000.

[208] Intel Corporation. *The Complete Guide to MMX Technology*. McGraw-Hill, 1997. Contributing authors: D. Bistry, C. Delong, M. Gutman, M. Julier, M. Keith, L. Mennemeier, M. Mittal, A. Peleg, and U. Weiser.

[209] ——. *Intel Pentium 4 and Intel Xeon Processor Optimization Reference Manual*, 2001. Number 248966-04, available from http://developer.intel.com.

[210] ——. *IA-32 Intel Architecture Software Developer's Manual, Volume 1: Basic Architecture*, 2002. Number 245470-007, available from http://developer.intel.com.

[211] ISO/IEC 15946-1. Information Technology – Security Techniques – Cryptographic Techniques Based on Elliptic Curves – Part 1: General, 2002.

[212] ISO/IEC 15946-2. Information Technology – Security Techniques – Cryptographic Techniques Based on Elliptic Curves – Part 2: Digital Signatures, 2002.

[213] ISO/IEC 15946-3. Information Technology – Security Techniques – Cryptographic Techniques Based on Elliptic Curves – Part 3: Key Establishment, 2002.

[214] ISO/IEC 15946-4. Information Technology – Security Techniques – Cryptographic Techniques Based on Elliptic Curves – Part 4: Digital Signatures Giving Message Recovery, draft 2003.

[215] ISO/IEC 18033-2. Information Technology – Security Techniques – Encryption Algorithms – Part 2: Asymmetric Ciphers, draft 2002.

[216] K. Itoh, M. Takenaka, N. Torii, S. Temma, and Y. Kurihara. Fast implementation of public-key cryptography on a DSP TMS320C6201. *Cryptographic Hardware and Embedded Systems—CHES '99* (LNCS 1717) [262], 61–72, 1999.

[217] T. Itoh and S. Tsujii. A fast algorithm for computing multiplicative inverses in $GF(2^m)$ using normal bases. *Information and Computation*, 78:171–177, 1988.

[218] T. Izu, J. Kogure, M. Noro, and K. Yokoyama. Efficient implementation of Schoof's algorithm. *Advances in Cryptology—ASIACRYPT '98* (LNCS 1514) [352], 66–79, 1998.

[219] T. IZU, B. MÖLLER, AND T. TAKAGI. Improved elliptic curve multiplication methods resistant against side channel attacks. *Progress in Cryptology—INDOCRYPT 2002* (LNCS 2551) [317], 296–313, 2002.

[220] T. IZU AND T. TAKAGI. A fast parallel elliptic curve multiplication resistant against side channel attacks. *Public Key Cryptography—PKC 2002* (LNCS 2274) [340], 280–296, 2002.

[221] ——. Exceptional procedure attack on elliptic curve cryptosystems. *Public Key Cryptography—PKC 2003* (LNCS 2567) [116], 224–239, 2003.

[222] M. JACOBSON, N. KOBLITZ, J. SILVERMAN, A. STEIN, AND E. TESKE. Analysis of the xedni calculus attack. *Designs, Codes and Cryptography*, 20:41–64, 2000.

[223] M. JACOBSON, A. MENEZES, AND A. STEIN. Solving elliptic curve discrete logarithm problems using Weil descent. *Journal of the Ramanujan Mathematical Society*, 16:231–260, 2001.

[224] D. JOHNSON. Key validation. Research contribution to IEEE P1363. Available from http://grouper.ieee.org/groups/1363/Research, 1997.

[225] ——. Public key validation: A piece of the PKI puzzle. Research contribution to IEEE P1363. Available from http://grouper.ieee.org/groups/1363/Research, 2000.

[226] D. JOHNSON, A. MENEZES, AND S. VANSTONE. The elliptic curve digital signature algorithm (ECDSA). *International Journal of Information Security*, 1:36–63, 2001.

[227] A. JOUX. A one round protocol for tripartite Diffie-Hellman. *Algorithmic Number Theory—ANTS-IV* (LNCS 1838) [65], 385–393, 2000.

[228] A. JOUX AND R. LERCIER. Improvements to the general Number Field Sieve for discrete logarithms in prime fields: A comparison with the Gaussian integer method. *Mathematics of Computation*, 72:953–967, 2003.

[229] A. JOUX AND K. NGUYEN. Separating decision Diffie-Hellman from computational Diffie-Hellman in cryptographic groups. *Journal of Cryptology*, to appear.

[230] M. JOYE, editor. *Topics in Cryptology—CT-RSA 2003*, volume 2612 of *Lecture Notes in Computer Science*. The Cryptographer's Track at the RSA Conference 2003, San Francisco, California, April 13-17, 2003, Springer-Verlag, 2003.

[231] M. JOYE AND J. QUISQUATER. Hessian elliptic curves and side-channel attacks. *Cryptographic Hardware and Embedded Systems—CHES 2001* (LNCS 2162) [261], 402–410, 2001.

[232] M. JOYE AND C. TYMEN. Protections against differential analysis for elliptic curve cryptography – an algebraic approach. *Cryptographic Hardware and Embedded Systems—CHES 2001* (LNCS 2162) [261], 377–390, 2001.

[233] B. KALISKI. One-way permutations on elliptic curves. *Journal of Cryptology*, 3:187–199, 1991.

[234] ——. The Montgomery inverse and its applications. *IEEE Transactions on Computers*, 44:1064–1065, 1995.

[235] ——, editor. *Advances in Cryptology—CRYPTO '97*, volume 1294 of *Lecture Notes in Computer Science*. 17th Annual International Cryptology Conference, Santa Barbara, California, August 1997, Springer-Verlag, 1997.

[236] ——. A chosen message attack on Demytko's elliptic curve cryptosystem. *Journal of Cryptology*, 10:71–72, 1997.

[237] ——. An unknown key-share attack on the MQV key agreement protocol. *ACM Transactions on Information and System Security*, 4:275–288, 2001.

[238] B. KALISKI, Ç. KOÇ, AND C. PAAR, editors. *Cryptographic Hardware and Embedded Systems—CHES 2002*, volume 2523 of *Lecture Notes in Computer Science*. Springer-Verlag, 2002.

[239] A. KARATSUBA AND Y. OFMAN. Multiplication of multidigit numbers on automata. *Soviet Physics — Doklady*, 7:595–596, 1963.

[240] K. KEDLAYA. Counting points on hyperelliptic curves using Monsky-Washnitzer cohomology. *Journal of the Ramanujan Mathematical Society*, 16:323–338, 2001.

[241] J. KILIAN, editor. *Advances in Cryptology—CRYPTO 2001*, volume 2139 of *Lecture Notes in Computer Science*. 21st Annual International Cryptology Conference, Santa Barbara, California, August 19-23, 2001, Springer-Verlag, 2001.

[242] D. KIM AND S. LIM. Integer decomposition for fast scalar multiplication on elliptic curves. *Selected Areas in Cryptography—SAC 2002* (LNCS 2595) [349], 13–20, 2003.

[243] H. KIM, J. PARK, J. CHEON, J. PARK, J. KIM, AND S. HAHN. Fast elliptic curve point counting using Gaussian normal basis. *Algorithmic Number Theory—ANTS-V* (LNCS 2369) [137], 292–207, 2002.

[244] K. KIM, editor. *Public Key Cryptography—PKC 2001*, volume 1992 of *Lecture Notes in Computer Science*. 4th International Workshop on Practice and Theory in Public Key Cryptosystems, Cheju Island, Korea, February 13-15, 2001, Springer-Verlag, 2001.

[245] K. KIM AND T. MATSUMOTO, editors. *Advances in Cryptology—ASIACRYPT '96*, volume 1163 of *Lecture Notes in Computer Science*. International Conference on the Theory and Application of Cryptology and Information Security, Kyongju, Korea, November 1996, Springer-Verlag, 1996.

[246] B. KING. An improved implementation of elliptic curves over $GF(2^n)$ when using projective point arithmetic. *Selected Areas in Cryptography—SAC 2001* (LNCS 2259) [468], 134–150, 2001.

[247] E. KNUDSEN. Elliptic scalar multiplication using point halving. *Advances in Cryptology—ASIACRYPT '99* (LNCS 1716) [274], 135–149, 1999.

[248] L. KNUDSEN, editor. *Advances in Cryptology—EUROCRYPT 2002*, volume 2332 of *Lecture Notes in Computer Science*. International Conference on the Theory and Applications of Cryptographic Techniques, Amsterdam, The Netherlands, April 28 – May 2, 2002, Springer-Verlag, 2002.

[249] D. KNUTH. *The Art of Computer Programming—Seminumerical Algorithms*. Addison-Wesley, 3rd edition, 1998.

[250] N. KOBLITZ. Elliptic curve cryptosystems. *Mathematics of Computation*, 48:203–209, 1987.

[251] ——. Hyperelliptic cryptosystems. *Journal of Cryptology*, 1:139–150, 1989.

[252] ——. Constructing elliptic curve cryptosystems in characteristic 2. *Advances in Cryptology—CRYPTO '90* (LNCS 537) [320], 156–167, 1991.

[253] ——. CM-curves with good cryptographic properties. *Advances in Cryptology—CRYPTO '91* (LNCS 576) [135], 279–287, 1992.

[254] ——. *A Course in Number Theory and Cryptography*. Springer-Verlag, 2nd edition, 1994.

[255] ——, editor. *Advances in Cryptology—CRYPTO '96*, volume 1109 of *Lecture Notes in Computer Science*. 16th Annual International Cryptology Conference, Santa Barbara, California, August 1996, Springer-Verlag, 1996.

[256] ——. An elliptic curve implementation of the finite field digital signature algorithm. *Advances in Cryptology—CRYPTO '98* (LNCS 1462) [270], 327–337, 1998.

[257] ——. Good and bad uses of elliptic curves in cryptography. *Moscow Mathematical Journal*, 2:693–715, 2002.

[258] Ç. KOÇ. High-speed RSA implementation. Technical Report TR-201, RSA Laboratories, 1994.

[259] Ç. KOÇ AND T. ACAR. Montgomery multiplication in $GF(2^k)$. *Designs, Codes and Cryptography*, 14:57–69, 1998.

[260] Ç. KOÇ, T. ACAR, AND B. KALISKI. Analyzing and comparing Montgomery multiplication algorithms. *IEEE Micro*, 16:26–33, 1996.

[261] Ç. KOÇ, D. NACCACHE, AND C. PAAR, editors. *Cryptographic Hardware and Embedded Systems—CHES 2001*, volume 2162 of *Lecture Notes in Computer Science*. Springer-Verlag, 2001.

[262] Ç. KOÇ AND C. PAAR, editors. *Cryptographic Hardware and Embedded Systems—CHES '99*, volume 1717 of *Lecture Notes in Computer Science*. Springer-Verlag, 1999.

[263] ——, editors. *Cryptographic Hardware and Embedded Systems—CHES 2000*, volume 1965 of *Lecture Notes in Computer Science*. Springer-Verlag, 2000.

[264] P. KOCHER. Timing attacks on implementations of Diffie-Hellman, RSA, DSS, and other systems. *Advances in Cryptology—CRYPTO '96* (LNCS 1109) [255], 104–113, 1996.

[265] P. KOCHER, J. JAFFE, AND B. JUN. Differential power analysis. *Advances in Cryptology—CRYPTO '99* (LNCS 1666) [480], 388–397, 1999.

[266] I. KOREN. *Computer Arithmetic Algorithms*. A.K. Peters, 2nd edition, 2002.

[267] K. KOYAMA, U. MAURER, T. OKAMOTO, AND S. VANSTONE. New public-key schemes based on elliptic curves over the ring $\mathbb{Z}_n$. *Advances in Cryptology—CRYPTO '91* (LNCS 576) [135], 252–266, 1992.

[268] D. KRAVITZ. Digital signature algorithm. U.S. patent # 5,231,668, 1993.

[269] H. KRAWCZYK. SKEME: A versatile secure key exchange mechanism for internet. *Proceedings of the Internet Society Symposium on Network and Distributed System Security*, 114–127, 1996.

[270] ——, editor. *Advances in Cryptology—CRYPTO '98*, volume 1462 of *Lecture Notes in Computer Science*. 18th Annual International Cryptology Conference, Santa Barbara, California, August 1998, Springer-Verlag, 1998.

[271] F. KUHN AND R. STRUIK. Random walks revisited: Extensions of Pollard's rho algorithm for computing multiple discrete logarithms. *Selected Areas in Cryptography—SAC 2001* (LNCS 2259) [468], 212–229, 2001.

[272] M. KUHN AND R. ANDERSON. Soft tempest: Hidden data transmission using electromagnetic emanations. *Information Hiding—IH '98* (LNCS 1525) [22], 124–142, 1998.

[273] K. KUROSAWA, K. OKAKA, AND S. TSUJII. Low exponent attack against elliptic curve RSA. *Advances in Cryptology—ASIACRYPT '94* (LNCS 917) [373], 376–383, 1995.

[274] K. LAM AND E. OKAMOTO, editors. *Advances in Cryptology—ASIACRYPT '99*, volume 1716 of *Lecture Notes in Computer Science*. International Conference on the Theory and Application of Cryptology and Information Security, Singapore, November 1999, Springer-Verlag, 1999.

[275] L. LAW, A. MENEZES, M. QU, J. SOLINAS, AND S. VANSTONE. An efficient protocol for authenticated key agreement. *Designs, Codes and Cryptography*, 28:119–134, 2003.

[276] G. LAY AND H. ZIMMER. Constructing elliptic curves with given group order over large finite fields. *Algorithmic Number Theory—ANTS-I* (LNCS 877) [3], 250–263, 1994.

[277] P. LEE AND C. LIM, editors. *Information Security and Cryptology 2002*, volume 2587 of *Lecture Notes in Computer Science*. 5th International Conference, November 28-29, 2002, Seoul, Korea, Springer-Verlag, 2003.

[278] D. LEHMER. Euclid's algorithm for large numbers. *American Mathematical Monthly*, 45:227–233, 1938.

[279] A. LENSTRA. Unbelievable security—matching AES security using public key systems. *Advances in Cryptology—ASIACRYPT 2001* (LNCS 2248) [67], 67–86, 2001.

[280] A. LENSTRA AND H. LENSTRA, editors. *The Development of the Number Field Sieve*. Springer-Verlag, 1993.

[281] A. LENSTRA AND A. SHAMIR. Analysis and optimization of the TWINKLE factoring device. *Advances in Cryptology—EUROCRYPT 2000* (LNCS 1807) [382], 35–52, 2000.

[282] A. LENSTRA, A. SHAMIR, J. TOMLINSON, AND E. TROMER. Analysis of Bernstein's factorization circuit. *Advances in Cryptology—ASIACRYPT 2002* (LNCS 2501) [489], 1–26, 2002.

[283] A. LENSTRA AND E. VERHEUL. The XTR public key system. *Advances in Cryptology—CRYPTO 2000* (LNCS 1880) [34], 1–19, 2000.

[284] ———. Selecting cryptographic key sizes. *Journal of Cryptology*, 14:255–293, 2001.

[285] H. LENSTRA. Factoring integers with elliptic curves. *Annals of Mathematics*, 126:649–673, 1987.

[286] P. LEONG AND K. LEUNG. A microcoded elliptic curve processor using FPGA technology. *IEEE Transactions on VLSI Systems*, 10:550–559, 2002.

[287] R. LERCIER. Finding good random elliptic curves for cryptosystems defined over $\mathbb{F}_{2^n}$. *Advances in Cryptology—EUROCRYPT '97* (LNCS 1233) [154], 379–392, 1997.

[288] R. LERCIER AND D. LUBICZ. Counting points on elliptic curves over finite fields of small characteristic in quasi quadratic time. *Advances in Cryptology—EUROCRYPT 2003* (LNCS 2656) [47], 360–373, 2003.

[289] R. LERCIER AND F. MORAIN. Counting the number of points on elliptic curves over finite fields: strategies and performances. *Advances in Cryptology—EUROCRYPT '95* (LNCS 921) [184], 79–94, 1995.

[290] S. LEVY. *Crypto: How the Code Rebels Beat the Government—Saving Privacy in the Digital Age*. Penguin Books, 2001.

[291] P. LIARDET AND N. SMART. Preventing SPA/DPA in ECC systems using the Jacobi form. *Cryptographic Hardware and Embedded Systems—CHES 2001* (LNCS 2162) [261], 391–401, 2001.

[292] R. LIDL AND H. NIEDERREITER. *Introduction to Finite Fields and Their Applications*. Cambridge University Press, revised edition, 1994.

[293] C. LIM AND H. HWANG. Fast implementation of elliptic curve arithmetic in $GF(p^n)$. *Public Key Cryptography—PKC 2000* (LNCS 1751) [207], 405–421, 2000.

[294] ——. Speeding up elliptic scalar multiplication with precomputation. *Information Security and Cryptology '99* (LNCS 1787) [448], 102–119, 2000.

[295] C. LIM AND P. LEE. More flexible exponentiation with precomputation. *Advances in Cryptology—CRYPTO '94* (LNCS 839) [115], 95–107, 1994.

[296] ——. A key recovery attack on discrete log-based schemes using a prime order subgroup. *Advances in Cryptology—CRYPTO '97* (LNCS 1294) [235], 249–263, 1997.

[297] ——. A study on the proposed Korean digital signature algorithm. *Advances in Cryptology—ASIACRYPT '98* (LNCS 1514) [352], 175–186, 1998.

[298] H. LIPMAA. IDEA: A cipher for multimedia architectures? *Selected Areas in Cryptography—SAC '98* (LNCS 1556) [457], 248–263, 1999.

[299] J. LÓPEZ AND R. DAHAB. Fast multiplication on elliptic curves over $GF(2^m)$ without precomputation. *Cryptographic Hardware and Embedded Systems—CHES '99* (LNCS 1717) [262], 316–327, 1999.

[300] ——. Improved algorithms for elliptic curve arithmetic in $GF(2^n)$. *Selected Areas in Cryptography—SAC '98* (LNCS 1556) [457], 201–212, 1999.

[301] ——. High-speed software multiplication in $\mathbb{F}_{2^m}$. *Progress in Cryptology—INDOCRYPT 2000* (LNCS 1977) [393], 203–212, 2000.

[302] J. LOUGHRY AND D. UMPHRESS. Information leakage from optical emanations. *ACM Transactions on Information and System Security*, 5:262–289, 2002.

[303] J. MANGER. A chosen ciphertext attack on RSA optimal asymmetric encryption padding (OAEP) as standardized in PKCS #1 v2.0. *Advances in Cryptology—CRYPTO 2001* (LNCS 2139) [241], 230–238, 2001.

[304] M. MAURER, A. MENEZES, AND E. TESKE. Analysis of the GHS Weil descent attack on the ECDLP over characteristic two finite fields of composite degree. *LMS Journal of Computation and Mathematics*, 5:127–174, 2002.

[305] U. MAURER. Towards the equivalence of breaking the Diffie-Hellman protocol and computing discrete logarithms. *Advances in Cryptology—CRYPTO '94* (LNCS 839) [115], 271–281, 1994.

[306] ——, editor. *Advances in Cryptology—EUROCRYPT '96*, volume 1070 of *Lecture Notes in Computer Science*. International Conference on the Theory and Application of Cryptographic Techniques, Saragossa, Spain, May 1996, Springer-Verlag, 1996.

[307] U. MAURER AND S. WOLF. The Diffie-Hellman protocol. *Designs, Codes and Cryptography*, 19:147–171, 2000.

[308] D. MAY, H. MULLER, AND N. SMART. Non-deterministic processors. *Information Security and Privacy 2001* (LNCS 2119) [465], 115–129, 2001.

[309] ——. Random register renaming to foil DPA. *Cryptographic Hardware and Embedded Systems—CHES 2001* (LNCS 2162) [261], 28–38, 2001.

[310] K. MCCURLEY. A key distribution system equivalent to factoring. *Journal of Cryptology*, 1:95–105, 1988.

[311] R. MCELIECE. *Finite Fields for Computer Scientists and Engineers*. Kluwer Academic Publishers, 1987.

[312] W. MEIER AND O. STAFFELBACH. Efficient multiplication on certain nonsupersingular elliptic curves. *Advances in Cryptology—CRYPTO '92* (LNCS 740) [71], 333–344, 1993.

[313] A. MENEZES. *Elliptic Curve Public Key Cryptosystems*. Kluwer Academic Publishers, 1993.

[314] A. MENEZES, T. OKAMOTO, AND S. VANSTONE. Reducing elliptic curve logarithms to logarithms in a finite field. *IEEE Transactions on Information Theory*, 39:1639–1646, 1993.

[315] A. MENEZES AND M. QU. Analysis of the Weil descent attack of Gaudry, Hess and Smart. *Topics in Cryptology—CT-RSA 2001* (LNCS 2020) [338], 308–318, 2001.

[316] A. MENEZES, M. QU, AND S. VANSTONE. Key agreement and the need for authentication. Presentation at PKS '95, Toronto, Canada, November 1995.

[317] A. MENEZES AND P. SARKAR, editors. *Progress in Cryptology—INDOCRYPT 2002*, volume 2551 of *Lecture Notes in Computer Science*. Third International Conference on Cryptology in India, Hyderabad, India, December 16-18, 2002, Springer-Verlag, 2002.

[318] A. MENEZES, E. TESKE, AND A. WENG. Weak fields for ECC. Cryptology ePrint Archive: Report 2003/128. Available from http://eprint.iacr.org/2003/128/, June 2003.

[319] A. MENEZES, P. VAN OORSCHOT, AND S. VANSTONE. *Handbook of Applied Cryptography*. CRC Press, 1996.

[320] A. MENEZES AND S. VANSTONE, editors. *Advances in Cryptology—CRYPTO '90*, volume 537 of *Lecture Notes in Computer Science*. Springer-Verlag, 1991.

[321] R. MERKLE. Secure communications over insecure channels. *Communications of the ACM*, 21:294–299, 1978.

[322] R. MERKLE AND M. HELLMAN. Hiding information and signatures in trapdoor knapsacks. *IEEE Transactions on Information Theory*, 24:525–530, 1978.

[323] T. MESSERGES, E. DABBISH, AND R. SLOAN. Examining smart-card security under the threat of power analysis attacks. *IEEE Transactions on Computers*, 51:541–552, 2002.

[324] J. MESTRE. Formules explicites et minoration de conducteurs de variétés algébriques. *Compositio Mathematica*, 58:209–232, 1986.

[325] V. MILLER. Use of elliptic curves in cryptography. *Advances in Cryptology—CRYPTO '85* (LNCS 218) [483], 417–426, 1986.

[326] B. MÖLLER. Algorithms for multi-exponentiation. *Selected Areas in Cryptography—SAC 2001* (LNCS 2259) [468], 165–180, 2001.

[327] ——. Securing elliptic curve point multiplication against side-channel attacks. *Information Security 2001* (LNCS 2200) [108], 324–334, 2001.

[328] ——. Parallelizable elliptic curve point multiplication method with resistance against side-channel attacks. *Information Security 2002* (LNCS 2433) [89], 402–413, 2002.

[329] ——. Improved techniques for fast exponentiation. *Information Security and Cryptology 2002* (LNCS 2587) [277], 298–312, 2003.

[330] P. MONTGOMERY. Modular multiplication without trial division. *Mathematics of Computation*, 44:519–521, 1985.

[331] ——. Speeding the Pollard and elliptic curve methods of factorization. *Mathematics of Computation*, 48:243–264, 1987.

[332] S. MOORE. Using streaming SIMD extensions (SSE2) to perform big multiplications. Application Note AP-941, Intel Corporation, 2000. Version 2.0, Order Number 248606-001.

[333] F. MORAIN AND J. OLIVOS. Speeding up the computations on an elliptic curve using addition-subtraction chains. *Informatique Théorique et Applications*, 24:531–544, 1990.

[334] V. MÜLLER. Fast multiplication on elliptic curves over small fields of characteristic two. *Journal of Cryptology*, 11:219–234, 1998.

[335] ———. Efficient point multiplication for elliptic curves over special optimal extension fields. *Public-Key Cryptography and Computational Number Theory*, 197–207. de Gruyter, 2001.

[336] V. MÜLLER, S. VANSTONE, AND R. ZUCCHERATO. Discrete logarithm based cryptosystems in quadratic function fields of characteristic 2. *Designs, Codes and Cryptography*, 14:159–178, 1998.

[337] R. MULLIN, I. ONYSZCHUK, S. VANSTONE, AND R. WILSON. Optimal normal bases in $GF(p^n)$. *Discrete Applied Mathematics*, 22:149–161, 1988/89.

[338] D. NACCACHE, editor. *Topics in Cryptology—CT-RSA 2001*, volume 2020 of *Lecture Notes in Computer Science*. The Cryptographers' Track at RSA Conference 2001, San Francisco, California, April 8-12, 2001, Springer-Verlag, 2001.

[339] D. NACCACHE AND D. M'RAÏHI. Cryptographic smart cards. *IEEE Micro*, 16(3):14–24, June 1996.

[340] D. NACCACHE AND P. PAILLIER, editors. *Public Key Cryptography—PKC 2002*, volume 2274 of *Lecture Notes in Computer Science*. 5th International Workshop on Practice and Theory in Public Key Cryptosystems, Paris, France, February 2002, Springer-Verlag, 2002.

[341] D. NACCACHE AND J. STERN. Signing on a postcard. *Financial Cryptography—FC 2000* (LNCS 1962) [148], 121–135, 2001.

[342] NATIONAL INSTITUTE OF STANDARDS AND TECHNOLOGY. NIST Special Publication 800-56: Recommendation on key establishment schemes, Draft 2.0. Available from http://csrc.nist.gov/CryptoToolkit/tkkeymgmt.html, January 2003.

[343] NATIONAL SECURITY AGENCY. NACSIM 5000 Tempest Fundamentals (U). Fort George G. Meade, Maryland, USA. Available from http://cryptome.org/nacsim-5000.htm.

[344] V. NECHAEV. Complexity of a determinate algorithm for the discrete logarithm problem. *Mathematical Notes*, 55:165–172, 1994.

[345] P. NGUYEN AND I. SHPARLINSKI. The insecurity of the digital signature algorithm with partially known nonces. *Journal of Cryptology*, 15:151–176, 2002.

[346] ———. The insecurity of the elliptic curve digital signature algorithm with partially known nonces. *Designs, Codes and Cryptography*, to appear.

[347] M. NIELSEN AND I. CHUANG. *Quantum Computation and Quantum Information*. Cambridge University Press, 2000.

[348] P. NING AND Y. YIN. Efficient software implementation for finite field multiplication in normal basis. *Information and Communications Security 2001* (LNCS 2229) [385], 177–189, 2001.

[349] K. NYBERG AND H. HEYS, editors. *Selected Areas in Cryptography—SAC 2002*, volume 2595 of *Lecture Notes in Computer Science*. 9th Annual International Workshop, St. John's, Newfoundland, Canada, August 15-16, 2002, Springer-Verlag, 2003.

[350] K. NYBERG AND R. RUEPPEL. Message recovery for signature schemes based on the discrete logarithm problem. *Designs, Codes and Cryptography*, 7:61–81, 1996.

[351] A. ODLYZKO, editor. *Advances in Cryptology—CRYPTO '86*, volume 263 of *Lecture Notes in Computer Science*. Springer-Verlag, 1987.

[352] K. OHTA AND D. PEI, editors. *Advances in Cryptology—ASIACRYPT '98*, volume 1514 of *Lecture Notes in Computer Science*. International Conference on the Theory and Application of Cryptology and Information Security, Beijing, China, October 1998, Springer-Verlag, 1998.

[353] S. OKADA, N. TORII, K. ITOH, AND M. TAKENAKA. Implementation of elliptic curve cryptographic coprocessor over $GF(2^m)$ on an FPGA. *Cryptographic Hardware and Embedded Systems—CHES 2000* (LNCS 1965) [263], 25–40, 2000.

[354] T. OKAMOTO. Provably secure and practical identification schemes and corresponding signature schemes. *Advances in Cryptology—CRYPTO '92* (LNCS 740) [71], 31–53, 1993.

[355] ———, editor. *Advances in Cryptology—ASIACRYPT 2000*, volume 1976 of *Lecture Notes in Computer Science*. 6th International Conference on the Theory and Application of Cryptology and Information Security, Kyoto, Japan, December 2000, Springer-Verlag, 2000.

[356] T. OKAMOTO AND D. POINTCHEVAL. The gap-problems: A new class of problems for the security of cryptographic schemes. *Public Key Cryptography—PKC 2001* (LNCS 1992) [244], 104–118, 2001.

[357] ———. REACT: Rapid Enhanced-security Asymmetric Cryptosystem Transform. *Topics in Cryptology—CT-RSA 2001* (LNCS 2020) [338], 159–175, 2001.

[358] K. OKEYA AND K. SAKURAI. Power analysis breaks elliptic curve cryptosystems even secure against the timing attack. *Progress in Cryptology—INDOCRYPT 2000* (LNCS 1977) [393], 178–190, 2000.

[359] ———. Efficient elliptic curve cryptosystems from a scalar multiplication algorithm with recovery of the y-coordinate on a Montgomery-form elliptic curve. *Cryptographic Hardware and Embedded Systems—CHES 2001* (LNCS 2162) [261], 126–141, 2001.

[360] OPEN MOBILE ALLIANCE LTD. Wireless Transport Layer Security. Version 06-Apr-2001.

[361] G. ORLANDO AND C. PAAR. A high-performance reconfigurable elliptic curve processor for $GF(2^m)$. *Cryptographic Hardware and Embedded Systems—CHES 2000* (LNCS 1965) [263], 41–56, 2000.

[362] ———. A scalable $GF(p)$ elliptic curve processor architecture for programmable hardware. *Cryptographic Hardware and Embedded Systems—CHES 2001* (LNCS 2162) [261], 348–363, 2001.

[363] H. ORMAN. The OAKLEY key determination protocol. Internet Request for Comments 2412, Available from http://www.ietf.org/rfc/rfc2412.txt, November 1998.

[364] E. OSWALD. Enhancing simple power-analysis attacks on elliptic curve cryptosystems. *Cryptographic Hardware and Embedded Systems—CHES 2002* (LNCS 2523) [238], 82–97, 2002.

[365] C. PAAR AND P. SORIA-RODRIGUEZ. Fast arithmetic architectures for public-key algorithms over Galois fields $GF((2^n)^m)$. *Advances in Cryptology—EUROCRYPT '97* (LNCS 1233) [154], 363–378, 1997.

[366] D. PAGE AND N. SMART. Hardware implementation of finite fields of characteristic three. *Cryptographic Hardware and Embedded Systems—CHES 2002* (LNCS 2523) [238], 529–539, 2002.

[367] C. PANDU RANGAN AND C. DING, editors. *Progress in Cryptology—INDOCRYPT 2001*, volume 2247 of *Lecture Notes in Computer Science*. Second International Conference on Cryptology in India, Chennai, India, December 16-20, 2001, Springer-Verlag, 2001.

[368] Y. PARK, S. JEONG, C. KIM, AND J. LIM. An alternate decomposition of an integer for faster point multiplication on certain elliptic curves. *Public Key Cryptography—PKC 2002* (LNCS 2274) [340], 323–334, 2002.

[369] Y. PARK, S. JEONG, AND J. LIM. Speeding up point multiplication on hyperelliptic curves with efficiently-computable endomorphisms. *Advances in Cryptology—EUROCRYPT 2002* (LNCS 2332) [248], 197–208, 2002.

[370] Y. PARK, S. OH, J. L. S. LEE, AND M. SUNG. An improved method of multiplication on certain elliptic curves. *Public Key Cryptography—PKC 2002* (LNCS 2274) [340], 310–322, 2002.

[371] R. PAUL. *SPARC Architecture, Assembly Language Programming, and C*. Prentice Hall, second edition, 2000.

[372] B. PFITZMANN, editor. *Advances in Cryptology—EUROCRYPT 2001*, volume 2045 of *Lecture Notes in Computer Science*. International Conference on the Theory and Application of Cryptographic Techniques, Innsbruck, Austria, May 6-10, 2001, Springer-Verlag, 2001.

[373] J. PIEPRZYK, editor. *Advances in Cryptology—ASIACRYPT '94*, volume 917 of *Lecture Notes in Computer Science*. 4th International Conference on the Theory and Application of Cryptology, Wollongong, Australia, November/December 1994, Springer-Verlag, 1995.

[374] R. PINCH. Extending the Wiener attack to RSA-type cryptosystems. *Electronics Letters*, 31:1736–1738, 1995.

[375] L. PINTSOV AND S. VANSTONE. Postal revenue collection in the digital age. *Financial Cryptography—FC 2000* (LNCS 1962) [148], 105–120, 2001.

[376] S. POHLIG AND M. HELLMAN. An improved algorithm for computing logarithms over $GF(p)$ and its cryptographic significance. *IEEE Transactions on Information Theory*, 24:106–110, 1978.

[377] D. POINTCHEVAL. Chosen-ciphertext security for any one-way cryptosystem. *Public Key Cryptography—PKC 2000* (LNCS 1751) [207], 129–146, 2000.

[378] D. POINTCHEVAL AND J. STERN. Security arguments for digital signatures and blind signatures. *Journal of Cryptology*, 13:361–396, 2000.

[379] J. POLLARD. Monte Carlo methods for index computation (mod p). *Mathematics of Computation*, 32:918–924, 1978.

[380] ———. Factoring with cubic integers. In Lenstra and Lenstra [280], 4–10.

[381] ———. Kangaroos, monopoly and discrete logarithms. *Journal of Cryptology*, 13:437–447, 2000.

[382] B. PRENEEL, editor. *Advances in Cryptology—EUROCRYPT 2000*, volume 1807 of *Lecture Notes in Computer Science*. International Conference on the Theory and Application of Cryptographic Techniques, Bruges, Belgium, May 2000, Springer-Verlag, 2000.

[383] J. PROOS. Joint sparse forms and generating zero columns when combing. Technical Report CORR 2003-23, Department of Combinatorics and Optimization, University of Waterloo, Canada, 2003.

[384] J. PROOS AND C. ZALKA. Shor's discrete logarithm quantum algorithm for elliptic curves. *Quantum Information and Computation*, 3:317–344, 2003.

[385] S. QING, T. OKAMOTO, AND J. ZHOU, editors. *Information and Communications Security 2001*, volume 2229 of *Lecture Notes in Computer Science*. Third Inernational Conference, November 13-16, 2001, Xian, China, Springer-Verlag, 2001.

[386] J. QUISQUATER AND D. SAMYDE. Electromagnetic analysis (EMA): Measures and countermeasures for smart cards. *Smart Card Programming and Security* (LNCS 2140) [21], 200–210, 2001.

[387] J. QUISQUATER AND B. SCHNEIER, editors. *Smart Card Research and Applications*, volume 1820 of *Lecture Notes in Computer Science*. Third International Conference (CARDIS'98), Louvain-la-Neuve, Belgium, September 14-16, 1998, Springer-Verlag, 2000.

[388] J. QUISQUATER AND J. VANDEWALLE, editors. *Advances in Cryptology — EUROCRYPT '89*, volume 434 of *Lecture Notes in Computer Science*. Workshop on the Theory and Application of Cryptographic Techniques, Houthalen, Belgium, April 1989, Springer-Verlag, 1990.

[389] C. RACKOFF AND D. SIMON. Non-interactive zero-knowledge proof of knowledge and chosen ciphertext attack. *Advances in Cryptology—CRYPTO '91* (LNCS 576) [135], 433–444, 1992.

[390] A. REYHANI-MASOLEH AND M. HASAN. Fast normal basis multiplication using general purpose processors. *Selected Areas in Cryptography—SAC 2001* (LNCS 2259) [468], 230–244, 2001.

[391] R. RIVEST, A. SHAMIR, AND L. ADLEMAN. A method for obtaining digital signatures and public-key cryptosystems. *Communications of the ACM*, 21:120–126, 1978.

[392] T. RÖMER AND J. SEIFERT. Information leakage attacks against smart card implementations of the elliptic curve digital signature algorithm. *Smart Card Programming and Security* (LNCS 2140) [21], 211–219, 2001.

[393] B. ROY AND E. OKAMOTO, editors. *Progress in Cryptology—INDOCRYPT 2000*, volume 1977 of *Lecture Notes in Computer Science*. First International Conference in Cryptology in India, Calcutta, India, December 2000, Springer-Verlag, 2000.

[394] RSA LABORATORIES. PKCS #1 v1.5: RSA Encryption Standard, November 1993.

[395] ———. PKCS #1 v2.1: RSA Cryptography Standard, June 2002.

[396] K. RUBIN AND A. SILVERBERG. The best and worst of supersingular abelian varieties in cryptology. *Advances in Cryptology—CRYPTO 2002* (LNCS 2442) [488], 336–353, 2002.

[397] H. RÜCK. On the discrete logarithm in the divisor class group of curves. *Mathematics of Computation*, 68:805–806, 1999.

[398] R. RUEPPEL, editor. *Advances in Cryptology—EUROCRYPT '92*, volume 658 of *Lecture Notes in Computer Science*. Workshop on the Theory and Application of Cryptographic Techniques, Balatonfüred, Hungary, May 1992, Springer-Verlag, 1993.

[399] R. SAFAVI-NAINI, editor. *Information Security and Privacy 2003*, volume 2727 of *Lecture Notes in Computer Science*. 8th Australasian Conference, July 9-11, 2003, Wollongong, Australia, Springer-Verlag, 2003.

[400] T. SATOH. The canonical lift of an ordinary elliptic curve over a prime field and its point counting. *Journal of the Ramanujan Mathematical Society*, 15:247–270, 2000.

[401] T. SATOH AND K. ARAKI. Fermat quotients and the polynomial time discrete log algorithm for anomalous elliptic curves. *Commentarii Mathematici Universitatis Sancti Pauli*, 47:81–92, 1998.

[402] T. SATOH, B. SKJERNAA, AND Y. TAGUCHI. Fast computation of canonical lifts of elliptic curves and its application to point counting. *Finite Fields and Their Applications*, 9:89–101, 2003.

[403] E. SAVAŞ AND Ç. KOÇ. The Montgomery inverse—revisited. *IEEE Transactions on Computers*, 49:763–766, 2000.

[404] E. SAVAŞ, A. TENCA, AND Ç. KOÇ. A scalable and unified multiplier architecture for finite fields $GF(p)$ and $GF(2^m)$. *Cryptographic Hardware and Embedded Systems—CHES 2000* (LNCS 1965) [263], 277–292, 2000.

[405] R. SCHEIDLER, J. BUCHMANN, AND H. WILLIAMS. A key-exchange protocol using real quadratic fields. *Journal of Cryptology*, 7:171–199, 1994.

[406] R. SCHEIDLER, A. STEIN, AND H. WILLIAMS. Key-exchange in real quadratic congruence function fields. *Designs, Codes and Cryptography*, 7:153–174, 1996.

[407] W. SCHINDLER. A timing attack against RSA with the Chinese Remainder Theorem. *Cryptographic Hardware and Embedded Systems—CHES 2000* (LNCS 1965) [263], 109–124, 2000.

[408] O. SCHIROKAUER. Discrete logarithms and local units. *Philosophical Transactions of the Royal Society of London A*, 345:409–423, 1993.

[409] B. SCHNEIER. *Applied Cryptography: Protocols, Algorithms, and Source Code in C*. Wiley, 2nd edition, 1996.

[410] C. SCHNORR. Efficient signature generation by smart cards. *Journal of Cryptology*, 4:161–174, 1991.

[411] R. SCHOOF. Elliptic curves over finite fields and the computation of square roots mod *p*. *Mathematics of Computation*, 44:483–494, 1985.

[412] R. SCHROEPPEL. Automatically solving equations in finite fields. US Patent Application No. 09/834,363, filed 12 April 2001.

[413] ———. Elliptic curves: Twice as fast! Presentation at the CRYPTO 2000 [34] Rump Session, 2000.

[414] R. SCHROEPPEL, C. BEAVER, R. GONZALES, R. MILLER, AND T. DRAELOS. A low-power design for an elliptic curve digital signature chip. *Cryptographic Hardware and Embedded Systems—CHES 2002* (LNCS 2523) [238], 366–280, 2002.

[415] R. SCHROEPPEL, H. ORMAN, S. O'MALLEY, AND O. SPATSCHECK. Fast key exchange with elliptic curve systems. *Advances in Cryptology—CRYPTO '95* (LNCS 963) [103], 43–56, 1995.

[416] M. SCOTT. Comparison of methods for modular exponentiation on 32-bit Intel 80x86 processors. Informal Draft 11 June 1996. Available from the MIRACL site http://indigo.ie/~mscott/.

[417] SEC 1. Standards for Efficient Cryptography Group: Elliptic Curve Cryptography. Version 1.0, 2000.

[418] SEC 2. Standards for Efficient Cryptography Group: Recommended Elliptic Curve Domain Parameters. Version 1.0, 2000.

[419] R. SEDGEWICK, T. SZYMANSKI, AND A. YAO. The complexity of finding cycles in periodic functions. *SIAM Journal on Computing*, 11:376–390, 1982.

[420] I. SEMAEV. Evaluation of discrete logarithms in a group of p-torsion points of an elliptic curve in characteristic p. *Mathematics of Computation*, 67:353–356, 1998.

[421] A. SHAMIR. Factoring large numbers with the TWINKLE device. *Cryptographic Hardware and Embedded Systems—CHES '99* (LNCS 1717) [262], 2–12, 1999.

[422] ———. Protecting smart cards from passive power analysis with detached power supplies. *Cryptographic Hardware and Embedded Systems—CHES 2000* (LNCS 1965) [263], 71–77, 2000.

[423] A. SHAMIR AND E. TROMER. Factoring large numbers with the TWIRL device. *Advances in Cryptology—CRYPTO 2003* (LNCS 2729) [55], 1–26, 2003.

[424] P. SHOR. Polynomial-time algorithms for prime factorization and discrete logarithms on a quantum computer. *SIAM Journal on Computing*, 26:1484–1509, 1997.

[425] V. SHOUP. Lower bounds for discrete logarithms and related problems. *Advances in Cryptology—EUROCRYPT '97* (LNCS 1233) [154], 256–266, 1997.

[426] ———. Using hash functions as a hedge against chosen ciphertext attack. *Advances in Cryptology—EUROCRYPT 2000* (LNCS 1807) [382], 275–288, 2000.

[427] ———. OAEP reconsidered. *Journal of Cryptology*, 15:223–249, 2002.

[428] F. SICA, M. CIET, AND J. QUISQUATER. Analysis of the Gallant-Lambert-Vanstone method based on efficient endomorphisms: Elliptic and hyperelliptic curves. *Selected Areas in Cryptography—SAC 2002* (LNCS 2595) [349], 21–36, 2003.

[429] J. SILVERMAN. *The Arithmetic of Elliptic Curves*. Springer-Verlag, 1986.

[430] ———. *Advanced Topics in the Arithmetic of Elliptic Curves*. Springer-Verlag, 1994.

[431] ———. The xedni calculus and the elliptic curve discrete logarithm problem. *Designs, Codes and Cryptography*, 20:5–40, 2000.

[432] J. SILVERMAN AND J. SUZUKI. Elliptic curve discrete logarithms and the index calculus. *Advances in Cryptology—ASIACRYPT '98* (LNCS 1514) [352], 110–125, 1998.

[433] J. SILVERMAN AND J. TATE. *Rational Points on Elliptic Curves*. Springer-Verlag, 1992.

[434] R. SILVERMAN AND J. STAPLETON. Contribution to the ANSI X9F1 working group, 1997.

[435] G. SIMMONS, editor. *Contemporary Cryptology: The Science of Information Integrity*. IEEE Press, 1992.

[436] B. SKJERNAA. Satoh's algorithm in characteristic 2. *Mathematics of Computation*, 72:477–487, 2003.

[437] S. SKOROBOGATOV AND R. ANDERSON. Optical fault induction analysis. *Cryptographic Hardware and Embedded Systems—CHES 2002* (LNCS 2523) [238], 2–12, 2002.

[438] N. SMART. The discrete logarithm problem on elliptic curves of trace one. *Journal of Cryptology*, 12:193–196, 1999.

[439] ——. Elliptic curve cryptosystems over small fields of odd characteristic. *Journal of Cryptology*, 12:141–151, 1999.

[440] ——. A comparison of different finite fields for elliptic curve cryptosystems. *Computers and Mathematics with Applications*, 42:91–100, 2001.

[441] ——. The exact security of ECIES in the generic group model. *Cryptography and Coding 2001*, volume 2260 of *Lecture Notes in Computer Science*, 73–84. Springer-Verlag, 2001.

[442] ——. The Hessian form of an elliptic curve. *Cryptographic Hardware and Embedded Systems—CHES 2001* (LNCS 2162) [261], 118–125, 2001.

[443] P. SMITH AND C. SKINNER. A public-key cryptosystem and a digital signature system based on the Lucas function analogue to discrete logarithms. *Advances in Cryptology—ASIACRYPT '94* (LNCS 917) [373], 357–364, 1995.

[444] J. SOLINAS. An improved algorithm for arithmetic on a family of elliptic curves. *Advances in Cryptology—CRYPTO '97* (LNCS 1294) [235], 357–371, 1997.

[445] ——. Generalized Mersenne numbers. Technical Report CORR 99-39, Department of Combinatorics and Optimization, University of Waterloo, Canada, 1999.

[446] ——. Efficient arithmetic on Koblitz curves. *Designs, Codes and Cryptography*, 19:195–249, 2000.

[447] ——. Low-weight binary representations for pairs of integers. Technical Report CORR 2001-41, Department of Combinatorics and Optimization, University of Waterloo, Canada, 2001.

[448] J. SONG, editor. *Information Security and Cryptology '99*, volume 1787 of *Lecture Notes in Computer Science*. Second International Conference, December 9-10, 1999, Seoul, Korea, Springer-Verlag, 2000.

[449] L. SONG AND K. PARHI. Low-energy digit-serial/parallel finite field multipliers. *Journal of VLSI Signal Processing*, 19:149–166, 1998.

[450] J. SORENSON. An analysis of Lehmer's Euclidean GCD algorithm. *Proceedings of the 1995 International Symposium on Symbolic and Algebraic Computation*, 254–258, 1995.

[451] J. STEIN. Computational problems associated with Racah algebra. *Journal of Computational Physics*, 1:397–405, 1967.

[452] J. STERN, D. POINTCHEVAL, J. MALONE-LEE, AND N. SMART. Flaws in applying proof methodologies to signature schemes. *Advances in Cryptology—CRYPTO 2002* (LNCS 2442) [488], 93–110, 2002.

[453] D. STINSON, editor. *Advances in Cryptology—CRYPTO '93*, volume 773 of *Lecture Notes in Computer Science*. 13th Annual International Cryptology Conference, Santa Barbara, California, August 1993, Springer-Verlag, 1994.

[454] ——. *Cryptography: Theory and Practice*. CRC Press, 2nd edition, 2002.

[455] D. STINSON AND S. TAVARES, editors. *Selected Areas in Cryptography—SAC 2000*, volume 2012 of *Lecture Notes in Computer Science*. 7th Annual International Workshop, Waterloo, Ontario, Canada, August 14-15, 2000, Springer-Verlag, 2001.

[456] B. SUNAR AND Ç. KOÇ. An efficient optimal normal basis type II multiplier. *IEEE Transactions on Computers*, 50:83–87, 2001.

[457] S. TAVARES AND H. MEIJER, editors. *Selected Areas in Cryptography—SAC '98*, volume 1556 of *Lecture Notes in Computer Science*. 5th Annual International Workshop, Kingston, Ontario, Canada, August 1998, Springer-Verlag, 1999.

[458] E. TESKE. Speeding up Pollard's rho method for computing discrete logarithms. *Algorithmic Number Theory—ANTS-III* (LNCS 1423) [82], 541–554, 1998.

[459] ———. On random walks for Pollard's rho method. *Mathematics of Computation*, 70:809–825, 2001.

[460] E. THOMÉ. Computation of discrete logarithms in $\mathbb{F}_{2^{607}}$. *Advances in Cryptology— ASIACRYPT 2001* (LNCS 2248) [67], 107–124, 2001.

[461] E. TRICHINA AND A. BELLEZZA. Implementation of elliptic curve cryptography with built-in counter measures against side channel attacks. *Cryptographic Hardware and Embedded Systems—CHES 2002* (LNCS 2523) [238], 98–113, 2002.

[462] P. VAN OORSCHOT AND M. WIENER. On Diffie-Hellman key agreement with short exponents. *Advances in Cryptology—EUROCRYPT '96* (LNCS 1070) [306], 332–343, 1996.

[463] ———. Parallel collision search with cryptanalytic applications. *Journal of Cryptology*, 12:1–28, 1999.

[464] M. VANDERSYPEN, M. STEFFEN, G. BREYTA, C. YANNONI, M. SHERWOOD, AND I. CHUANG. Experimental realization of Shor's quantum factoring algorithm using nuclear magnetic resonance. *Nature*, 414:883–887, 2001.

[465] V. VARADHARAJAN AND Y. MU, editors. *Information Security and Privacy 2001*, volume 2119 of *Lecture Notes in Computer Science*. 6th Australasian Conference, July 11-13, 2001, Sydney, Australia, Springer-Verlag, 2001.

[466] S. VAUDENAY. Security flaws induced by CBC padding—applications, to SSL, IPSEC, WTLS... *Advances in Cryptology—EUROCRYPT 2002* (LNCS 2332) [248], 534–545, 2002.

[467] ———. The security of DSA and ECDSA. *Public Key Cryptography—PKC 2003* (LNCS 2567) [116], 309–323, 2003.

[468] S. VAUDENAY AND A. YOUSSEF, editors. *Selected Areas in Cryptography—SAC 2001*, volume 2259 of *Lecture Notes in Computer Science*. 8th Annual International Workshop, Toronto, Ontario, Canada, August 16-17, 2001, Springer-Verlag, 2001.

[469] F. VERCAUTEREN. Computing zeta functions of hyperelliptic curves over finite fields of characteristic 2. *Advances in Cryptology—CRYPTO 2002* (LNCS 2442) [488], 369–384, 2002.

[470] F. VERCAUTEREN, B. PRENEEL, AND J. VANDEWALLE. A memory efficient version of Satoh's algorithm. *Advances in Cryptology—EUROCRYPT 2001* (LNCS 2045) [372], 1–13, 2001.

[471] E. VERHEUL. Evidence that XTR is more secure than supersingular elliptic curve cryptosystems. *Advances in Cryptology—EUROCRYPT 2001* (LNCS 2045) [372], 195–210, 2001.

[472] ——. Self-blindable credential certificates from the Weil pairing. *Advances in Cryptology—ASIACRYPT 2001* (LNCS 2248) [67], 533–551, 2001.

[473] J. VIEGA AND G. McGRAW. *Building Secure Software: How to Avoid Security Problems the Right Way.* Addison-Wesley, 2001.

[474] L. WASHINGTON. *Elliptic Curves: Number Theory and Cryptography.* CRC Press, 2003.

[475] W. WATERHOUSE. Abelian varieties over finite fields. *Annales Scientifiques de l'École Normale Supérieure, 4e Série*, 2:521–560, 1969.

[476] D. WEAVER AND T. GERMOND, editors. *The SPARC Architecture Manual, Version 9.* Prentice Hall, 1994.

[477] A. WEIMERSKIRCH, C. PAAR, AND S. CHANG SHANTZ. Elliptic curve cryptography on a Palm OS device. *Information Security and Privacy 2001* (LNCS 2119) [465], 502–513, 2001.

[478] A. WEIMERSKIRCH, D. STEBILA, AND S. CHANG SHANTZ. Generic $GF(2^m)$ arithmetic in software and its application to ECC. *Information Security and Privacy 2003* (LNCS 2727) [399], 79–92, 2003.

[479] A. WENG. Constructing hyperelliptic curves of genus 2 suitable for cryptography. *Mathematics of Computation*, 72:435–458, 2003.

[480] M. WIENER, editor. *Advances in Cryptology—CRYPTO '99*, volume 1666 of *Lecture Notes in Computer Science.* 19th Annual International Cryptology Conference, Santa Barbara, California, August 1999, Springer-Verlag, 1999.

[481] ——. The full cost of cryptanalytic attacks. *Journal of Cryptology*, to appear.

[482] M. WIENER AND R. ZUCCHERATO. Faster attacks on elliptic curve cryptosystems. *Selected Areas in Cryptography—SAC '98* (LNCS 1556) [457], 190–200, 1999.

[483] H. WILLIAMS, editor. *Advances in Cryptology—CRYPTO '85*, volume 218 of *Lecture Notes in Computer Science.* Springer-Verlag, 1986.

[484] C. WITTMANN. Group structure of elliptic curves over finite fields. *Journal of Number Theory*, 88:335–344, 2001.

[485] J. WOLKERSTORFER. Dual-field arithmetic unit for $GF(p)$ and $GF(2^m)$. *Cryptographic Hardware and Embedded Systems—CHES 2002* (LNCS 2523) [238], 500–514, 2002.

[486] A. WOODBURY, D. BAILEY, AND C. PAAR. Elliptic curve cryptography on smart cards without coprocessors. *Smart Card Research and Advanced Applications* [125], 71–92, 2000.

[487] S. YEN, C. LAIH, AND A. LENSTRA. Multi-exponentiation. *IEE Proceedings—Computers and Digital Techniques*, 141:325–326, 1994.

[488] M. YUNG, editor. *Advances in Cryptology—CRYPTO 2002*, volume 2442 of *Lecture Notes in Computer Science.* 22nd Annual International Cryptology Conference, Santa Barbara, California, August 18-22, 2002, Springer-Verlag, 2002.

[489] Y. ZHENG, editor. *Advances in Cryptology—ASIACRYPT 2002*, volume 2501 of *Lecture Notes in Computer Science.* 8th International Conference on the Theory and Application of Cryptology and Information Security, Queenstown, New Zealand, December 1-5, 2002, Springer-Verlag, 2002.

Index

Printed in the United States
154355LV00008B/2/P